Wiley's Level III CFA® Program 11th Hour Final Review Study Guide 2020

Thousands of candidates from more than 100 countries have relied on these Study Guides to pass the CFA® Exam. Covering every Learning Outcome Statement (LOS) on the exam, these review materials are an invaluable tool for anyone who wants a deep-dive review of all the concepts, formulas, and topics required to pass.

Wiley study materials are produced by expert CFA charterholders, CFA Institute members, and investment professionals from around the globe. For more information, contact us at www.efficientlearning.com.

Wiley's Level III CFA® Program 11th Hour Final Review Study Guide 2020

WILEY

V10017451_021020

Contents

Foreword

Wiley's Level III CFA® Program 11th Hour Final Review Study Guide 2020 is a concise and easy-to-understand review book that is meant to supplement your review for the CFA® Level III Program Exam. It becomes extremely difficult to go through the entire curriculum in the last few weeks leading up to the exam, so we have condensed the material for you. You must remember, though, that this book is not meant to be a primary study tool for the exam. It is designed to help you review the material in an efficient and effective manner so that you can be confident on exam day.

About the Author

Wiley's Study Guides are written by a team of highly qualified CFA charterholders and leading CFA instructors from around the globe. Our team of CFA experts work collaboratively to produce the best study materials for CFA candidates available today.

Wiley's expert team of contributing authors and instructors is led by Content Director Basit Shajani, CFA. Basit founded online education start-up Élan Guides in 2009 to help address CFA candidates' need for better study materials. As lead writer, lecturer, and curriculum developer, Basit's unique ability to break down complex topics helped the company grow organically to be a leading global provider of CFA Exam prep materials. In January 2014, Élan Guides was acquired by John Wiley & Sons, Inc., where Basit continues his work as Director of CFA Content. Basit graduated magna cum laude from the Wharton School of Business at the University of Pennsylvania with majors in finance and legal studies. He went on to obtain his CFA charter in 2006, passing all three levels on the first attempt. Prior to Élan Guides, Basit ran his own private wealth management business. He is a past president of the Pakistani CFA Society.

There are many more expert CFA charterholders who contribute to the creation of Wiley materials. We are thankful for their invaluable expertise and diligent work. To learn more about Wiley's team of subject matter experts, please visit: www.efficientlearning.com/cfa/why-wiley/

CODE OF ETHICS AND STANDARDS OF PROFESSIONAL CONDUCT
Cross-Reference to CFA Institute Assigned Reading #1

The Code of Ethics consists of high-level objectives that are expected of all CFA Institute members and candidates. Be sure that you know the six components of the Code of Ethics and how the Professional Conduct Program (PCP) operates, including investigations into alleged violations of the Code and Standards.

CFA Institute Professional Conduct Program

All CFA Institute members and candidates enrolled in the CFA Program are required to comply with the Code and Standards. The CFA Institute Board of Governors maintains oversight and responsibility for the Professional Conduct Program (PCP) which, in conjunction with the Disciplinary Review Committee (DRC), is responsible for enforcement of the Code and Standards. The DRC is a volunteer committee of CFA charterholders who serve on panels to review conduct and partner with Professional Conduct staff to establish and review professional conduct policies. The CFA Institute Bylaws and Rules of Procedure for Professional Conduct (Rules of Procedure) form the basic structure for enforcing the Code and Standards. The Professional Conduct division is also responsible for enforcing testing policies of other CFA Institute education programs as well as the professional conduct of Certificate in Investment Performance Measurement (CIPM) certificants.

Professional Conduct inquiries come from a number of sources.

- Members and candidates must self-disclose on the annual Professional Conduct Statement all matters that question their professional conduct, such as involvement in civil litigation or a criminal investigation or being the subject of a written complaint.
- Written complaints received by Professional Conduct staff can bring about an investigation.
- CFA Institute staff may become aware of questionable conduct by a member or candidate through the media, regulatory notices, or another public source.
- Candidate conduct is monitored by proctors who complete reports on candidates suspected to have violated testing rules on exam day.
- CFA Institute may also conduct analyses of scores and exam materials after the exam, as well as monitor online and social media to detect disclosure of confidential exam information.

When an inquiry is initiated, the Professional Conduct staff conducts an investigation that may include:

- Requesting a written explanation from the member or candidate.
- Interviewing the member or candidate, complaining parties, and third parties.
- Collecting documents and records relevant to the investigation.

Upon reviewing the material obtained during the investigation, the Professional Conduct staff may:

- Take no disciplinary sanction.
- Issue a cautionary letter.
- Continue proceedings to discipline the member or candidate.

If the Professional Conduct staff believes a violation of the Code and Standards or testing policies has occurred, the member or candidate has the opportunity to reject or accept any charges and the proposed sanctions. If the member or candidate does not accept the charges and proposed sanction, the matter is referred to a panel composed of DRC members. Panels review materials and presentations from Professional Conduct staff and from the member or candidate. The panel's task is to determine whether a violation of the Code and Standards or testing policies occurred and, if so, what sanction should be imposed.

Sanctions imposed by CFA Institute may have significant consequences; they include public censure, suspension of membership and use of the CFA designation, and revocation of the CFA charter. Candidates enrolled in the CFA Program who have violated the Code and Standards or testing policies may be suspended or prohibited from further participation in the CFA Program CFA Institute does not impose fines on those who have violated the Standards.

Adoption of the Code and Standards

The Code and Standards apply to individual members of CFA Institute and candidates in the CFA Program. CFA Institute does encourage firms to adopt the Code and Standards, however, as part of their code of ethics. Those who claim compliance should fully understand the requirements of each of the principles of the Code and Standards.

Once a party—nonmember or firm—ensures its code of ethics meets the principles of the Code and Standards, that party should make the following statement whenever claiming compliance:

"[Insert name of party] claims compliance with the CFA Institute Code of Ethics and Standards of Professional Conduct. This claim has not been verified by CFA Institute."

CFA Institute welcomes public acknowledgment, when appropriate, that firms are complying with the CFA Institute Code of Ethics and Standards of Professional Conduct and encourages firms to notify it of the adoption plans.

CFA INSTITUTE CODE OF ETHICS AND STANDARDS OF PROFESSIONAL CONDUCT

The Code of Ethics

Members of CFA Institute (including CFA charterholders) and candidates for the CFA designation ("Members and Candidates") must:

- Act with integrity, competence, diligence, and respect and in an ethical manner with the public, clients, prospective clients, employers, employees, colleagues in the investment profession, and other participants in the global capital markets.
- Place the integrity of the investment profession and the interests of clients above their own personal interests.
- Use reasonable care and exercise independent professional judgment when conducting investment analysis, making investment recommendations, taking investment actions, and engaging in other professional activities.
- Practice and encourage others to practice in a professional and ethical manner that will reflect credit on themselves and the profession.
- Promote the integrity and viability of the global capital markets for the ultimate benefit of society.
- Maintain and improve their professional competence and strive to maintain and improve the competence of other investment professionals.

STANDARDS OF PROFESSIONAL CONDUCT

I. Professionalism
   A. Knowledge of the Law
   B. Independence and Objectivity
   C. Misrepresentation
   D. Misconduct
II. Integrity of Capital Markets
   A. Material Nonpublic Information
   B. Market Manipulation
III. Duties to Clients
   A. Loyalty, Prudence and Care
   B. Fair Dealing
   C. Suitability
   D. Performance Presentation
   E. Preservation of Confidentiality
IV. Duties to Employers
   A. Loyalty
   B. Additional Compensation Arrangements
   C. Responsibilities of Supervisors
V. Investment Analysis, Recommendations and Actions
   A. Diligence and Reasonable Basis
   B. Communication with Clients and Prospective Clients
   C. Record Retention
VI. Conflicts of Interest
   A. Disclosure of Conflicts
   B. Priority of Transactions
   C. Referral Fees

VII. Responsibilities as a CFA Institute Member or CFA Candidate
    A. Conduct as Participants in CFA Institute Programs
    B. Reference to CFA Institute, the CFA Designation, and the CFA Program

The Code of Ethics and the Standards of Practice apply to all candidates in the CFA program and members of CFA Institute. All examples and other extracts from the Standards of Practice Handbook that are included in this reading are reprinted with permission of CFA Institute.

GUIDANCE FOR STANDARDS I–VII
Cross-Reference to CFA Institute Assigned Reading #2

The seven Standards of Professional Conduct contain detailed rules of minimum behavior that are required of all CFA candidates and charterholders. As in previous levels, you do not need to know the standard letter and number but must know all the requirements, recommendations, and best practices relevant to each section.

STANDARD I(A): KNOWLEDGE OF THE LAW

The Standard

Members and candidates must understand and comply with all applicable laws, rules, and regulations (including the CFA Institute Code of Ethics and Standards of Professional Conduct) of any government, regulatory organization, licensing agency, or professional association governing their professional activities. In the event of conflict, members and candidates must comply with the more strict law, rule, regulation or CFA Institute standard. Members and candidates must not knowingly participate or assist in and must dissociate from any violation of such laws, rules, or regulations.

Guidance
- Members and candidates must understand the applicable laws and regulations of the countries and jurisdictions where they engage in professional activities.
- On the basis of their reasonable and good faith understanding, members and candidates must comply with the laws and regulations that directly govern their professional activities.
- When questions arise, members and candidates should know their firm's policies and procedures for accessing compliance guidance.
- Members and candidates must remain vigilant in maintaining their knowledge of the requirements for their professional activities.

Relationship between the Code and Standards and Applicable Law
- When applicable law and the Code and Standards require different conduct, members and candidates must follow the stricter of the applicable law or the Code and Standards.
  - "Applicable law" is the law that governs the member's or candidate's conduct. Which law applies will depend on the particular facts and circumstances of each case.
  - The "more strict" law or regulation is the law or regulation that imposes greater restrictions on the action of the member or candidate, or calls for the member or candidate to exert a greater degree of action that protects the interests of investors.

Global Application of the Code and Standards

Members and candidates who practice in multiple jurisdictions may be subject to varied securities laws and regulations. The following chart provides illustrations involving a member who may be subject to the securities laws and regulations of three different types of countries:

NS: country with no securities laws or regulations

LS: country with *less* strict securities laws and regulations than the Code and Standards

MS: country with *more* strict securities laws and regulations than the Code and Standards

Applicable Law	Duties	Explanation
Member resides in NS country, does business in LS country; LS law applies.	Member must adhere to the Code and Standards.	Because applicable law is less strict than the Code and Standards, the member must adhere to the Code and Standards.
Member resides in NS country, does business in MS country; MS law applies.	Member must adhere to the law of MS country.	Because applicable law is stricter than the Code and Standards, member must adhere to the more strict applicable law.
Member resides in LS country, does business in NS country; LS law applies.	Member must adhere to the Code and Standards.	Because applicable law is less strict than the Code and Standards, member must adhere to the Code and Standards.
Member resides in LS country, does business in MS country; MS law applies.	Member must adhere to the law of MS country.	Because applicable law is stricter than the Code and Standards, member must adhere to the more strict applicable law.
Member resides in LS country, does business in NS country; LS law applies, but it states that law of locality where business is conducted governs.	Member must adhere to the Code and Standards.	Because applicable law states that the law of the locality where the business is conducted governs and there is no local law, the member must adhere to the Code and Standards.
Member resides in LS country, does business in MS country; LS law applies, but it states that law of locality where business is conducted governs.	Member must adhere to the law of MS country.	Because applicable law of the locality where the business is conducted governs and local law is stricter than the Code and Standards, member must adhere to the more strict applicable law.
Member resides in MS country, does business in LS country; MS law applies.	Member must adhere to the law of MS country.	Because applicable law is stricter than the Code and Standards, member must adhere to the more strict applicable law.
Member resides in MS country, does business in LS country; MS law applies, but it states that law of locality where business is conducted governs.	Member must adhere to the Code and Standards.	Because applicable law states that the law of the locality where the business is conducted governs and local law is less strict than the Code and Standards, member must adhere to the Code and Standards.
Member resides in MS country, does business in LS country with a client who is a citizen of LS country; MS law applies, but it states that the law of the client's home country governs.	Member must adhere to the Code and Standards.	Because applicable law states that the law of the client's home country governs (which is less strict than the Code and Standards), member must adhere to the Code and Standards.
Member resides in MS country, does business in LS country with a client who is a citizen of MS country; MS law applies, but it states that the law of the client's home country governs.	Member must adhere to the law of MS country.	Because applicable law states that the law of the client's home country governs and the law of the client's home country is stricter than the Code and Standards, the member must adhere to the more strict applicable law.

Participation in or Association with Violations by Others

- Members and candidates are responsible for violations in which they knowingly participate or assist. Standard I(A) applies when members and candidates know or should know that their conduct may contribute to a violation of applicable laws, rules, or regulations or the Code and Standards.
- If a member or candidate has reasonable grounds to believe that imminent or ongoing client or employer activities are illegal or unethical, the member or candidate must dissociate, or separate, from the activity.
- In extreme cases, dissociation may require a member or candidate to leave his or her employment.
- Members and candidates may take the following steps before dissociating from ethical violations of others when direct discussions with the person or persons committing the violation are unsuccessful.
  - Attempt to stop the behavior by bringing it to the attention of the employer through a supervisor or the firm's compliance department.
  - If this attempt is unsuccessful, then members and candidates have a responsibility to step away and dissociate from the activity. Inaction combined with continuing association with those involved in illegal or unethical conduct may be construed as participation or assistance in the illegal or unethical conduct.
- CFA Institute strongly encourages members and candidates to report potential violations of the Code and Standards committed by fellow members and candidates, although a failure to report is less likely to be construed as a violation than a failure to dissociate from unethical conduct.

Investment Products and Applicable Laws

- Members and candidates involved in creating or maintaining investment services or investment products or packages of securities and/or derivatives should be mindful of where these products or packages will be sold as well as their places of origination.
- They should understand the applicable laws and regulations of the countries or regions of origination and expected sale, and should make reasonable efforts to review whether associated firms that are distributing products or services developed by their employing firms also abide by the laws and regulations of the countries and regions of distribution.
- Finally, they should undertake the necessary due diligence when transacting cross-border business to understand the multiple applicable laws and regulations in order to protect the reputation of their firms and themselves.

Recommended Procedures for Compliance

Members and Candidates

Suggested methods by which members and candidates can acquire and maintain understanding of applicable laws, rules, and regulations include the following:

- **Stay informed:** Members and candidates should establish or encourage their employers to establish a procedure by which employees are regularly informed about changes in applicable laws, rules, regulations, and case law.
- **Review procedures:** Members and candidates should review, or encourage their employers to review, the firm's written compliance procedures on a regular basis to ensure that the procedures reflect current law and provide adequate guidance to employees about what is permissible conduct under the law and/or the Code and Standards.

- **Maintain current files:** Members and candidates should maintain or encourage their employers to maintain readily accessible current reference copies of applicable statutes, rules, regulations, and important cases.

Distribution Area Laws
- Members and candidates should make reasonable efforts to understand the applicable laws—both country and regional—for the countries and regions where their investment products are developed and are most likely to be distributed to clients.

Legal Counsel
- When in doubt about the appropriate action to undertake, it is recommended that a member or candidate seek the advice of compliance personnel or legal counsel concerning legal requirements.
- If a potential violation is being committed by a fellow employee, it may also be prudent for the member or candidate to seek the advice of the firm's compliance department or legal counsel.

Dissociation
- When dissociating from an activity that violates the Code and Standards, members and candidates should document the violation and urge their firms to attempt to persuade the perpetrator(s) to cease such conduct. Note that in order to dissociate from the conduct, a member or candidate may have to resign his or her employment.

Firms

Members and candidates should encourage their firms to consider the following policies and procedures to support the principles of Standard I(A):

- Develop and/or adopt a code of ethics.
- Provide information on applicable laws.
- Establish procedures for reporting violations.

STANDARD I(B) INDEPENDENCE AND OBJECTIVITY

The Standard

Members and candidates must use reasonable care and judgment to achieve and maintain independence and objectivity in their professional activities. Members and candidates must not offer, solicit, or accept any gift, benefit, compensation, or consideration that reasonably could be expected to compromise their own or another's independence and objectivity.

Guidance
- Members and candidates should endeavor to avoid situations that could cause or be perceived to cause a loss of independence or objectivity in recommending investments or taking investment action.
- Modest gifts and entertainment are acceptable, but special care must be taken by members and candidates to resist subtle and not-so-subtle pressures to act in conflict with the interests of their clients. Best practice dictates that members and candidates reject any offer of gift or entertainment that could be expected to threaten their independence and objectivity.

- Receiving a gift, benefit, or consideration from a client can be distinguished from gifts given by entities seeking to influence a member or candidate to the detriment of other clients.
- When possible, prior to accepting "bonuses" or gifts from clients, members and candidates should disclose to their employers such benefits offered by clients. If notification is not possible prior to acceptance, members and candidates must disclose to their employer benefits previously accepted from clients.
- Members and candidates are personally responsible for maintaining independence and objectivity when preparing research reports, making investment recommendations, and taking investment action on behalf of clients. Recommendations must convey the member's or candidate's true opinions, free of bias from internal or external pressures, and be stated in clear and unambiguous language.
- When seeking corporate financial support for conventions, seminars, or even weekly society luncheons, the members or candidates responsible for the activities should evaluate both the actual effect of such solicitations on their independence and whether their objectivity might be perceived to be compromised in the eyes of their clients.

Investment-Banking Relationships

- Some sell-side firms may exert pressure on their analysts to issue favorable research reports on current or prospective investment banking clients. Members and candidates must not succumb to such pressures.
- Allowing analysts to work with investment bankers is appropriate only when the conflicts are adequately and effectively managed and disclosed. Firm managers have a responsibility to provide an environment in which analysts are neither coerced nor enticed into issuing research that does not reflect their true opinions. Firms should require public disclosure of actual conflicts of interest to investors.
- Any "firewalls" between the investment banking and research functions must be managed to minimize conflicts of interest. Key elements of enhanced firewalls include:
  - Separate reporting structures for personnel on the research side and personnel on the investment banking side.
  - Compensation arrangements that minimize pressures on research analysts and reward objectivity and accuracy. Ideally, compensation should be tied to the quality of the research and not the operating performance of the investment bank.

Public Companies

- Analysts may be pressured to issue favorable reports and recommendations by the companies they follow. In making an investment recommendation, the analyst is responsible for anticipating, interpreting, and assessing a company's prospects and stock price performance in a factual manner.
- Due diligence in financial research and analysis involves gathering information from a wide variety of sources, including public disclosure documents (such as proxy statements, annual reports, and other regulatory filings) and also company management and investor-relations personnel, suppliers, customers, competitors, and other relevant sources. Research analysts may justifiably fear that companies will limit their ability to conduct thorough research by denying analysts who have "negative" views direct access to company managers and/or barring them from conference calls and other communication venues. This concern may make it difficult for them to conduct the comprehensive research needed to make objective recommendations.

Buy-Side Clients

- Portfolio managers may have significant positions in the security of a company under review. A rating downgrade may adversely affect portfolio performance, particularly in the short term, because the sensitivity of stock prices to ratings changes has increased in recent years. A downgrade may also affect the manager's compensation, which is usually tied to portfolio performance. Moreover, portfolio performance is subject to media and public scrutiny, which may affect the manager's professional reputation. Consequently, some portfolio managers implicitly or explicitly support sell-side ratings inflation.
- Portfolio managers have a responsibility to respect and foster the intellectual honesty of sell-side research. Therefore, it is improper for portfolio managers to threaten or engage in retaliatory practices, such as reporting sell-side analysts to the covered company in order to instigate negative corporate reactions.

Fund Manager and Custodial Relationships

- Research analysts are not the only people who must be concerned with maintaining their independence. Members and candidates who are responsible for hiring and retaining outside managers and third-party custodians should not accepts gifts, entertainment, or travel funding that may be perceived as impairing their decisions.

Credit Rating Agency Opinions

- Members and candidates employed at rating agencies should ensure that procedures and processes at the agencies prevent undue influences from a sponsoring company during the analysis. Members and candidates should abide by their agencies' and the industry's standards of conduct regarding the analytical process and the distribution of their reports.
- When using information provided by credit rating agencies, members and candidates should be mindful of the potential conflicts of interest. And because of the potential conflicts, members and candidates may need to independently validate the rating granted.

Issuer-Paid Research

- Some companies hire analysts to produce research reports in case of lack of coverage from sell-side research, or to increase the company's visibility in financial markets.
- Analysts must engage in thorough, independent, and unbiased analysis and must fully disclose potential conflicts, including the nature of their compensation. It should also be clearly mentioned in the report that the research has been paid for by the subject company. At a minimum, research should include a thorough analysis of the company's financial statements based on publicly disclosed information, benchmarking within a peer group, and industry analysis.
- Analysts must try to limit the type of compensation they accept for conducting research. This compensation can be direct, such as payment based on the conclusions of the report or more indirect, such as stock warrants or other equity instruments that could increase in value based on positive coverage in the report. In those instances, analysts would have an incentive to avoid negative information or conclusions that would diminish their potential compensation.
- Best practice is for analysts to accept only a flat fee for their work prior to writing the report, without regard to their conclusions or the report's recommendations.

Travel Funding

- The benefits related to accepting paid travel extend beyond the cost savings to the member or candidate and his firm, such as the chance to talk exclusively with the executives of a company or learning more about the investment options provided by an investment organization. Acceptance also comes with potential concerns; for example, members and candidates may be influenced by these discussions when flying on a corporate or chartered jet, or attending sponsored conferences where many expenses, including airfare and lodging, are covered.

- To avoid the appearance of compromising their independence and objectivity, best practice dictates that analysts always use commercial transportation at their expense or at the expense of their firm rather than accept paid travel arrangements from an outside company.
- In case of unavailability of commercial travel, they may accept modestly arranged travel to participate in appropriate information gathering events, such as a property tour.

Performance Measurement and Attribution

- Members and candidates working within a firm's investment performance measurement department may also be presented with situations that challenge their independence and objectivity. As performance analysts, their analyses may reveal instances where managers may appear to have strayed from their mandate. Additionally, the performance analyst may receive requests to alter the construction of composite indices owing to negative results for a selected account or fund. Members or candidates must not allow internal or external influences to affect their independence and objectivity as they faithfully complete their performance calculation and analysis-related responsibilities.

Influence During the Manager Selection/Procurement Process

- When serving in a hiring capacity, members and candidates should not solicit gifts, contributions, or other compensation that may affect their independence and objectivity. Solicitations do not have to benefit members and candidates personally to conflict with Standard I(B). Requesting contributions to a favorite charity or political organization may also be perceived as an attempt to influence the decision-making process. Additionally, members and candidates serving in a hiring capacity should refuse gifts, donations, and other offered compensation that may be perceived to influence their decision-making process.
- When working to earn a new investment allocation, members and candidates should not offer gifts, contributions, or other compensation to influence the decision of the hiring representative. The offering of these items with the intent to impair the independence and objectivity of another person would not comply with Standard I(B). Such prohibited actions may include offering donations to a charitable organization or political candidate referred by the hiring representative.

Recommended Procedures for Compliance

Members and candidates should adhere to the following practices and should encourage their firms to establish procedures to avoid violations of Standard I(B):

- **Protect the integrity of opinions:** Members, candidates, and their firms should establish policies stating that every research report concerning the securities of a corporate client should reflect the unbiased opinion of the analyst.
- **Create a restricted list:** If the firm is unwilling to permit dissemination of adverse opinions about a corporate client, members and candidates should encourage the firm to remove the controversial company from the research universe and put it on a restricted list so that the firm disseminates only factual information about the company and not the analyst's recommendation.
- **Restrict special cost arrangements:** When attending meetings at an issuer's headquarters, members and candidates should pay for commercial transportation and

hotel charges. No corporate issuer should reimburse members or candidates for air transportation. Members and candidates should encourage issuers to limit the use of corporate aircraft to situations in which commercial transportation is not available or in which efficient movement could not otherwise be arranged.

- **Limit gifts:** Members and candidates must limit the acceptance of gratuities and/or gifts to token items. Standard I(B) does not preclude customary, ordinary business-related entertainment as long as its purpose is not to influence or reward members or candidates. Firms should consider a strict value limit for acceptable gifts that is based on the local or regional customs and should address whether the limit is per gift or an aggregate annual value.

- **Restrict investments:** Members and candidates should encourage their investment firms to develop formal polices related to employee purchases of equity or equity-related IPOs. Firms should require prior approval for employee participation in IPOs, with prompt disclosure of investment actions taken following the offering. Strict limits should be imposed on investment personnel acquiring securities in private placements. Note that a restriction is not a complete prohibition.

- **Review procedures:** Members and candidates should encourage their firms to implement effective supervisory and review procedures to ensure that analysts and portfolio managers comply with policies relating to their personal investment activities.

- **Independence policy:** Members, candidates, and their firms should establish a formal written policy on the independence and objectivity of research and implement reporting structures and review procedures to ensure that research analysts do not report to and are not supervised or controlled by any department of the firm that could compromise the independence of the analyst.

- **Appointed officer:** Firms should appoint a senior officer with oversight responsibilities for compliance with the firm's code of ethics and all regulations concerning its business.

STANDARD I(C) MISREPRESENTATION

The Standard

Members and candidates must not knowingly make any misrepresentations relating to investment analysis, recommendations, actions, or other professional activities.

Guidance
- A misrepresentation is any untrue statement or omission of a fact or any statement that is otherwise false or misleading.
- A member or candidate must not knowingly omit or misrepresent information or give a false impression of a firm, organization, or security in the member's or candidate's oral representations, advertising (whether in the press or through brochures), electronic communications, or written materials (whether publicly disseminated or not).
  - In this context, "knowingly" means that the member or candidate either knows or should have known that the misrepresentation was being made or that omitted information could alter the investment decision-making process.
- Members and candidates who use webpages should regularly monitor materials posted on these sites to ensure that they contain current information. Members and candidates should also ensure that all reasonable precautions have been taken to protect the site's integrity and security and that the site does not misrepresent any information and does provide full disclosure.
- Members and candidates should not guarantee clients any specific return on volatile investments. Most investments contain some element of risk that makes their return inherently unpredictable. For such investments, guaranteeing either a particular rate of

return or a guaranteed preservation of investment capital (e.g., "I can guarantee that you will earn 8% on equities this year" or "I can guarantee that you will not lose money on this investment") is misleading to investors.

- Note that Standard I(C) does not prohibit members and candidates from providing clients with information on investment products that have guarantees built into the structure of the products themselves or for which an institution has agreed to cover any losses.

Impact on Investment Practice

- Members and candidates must not misrepresent any aspect of their practice, including (but not limited to) their qualifications or credentials, the qualifications or services provided by their firm, their performance record and the record of their firm, and the characteristics of an investment.
- Members and candidates should exercise care and diligence when incorporating third-party information. Misrepresentations resulting from the use of the credit ratings, research, testimonials, or marketing materials of outside parties become the responsibility of the investment professional when it affects that professional's business practices.
- Members and candidates must disclose their intended use of external managers and must not represent those managers' investment practices as their own.

Performance Reporting

- Members and candidates should not misrepresent the success of their performance record by presenting benchmarks that are not comparable to their strategies. The benchmark's results should be reported on a basis comparable to that of the fund's or client's results.
- Note that Standard I(C) does not require that a benchmark always be provided in order to comply. Some investment strategies may not lend themselves to displaying an appropriate benchmark because of the complexity or diversity of the investments included.
- Members and candidates should discuss with clients on a continuous basis the appropriate benchmark to be used for performance evaluations and related fee calculations.
- Members and candidates should take reasonable steps to provide accurate and reliable security pricing information to clients on a consistent basis. Changing pricing providers should not be based solely on the justification that the new provider reports a higher current value of a security.

Social Media

- When communicating through social media channels, members and candidates should provide only the same information they are allowed to distribute to clients and potential clients through other traditional forms of communication.
- Along with understanding and following existing and newly developing rules and regulations regarding the allowed use of social media, members and candidates should also ensure that all communications in this format adhere to the requirements of the Code and Standards.
- The perceived anonymity granted through these platforms may entice individuals to misrepresent their qualifications or abilities or those of their employer. Actions undertaken through social media that knowingly misrepresent investment recommendations or professional activities are considered a violation of Standard I(C).

Omissions

- Members and candidates should not knowingly omit inputs used in any models and processes they use to scan for new investment opportunities, to develop investment vehicles, and to produce investment recommendations and ratings as resulting outcomes may provide misleading information. Further, members and candidates should not present outcomes from their models as facts because they only represent expected results.
- Members and candidates should encourage their firms to develop strict policies for composite development to prevent cherry picking—situations in which selected accounts are presented as representative of the firm's abilities. The omission of any accounts appropriate for the defined composite may misrepresent to clients the success of the manager's implementation of its strategy.

Plagiarism

- Plagiarism refers to the practice of copying, or using in substantially the same form, materials prepared by others without acknowledging the source of the material or identifying the author and publisher of the material. Plagiarism includes:
  - Taking a research report or study performed by another firm or person, changing the names, and releasing the material as one's own original analysis.
  - Using excerpts from articles or reports prepared by others either verbatim or with only slight changes in wording without acknowledgment.
  - Citing specific quotations supposedly attributable to "leading analysts" and "investment experts" without specific reference.
  - Presenting statistical estimates of forecasts prepared by others with the source identified but without qualifying statements or caveats that may have been used.
  - Using charts and graphs without stating their sources.
  - Copying proprietary computerized spreadsheets or algorithms without seeking the cooperation or authorization of their creators.
- In the case of distributing third-party, outsourced research, members and candidates can use and distribute these reports as long as they do not represent themselves as the author of the report. They may add value to clients by sifting through research and repackaging it for them, but should disclose that the research being presented to clients comes from an outside source.
- The standard also applies to plagiarism in oral communications, such as through group meetings; visits with associates, clients, and customers; use of audio/video media (which is rapidly increasing); and telecommunications, such as through electronic data transfer and the outright copying of electronic media. One of the most egregious practices in violation of this standard is the preparation of research reports based on multiple sources of information without acknowledging the sources. Such information would include, for example, ideas, statistical compilations, and forecasts combined to give the appearance of original work.

Work Completed for Employer

- Members and candidates may use research conducted by other analysts within their firm. Any research reports prepared by the analysts are the property of the firm and may be issued by it even if the original analysts are no longer with the firm.
- Therefore, members and candidates are allowed to use the research conducted by analysts who were previously employed at their firms. However, they cannot reissue a previously released report solely under their own name.

Recommended Procedures for Compliance

Factual presentations: Firms should provide guidance for employees who make written or oral presentations to clients or potential clients by providing a written list of the firm's available services and a description of the firm's qualifications. Firms can also help prevent misrepresentation by specifically designating which employees are authorized to speak on behalf of the firm.

Qualification summary: In order to ensure accurate presentations to clients, the member or candidate should prepare a summary of her own qualifications and experience, as well as a list of the services she is capable of performing.

Verify outside information: When providing information to clients from third parties, members and candidates should ensure the accuracy of the marketing and distribution materials that pertain to the third party's capabilities, services, and products. This is because inaccurate information can damage their individual and their firm's reputations as well as the integrity of the capital markets.

Maintain webpages: If they publish a webpage, members and candidates should regularly monitor materials posted to the site to ensure the site maintains current information.

Plagiarism policy: To avoid plagiarism in preparing research reports or conclusions of analysis, members and candidates should take the following steps:

- **Maintain copies:** Keep copies of all research reports, articles containing research ideas, material with new statistical methodology, and other materials that were relied on in preparing the research report.
- **Attribute quotations:** Attribute to their sources any direct quotations, including projections, tables, statistics, model/product ideas, and new methodologies prepared by persons other than recognized financial and statistical reporting services or similar sources.
- **Attribute summaries:** Attribute to their sources paraphrases or summaries of material prepared by others.

STANDARD I(D) MISCONDUCT

The Standard

Members and candidates must not engage in any professional conduct involving dishonesty, fraud, or deceit, or commit any act that reflects adversely on their professional reputation, integrity, or competence.

Guidance
- While Standard I(A) addresses the obligation of members and candidates to comply with applicable law that governs their professional activities, Standard I(D) addresses all conduct that reflects poorly on the professional integrity, good reputation, or competence of members and candidates. Any act that involves lying, cheating, stealing, or other dishonest conduct is a violation of this standard if the offense reflects adversely on a member's or candidate's professional activities.
- Conduct that damages trustworthiness or competence may include behavior that, although not illegal, nevertheless negatively affects a member's or candidate's ability to perform his or her responsibilities. For example:

- ○ Abusing alcohol during business hours might constitute a violation of this standard because it could have a detrimental effect on the member's or candidate's ability to fulfill his or her professional responsibilities.
  - ○ Personal bankruptcy may not reflect on the integrity or trustworthiness of the person declaring bankruptcy, but if the circumstances of the bankruptcy involve fraudulent or deceitful business conduct, the bankruptcy may be a violation of this standard.
- In some cases, the absence of appropriate conduct or the lack of sufficient effort may be a violation of Standard I(D). The integrity of the investment profession is built on trust. A member or candidate—whether an investment banker, rating or research analyst, or portfolio manager—is expected to conduct the necessary due diligence to properly understand the nature and risks of an investment before making an investment recommendation. By not taking these steps and, instead, relying on someone else in the process to perform them, members or candidates may violate the trust their clients have placed in them. This loss of trust may have a significant impact on the reputation of the member or candidate and the operations of the financial market as a whole.
- Note that Standard I(D) or any other standard should not be used to settle personal, political, or other disputes unrelated to professional ethics.

Recommended Procedures for Compliance

Members and candidates should encourage their firms to adopt the following policies and procedures to support the principles of Standard I(D):

- **Code of ethics:** Develop and/or adopt a code of ethics to which every employee must subscribe, and make clear that any personal behavior that reflects poorly on the individual involved, the institution as a whole, or the investment industry will not be tolerated.
- **List of violations:** Disseminate to all employees a list of potential violations and associated disciplinary sanctions, up to and including dismissal from the firm.
- **Employee references:** Check references of potential employees to ensure that they are of good character and not ineligible to work in the investment industry because of past infractions of the law.

STANDARD II(A) MATERIAL NONPUBLIC INFORMATION

The Standard

Members and candidates who possess material nonpublic information that could affect the value of an investment must not act or cause others to act on the information.

Guidance

- Standard II(A) is related to information that is material and is nonpublic. Such information must not be used for direct buying and selling of individual securities or bonds, nor to influence investment actions related to derivatives, mutual funds, or other alternative investments.

Material Information

Information is "material" if its disclosure would likely have an impact on the price of a security, or if reasonable investors would want to know the information before making an investment decision. Material information may include, but is not limited to, information relating to the following:

- Earnings.
- Mergers, acquisitions, tender offers, or joint ventures.
- Changes in assets.
- Innovative products, processes, or discoveries.
- New licenses, patents, registered trademarks, or regulatory approval/rejection of a product.
- Developments regarding customers or suppliers (e.g., the acquisition or loss of a contract).
- Changes in management.
- Change in auditor notification or the fact that the issuer may no longer rely on an auditor's report or qualified opinion.
- Events regarding the issuer's securities (e.g., defaults on senior securities, calls of securities for redemption, repurchase plans, stock splits, changes in dividends, changes to the rights of security holders, public or private sales of additional securities, and changes in credit ratings).
- Bankruptcies.
- Significant legal disputes.
- Government reports of economic trends (employment, housing starts, currency information, etc.).
- Orders for large trades before they are executed.
- New or changing equity or debt ratings issued by a third party (e.g., sell-side recommendations and credit ratings).
- To determine if information is material, members and candidates should consider the source of information and the information's likely effect on the relevant stock price.
  - The less reliable a source, such as a rumor, the less likely the information provided would be considered material.
  - The more ambiguous the effect on price, the less material the information becomes.
  - If it is unclear whether the information will affect the price of a security and to what extent, information may not be considered material.

Nonpublic Information

- Information is "nonpublic" until it has been disseminated or is available to the marketplace in general (as opposed to a select group of investors). "Disseminated" can be defined as "made known."
  - For example, a company report of profits that is posted on the Internet and distributed widely through a press release or accompanied by a filing has been effectively disseminated to the marketplace.
- Members and candidates must be particularly aware of information that is selectively disclosed by corporations to a small group of investors, analysts, or other market participants. Information that is made available to analysts remains nonpublic until it is disseminated to investors in general.
- Analysts should also be alert to the possibility that they are selectively receiving material nonpublic information when a company provides them with guidance or interpretation of such publicly available information as financial statements or regulatory filings.
- A member or candidate may use insider information provided legitimately by the source company for the specific purpose of conducting due diligence according to the business agreement between the parties for such activities as mergers, loan underwriting, credit ratings, and offering engagements. However, the use of insider information provided by

the source company for other purposes, especially to trade or entice others to trade the securities of the firm, conflicts with this standard.

Mosaic Theory

- A financial analyst may use significant conclusions derived from the analysis of public information and nonmaterial nonpublic information as the basis for investment recommendations and decisions. Under the "mosaic theory," financial analysts are free to act on this collection, or mosaic, of information without risking violation, even when the conclusion they reach would have been material inside information had the company communicated the same.
- Investment professionals should note, however, that although analysts are free to use mosaic information in their research reports, they should save and document all their research [see Standard V(C)].

Social Media

- Members and candidates participating in online discussion forums/groups with membership limitations should verify that material information obtained from these sources can also be accessed from a source that would be considered available to the public (e.g., company filings, webpages, and press releases).
- Members and candidates may use social media platforms to communicate with clients or investors without conflicting with this standard.
- Members and candidates, as required by Standard I(A), should also complete all appropriate regulatory filings related to information distributed through social media platforms.

Using Industry Experts

- The increased demand for insights for understanding the complexities of some industries has led to an expansion of engagement with outside experts. Members and candidates may provide compensation to individuals for their insights without violating this standard.
- However, members and candidates are ultimately responsible for ensuring that they are not requesting or acting on confidential information received from external experts, which is in violation of security regulations and laws or duties to others.

Investment Research Reports

- It might often be the case that reports prepared by well-known analysts may have an effect on the market and thus may be considered material information. Theoretically, such a report might have to be made public before it was distributed to clients. However, since the analyst is not a company insider, and presumably prepared the report based on publicly available information, the report does not need to be made public just because its conclusions are material. Investors who want to use that report can become clients of the analyst.

Recommended Procedures for Compliance

Achieve public dissemination: If a member or candidate determines that some nonpublic information is material, she should encourage the issuer to make the information public. If public dissemination is not possible, she must communicate the information only to the designated supervisory and compliance personnel in her firm and must not take investment action on the basis of the information.

Adopt compliance procedures: Members and candidates should encourage their firms to adopt compliance procedures to prevent the misuse of material nonpublic information. Particularly important is improving compliance in areas such as review of employee and proprietary trading, documentation of firm procedures, and the supervision of interdepartmental communications in multi-service firms.

Adopt disclosure procedures: Members and candidates should encourage their firms to develop and follow disclosure policies designed to ensure that information is disseminated in the marketplace in an equitable manner. An issuing company should not discriminate among analysts in the provision of information or blackball particular analysts who have given negative reports on the company in the past.

Issue press releases: Companies should consider issuing press releases prior to analyst meetings and conference calls and scripting those meetings and calls to decrease the chance that further information will be disclosed.

Firewall elements: An information barrier commonly referred to as a "firewall" is the most widely used approach to prevent communication of material nonpublic information within firms. The minimum elements of such a system include, but are not limited to, the following:

- Substantial control of relevant interdepartmental communications, preferably through a clearance area within the firm in either the compliance or legal department;
- Review of employee trading through the maintenance of "watch," "restricted," and "rumor" lists;
- Documentation of the procedures designed to limit the flow of information between departments and of the enforcement actions taken pursuant to those procedures;
- Heightened review or restriction of proprietary trading while a firm is in possession of material nonpublic information.

Appropriate interdepartmental communications: Based on the size of the firm, procedures concerning interdepartmental communication, the review of trading activity, and the investigation of possible violations should be compiled and formalized.

Physical separation of departments: As a practical matter, to the extent possible, firms should consider the physical separation of departments and files to prevent the communication of sensitive information.

Prevention of personnel overlap: There should be no overlap of personnel between the investment banking and corporate finance areas of a brokerage firm and the sales and research departments or between a bank's commercial lending department and its trust and research departments. For a firewall to be effective in a multi-service firm, an employee can be allowed to be on only one side of the wall at any given time.

A reporting system: The least a firm should do to protect itself from liability is have an information barrier in place. It should authorize people to review and approve communications between departments. A single supervisor or compliance officer should have the specific authority and responsibility of deciding whether or not information is material and whether it is sufficiently public to be used as the basis for investment decisions.

Personal trading limitations: Firms should also consider restrictions or prohibitions on personal trading by employees and should carefully monitor both proprietary trading and personal trading by employees. Further, they should require employees to make periodic reports (to the extent that such reporting is not already required by securities laws) of their own transactions and transactions made for the benefit of family members.

Securities should be placed on a restricted list when a firm has or may have material nonpublic information. Further, the watch list (seen only by compliance personnel) should be shown to only the few people responsible for compliance to monitor transactions in specified securities. The use of a watch list in combination with a restricted list has become a common means of ensuring an effective procedure.

Record maintenance: Multi-service firms should maintain written records of communications among various departments. Firms should place a high priority on training and should consider instituting comprehensive training programs, to enable employees to make informed decisions.

Proprietary trading procedures: Procedures concerning the restriction or review of a firm's proprietary trading while it possesses material nonpublic information will necessarily depend on the types of proprietary trading in which a firm may engage. For example, when a firm acts as a market maker, a prohibition on proprietary trading may be counterproductive to the goals of maintaining the confidentiality of information and market liquidity. However, a firm should suspend arbitrage activity when a security is placed on the watch list.

Communication to all employees: Written compliance policies and guidelines should be circulated to all employees of a firm. Further, they must be given sufficient training to either be able to make an informed decision or to realize that they need to consult a compliance officer before engaging in questionable transactions.

STANDARD II(B) MARKET MANIPULATION

The Standard

Members and candidates must not engage in practices that distort prices or artificially inflate trading volume with the intent to mislead market participants.

Guidance
- Members and candidates must uphold market integrity by prohibiting market manipulation. Market manipulation includes practices that distort security prices or trading volume with the intent to deceive people or entities that rely on information in the market.
- Market manipulation includes (1) the dissemination of false or misleading information and (2) transactions that deceive or would be likely to mislead market participants by distorting the price-setting mechanism of financial instruments.

Information-Based Manipulation
- Information-based manipulation includes, but is not limited to, spreading false rumors to induce trading by others.
  - For example, members and candidates must refrain from "pumping up" the price of an investment by issuing misleading positive information or overly optimistic projections of a security's worth only to later "dump" the investment (i.e., sell it) once the price, fueled by the misleading information's effect on other market participants, reaches an artificially high level.

Transaction-Based Manipulation

- Transaction-based manipulation involves instances where a member or candidate knew or should have known that his or her actions could affect the pricing of a security. This type of manipulation includes, but is not limited to, the following:
  - ○ Transactions that artificially affect prices or volume to give the impression of activity or price movement in a financial instrument, which represent a diversion from the expectations of a fair and efficient market.
  - ○ Securing a controlling, dominant position in a financial instrument to exploit and manipulate the price of a related derivative and/or the underlying asset.

Note that Standard II(B) is not intended to preclude transactions undertaken on legitimate trading strategies based on perceived market inefficiencies. The *intent* of the action is critical to determining whether it is a violation of this standard.

STANDARD III(A) LOYALTY, PRUDENCE, AND CARE

The Standard

Members and candidates have a duty of loyalty to their clients and must act with reasonable care and exercise prudent judgment. Members and candidates must act for the benefit of their clients and place their clients' interests before their employer's or their own interests.

Guidance

- Standard III(A) clarifies that client interests are paramount. A member's or candidate's responsibility to a client includes a duty of loyalty and a duty to exercise reasonable care. Investment actions must be carried out for the sole benefit of the client and in a manner the member or candidate believes, given the known facts and circumstances, to be in the best interest of the client. Members and candidates must exercise the same level of prudence, judgment, and care that they would apply in the management and disposition of their own interests in similar circumstances.
- Prudence requires caution and discretion. The exercise of prudence by investment professionals requires that they act with the care, skill, and diligence that a reasonable person acting in a like capacity and familiar with such matters would use. In the context of managing a client's portfolio, prudence requires following the investment parameters set forth by the client and balancing risk and return. Acting with care requires members and candidates to act in a prudent and judicious manner in avoiding harm to clients.
- Standard III(A), however, is not a substitute for a member's or candidate's legal or regulatory obligations. As stated in Standard I(A), members and candidates must abide by the most strict requirements imposed on them by regulators or the Code and Standards, including any legally imposed fiduciary duty.
- Members and candidates must also be aware of whether they have "custody" or effective control of client assets. If so, a heightened level of responsibility arises. Members and candidates are considered to have custody if they have any direct or indirect access to client funds. Members and candidates must manage any pool of assets in their control in accordance with the terms of the governing documents (such as trust documents and investment management agreements), which are the primary determinant of the manager's powers and duties.

Understanding the Application of Loyalty, Prudence, and Care

- Standard III(A) establishes a minimum benchmark for the duties of loyalty, prudence, and care that are required of all members and candidates regardless of whether a legal fiduciary duty applies. Although fiduciary duty often encompasses the principles of loyalty, prudence, and care, Standard III(A) does not render all members and candidates fiduciaries. The responsibilities of members and candidates for fulfilling their obligations under this standard depend greatly on the nature of their professional responsibilities and the relationships they have with clients.

- There is a large variety of professional relationships that members and candidates have with their clients. Standard III(A) requires them to fulfill the obligations outlined explicitly or implicitly in the client agreements to the best of their abilities and with loyalty, prudence, and care. Whether a member or candidate is structuring a new securitization transaction, completing a credit rating analysis, or leading a public company, he or she must work with prudence and care in delivering the agreed-on services.

Identifying the Actual Investment Client

- The first step for members and candidates in fulfilling their duty of loyalty to clients is to determine the identity of the "client" to whom the duty of loyalty is owed. In the context of an investment manager managing the personal assets of an individual, the client is easily identified. When the manager is responsible for the portfolios of pension plans or trusts, however, the client is not the person or entity who hires the manager but, rather, the beneficiaries of the plan or trust. The duty of loyalty is owed to the ultimate beneficiaries.
- Members and candidates managing a fund to an index or an expected mandate owe the duty of loyalty, prudence, and care to invest in a manner consistent with the stated mandate. The decisions of a fund's manager, although benefiting all fund investors, do not have to be based on an individual investor's requirements and risk profile. Client loyalty and care for those investing in the fund are the responsibility of members and candidates who have an advisory relationship with those individuals.

Developing the Client's Portfolio

- Professional investment managers should ensure that the client's objectives and expectations for the performance of the account are realistic and suitable to the client's circumstances and that the risks involved are appropriate. In most circumstances, recommended investment strategies should relate to the long-term objectives and circumstances of the client.
- When members and candidates cannot avoid potential conflicts between their firm and clients' interests, they must provide clear and factual disclosures of the circumstances to the clients.
- Members and candidates must follow any guidelines set by their clients for the management of their assets.
- Investment decisions must be judged in the context of the total portfolio rather than by individual investments within the portfolio. The member's or candidate's duty is satisfied with respect to a particular investment if the individual has thoroughly considered the investment's place in the overall portfolio, the risk of loss and opportunity for gains, tax implications, and the diversification, liquidity, cash flow, and overall return requirements of the assets or the portion of the assets for which the manager is responsible.

Soft Commission Policies

- An investment manager often has discretion over the selection of brokers executing transactions. Conflicts may arise when an investment manager uses client brokerage to purchase research services, a practice commonly called "soft dollars" or "soft commissions." A member or candidate who pays a higher brokerage commission than he or she would normally pay to allow for the purchase of goods or services, without corresponding benefit to the client, violates the duty of loyalty to the client.

- From time to time, a client will direct a manager to use the client's brokerage to purchase goods or services for the client, a practice that is commonly called "directed brokerage." Because brokerage commission is an asset of the client and is used to benefit that client, not the manager, such a practice does not violate any duty of loyalty. However, a member or candidate is obligated to seek "best price" and "best execution" and be assured by the client that the goods or services purchased from the brokerage will benefit the account beneficiaries. In addition, the member or candidate should disclose to the client that the client may not be getting best execution from the directed brokerage.
  - ○ "Best execution" refers to a trading process that seeks to maximize the value of the client's portfolio within the client's stated investment objectives and constraints.

Proxy Voting Policies

- Part of a member's or candidate's duty of loyalty includes voting proxies in an informed and responsible manner. Proxies have economic value to a client, and members and candidates must ensure that they properly safeguard and maximize this value.
- An investment manager who fails to vote, casts a vote without considering the impact of the question, or votes blindly with management on non-routine governance issues (e.g., a change in company capitalization) may violate this standard. Voting of proxies is an integral part of the management of investments.
- A cost-benefit analysis may show that voting all proxies may not benefit the client, so voting proxies may not be necessary in all instances.
- Members and candidates should disclose to clients their proxy voting policies.

Recommended Procedures for Compliance

Regular Account Information

Members and candidates with control of client assets should:

- Submit to each client, at least quarterly, an itemized statement showing the funds and securities in the custody or possession of the member or candidate plus all debits, credits, and transactions that occurred during the period.
- Disclose to the client where the assets are to be maintained, as well as where or when they are moved.
- Separate the client's assets from any other party's assets, including the member's or candidate's own assets.

Client Approval

- If a member or candidate is uncertain about the appropriate course of action with respect to a client, the member or candidate should consider what he or she would expect or demand if the member or candidate were the client.
- If in doubt, a member or candidate should disclose the questionable matter in writing to the client and obtain client approval.

Firm Policies

Members and candidates should address and encourage their firms to address the following topics when drafting the statements or manuals containing their policies and procedures regarding responsibilities to clients:

- **Follow all applicable rules and laws:** Members and candidates must follow all legal requirements and applicable provisions of the Code and Standards.
- **Establish the investment objectives of the client:** Make a reasonable inquiry into a client's investment experience, risk and return objectives, and financial constraints prior to making investment recommendations or taking investment actions.
- **Consider all the information when taking actions:** When taking investment actions, members and candidates must consider the appropriateness and suitability of the investment relative to (1) the client's needs and circumstances, (2) the investment's basic characteristics, and (3) the basic characteristics of the total portfolio.
- **Diversify:** Members and candidates should diversify investments to reduce the risk of loss, unless diversification is not consistent with plan guidelines or is contrary to the account objectives.
- **Carry out regular reviews:** Members and candidates should establish regular review schedules to ensure that the investments held in the account adhere to the terms of the governing documents.
- **Deal fairly with all clients with respect to investment actions:** Members and candidates must not favor some clients over others and should establish policies for allocating trades and disseminating investment recommendations.
- **Disclose conflicts of interest:** Members and candidates must disclose all actual and potential conflicts of interest so that clients can evaluate those conflicts.
- **Disclose compensation arrangements:** Members and candidates should make their clients aware of all forms of manager compensation.
- **Vote proxies:** In most cases, members and candidates should determine who is authorized to vote shares and vote proxies in the best interests of the clients and ultimate beneficiaries.
- **Maintain confidentiality:** Members and candidates must preserve the confidentiality of client information.
- **Seek best execution:** Unless directed by the client as ultimate beneficiary, members and candidates must seek best execution for their clients. (Best execution is defined in the preceding text.)
- **Place client interests first:** Members and candidates must serve the best interests of clients.

Standard III(B) Fair Dealing

The Standard

Members and candidates must deal fairly and objectively with all clients when providing investment analysis, making investment recommendations, taking investment action, or engaging in other professional activities.

Guidance

- Standard III(B) requires members and candidates to treat all clients fairly when disseminating investment recommendations or making material changes to prior investment recommendations, or when taking investment action with regard to general purchases, new issues, or secondary offerings.
- The term "fairly" implies that the member or candidate must take care not to discriminate against any clients when disseminating investment recommendations or taking investment action. Standard III(B) does not state "equally" because members and candidates could not possibly reach all clients at exactly the same time. Further, each client has unique needs, investment criteria, and investment objectives, so not all investment opportunities are suitable for all clients.

- Members and candidates may provide more personal, specialized, or in-depth service to clients who are willing to pay for premium services through higher management fees or higher levels of brokerage. Members and candidates may differentiate their services to clients, but different levels of service must not disadvantage or negatively affect clients. In addition, the different service levels should be disclosed to clients and prospective clients and should be available to everyone (i.e., different service levels should not be offered selectively).

Investment Recommendations

- An investment recommendation is any opinion expressed by a member or candidate in regard to purchasing, selling, or holding a given security or other investment. The opinion may be disseminated to customers or clients through an initial detailed research report, through a brief update report, by addition to or deletion from a list of recommended securities, or simply by oral communication. A recommendation that is distributed to anyone outside the organization is considered a communication for general distribution under Standard III(B).
- Each member or candidate is obligated to ensure that information is disseminated in such a manner that all clients have a fair opportunity to act on every recommendation. Members and candidates should encourage their firms to design an equitable system to prevent selective or discriminatory disclosure and should inform clients about what kind of communications they will receive.
- The duty to clients imposed by Standard III(B) may be more critical when members or candidates change their recommendations than when they make initial recommendations. Material changes in a member's or candidate's prior investment recommendations because of subsequent research should be communicated to all current clients; particular care should be taken that the information reaches those clients who the member or candidate knows have acted on or been affected by the earlier advice.
- Clients who do not know that the member or candidate has changed a recommendation and who, therefore, place orders contrary to a current recommendation should be advised of the changed recommendation before the order is accepted.

Investment Action

- Members or candidates must treat all clients fairly in light of their investment objectives and circumstances. For example, when making investments in new offerings or in secondary financings, members and candidates should distribute the issues to all customers for whom the investments are appropriate in a manner consistent with the policies of the firm for allocating blocks of stock. If the issue is oversubscribed, then the issue should be prorated to all subscribers. If the issue is oversubscribed, members and candidates should forgo any sales to themselves or their immediate families in order to free up additional shares for clients.
  - If the investment professional's family-member accounts are managed similarly to the accounts of other clients of the firm, however, the family-member accounts should not be excluded from buying such shares.
- Members and candidates must make every effort to treat all individual and institutional clients in a fair and impartial manner.
- Members and candidates should disclose to clients and prospective clients the documented allocation procedures they or their firms have in place and how the procedures would affect the client or prospect. The disclosure should be clear and complete so that the client can make an informed investment decision. Even when complete disclosure is made, however, members and candidates must put client interests ahead of their own. A member's or candidate's duty of fairness and loyalty to clients can never be overridden by client consent to patently unfair allocation procedures.

- Treating clients fairly also means that members and candidates should not take advantage of their position in the industry to the detriment of clients. For instance, in the context of IPOs, members and candidates must make bona fide public distributions of "hot issue" securities (defined as securities of a public offering that are trading at a premium in the secondary market whenever such trading commences because of the great demand for the securities). Members and candidates are prohibited from withholding such securities for their own benefit and must not use such securities as a reward or incentive to gain benefit.

Recommended Procedures for Compliance

Develop Firm Policies

- A member or candidate should recommend appropriate procedures to management if none are in place.
- A member or candidate should make management aware of possible violations of fair-dealing practices within the firm when they come to the attention of the member or candidate.
- Although a member or candidate need not communicate a recommendation to all customers, the selection process by which customers receive information should be based on suitability and known interest, not on any preferred or favored status.

A common practice to assure fair dealing is to communicate recommendations simultaneously within the firm and to customers. Members and candidates should consider the following points when establishing fair-dealing compliance procedures:

- Limit the number of people involved.
- Shorten the time frame between decision and dissemination.
- Publish guidelines for pre-dissemination behavior.
- Simultaneous dissemination.
- Maintain a list of clients and their holdings.
- Develop and document trade allocation procedures that ensure:
  - Fairness to advisory clients, both in priority of execution of orders and in the allocation of the price obtained in execution of block orders or trades.
  - Timeliness and efficiency in the execution of orders.
  - Accuracy of the member's or candidate's records as to trade orders and client account positions.

With these principles in mind, members and candidates should develop or encourage their firm to develop written allocation procedures, with particular attention to procedures for block trades and new issues. Procedures to consider are as follows:

- Requiring orders and modifications or cancellations of orders to be documented and time stamped.
- Processing and executing orders on a first-in, first-out basis with consideration of bundling orders for efficiency as appropriate for the asset class or the security.
- Developing a policy to address such issues as calculating execution prices and "partial fills" when trades are grouped, or in a block, for efficiency.
- Giving all client accounts participating in a block trade the same execution price and charging the same commission.
- When the full amount of the block order is not executed, allocating partially executed orders among the participating client accounts pro rata on the basis of order size while not going below an established minimum lot size for some securities (e.g., bonds).

- When allocating trades for new issues, obtaining advance indications of interest, allocating securities by client (rather than portfolio manager), and providing a method for calculating allocations.

Disclose Trade Allocation Procedures
- Members and candidates should disclose to clients and prospective clients how they select accounts to participate in an order and how they determine the amount of securities each account will buy or sell. Trade allocation procedures must be fair and equitable, and disclosure of inequitable allocation methods does not relieve the member or candidate of this obligation.

Establish Systematic Account Review
- Member and candidate supervisors should review each account on a regular basis to ensure that no client or customer is being given preferential treatment and that the investment actions taken for each account are suitable for each account's objectives.
- Because investments should be based on individual needs and circumstances, an investment manager may have good reasons for placing a given security or other investment in one account while selling it from another account and should fully document the reasons behind both sides of the transaction.
- Members and candidates should encourage firms to establish review procedures, however, to detect whether trading in one account is being used to benefit a favored client.

Disclose Levels of Service
- Members and candidates should disclose to all clients whether the organization offers different levels of service to clients for the same fee or different fees.
- Different levels of service should not be offered to clients selectively.

Standard III(C) Suitability

The Standard
1. When members and candidates are in an **advisory relationship with a client**, they must:
   a. Make a reasonable inquiry into a client's or prospective client's investment experience, risk and return objectives, and financial constraints prior to making any investment recommendation or taking investment action and must reassess and update this information regularly.
   b. Determine that an investment is suitable to the client's financial situation and consistent with the client's written objectives, mandates, and constraints before making an investment recommendation or taking investment action.
   c. Judge the suitability of investments in the context of the client's total portfolio.
2. When members and candidates are **responsible for managing a portfolio to a specific mandate, strategy, or style**, they must make only investment recommendations or take only investment actions that are consistent with the stated objectives and constraints of the portfolio. In other words, there is no need for an investment policy statement when managing to a specific mandate.

Guidance
- Standard III(C) requires that members and candidates who are in an investment advisory relationship with clients consider carefully the needs, circumstances, and objectives of

the clients when determining the appropriateness and suitability of a given investment or course of investment action.

- In judging the suitability of a potential investment, the member or candidate should review many aspects of the client's knowledge, experience related to investing, and financial situation. These aspects include, but are not limited to, the risk profile of the investment as compared with the constraints of the client, the impact of the investment on the diversity of the portfolio, and whether the client has the means or net worth to assume the associated risk. The investment professional's determination of suitability should reflect only the investment recommendations or actions that a prudent person would be willing to undertake. Not every investment opportunity will be suitable for every portfolio, regardless of the potential return being offered.
- The responsibilities of members and candidates to gather information and make a suitability analysis prior to making a recommendation or taking investment action fall on those members and candidates who provide investment advice in the course of an advisory relationship with a client. Other members and candidates who are simply executing specific instructions for retail clients when buying or selling securities, may not have the opportunity to judge the suitability of a particular investment for the ultimate client.

Developing an Investment Policy When an Advisory Relationship Exists
- When an advisory relationship exists, members and candidates must gather client information at the inception of the relationship. Such information includes the client's financial circumstances, personal data (such as age and occupation) that are relevant to investment decisions, attitudes toward risk, and objectives in investing. This information should be incorporated into a written investment policy statement (IPS) that addresses the client's risk tolerance, return requirements, and all investment constraints (including time horizon, liquidity needs, tax concerns, legal and regulatory factors, and unique circumstances).
- The IPS also should identify and describe the roles and responsibilities of the parties to the advisory relationship and investment process, as well as schedules for review and evaluation of the IPS.
- After formulating long-term capital market expectations, members and candidates can assist in developing an appropriate strategic asset allocation and investment program for the client, whether these are presented in separate documents or incorporated in the IPS or in appendices to the IPS.

Understanding the Client's Risk Profile
- The investment professional must consider the possibilities of rapidly changing investment environments and their likely impact on a client's holdings, both individual securities and the collective portfolio.
- The risk of many investment strategies can and should be analyzed and quantified in advance.
- Members and candidates should pay careful attention to the leverage inherent in many synthetic investment vehicles or products when considering them for use in a client's investment program.

Updating an Investment Policy
- Updating the IPS should be repeated at least annually and also prior to material changes to any specific investment recommendations or decisions on behalf of the client.
  - For an individual client, important changes might include the number of dependents, personal tax status, health, liquidity needs, risk tolerance, amount of

wealth beyond that represented in the portfolio, and extent to which compensation and other income provide for current income needs.
  - For an institutional client, such changes might relate to the magnitude of unfunded liabilities in a pension fund, the withdrawal privileges in an employee savings plan, or the distribution requirements of a charitable foundation.
- If clients withhold information about their financial portfolios, the suitability analysis conducted by members and candidates cannot be expected to be complete; it must be based on the information provided.

The Need for Diversification
- The unique characteristics (or risks) of an individual investment may become partially or entirely neutralized when it is combined with other individual investments within a portfolio. Therefore, a reasonable amount of diversification is thus the norm for many portfolios.
- An investment with high relative risk on its own may be a suitable investment in the context of the entire portfolio or when the client's stated objectives contemplate speculative or risky investments.
- Members and candidates can be responsible for assessing the suitability of an investment only on the basis of the information and criteria actually provided by the client.

Addressing Unsolicited Trading Requests
- If an unsolicited request is expected to have only a minimum impact on the entire portfolio because the size of the requested trade is small or the trade would result in a limited change to the portfolio's risk profile, the member or candidate should focus on educating the investor on how the request deviates from the current policy statement, and then she may follow her firm's policies regarding the necessary client approval for executing unsuitable trades. At a minimum, the client should acknowledge the discussion and accept the conditions that make the recommendation unsuitable.
- If an unsolicited request is expected to have a material impact on the portfolio, the member or candidate should use this opportunity to update the investment policy statement. Doing so would allow the client to fully understand the potential effect of the requested trade on his or her current goals or risk levels.
- If the client declines to modify her policy statements while insisting an unsolicited trade be made, the member or candidate will need to evaluate the effectiveness of her services to the client. The options available to the members or candidates will depend on the services provided by their employer. Some firms may allow for the trade to be executed in a new unmanaged account. If alternative options are not available, members and candidates ultimately will need to determine whether they should continue the advisory arrangement with the client.

Managing to an Index or Mandate
Some members and candidates do not manage money for individuals but are responsible for managing a fund to an index or an expected mandate. The responsibility of these members and candidates is to invest in a manner consistent with the stated mandate but without having to prepare the IPS for the client.

Recommended Procedures for Compliance

Investment Policy Statement
In formulating an investment policy for the client, the member or candidate should take the following into consideration:

- *Client identification*—(1) type and nature of client, (2) the existence of separate beneficiaries, and (3) approximate portion of total client assets that the member or candidate is managing.
- *Investor objectives*—(1) return objectives (income, growth in principal, maintenance of purchasing power) and (2) risk tolerance (suitability, stability of values).
- *Investor constraints*—(1) liquidity needs, (2) expected cash flows (patterns of additions and/or withdrawals), (3) investable funds (assets and liabilities or other commitments), (4) time horizon, (5) tax considerations, (6) regulatory and legal circumstances, (7) investor preferences, prohibitions, circumstances, and unique needs, and (8) proxy voting responsibilities and guidance.
- *Performance measurement benchmarks.*

Regular Updates
- The investor's objectives and constraints should be maintained and reviewed periodically to reflect any changes in the client's circumstances.

Suitability Test Policies
- With the increase in regulatory required suitability tests, members and candidates should encourage their firms to develop related policies and procedures. The test procedures should require the investment professional to look beyond the potential return of the investment and include the following:
  - An analysis of the impact on the portfolio's diversification.
  - A comparison of the investment risks with the client's assessed risk tolerance.
  - The fit of the investment with the required investment strategy.

Standard III(D) Performance Presentation

The Standard
When communicating investment performance information, members and candidates must make reasonable efforts to ensure that it is fair, accurate, and complete.

Guidance
- Members and candidates must provide credible performance information to clients and prospective clients and to avoid misstating performance or misleading clients and prospective clients about the investment performance of members or candidates or their firms.
- Standard III(D) covers any practice that would lead to misrepresentation of a member's or candidate's performance record, whether the practice involves performance presentation or performance measurement.
- Members and candidates should not state or imply that clients will obtain or benefit from a rate of return that was generated in the past.
- Research analysts promoting the success or accuracy of their recommendations must ensure that their claims are fair, accurate, and complete.
- If the presentation is brief, the member or candidate must make available to clients and prospects, on request, the detailed information supporting that communication. Best practice dictates that brief presentations include a reference to the limited nature of the information provided.

Recommended Procedures for Compliance

Apply the GIPS Standards
- Compliance with the GIPS standards is the best method to meet their obligations under Standard III(D).

Compliance without Applying GIPS Standards
Members and candidates can also meet their obligations under Standard III(D) by:

- Considering the knowledge and sophistication of the audience to whom a performance presentation is addressed.
- Presenting the performance of the weighted composite of similar portfolios rather than using a single representative account.
- Including terminated accounts as part of performance history with a clear indication of when the accounts were terminated.
- Including disclosures that fully explain the performance results being reported (for example, stating, when appropriate, that results are simulated when model results are used, clearly indicating when the performance record is that of a prior entity, or disclosing whether the performance is gross of fees, net of fees, or after tax).
- Maintaining the data and records used to calculate the performance being presented.

Standard III(E) Preservation of Confidentiality

The Standard
Members and candidates must keep information about current, former, and prospective clients confidential unless:

1. The information concerns illegal activities on the part of the client;
2. Disclosure is required by law; or
3. The client or prospective client permits disclosure of the information.

Guidance
- Members and candidates must preserve the confidentiality of information communicated to them by their clients, prospective clients, and former clients. This standard is applicable when (1) the member or candidate receives information because of his or her special ability to conduct a portion of the client's business or personal affairs and (2) the member or candidate receives information that arises from or is relevant to that portion of the client's business that is the subject of the special or confidential relationship.
- If disclosure of the information is required by law or the information concerns illegal activities by the client, however, the member or candidate may have an obligation to report the activities to the appropriate authorities.

Status of Client
- This standard protects the confidentiality of client information even if the person or entity is no longer a client of the member or candidate. Therefore, members and candidates must continue to maintain the confidentiality of client records even after the client relationship has ended.
- If a client or former client expressly authorizes the member or candidate to disclose information, however, the member or candidate may follow the terms of the authorization and provide the information.

Compliance with Laws

- As a general matter, members and candidates must comply with applicable law. If applicable law requires disclosure of client information in certain circumstances, members and candidates must comply with the law. Similarly, if applicable law requires members and candidates to maintain confidentiality, even if the information concerns illegal activities on the part of the client, members and candidates must not disclose such information.
- When in doubt, members and candidates should consult with their employer's compliance personnel or legal counsel before disclosing confidential information about clients.

Electronic Information and Security

- Standard III(E) does not require members or candidates to become experts in information security technology, but they should have a thorough understanding of the policies of their employer.
- Members and candidates should encourage their firm to conduct regular periodic training on confidentiality procedures for all firm personnel, including portfolio associates, receptionists, and other non-investment staff who have routine direct contact with clients and their records.

Professional Conduct Investigations by CFA Institute

- The requirements of Standard III(E) are not intended to prevent members and candidates from cooperating with an investigation by the CFA Institute Professional Conduct Program (PCP). When permissible under applicable law, members and candidates shall consider the PCP an extension of themselves when requested to provide information about a client in support of a PCP investigation into their own conduct.

Recommended Procedures for Compliance

The simplest, most conservative, and most effective way to comply with Standard III(E) is to avoid disclosing any information received from a client except to authorized fellow employees who are also working for the client. In some instances, however, a member or candidate may want to disclose information received from clients that is outside the scope of the confidential relationship and does not involve illegal activities. Before making such a disclosure, a member or candidate should ask the following:

- In what context was the information disclosed? If disclosed in a discussion of work being performed for the client, is the information relevant to the work?
- Is the information background material that, if disclosed, will enable the member or candidate to improve service to the client?

Communicating with Clients

- Members and candidates should make reasonable efforts to ensure that firm-supported communication methods and compliance procedures follow practices designed for preventing accidental distribution of confidential information.
- Members and candidates should be diligent in discussing with clients the appropriate methods for providing confidential information. It is important to convey to clients that not all firm-sponsored resources may be appropriate for such communications.

Standard IV(A) Loyalty

The Standard
In matters related to their employment, members and candidates must act for the benefit of their employer and not deprive their employer of the advantage of their skills and abilities, divulge confidential information, or otherwise cause harm to their employer.

Guidance
- Members and candidates should protect the interests of their firm by refraining from any conduct that would injure the firm, deprive it of profit, or deprive it of the member's or candidate's skills and ability.
- Members and candidates must always place the interests of clients above the interests of their employer but should also consider the effects of their conduct on the sustainability and integrity of the employer firm.
- In matters related to their employment, members and candidates must comply with the policies and procedures established by their employers that govern the employer-employee relationship—to the extent that such policies and procedures do not conflict with applicable laws, rules, or regulations or the Code and Standards.
- The standard does not require members and candidates to subordinate important personal and family obligations to their work.

Employer Responsibilities
- Employers must recognize the duties and responsibilities that they owe to their employees if they expect to have content and productive employees.
- Members and candidates are encouraged to provide their employer with a copy of the Code and Standards.
- Employers are not obligated to adhere to the Code and Standards. In expecting to retain competent employees who are members and candidates, however, they should not develop conflicting policies and procedures.

Independent Practice
- Members and candidates must abstain from independent competitive activity that could conflict with the interests of their employer.
- Members and candidates who plan to engage in independent practice for compensation must notify their employer and describe the types of services they will render to prospective independent clients, the expected duration of the services, and the compensation for the services.
- Members and candidates should not render services until they receive consent from their employer to all of the terms of the arrangement.
  - "Practice" means any service that the employer currently makes available for remuneration.
  - "Undertaking independent practice" means engaging in competitive business, as opposed to making preparations to begin such practice.

Leaving an Employer
- When members and candidates are planning to leave their current employer, they must continue to act in the employer's best interest. They must not engage in any activities that would conflict with this duty until their resignation becomes effective.
- Activities that might constitute a violation, especially in combination, include the following:
  - Misappropriation of trade secrets.
  - Misuse of confidential information.

- ○ Solicitation of the employer's clients prior to cessation of employment.
- ○ Self-dealing (appropriating for one's own property a business opportunity or information belonging to one's employer).
- ○ Misappropriation of clients or client lists.
- A departing employee is generally free to make arrangements or preparations to go into a competitive business before terminating the relationship with his or her employer as long as such preparations do not breach the employee's duty of loyalty.
- A member or candidate who is contemplating seeking other employment must not contact existing clients or potential clients prior to leaving his or her employer for purposes of soliciting their business for the new employer. Once notice is provided to the employer of the intent to resign, the member or candidate must follow the employer's policies and procedures related to notifying clients of his or her planned departure. In addition, the member or candidate must not take records or files to a new employer without the written permission of the previous employer.
- Once an employee has left the firm, the skills and experience that an employee obtained while employed are not "confidential" or "privileged" information. Similarly, simple knowledge of the names and existence of former clients is generally not confidential information unless deemed such by an agreement or by law.
- Standard IV(A) does not prohibit experience or knowledge gained at one employer from being used at another employer. Firm records or work performed on behalf of the firm that is stored in paper copy or electronically for the member's or candidate's convenience while employed, however, should be erased or returned to the employer unless the firm gives permission to keep those records after employment ends.
- The standard does not prohibit former employees from contacting clients of their previous firm as long as the contact information does not come from the records of the former employer or violate an applicable "non-compete agreement." Members and candidates are free to use public information after departing to contact former clients without violating Standard IV(A) as long as there is no specific agreement not to do so.

Use of Social Media

- Members and candidates should understand and abide by all applicable firm policies and regulations as to the acceptable use of social media platforms to interact with clients and prospective clients.
- Specific accounts and user profiles of members and candidates may be created for solely professional reasons, including firm-approved accounts for client engagements. Such firm-approved business-related accounts would be considered part of the firm's assets, thus requiring members and candidates to transfer or delete the accounts as directed by their firm's policies and procedures.
- Best practice for members and candidates is to maintain separate accounts for their personal and professional social media activities. Members and candidates should discuss with their employers how profiles should be treated when a single account includes personal connections and also is used to conduct aspects of their professional activities.

Whistleblowing

Sometimes, circumstances may arise (e.g., when an employer is engaged in illegal or unethical activity) in which members and candidates must act contrary to their employer's interests in order to comply with their duties to the market and clients. In such instances, activities that would normally violate a member's or candidate's duty to his or her employer (such as contradicting employer instructions, violating certain policies and procedures, or preserving a record by copying employer records) may be justified. However, such action would be permitted only if the intent is clearly aimed at protecting clients or the integrity of the market, not for personal gain.

Nature of Employment

- Members and candidates must determine whether they are employees or independent contractors in order to determine the applicability of Standard IV(A). This issue will be decided largely by the degree of control exercised by the employing entity over the member or candidate. Factors determining control include whether the member's or candidate's hours, work location, and other parameters of the job are set; whether facilities are provided to the member or candidate; whether the member's or candidate's expenses are reimbursed; whether the member or candidate seeks work from other employers; and the number of clients or employers the member or candidate works for.
- A member's or candidate's duties within an independent contractor relationship are governed by the oral or written agreement between the member and the client. Members and candidates should take care to define clearly the scope of their responsibilities and the expectations of each client within the context of each relationship. Once a member or candidate establishes a relationship with a client, the member or candidate has a duty to abide by the terms of the agreement.

Recommended Procedures for Compliance

Competition Policy

- A member or candidate must understand any restrictions placed by the employer on offering similar services outside the firm while employed by the firm.
- If a member's or candidate's employer elects to have its employees sign a non-compete agreement as part of the employment agreement, the member or candidate should ensure that the details are clear and fully explained prior to signing the agreement.

Termination Policy

- Members and candidates should clearly understand the termination policies of their employer. Termination policies should:
  - Establish clear procedures regarding the resignation process, including addressing how the termination will be disclosed to clients and staff and whether updates posted through social media platforms will be allowed.
  - Outline the procedures for transferring ongoing research and account management responsibilities.
  - Address agreements that allow departing employees to remove specific client-related information upon resignation.

Incident-Reporting Procedures

- Members and candidates should be aware of their firm's policies related to whistleblowing and encourage their firm to adopt industry best practices in this area.

Employee Classification

- Members and candidates should understand their status within their employer firm.

Standard IV(B) Additional Compensation Arrangements

The Standard

Members and candidates must not accept gifts, benefits, compensation, or consideration that competes with or might reasonably be expected to create a conflict of interest with their employer's interest unless they obtain written consent from all parties involved.

Guidance

- Members and candidates must obtain permission from their employer before accepting compensation or other benefits from third parties for the services rendered to the employer or for any services that might create a conflict with their employer's interest.
  - Compensation and benefits include direct compensation by the client and any indirect compensation or other benefits received from third parties.
  - "Written consent" includes any form of communication that can be documented (for example, communication via e-mail that can be retrieved and documented).

Recommended Procedures for Compliance

- Members and candidates should make an immediate written report to their supervisor and compliance officer specifying any compensation they propose to receive for services in addition to the compensation or benefits received from their employer.
- The details of the report should be confirmed by the party offering the additional compensation, including performance incentives offered by clients.
- This written report should state the terms of any agreement under which a member or candidate will receive additional compensation; "terms" include the nature of the compensation, the approximate amount of compensation, and the duration of the agreement.

Standard IV(C) Responsibilities of Supervisors

The Standard

Members and candidates must make reasonable efforts to ensure that anyone subject to their supervision or authority complies with applicable laws, rules, regulations, and the Code and Standards.

Guidance

- Members and candidates must promote actions by all employees under their supervision and authority to comply with applicable laws, rules, regulations, and firm policies, and the Code and Standards.
- A member's or candidate's responsibilities under Standard IV(C) include instructing those subordinates to whom supervision is delegated about methods to promote compliance, including preventing and detecting violations of laws, rules, regulations, firm policies, and the Code and Standards.
- At a minimum, Standard IV(C) requires that members and candidates with supervisory responsibility make reasonable efforts to prevent and detect violations by ensuring the establishment of effective compliance systems. However, an effective compliance system goes beyond enacting a code of ethics, establishing policies and procedures to achieve compliance with the code and applicable law, and reviewing employee actions to determine whether they are following the rules.
- To be effective supervisors, members and candidates should implement education and training programs on a recurring or regular basis for employees under their supervision. Further, establishing incentives—monetary or otherwise—for employees not only to meet business goals but also to reward ethical behavior offers supervisors another way to assist employees in complying with their legal and ethical obligations.
- A member or candidate with supervisory responsibility should bring an inadequate compliance system to the attention of the firm's senior managers and recommend corrective action. If the member or candidate clearly cannot discharge supervisory responsibilities because of the absence of a compliance system or because of an inadequate compliance system, the member or candidate should decline in writing to

accept supervisory responsibility until the firm adopts reasonable procedures to allow adequate exercise of supervisory responsibility.

System for Supervision
- Members and candidates with supervisory responsibility must understand what constitutes an adequate compliance system for their firms and make reasonable efforts to see that appropriate compliance procedures are established, documented, communicated to covered personnel, and followed.
    - "Adequate" procedures are those designed to meet industry standards, regulatory requirements, the requirements of the Code and Standards, and the circumstances of the firm.
    - To be effective, compliance procedures must be in place prior to the occurrence of a violation of the law or the Code and Standards.
- Once a supervisor learns that an employee has violated or may have violated the law or the Code and Standards, the supervisor must promptly initiate an assessment to determine the extent of the wrongdoing. Relying on an employee's statements about the extent of the violation or assurances that the wrongdoing will not reoccur is not enough. Reporting the misconduct up the chain of command and warning the employee to cease the activity are also not enough. Pending the outcome of the investigation, a supervisor should take steps to ensure that the violation will not be repeated, such as placing limits on the employee's activities or increasing the monitoring of the employee's activities.

Supervision Includes Detection
- Members and candidates with supervisory responsibility must also make reasonable efforts to detect violations of laws, rules, regulations, firm policies, and the Code and Standards. If a member or candidate has adopted reasonable procedures and taken steps to institute an effective compliance program, then the member or candidate may not be in violation of Standard IV(C) if he or she does not detect violations that occur despite these efforts. The fact that violations do occur may indicate, however, that the compliance procedures are inadequate.
- In addition, in some cases, merely enacting such procedures may not be sufficient to fulfill the duty required by Standard IV(C). A member or candidate may be in violation of Standard IV(C) if he or she knows or should know that the procedures designed to promote compliance, including detecting and preventing violations, are not being followed.

Recommended Procedures for Compliance

Codes of Ethics or Compliance Procedures
- Members and candidates are encouraged to recommend that their employers adopt a code of ethics, and put in place specific policies and procedures needed to ensure compliance with the codes and with securities laws and regulations.
- Members and candidates should encourage their employers to provide their codes of ethics to clients.

Adequate Compliance Procedures
Adequate compliance procedures should:

- Be contained in a clearly written and accessible manual that is tailored to the firm's operations.
- Be drafted so that the procedures are easy to understand.

- Designate a compliance officer whose authority and responsibility are clearly defined and who has the necessary resources and authority to implement the firm's compliance procedures.
- Describe the hierarchy of supervision and assign duties among supervisors.
- Implement a system of checks and balances.
- Outline the scope of the procedures.
- Outline procedures to document the monitoring and testing of compliance procedures.
- Outline permissible conduct.
- Delineate procedures for reporting violations and sanctions.

Once a compliance program is in place, a supervisor should:

- Disseminate the contents of the program to appropriate personnel.
- Periodically update procedures to ensure that the measures are adequate under the law.
- Continually educate personnel regarding the compliance procedures.
- Issue periodic reminders of the procedures to appropriate personnel.
- Incorporate a professional conduct evaluation as part of an employee's performance review.
- Review the actions of employees to ensure compliance and identify violators.
- Take the necessary steps to enforce the procedures once a violation has occurred.

Once a violation is discovered, a supervisor should:

- Respond promptly.
- Conduct a thorough investigation of the activities to determine the scope of the wrongdoing.
- Increase supervision or place appropriate limitations on the wrongdoer pending the outcome of the investigation.
- Review procedures for potential changes necessary to prevent future violations from occurring.

Implementation of Compliance Education and Training
- Regular ethics and compliance training, in conjunction with the adoption of a code of ethics, is critical to investment firms seeking to establish a strong culture of integrity and to provide an environment in which employees routinely engage in ethical conduct in compliance with the law.

Establish an Appropriate Incentive Structure
- Supervisors and firms must look closely at their incentive structure to determine whether the structure encourages profits and returns at the expense of ethically appropriate conduct. Only when compensation and incentives are firmly tied to client interests and how outcomes are achieved, rather than how much is generated for the firm, will employees work to achieve a culture of integrity.

Standard V(A) Diligence and Reasonable Basis

The Standard
Members and candidates must:

1. Exercise diligence, independence, and thoroughness in analyzing investments, making investment recommendations, and taking investment actions.

2. Have a reasonable and adequate basis, supported by appropriate research and investigation, for any investment analysis, recommendation, or action.

Guidance

- The requirements for issuing conclusions based on research will vary in relation to the member's or candidate's role in the investment decision-making process, but the member or candidate must make reasonable efforts to cover all pertinent issues when arriving at a recommendation.
- Members and candidates enhance transparency by providing or offering to provide supporting information to clients when recommending a purchase or sale or when changing a recommendation.

Defining Diligence and Reasonable Basis

- As with determining the suitability of an investment for the client, the necessary level of research and analysis will differ with the product, security, or service being offered. The following list provides some, but definitely not all, examples of attributes to consider while forming the basis for a recommendation:
  - Global, regional, and country macroeconomic conditions.
  - A company's operating and financial history.
  - The industry's and sector's current conditions and the stage of the business cycle.
  - A mutual fund's fee structure and management history.
  - The output and potential limitations of quantitative models.
  - The quality of the assets included in a securitization.
  - The appropriateness of selected peer-group comparisons.
- The steps taken in developing a diligent and reasonable recommendation should minimize unexpected downside events.

Using Secondary or Third-Party Research

- If members and candidates rely on secondary or third-party research, they must make reasonable and diligent efforts to determine whether such research is sound.
  - Secondary research is defined as research conducted by someone else in the member's or candidate's firm.
  - Third-party research is research conducted by entities outside the member's or candidate's firm, such as a brokerage firm, bank, or research firm.
- Members and candidates should make reasonable inquiries into the source and accuracy of all data used in completing their investment analysis and recommendations.
- Criteria that a member or candidate can use in forming an opinion on whether research is sound include the following:
  - Assumptions used.
  - Rigor of the analysis performed.
  - Date/timeliness of the research.
  - Evaluation of the objectivity and independence of the recommendations.
- A member or candidate may rely on others in his or her firm to determine whether secondary or third-party research is sound and use the information in good faith unless the member or candidate has reason to question its validity or the processes and procedures used by those responsible for the research.
- A member or candidate should verify that the firm has a policy about the timely and consistent review of approved research providers to ensure that the quality of the research continues to meet the necessary standards. If such a policy is not in place at the firm, the member or candidate should encourage the development and adoption of a formal review practice.

ET

Using Quantitatively Oriented Research

- Members and candidates must have an understanding of the parameters used in models and quantitative research that are incorporated into their investment recommendations. Although they are not required to become experts in every technical aspect of the models, they must understand the assumptions and limitations inherent in any model and how the results were used in the decision-making process.
- Members and candidates should make reasonable efforts to test the output of investment models and other pre-programmed analytical tools they use. Such validation should occur before incorporating the process into their methods, models, or analyses.
- Although not every model can test for every factor or outcome, members and candidates should ensure that their analyses incorporate a broad range of assumptions sufficient to capture the underlying characteristics of investments. The omission from the analysis of potentially negative outcomes or of levels of risk outside the norm may misrepresent the true economic value of an investment. The possible scenarios for analysis should include factors that are likely to have a substantial influence on the investment value and may include extremely positive and negative scenarios.

Developing Quantitatively Oriented Techniques

- Members and candidates involved in the development and oversight of quantitatively oriented models, methods, and algorithms must understand the technical aspects of the products they provide to clients. A thorough testing of the model and resulting analysis should be completed prior to product distribution.
- In reviewing the computer models or the resulting output, members and candidates need to pay particular attention to the assumptions used in the analysis and the rigor of the analysis to ensure that the model incorporates a wide range of possible input expectations, including negative market events.

Selecting External Advisers and Sub-Advisers

- Members and candidates must review managers as diligently as they review individual funds and securities.
- Members and candidates who are directly involved with the use of external advisers need to ensure that their firms have standardized criteria for reviewing these selected external advisers and managers. Such criteria would include, but would not be limited to, the following:
  - Reviewing the adviser's established code of ethics,
  - Understanding the adviser's compliance and internal control procedures,
  - Assessing the quality of the published return information, and
  - Reviewing the adviser's investment process and adherence to its stated strategy.

Group Research and Decision Making

In some instances, a member or candidate will not agree with the view of the group. If, however, the member or candidate believes that the consensus opinion has a reasonable and adequate basis and is independent and objective, the member or candidate need not decline to be identified with the report. If the member or candidate is confident in the process, the member or candidate does not need to dissociate from the report even if it does not reflect his or her opinion.

Recommended Procedures for Compliance

Members and candidates should encourage their firms to consider the following policies and procedures to support the principles of Standard V(A):

- Establish a policy requiring that research reports, credit ratings, and investment recommendations have a basis that can be substantiated as reasonable and adequate.
- Develop detailed, written guidance for analysts (research, investment, or credit), supervisory analysts, and review committees that establishes the due diligence procedures for judging whether a particular recommendation has a reasonable and adequate basis.
- Develop measurable criteria for assessing the quality of research, the reasonableness and adequacy of the basis for any recommendation or rating, and the accuracy of recommendations over time.
- Develop detailed, written guidance that establishes minimum levels of scenario testing of all computer-based models used in developing, rating, and evaluating financial instruments.
- Develop measurable criteria for assessing outside providers, including the quality of information being provided, the reasonableness and adequacy of the provider's collection practices, and the accuracy of the information over time.
  - Adopt a standardized set of criteria for evaluating the adequacy of external advisers.

Standard V(B) Communication with Clients and Prospective Clients

The Standard

Members and candidates must:

1. Disclose to clients and prospective clients the basic format and general principles of the investment processes they use to analyze investments, select securities, and construct portfolios, and must promptly disclose any changes that might materially affect those processes.
2. Disclose to clients and prospective clients significant limitations and risks associated with the investment process.
3. Use reasonable judgment in identifying which factors are important to their investment analyses, recommendations, or actions, and include those factors in communications with clients and prospective clients.
4. Distinguish between fact and opinion in the presentation of investment analyses and recommendations.

Guidance

- Members and candidates should communicate in a recommendation the factors that were instrumental in making the investment recommendation. A critical part of this requirement is to distinguish clearly between opinions and facts.
- Follow-up communication of significant changes in the risk characteristics of a security or asset strategy is required.
- Providing regular updates to any changes in the risk characteristics is recommended.

Informing Clients of the Investment Process

- Members and candidates must adequately describe to clients and prospective clients the manner in which they conduct the investment decision-making process. Such disclosure should address factors that have positive and negative influences on the recommendations, including significant risks and limitations of the investment process used.
- The member or candidate must keep clients and other interested parties informed on an ongoing basis about changes to the investment process, especially newly identified significant risks and limitations.

- Members and candidates should inform the clients about the specialization or diversification expertise provided by the external adviser(s).

Different Forms of Communication

- Members and candidates using any social media service to communicate business information must be diligent in their efforts to avoid unintended problems because these services may not be available to all clients. When providing information to clients through new technologies, members and candidates should take reasonable steps to ensure that such delivery would treat all clients fairly and, if necessary, be considered publicly disseminated.
- If recommendations are contained in capsule form (such as a recommended stock list), members and candidates should notify clients that additional information and analyses are available from the producer of the report.

Identifying Risks and Limitations

- Members and candidates must outline to clients and prospective clients significant risks and limitations of the analysis contained in their investment products or recommendations.
- The appropriateness of risk disclosure should be assessed on the basis of what was known at the time the investment action was taken (often called an ex ante basis). Members and candidates must disclose significant risks known to them at the time of the disclosure.
- Members and candidates cannot be expected to disclose risks they are unaware of at the time recommendations or investment actions are made.
- Having no knowledge of a risk or limitation that subsequently triggers a loss may reveal a deficiency in the diligence and reasonable basis of the research of the member or candidate but may not reveal a breach of Standard V(B).

Report Presentation

- A report writer who has done adequate investigation may emphasize certain areas, touch briefly on others, and omit certain aspects deemed unimportant.
- Investment advice based on quantitative research and analysis must be supported by readily available reference material and should be applied in a manner consistent with previously applied methodology. If changes in methodology are made, they should be highlighted.

Distinction between Facts and Opinions in Reports

- Violations often occur when reports fail to separate the past from the future by not indicating that earnings estimates, changes in the outlook for dividends, or future market price information are opinions subject to future circumstances.
- In the case of complex quantitative analyses, members and candidates must clearly separate fact from statistical conjecture and should identify the known limitations of an analysis.
- Members and candidates should explicitly discuss with clients and prospective clients the assumptions used in the investment models and processes to generate the analysis. Caution should be used in promoting the perceived accuracy of any model or process to clients because the ultimate output is merely an estimate of future results and not a certainty.

Recommended Procedures for Compliance
- Members and candidates should encourage their firms to have a rigorous methodology for reviewing research that is created for publication and dissemination to clients.
- To assist in the after-the-fact review of a report, the member or candidate must maintain records indicating the nature of the research and should, if asked, be able to supply additional information to the client (or any user of the report) covering factors not included in the report.

Standard V(C) Record Retention

The Standard
Members and candidates must develop and maintain appropriate records to support their investment analyses, recommendations, actions, and other investment-related communications with clients and prospective clients.

Guidance
- Members and candidates must retain records that substantiate the scope of their research and reasons for their actions or conclusions. The retention requirement applies to decisions to buy or sell a security as well as reviews undertaken that do not lead to a change in position.
- Records may be maintained either in hard copy or electronic form.

New Media Records
- Members and candidates should understand that although employers and local regulators are developing digital media retention policies, these policies may lag behind the advent of new communication channels. Such lag places greater responsibility on the individual for ensuring that all relevant information is retained. Examples of non-print media formats that should be retained include, but are not limited to e-mails, text messages, blog posts, and Twitter posts.

Records Are Property of the Firm
- As a general matter, records created as part of a member's or candidate's professional activity on behalf of his or her employer are the property of the firm.
- When a member or candidate leaves a firm to seek other employment, the member or candidate cannot take the property of the firm, including original forms or copies of supporting records of the member's or candidate's work, to the new employer without the express consent of the previous employer.
- The member or candidate cannot use historical recommendations or research reports created at the previous firm because the supporting documentation is unavailable.
- For future use, the member or candidate must re-create the supporting records at the new firm with information gathered through public sources or directly from the covered company and not from memory or sources obtained at the previous employer.

Local Requirements
- Local regulators and firms may also implement policies detailing the applicable time frame for retaining research and client communication records. Fulfilling such regulatory and firm requirements satisfies the requirements of Standard V(C).
- In the absence of regulatory guidance or firm policies, CFA Institute recommends maintaining records for at least seven years. If there is a regulatory mandate to maintain records for less than seven years, then the member or candidate must follow this mandate.

Recommended Procedures for Compliance
The responsibility to maintain records that support investment action generally falls with the firm rather than individuals. Members and candidates must, however, archive research notes and other documents, either electronically or in hard copy, that support their current investment-related communications.

Standard VI(A) Disclosure of Conflicts

The Standard
Members and candidates must make full and fair disclosure of all matters that could reasonably be expected to impair their independence and objectivity or interfere with respective duties to their clients, prospective clients, and employer. Members and candidates must ensure that such disclosures are prominent, are delivered in plain language, and communicate the relevant information effectively.

Guidance
- Best practice is to avoid actual conflicts or the appearance of conflicts of interest when possible. Conflicts of interest often arise in the investment profession.
- When conflicts cannot be reasonably avoided, clear and complete disclosure of their existence is necessary.
- In making and updating disclosures of conflicts of interest, members and candidates should err on the side of caution to ensure that conflicts are effectively communicated.

Disclosure of Conflicts to Employers
- When reporting conflicts of interest to employers, members and candidates must give their employers enough information to assess the impact of the conflict.
- Members and candidates must take reasonable steps to avoid conflicts and, if they occur inadvertently, must report them promptly so that the employer and the member or candidate can resolve them as quickly and effectively as possible.
- Any potential conflict situation that could prevent clear judgment about or full commitment to the execution of a member's or candidate's duties to the employer should be reported to the member's or candidate's employer and promptly resolved.

Disclosure to Clients
- The most obvious conflicts of interest, which should always be disclosed, are relationships between an issuer and the member, the candidate, or his or her firm (such as a directorship or consultancy by a member; investment banking, underwriting, and financial relationships; broker/dealer market-making activities; and material beneficial ownership of stock).
- Disclosures should be made to clients regarding fee arrangements, sub-advisory agreements, or other situations involving nonstandard fee structures. Equally important is the disclosure of arrangements in which the firm benefits directly from investment recommendations. An obvious conflict of interest is the rebate of a portion of the service fee some classes of mutual funds charge to investors.

Cross-Departmental Conflicts
- Other circumstances can give rise to actual or potential conflicts of interest. For instance:
  - A sell-side analyst working for a broker/dealer may be encouraged, not only by members of her or his own firm but by corporate issuers themselves, to write research reports about particular companies.
  - A buy-side analyst is likely to be faced with similar conflicts as banks exercise their underwriting and security-dealing powers.

- The marketing division may ask an analyst to recommend the stock of a certain company in order to obtain business from that company.
- Members, candidates, and their firms should attempt to resolve situations presenting potential conflicts of interest or disclose them in accordance with the principles set forth in Standard VI(A).

Conflicts with Stock Ownership

- The most prevalent conflict requiring disclosure under Standard VI(A) is a member's or candidate's ownership of stock in companies that he or she recommends to clients or that clients hold. Clearly, the easiest method for preventing a conflict is to prohibit members and candidates from owning any such securities, but this approach is overly burdensome and discriminates against members and candidates. Therefore:
  - Sell-side members and candidates should disclose any materially beneficial ownership interest in a security or other investment that the member or candidate is recommending.
  - Buy-side members and candidates should disclose their procedures for reporting requirements for personal transactions.

Conflicts as a Director

- Service as a director poses three basic conflicts of interest.
  - A conflict may exist between the duties owed to clients and the duties owed to shareholders of the company.
  - Investment personnel who serve as directors may receive the securities or options to purchase securities of the company as compensation for serving on the board, which could raise questions about trading actions that might increase the value of those securities.
  - Board service creates the opportunity to receive material nonpublic information involving the company.
- When members or candidates providing investment services also serve as directors, they should be isolated from those making investment decisions by the use of firewalls or similar restrictions.

Recommended Procedures for Compliance

- Members or candidates should disclose special compensation arrangements with the employer that might conflict with client interests, such as bonuses based on short-term performance criteria, commissions, incentive fees, performance fees, and referral fees.
- Members' and candidates' firms are encouraged to include information on compensation packages in firms' promotional literature.

Standard VI(B) Priority of Transactions

The Standard

Investment transactions for clients and employers must have priority over investment transactions in which a member or candidate is the beneficial owner.

Guidance

- This standard is designed to prevent any potential conflict of interest or the appearance of a conflict of interest with respect to personal transactions.
- Client interests have priority. Client transactions must take precedence over transactions made on behalf of the member's or candidate's firm or personal transactions.

Avoiding Potential Conflicts

- Although conflicts of interest exist, nothing is inherently unethical about individual managers, advisers, or mutual fund employees making money from personal investments as long as (1) the client is not disadvantaged by the trade, (2) the investment professional does not benefit personally from trades undertaken for clients, and (3) the investment professional complies with applicable regulatory requirements.
- Some situations occur in which a member or candidate may need to enter a personal transaction that runs counter to current recommendations or what the portfolio manager is doing for client portfolios such as personal financial hardship. In these situations, the same three criteria given in the preceding paragraph should be applied in the transaction so as to not violate Standard VI(B).

Personal Trading Secondary to Trading for Clients

- The objective of the standard is to prevent personal transactions from adversely affecting the interests of clients or employers. A member or candidate having the same investment positions or being co-invested with clients does not always create a conflict.
- Personal investment positions or transactions of members or candidates or their firm should never, however, adversely affect client investments.

Standards for Nonpublic Information

- Standard VI(B) covers the activities of members and candidates who have knowledge of pending transactions that may be made on behalf of their clients or employers, who have access to nonpublic information during the normal preparation of research recommendations, or who take investment actions.
- Members and candidates are prohibited from conveying nonpublic information to any person whose relationship to the member or candidate makes the member or candidate a beneficial owner of the person's securities.
- Members and candidates must not convey this information to any other person if the nonpublic information can be deemed material.

Impact on All Accounts with Beneficial Ownership

- Members or candidates may undertake transactions in accounts for which they are a beneficial owner only after their clients and employers have had adequate opportunity to act on a recommendation.
- Personal transactions include those made for the member's or candidate's own account, for family (including spouse, children, and other immediate family members) accounts, and for accounts in which the member or candidate has a direct or indirect pecuniary interest, such as a trust or retirement account.
- Family accounts that are client accounts should be treated like any other firm account and should neither be given special treatment nor be disadvantaged because of the family relationship. If a member or candidate has a beneficial ownership in the account, however, the member or candidate may be subject to preclearance or reporting requirements of the employer or applicable law.

Recommended Procedures for Compliance

- Members and candidates should urge their firms to establish such policies and procedures.
- The specific provisions of each firm's standards will vary, but all firms should adopt certain basic procedures to address the conflict areas created by personal investing. These procedures include the following:
  - Limited participation in equity IPOs.

- ○ Restrictions on private placements.
- ○ Establish blackout/restricted periods.
- ○ Reporting requirements, including:
    - ▪ Disclosure of holdings in which the employee has a beneficial interest.
    - ▪ Providing duplicate confirmations of transactions.
    - ▪ Preclearance procedures.
- • Disclosure of policies to investors.

Standard VI(C) Referral Fees

The Standard
Members and candidates must disclose to their employer, clients, and prospective clients, as appropriate, any compensation, consideration, or benefit received from or paid to others for the recommendation of products or services.

Guidance
- • Members and candidates must inform their employer, clients, and prospective clients of any benefit received for referrals of customers and clients.
- • Members and candidates must disclose when they pay a fee or provide compensation to others who have referred prospective clients to the member or candidate.
- • Appropriate disclosure means that members and candidates must advise the client or prospective client, before entry into any formal agreement for services, of any benefit given or received for the recommendation of any services provided by the member or candidate. In addition, the member or candidate must disclose the nature of the consideration or benefit.

Recommended Procedures for Compliance
- • Members and candidates should encourage their employers to develop procedures related to referral fees. The firm may completely restrict such fees. If the firm does not adopt a strict prohibition of such fees, the procedures should indicate the appropriate steps for requesting approval.
- • Employers should have investment professionals provide to the clients notification of approved referral fee programs and provide the employer regular (at least quarterly) updates on the amount and nature of compensation received.

Standard VII(A) Conduct as Participants in CFA Institute Programs

The Standard
Members and candidates must not engage in any conduct that compromises the reputation or integrity of CFA Institute or the CFA designation or the integrity, validity, or security of CFA Institute programs.

Guidance
- • Standard VII(A) prohibits any conduct that undermines the public's confidence that the CFA charter represents a level of achievement based on merit and ethical conduct.
- • Conduct covered includes but is not limited to:
    - ○ Giving or receiving assistance (cheating) on any CFA Institute examinations,
    - ○ Violating the rules, regulations, and testing policies of CFA Institute programs,
    - ○ Providing confidential program or exam information to candidates or the public,
    - ○ Disregarding or attempting to circumvent security measures established for any CFA Institute examinations,

- ○ Improperly using an association with CFA Institute to further personal or professional goals, and
- ○ Misrepresenting information on the Professional Conduct Statement or in the CFA Institute Continuing Education Program.

Confidential Program Information
- Examples of information that cannot be disclosed by candidates sitting for an exam include but are not limited to:
  - ○ Specific details of questions appearing on the exam and
  - ○ Broad topical areas and formulas tested or not tested on the exam.
- All aspects of the exam, including questions, broad topical areas, and formulas, tested or not tested, are considered confidential until such time as CFA Institute elects to release them publicly.

Additional CFA Program Restrictions
- Violating any of the testing policies, such as the calculator policy, personal belongings policy, or the Candidate Pledge, constitutes a violation of Standard VII(A).
- Examples of information that cannot be shared by members involved in developing, administering, or grading the exams include but are not limited to:
  - ○ Questions appearing on the exam or under consideration.
  - ○ Deliberation related to the exam process.
  - ○ Information related to the scoring of questions.

Expressing an Opinion
- Standard VII(A) does not cover expressing opinions regarding CFA Institute, the CFA Program, or other CFA Institute programs.
- However, when expressing a personal opinion, a candidate is prohibited from disclosing content-specific information, including any actual exam question and the information as to subject matter covered or not covered in the exam.

Standard VII(B) Reference to CFA Institute, the CFA Designation, and the CFA Program

The Standard
When referring to CFA Institute, CFA Institute membership, the CFA designation, or candidacy in the CFA Program, members and candidates must not misrepresent or exaggerate the meaning or implications of membership in CFA Institute, holding the CFA designation, or candidacy in the CFA Program.

Guidance
- Standard VII(B) is intended to prevent promotional efforts that make promises or guarantees that are tied to the CFA designation. Individuals may refer to their CFA designation, CFA Institute membership, or candidacy in the CFA Program but must not exaggerate the meaning or implications of membership in CFA Institute, holding the CFA designation, or candidacy in the CFA Program.
- Standard VII(B) is not intended to prohibit factual statements related to the positive benefit of earning the CFA designation. However, statements referring to CFA Institute, the CFA designation, or the CFA Program that overstate the competency of an individual or imply, either directly or indirectly, that superior performance can be expected from someone with the CFA designation are not allowed under the standard.
- Statements that highlight or emphasize the commitment of CFA Institute members, CFA charterholders, and CFA candidates to ethical and professional conduct or mention the thoroughness and rigor of the CFA Program are appropriate.

- Members and candidates may make claims about the relative merits of CFA Institute, the CFA Program, or the Code and Standards as long as those statements are implicitly or explicitly stated as the opinion of the speaker.
- Standard VII(B) applies to any form of communication, including but not limited to communications made in electronic or written form (such as on firm letterhead, business cards, professional biographies, directory listings, printed advertising, firm brochures, or personal resumes), and oral statements made to the public, clients, or prospects.

CFA Institute Membership

The term "CFA Institute member" refers to "regular" and "affiliate" members of CFA Institute who have met the membership requirements as defined in the CFA Institute Bylaws. Once accepted as a CFA Institute member, the member must satisfy the following requirements to maintain his or her status:

- Remit annually to CFA Institute a completed Professional Conduct Statement, which renews the commitment to abide by the requirements of the Code and Standards and the CFA Institute Professional Conduct Program.
- Pay applicable CFA Institute membership dues on an annual basis.

If a CFA Institute member fails to meet any of these requirements, the individual is no longer considered an active member. Until membership is reactivated, individuals must not present themselves to others as active members. They may state, however, that they were CFA Institute members in the past or refer to the years when their membership was active.

Using the CFA Designation
- Those who have earned the right to use the Chartered Financial Analyst designation may use the trademarks or registered marks "Chartered Financial Analyst" or "CFA" and are encouraged to do so but only in a manner that does not misrepresent or exaggerate the meaning or implications of the designation.
- The use of the designation may be accompanied by an accurate explanation of the requirements that have been met to earn the right to use the designation.
- "CFA charterholders" are those individuals who have earned the right to use the CFA designation granted by CFA Institute. These people have satisfied certain requirements, including completion of the CFA Program and required years of acceptable work experience. Once granted the right to use the designation, individuals must also satisfy the CFA Institute membership requirements (see above) to maintain their right to use the designation.
- If a CFA charterholder fails to meet any of the membership requirements, he or she forfeits the right to use the CFA designation. Until membership is reactivated, individuals must not present themselves to others as CFA charterholders. They may state, however, that they were charterholders in the past.
- Given the growing popularity of social media, where individuals may anonymously express their opinions, pseudonyms or online profile names created to hide a member's identity should not be tagged with the CFA designation.

Referring to Candidacy in the CFA Program
- Candidates in the CFA Program may refer to their participation in the CFA Program, but such references must clearly state that an individual is a candidate in the CFA Program and must not imply that the candidate has achieved any type of partial designation. A person is a candidate in the CFA Program if:

- ○ The person's application for registration in the CFA Program has been accepted by CFA Institute, as evidenced by issuance of a notice of acceptance, and the person is enrolled to sit for a specified examination; or
  - ○ The registered person has sat for a specified examination but exam results have not yet been received.
- If an individual is registered for the CFA Program but declines to sit for an exam or otherwise does not meet the definition of a candidate as described in the CFA Institute Bylaws, then that individual is no longer considered an active candidate. Once the person is enrolled to sit for a future examination, his or her CFA candidacy resumes.
- CFA candidates must never state or imply that they have a partial designation as a result of passing one or more levels, or cite an expected completion date of any level of the CFA Program. Final award of the charter is subject to meeting the CFA Program requirements and approval by the CFA Institute Board of Governors.
- If a candidate passes each level of the exam in consecutive years and wants to state that he or she did so, that is not a violation of Standard VII(B) because it is a statement of fact. If the candidate then goes on to claim or imply superior ability by obtaining the designation in only three years, however, he or she is in violation of Standard VII(B).

Proper and Improper References to the CFA Designation

Proper References	Improper References
"Completion of the CFA Program has enhanced my portfolio management skills."	"CFA charterholders achieve better performance results."
"John Smith passed all three CFA examinations in three consecutive years."	"John Smith is among the elite, having passed all three CFA examinations in three consecutive attempts."
"The CFA designation is globally recognized and attests to a charterholder's success in a rigorous and comprehensive study program in the field of investment management and research analysis."	"As a CFA charterholder, I am the most qualified to manage client investments."
"The credibility that the CFA designation affords and the skills the CFA Program cultivates are key assets for my future career development."	"As a CFA charterholder, Jane White provides the best value in trade execution."
"I enrolled in the CFA Program to obtain the highest set of credentials in the global investment management industry."	"Enrolling as a candidate in the CFA Program ensures one of becoming better at valuing debt securities."
"I passed Level I of the CFA exam."	"CFA, Level II"
"I am a 2010 Level III candidate in the CFA Program."	"CFA, Expected 2011"
"I passed all three levels of the CFA Program and will be eligible for the CFA charter upon completion of the required work experience."	"Level III CFA Candidate"
"As a CFA charterholder, I am committed to the highest ethical standards."	"CFA, Expected 2011" "John Smith, Charter Pending"

Recommended Procedures for Compliance

Members and candidates can reduce the risk of misrepresenting the CFA credential or misusing the CFA designation or CFA Institute marks by disseminating written guidance on Standard VII(B) to their firm's compliance, legal, public relations, and marketing departments.

Covered persons should encourage their firms to create compliance department–approved templates consistent with the Standard.

APPLICATION OF THE CODE AND STANDARDS
Cross-Reference to CFA Institute Assigned Reading #3

Marcia Lopez

Lopez asks Hockett, her supervisor, to approve her business card request form, on which she appends "CFA, Level I" after her name. Hockett tells Lopez to include the year she expects to receive her CFA charter.

Lopez violated Standard VII(B): Responsibilities as a CFA Institute Member or CFA Candidate, Reference to CFA Institute, the CFA Designation, and the CFA Program. While she can indicate participation in the program, she may not indicate an expected completion date for the designation or any level of the program.

Hockett violated Standard IV(C): Duties to Employers, Responsibilities of Supervisors by failing to ensure that anyone subject to their supervision or authority complies with applicable laws, rules, regulations, and the Code and Standards.

David Hockett and Team

Hockett's wealth management team at BankGlobal receives calls directly from analysts with coverage information. This avoids the 45-minute period necessary to update BankGlobal's website and email the changes to clients. Hockett's team, however, acts immediately in discretionary accounts when they receive these analyst calls. This allows them to prevent discretionary accounts from being negatively affected when other clients receive and act on the information.

Hockett's team violated Standard III(B): Duties to Clients, Fair Dealing by failing to ensure all clients are treated fairly in the dissemination of information. Hockett's team favors their own preferential accounts over non-discretionary accounts and other accounts managed by other BankGlobal wealth teams.

[There was some initial confusion as to whether the reports themselves are considered "material nonpublic information." In general, analyst reports which contain information that could affect an investor's decisions are considered material and are considered nonpublic until appropriately disseminated. You do not need to be a company insider to possess and misuse material nonpublic information.]

The Kochanskis

Lopez recommends a balanced portfolio to clients without first determining their investment objectives, risk tolerance, investment horizon, and internal and external constraints.

Lopez violated Standard III(C): Duties to Clients, Suitability by failing to make proper inquiries into their investment experience, objectives, and constraints prior to making a recommendation. Lopez should have developed an investment policy statement (IPS) for her clients prior to making a recommendation. Further, such information should be regularly reassessed and updated if necessary.

Lopez develops the balanced portfolio and creates reports for the strategy based on only two equity and two fixed income top-performing portfolios. She averages returns from these four funds for each of the five years. She compares this to annual rates of return over a five-year horizon for a composite portfolio of balanced-objective discretionary accounts of similar size. She does not include terminated accounts.

Lopez violated Standard III(D): Duties to Clients, Performance Presentation by failing to include terminated accounts and accounts of dissimilar size but with similar strategy.

Lopez did not violate the Standards by averaging returns for the four funds for each of the five years because she does not know the Kochanskis' level of investment knowledge and can use this easy-to-understand method.

After finally meeting with the Kochanskis, Hockett discloses to a referring party that BankGlobal's wealth management division achieves alpha in long-horizon conservative accounts by investing 15–20% of the portfolio in high-beta, apparently low-risk stocks. This allows the wealth management division to receive performance bonuses on quarterly results and avoids the need to revise each conservative client's IPS.

Hockett violated Standard III(C)(2): Duties to Clients, Suitability, which states "When Members and Candidates are responsible for managing a portfolio to a specific mandate, strategy, or style, they must make only investment recommendations or take only investment actions that are consistent with the stated objectives and constraints of the portfolio."

He violated this standard by (1) investing in inherently risk-high beta stocks and (2) managing portfolios with a long horizon to a short-term performance target to make his bonus.

Lopez then tweets that she opened an account for "Mr. Kochanski and his wife, Mary."

Lopez violated Standard III(E): Duties to Clients, Preservation of Confidentiality. Members and candidates must maintain confidentiality of former, current, and prospective client personal information unless (1) the information concerns illegal activities, (2) the law requires disclosure, or (3) the parties permit disclosure.

Castle Biotechnology

David Plume

Plume was a biochemist at Castle Biotechnology (CB), a pharmaceutical holding company, for 15 years prior to becoming a biotech analyst at Global Capital Management (Global), which was acquired by CB. He was encouraged to become an analyst for Global because he could write perceptive research reports and help identify takeover targets. Plume receives 0.10% of gross proceeds for each IPO he works on for Global.

CB's portfolio includes APBX and STRX, which Plume helped take public. Shortly after taking them public, Plume wrote a report claiming for each company that it was developing extraordinary drugs and that their share prices would double in 9–12 months. Three months after issuing the report, Plume shorts APBX in his personal portfolio and does not disclose the sale because he was never a beneficial owner of APBX's stock.

Although the offering materials and prospectus indicated the relationship between CB, Global, and the two portfolio companies, Plume does not mention this in his research reports. He also does not disclose that he owns class A shares and options on CB's stock. He does state, however, that "One or more directors, officers, and/or employees of Global Capital and its affiliated companies, or independent contractors affiliated with Global, may be a director of the issuer of the securities mentioned herein."

Plume violated Standard I(B): Professionalism, Independence and Objectivity, because his annual bonus as an analyst depended on his IPO work, which obviously presents an opportunity for conflict of interest. This Standard states: "Members and Candidates must use reasonable care and judgment to achieve and maintain independence and objectivity in their professional activities. Members and Candidates must not offer, solicit, or accept any gift, benefit, compensation, or consideration that reasonably could be expected to compromise their own or another's independence and objectivity." There is evidence of this in his short sale of APBX shares shortly after the IPO. In addition to favoring APBX and STRX in his analytical reports, he may have excluded other more suitable companies from research reports.

Plume violated Standard VI(A): Conflicts of Interest, Disclosure of Conflicts, because he failed to disclose in his research reports that Global, his employer, was owned by CB, which also owned the biotech companies that were the report subject. Disclosure in the IPO materials was necessary but insufficient to prevent the violation. He also violated the Standard by failing to disclose his ownership of the preferred shares and options on CB stock. This indicates an indirect beneficial ownership in APBX and STRX.

[Note that the corporate chain of ownership is not *ex ante* a conflict of interest as was receiving a bonus based on the IPOs he analyzes.]

Sandra Benning
Benning worked at Kodiak securities prior to joining Global. While at Kodiak, Benning communicated with clients through personal accounts at Facebook, LinkedIn, and Twitter and through personal email. After leaving Kodiak, she communicated her departure through these platforms and encouraged her former clients to follow her to Global. Global paid her a signing bonus dependent on a percentage of former Kodiak clients following her to Global. Global also pays investment advisers a year-end bonus based on their clients' IPO participation. Benning does not disclose either bonus.

Unless there is a noncompete agreement, Benning has not violated Standard IV(A): Duties to Employers, Loyalty, because Benning did not solicit Kodiak's clients until she left and did not use Kodiak's materials to do so.

Benning violated Standard VI(A): Conflicts of Interest, Disclosure of Conflicts by failing to disclose additional compensation. The sign-on bonus and bonus based on client IPO participation both present conflict of interest opportunities that must be disclosed.

Global plans a highly anticipated IPO for FTSX, one of CB's portfolio companies. Global allocates shares of "hot issues" to institutional clients who plan on purchasing additional shares on the first day of trading in order to boost the post-issue price. Benning notifies clients on various business and personal platforms that confirming an indication of interest does not mean the order will be filled in full or in part.

Global uses the following criteria for allocating shares to clients indicating interest in an allocation and subsequent additional purchases after IPO:

- Account AUM
- Track record of similar investments
- Level of previous business with Global
- Size of a client's anticipated long-term investment
- Existing or potential business relationships with Global
- Attendance at road shows and other indications of interest

On one day prior to the IPO, Benning telephones high-net-worth clients who had received allocations to tell them they will be excluded from future allocations if they "flip" (i.e., sell) the IPO shares immediately after issuance. She then calls her institutional clients to tell them they may flip their shares at the end of the first trading day.

Benning violated Standard II(B): Integrity of Capital Markets, Market Manipulation by allocating FTSX shares to institutional clients who plan to purchase additional shares when it begins trading. Such requirements are called "tie-in" agreements, which have a tendency to distort security prices to the detriment of market participants.

The practices described also violate Standard III(B): Duties to Clients, Fair Dealing.

Claris Deacon
Benning's newest client Claris Deacon completed the following actions on each of three successive visits:

1. Signed a New Account Agreement and a Limited Trade Authorization form that gives Benning discretionary authority to transact securities,
2. Opened a cash management account that linked her brokerage account to an in-house checking (transaction) account, and
3. Signed an Option Account Application and Agreement authorizing equity option transactions in her account.

After the third meeting, Benning changed the language on Deacon's form describing the types of suitable options and initialed the form on her behalf.

A week later, Deacon is traveling with her husband and calls Benning to tell her she's having trouble transferring money from her brokerage account to her checking account. Benning finds that Global had not activated that linkage and receives Deacon's verbal authorization to sign the account-linking form on Deacon's behalf.

A month later, Deacon's husband Steve calls to let Benning know that Claris has serious health issues. He convinces Benning to redeem $15,000 from Claris' account and several additional redemptions and withdrawals over the next few weeks. Benning makes a note on the trade form each time Steve transacts in Claris' account.

Benning violated Standard I(D): Professionalism, Misconduct by signing or initialing a form on behalf of a client. A telephone authorization is not enough.

Benning violated Standard III(A): Duties to Clients, Loyalty, Prudence, and Care by redeeming shares in Deacon's account at Steve's request without Claris' signed authorization.

Lionsgate Limited & Bank of Australia

Tony Hill and Team
All employees aged 18 to 70 in Australia are required to contribute a percentage of earnings to a tax-advantaged retirement account known as a "superannuation fund." Lionsgate Limited (LL) is a publicly listed Australian fund manager among the financial services firms that benefit from employees investing their money in the scheme. LL's Victory Capital Fund (VCF) is an equity mutual fund managed by Tony Hill and his team.

ET

Hill's marketing material for VCF states that the fund delivered high gross-of-fees returns over that period, the best among Australian equity funds, and goes on to describe high annual returns and growing AUM.

Hill does not violate any standards with his statements. Standard III(D): Duties to Clients, Performance Presentation, only requires that covered persons make reasonable efforts to ensure the reporting is fair, accurate, and complete. Guidance to the Standard suggests methods to ensure compliance:

"Members and candidates can also meet their obligations under Standard III(D) by including disclosures that fully explain the performance results being reported (for example, stating, when appropriate, that results are simulated when model results are used, clearly indicating when the performance record is that of a prior entity, or disclosing whether the performance is gross of fees, net of fees, or after tax.)"[1]

Hill makes a variety of uncompensated appearances in media, although the shows' sponsors give "thank-you" bags containing wine, retail gift cards, restaurant gift certificates, and travel discounts on hotels and airfare. Hill does not disclose receipt of the gift bags.

Hill does not violate any standards by accepting the gifts. Standard IV(B): Duties to Employers, Additional Compensation Arrangements, only requires that covered persons not accept gifts, benefits, compensation, or consideration that might create or could be expected to create a conflict with an employer's interest.

Note here that there is no indication Hill changed any position as the result of the gifts without written consent from all parties. Accepting the nominal gifts does not conflict with an employer's interests

As Hill became more of a media personality, Nicole Martin assumed more responsibility for investment decision-making. Although she and Hill both state publicly that he is in charge of investment decision-making, the last three years results were directly attributable to her and the other analysts.

Hill and Martin have both violated Standard V(B)1: Investment Analysis, Recommendations, and Actions, Communication with Clients and Prospective Clients by failing to disclose changes in investment management and reasons for performance.

Hill announces his resignation at a board meeting and indicated he is leaving to start his own firm. The board asks Hill to keep his resignation confidential until the end of LL's fiscal year in two weeks. Hill agrees and, after the meeting, announces to his team a plan to resign and start his own firm. He asks his team to join him. Ten analysts agree to follow him; five decline and leave the meeting. Hill indicates the team will have to work after company hours to get things ready when he departs in two weeks. In their off hours, they file registration paperwork, lease office space, and make other preparations, telling their team they will begin to solicit former clients as soon as they leave LL.

Hill violated Standard IV(A): Duties to Employers, Loyalty by announcing his resignation to his team after agreeing in the board meeting to keep the news confidential. Hill would not have violated this Standard by discussing his resignation with his team prior to the board's request for confidentiality.

---

[1] CFAI Curriculum, 2020.

Hill did not violate this standard by asking his team to join him at his new firm or to work during the interim two weeks because it was outside office hours. Guidance to Standard IV(A) states: "A departing employee is generally free to make arrangements or preparations to go into a competitive business before terminating the relationship with his or her employer as long as such preparations do not breach the employee's duty of loyalty."

Hill did not violate this standard by soliciting former clients after leaving LL unless he used client information obtained from LL without agreement.

Rob Portman

Rob Portman sells VCF to high net worth (HNW) individuals and to institutions. To make the fund more attractive to these investors, Portman always touts Tony Hill as the investments decision maker and refers to Martin as Hill's assistant, although he knows Hill has assumed most responsibilities.

Portman violated Standard I(C): Professionalism, Misrepresentation. "Members and Candidates must not knowingly make any misrepresentations relating to investment analysis, recommendations, actions, or other professional activities."

Portman asked LL's Chief Investment Officer (CIO), who attended the board meeting at which Hill resigned, to verify the rumor. The CIO told him to ignore the rumor and go on with a planned event for prospective clients. Portman sells his shares in LL and VCF when he learns from Sky New Business Channel that the CIO and two other directors sold their own shares.

The directors violated Standard II(A): Integrity of Capital Markets, Material Nonpublic Information. They did not violate Standard IV(A): Duties to Employers, Loyalty by selling their shares in LL and VCF.

Kirk Graeme

Bank of Australia Financial Group (BOA) is part owner of LL, which is part of its wealth management group. Kirk Graeme, an LL analyst broadly respected for his insight on IPO shares, receives additional, issuer-paid compensation for new issue purchases. BOA's Capital Markets Group is a member of the syndicate for new issues that Graeme purchases. As a syndicate member, BOA also shares in fees and commissions paid by the issuer although he receives only fee-based compensation from his wealth management clients.

BOA's policy does not require disclosure on commission received for new issues because clients receive prospectuses that disclose commissions paid to the syndicate member. Graeme discloses his new issue commissions to clients who ask for the information.

Graeme violated Standard VI(A): Conflicts of Interest, Disclosure of Conflicts by failing to notify all clients of the conflict, not just clients who ask.

The Delaneys

The Delaney's told Graeme, their advisor, that their account represented most of their investable assets, their horizon was 15 to 20 years, and they had low risk tolerance. Graeme purchased IPOs for their account, many of which were held for only five months.

Graeme violated Standard III(C)1: Duties to Clients, Suitability by failing to adhere to the Delaneys' investment mandate relating to risk.

[Note that CFA Institute materials declare that the time horizon mandate was not violated by Graeme's management of the Delaney's account, although no rationale for this position was offered.]

Jane Balmer, Graeme's supervisor, raised concerns about extensive IPO purchases and subsequent turnover in Graeme's accounts. Balmer also reported this to the compliance officer. Graeme reduced his new issue purchases and turnover after his meeting with Balmer.

Balmer violated Standard IV(C): Duties to Employers, Responsibilities of Supervisors by relying solely on Graeme's account and failing to initiate an investigation into the extent of Graeme's wrongdoing.

David Milgram

David Milgram's account has operated under his original IPS since Graeme opened his account five years ago. Milgram sent a letter to Balmer regarding the dismal performance of his account. Balmer discusses the account with Graeme but does not escalate the matter to the compliance director. Graeme and Balmer meet with Milgram and update his IPS during the meeting.

Graeme violated Standard III(C): Duties to Clients, Suitability by failing to properly update Milgram's IPS. Guidance states that update should occur at least annually or whenever the investor's situation undergoes material changes.

Balmer did not violate Standard IV(C): Duties to Employers, Responsibilities of Supervisors, because she initiated an investigation into the extent of Graeme's wrongdoing and sat in on a meeting where he updated Milgram's IPS. Guidance to this standard does not require escalation unless a resolution fails to occur.

Gabby Sim

Gabby Sim was recently hired by Global Harvest Bank (GHB) and received her orientation from Ahmed Yousoff, GHB's chief investment officer (CIO). Yousoff meets with GHB's president, Irene Wong, and board members David Tan and Audrey Chuong to discuss a memorandum of understanding with MGM2. The government of Saspara, through its Ministry of Finance, wholly owns MGM2, a strategic investment and development company charged with investments that establish global partnerships leading to foreign direct investment. Yousoff and Wong decide to pay a portion of their fee to Tan and Chuong, who worked tirelessly on the MGM2 deal, but do not disclose the payment in the MOU. Chuong does not tell Yousoff that Bo Hie, a Sasparian businessman who helped start MGM2, recently hired her son into an executive role in GHB.

Yousoff does not violate Standard VI(C): Conflicts of Interest, Referral Fees, because the fee was paid to Yousoff, who does not need to explain the fee sharing arrangement. Tan and Chuong receive the reward for their efforts to bring MGM2 on as a client for GHB, not as a referral.

Chuong violated Standard VI(A): Conflicts of Interest, Disclosure of Conflicts by failing to disclose that Hie recently hired her son. Standard VI(A) requires members and candidates to fully disclose to clients, potential clients, and employers all actual and potential conflicts of interest. Hie hiring Chuong's son could have resulted in GHB offering a special deal for MGM2 of which Yousoff was unaware.

Hie tells Sim that he wants to open an account under the name of his firm Bad Moon Rising, LTD, on which Hie has sole signatory authority. Hie refuses to answer discovery questions on the new account information form and writes Sim a $15 million check drawn on a Cayman Island bank account. Hie asks Sim to destroy all notes taken during their meeting and hands her a brief but insufficient information statement. Hie tells Sim that if she needs more information she should contact Tan and Chuong. She uses the information statement to prepare Hie's IPS. Sim does not advise Yousoff that Hie promised her a year-end bonus.

Sim violated Standard V(C): Investment Analysis, Recommendations, and Actions, Record Retention, which states: "Members and Candidates must develop and maintain appropriate records to support their investment analyses, recommendations, actions, and other investment-related communications with clients and prospective clients."

Sim does not violate Standard III(A): Duties to Clients, Loyalty, Prudence, and Care or III(E): Duties to Clients, Preservation of Confidentiality by keeping the notes as part of her file.

Sim also violated Standard III(C): Duties to Clients, Suitability by failing to gain enough information relevant to Sims investment situation. Guidance to the Standard states: "When an advisory relationship exists, members and candidates must gather client information at the inception of the relationship. Such information includes the client's financial circumstances, personal data (such as age and occupation) that are relevant to investment decisions, attitudes toward risk, and objectives in investing. This information should be incorporated into a written investment policy statement (IPS) that addresses the client's risk tolerance, return requirements, and all investment constraints (including time horizon, liquidity needs, tax concerns, legal and regulatory factors, and unique circumstances)." At the very least, the client's statement of risk tolerance is insufficient.

Shortly after Sim opens the account, an MGM2 account in Saspara wires $70 million into Hie's account. Hie provides a copy of an agreement between Bad Moon Rising and MGM2 and advises Sim that the money will be used by MGM2 to purchase United States real estate. She tells Yousoff, who tells her to contact Tan and Chuong. Sim calls Tan and Chuong to tell them about the deposit and faxes them a copy of the investment agreement Hie provided. After reviewing this information, the two board members confirm Hie's identity and his role with MGM2.

Yousoff violated Standard IV(C): Duties to Employers, Responsibilities of Supervisors by failing to have Sim arrange a meeting for him with Hie and an official of MGM2.

Sim did not violate Standard III(E): Duties to Clients, Preservation of Confidentiality by discussing Hie's information with Tan and Chuong because he had instructed her to do so. That the two board members also worked on the deal with MGM2 does not, by itself, allow Sim to share Hie's information.

Sim later becomes suspicious regarding Hie's behavior and is not reassured by Yousoff's comments that the speed of Hie's transactions are the important consideration, not their impropriety.

Sim's first course of action in this matter should be to refer her concerns to GHB's compliance department. Regarding potential violations by a fellow employee, Guidance to Standard I(A): Professionalism, Knowledge of the Law states: "When in doubt about the appropriate action to undertake, it is recommended that a member or candidate seek the advice of compliance personnel or legal counsel concerning legal requirements."

Sim meets with Madam Tan Swee Neo, a retiree with most of her money in fixed certificates of deposit. She invests the remainder in lower-risk, dividend-paying securities of utilities. She wants to allocate more to conservative equities to earn money to pay for her grandson's education.

Madame Tan says she wants to know more about GHB's oil-linked structured notes with a high return. Sim provides Madame Tan with a brochure in English, which Tan does not understand. Sim proceeds to describe the notes in some detail, including the lack of guaranteed income and heavy withdrawal penalties, but Tan does not understand. Sim allows Tan to invest a large sum in the notes.

Sim violated Standard III(C): Duties to Clients, Suitability, when Madame Tan invested against her own mandate of low-risk fixed income and equity. Guidance states: "Members and candidates will need to make reasonable efforts to balance their clients' trading requests with their responsibilities to follow the agreed-on investment policy statement." Although Tan has some experience in real estate, she does not understand the investment she is making. Handing her a brochure in a different language and simply explaining there is no income guarantee is not enough if Tan does not understand the risk to her portfolio. In any event, Sim should update Tan's IPS prior to making the investment.

One year later, Tan wants to change investment direction away from the structured notes due to underperformance and lack of confidence in oil prices. Sim reminds her of the withdrawal penalty but Tan refuses to listen and wants to redeem anyway. She is shocked to find her large investment became a small investment after she redeemed the oil-linked structured notes.

Sim violated Standard III(A): Duties to Clients, Loyalty, Prudence, and Care by immediately processing the redemption without helping Tan understand the redemption costs and ensuring her client had correct understanding of the economic environment.

Sim violated Standard III(C): Duties to Clients, Suitability by making the transaction when Tan's behavior suggested she did not fully understand how this would affect her ability to pay for her grandchild's education. Guidance to the Standard states: "Members and candidates will need to make reasonable efforts to balance their clients' trading requests with their responsibilities to follow the agreed-on investment policy statement."

STUDY SESSION 2: ETHICAL AND PROFESSIONAL STANDARDS (2)

PROFESSIONALISM IN INVESTMENT MANAGEMENT
Cross-Reference to CFA Institute Assigned Reading #4

A profession identifies an occupational group that develops specific education, knowledge, and practice behaviors that engender community recognition and trust. Professions establish trust by normalizing practice behaviors, which are, in turn, promoted through the occupation's code of ethics and standards of professional conduct.

Professions establish trust by:

- Providing a service to society
- Focusing on client needs
- Maintaining high entry standards
- Sharing established knowledge with new practitioners
- Encouraging and facilitating professional development
- Monitoring professional conduct
- Promoting collegial conduct
- Encouraging member engagement

To establish trust in the investment profession, practitioners must disclose and make sure clients understand conflicts, risks, and fees involved in a way that best serves client interests.

Investment professionals are expected to uphold professional standards and be reliable, accountable, and responsible in their work. Investment professionals provide independent advice, avoid or disclose conflicts, respect confidentiality, and provide objective and transparent recommendations. Professional development involves filling knowledge or information gaps, implementing new learnings, and evaluating results in order to begin the next cycle.

ASSET MANAGER CODE OF PROFESSIONAL CONDUCT
Cross-Reference to CFA Institute Assigned Reading #5

Unlike GIPS, don't worry about the difference between required and recommended standards; firms of all sizes will be able to adapt it. On the exam, expect the questions to read: "Is the action consistent with both the required and recommended standards?"

The AM Code is a firm-wide set of voluntary professional standards aimed at investment firms around the world who manage money for clients. Investors seeking ethically sound investment managers may take some assurance in firms that have adopted and adhere to the AM Code, regardless of whether they are subject to securities regulations.

As ethical leadership begins at the top of any company, it is recommended that AM Code be adopted by senior management and the board of directors.

There are four main points to consider before discussing the main standards:

1. There is no partial claim of compliance. If the firm does not follow all parts of the AM Code, then the firm cannot claim partial compliance.
2. A compliant firm must use an exactly worded statement consisting of two sentences whenever it claims compliance: "[Insert name of firm] claims compliance with the CFA Institute Asset Manager Code of Professional Conduct. This claim has not been verified by CFA Institute."
3. Firms must notify CFA Institute that they are claiming compliance. This is done for information purposes only.
4. Like the GIPS standards, CFA Institute does not enforce the quality control of a firm's claim of compliance with the AM Code. CFA Institute does not verify the manager's claim of compliance.

General Principles of Conduct
The Asset Manager Code of Professional Conduct mandates the following when asset managers work with clients:

1. Act in a professional and ethical manner at all times.
2. Act for the benefit of clients.
3. Act with independence and objectivity.
4. Act with skill, competence, and diligence.
5. Communicate with clients in a timely and accurate manner.
6. Uphold the applicable rules governing capital markets.

Asset Manager Code of Professional Conduct

Loyalty to Clients
Managers must:

1. Place client interests ahead of their own interests.
   The interests of the client are paramount over all other interests. Firms should develop and implement policies and procedures to detect and prevent abuses in all aspects of the manager-client relationship (e.g., investment selection, transactions, monitoring, and custody). The firm's compensation arrangement should align the financial interests of clients and managers to eliminate incentives that could result in conflicts of interest.
2. Preserve the confidentiality of information communicated by clients within the scope of the manager-client relationship.
   Managers should draft a privacy policy that addresses the collection, retention, protection, and dissemination of confidential client information. The policy should be

written with specific mention of anti-money-laundering procedures and implemented to prevent the firm from being implicated in criminal activity. Although managers must maintain client confidentiality, they should consider reporting illegal activities to authorities unless prevented from doing so by local law.

3. Refuse to participate in any business relationship or accept any gift that could reasonably be expected to affect their independence, objectivity, or loyalty to clients. Managers must establish policies and procedures for accepting and reporting gifts, including entertainment. Firms should create specific limits for accepting gifts and prohibit the acceptance of any cash gifts. Managers may maintain multiple business relationships with a client as long as they manage and disclose any potential conflicts of interest.

> Be sure to note the prohibition against the acceptance of cash gifts. This is more stringent than the Code and Standards.

Investment Process and Actions

Managers must:

1. Use reasonable care and prudent judgment when managing client assets.
   Managers must exhibit the same level of care, skill, and diligence that a trained professional acting in the same capacity would use in managing the client's assets. Prudence requires managing assets that balances risk and return while acting in a prudent and judicious manner in avoiding harm to clients.

> "Sidecar" or "side-letter" investments are not explained in the official curriculum but are use to indicate special arrangements between a specific limited partner (LP) and the general partner (GP). These arrangements would often be advantageous to other LPs.

2. Not engage in practices designed to distort prices or artificially inflate trading volume.
   Market manipulation is illegal, erodes investor confidence, and disrupts efficient functioning of financial markets. Managers should refrain from practices that distort market prices and/or trading volumes to give an illusion of activity. Information-based manipulation including spreading false rumors with the intent to motivate trading by others in such a way that benefits the firm or its clients is also prohibited by this standard.

3. Deal fairly and objectively with all clients when providing investment information, making investment recommendations, or taking investment action.
   Preferential treatment should not be granted to certain clients at the expense of others. Violation of this standard would include communicating recommendations to favored clients to the detriment of other clients or allocating over-subscribed offerings at the exclusion of some clients. Firms are not prohibited from offering varied levels of service, but the qualification for such services must be disclosed and made available to all. Secondary investment opportunities such as "side-letter," "sidecar," or "tag-along" deals with certain clients is permissible as long as they are fairly allocated among those clients that meet the suitability criteria.

4. Have a reasonable and adequate basis for investment decisions.
   Investment action should only be taken after the manager has conducted thorough research and established a reasonable basis for a decision. Managers may employ third-party research as long as they perform appropriate due diligence to ensure that the source is reliable and has a reasonable basis for its conclusions. Managers should thoroughly understand complex strategies and communicate these in a way that their clients can understand.

5. When managing a portfolio or pooled fund according to a specific mandate, strategy, or style:
   a. Take only investment actions that are consistent with the stated objectives and constraints of that portfolio or fund.
      Managers should not deviate from their specified mandate or strategies, especially in the case of pooled funds for which the managers do not know the specific financial situation of each client in the fund. Clients must be able to evaluate the

        suitability of the investment funds or strategies for themselves and trust that managers will not diverge from the stated mandates or strategies.

   b. Provide adequate disclosures and information so investors can consider whether any proposed changes in the investment style or strategy meet their investment needs.

       Managers must disclose to clients when a change in style is proposed, proposing enough time for clients to react to the change. If a client then wishes to redeem his shares, the manager should not penalize him for doing so and ought to waive any redemption charges, if any.

6. When managing separate accounts and before providing investment advice or taking investment action on behalf of the client:

   a. Evaluate and understand the client's investment objectives, tolerance for risk, time horizon, liquidity needs, financial constraints, any unique circumstances (including tax considerations, legal or regulatory constraints, etc.) and any other relevant information that would affect investment policy.

   b. Determine that an investment is suitable to a client's financial situation. Managers must make an effort to understand the client's investment requirements and develop an investment policy statement (IPS) prior to taking any investment actions for clients. Managers should review the IPS with the client at least annually or when changes necessitate the need and discuss risk tolerances (both the ability and willingness of the client to bear risk), return objectives, time horizon, liquidity requirements, liabilities, tax considerations, and any legal, regulatory, or other unique circumstances. The IPS should be used to assess the suitability of investment opportunities in the context of the investor's entire portfolio.

Trading

Managers must:

1. Not act or cause others to act on material nonpublic information that could affect the value of a publicly traded investment.

    Managers must adopt compliance procedures that prohibit trading on material nonpublic information. When in possession of nonpublic information, managers must take appropriate steps to keep such information confidential. This provision is not meant to prevent managers from using the mosaic theory to draw conclusions—that is, combine pieces of material public information with pieces of immaterial nonpublic information to draw actionable conclusions.

2. Give priority to investments made on behalf of the client over those that benefit the manager's interests.

    Managers must not trade ahead of clients or take advantage of information or recommendations before clients have had a chance to act first. Arrangements are permissible in pooled funds where managers put their own capital at risk alongside that of their clients so long as clients are not disadvantaged. Managers should develop reporting procedures that require employees to disclose personal holding, provide trade confirmations for personal investment transactions, and submit preclearance requests prior to making personal trades.

3. Use commissions generated from client trades to pay for only investment-related products or services that directly assist the manager in its investment decision-making process, and not in the management of the firm.

    Managers should use client brokerage for the client's benefit, including "soft dollars," and disclose methods or policies followed when such brokerage is used. Soft dollars must only be used to benefit clients by aiding the manager in making investment decisions on their behalf.

4. Maximize client portfolio value by seeking best execution for all client transactions. Managers have the obligation to seek best execution (lowest cost/highest value) for all trades made on behalf of clients. Some clients may request that the manager place trades through a specific broker to obtain research from that broker, known as "client-directed" brokerage. In such cases, the client must be informed that he might not be getting the best execution and the client is required to provide written acknowledgment to the manager that best execution might not be achieved.

5. Establish policies to ensure fair and equitable trade allocation among client accounts. When taking investment actions, managers must treat clients fairly. This includes access to oversubscribed issues and IPOs, which must be allocated fairly (pro rata in round-lots) among interested clients for whom such investments are suitable. Managers should disclose written allocation procedures on how initial public offerings and private placements will be handled.

Risk Management, Compliance, and Support

Managers must:

1. Develop and maintain policies and procedures to ensure that their activities comply with the provisions of this Code and all applicable legal and regulatory requirements.
   Firms should document applicable laws, rules, and regulations in a written compliance manual to ensure that managers meet their legal requirements when managing client assets. Firms should also develop or adopt a written code of ethics and disseminate written procedures for reporting violations.

2. Appoint a compliance officer responsible for administering the policies and procedures and for investigating complaints regarding the conduct of the manager or its personnel.
   The manager should designate a competent compliance officer and establish a clear chain of command for reporting, investigating, and enforcing compliance issues. Managers may designate an existing employee or hire a separate individual who is independent from the investment personnel and reports directly to the CEO or board of directors.

3. Ensure that portfolio information provided to clients by the manager is accurate and complete and arrange for independent third-party confirmation or review of such information.
   Managers should undertake independent third-party verification of information through regular audits. Not only does such verification improve client trust, it can help managers recognize and prevent potential problems.

4. Maintain records for an appropriate period of time in an easily accessible format.
   Managers must maintain records that support their investment recommendations and actions on behalf of clients. Managers should also maintain records that substantiate their compliance with the Code, related policies and procedures, and any violations that occur. Records may be maintained either in hard copy or electronic form, but must be easily accessible by clients. Managers must determine the appropriate minimum time frame for keeping records. **In the absence of regulatory or firm policies**, this period must be a minimum of seven years.

> This standard is exactly the same as the Code and Standards of Professional Conduct. Note that if other requirements apply, then those will apply, even if they state a shorter period of time than seven years. Use seven years ONLY when there is no local regulatory or company-specific guidance.

5. Employ qualified staff and sufficient human and technological resources to thoroughly investigate, analyze, implement, and monitor investment decisions and actions.
   Managers must ensure that client assets are invested, administered, and protected by a qualified and honest staff. Managers must employ adequate resources to effectively analyze and implement investment strategies. Managers must have adequate resources to monitor such portfolio holdings and strategies. This provision is not meant to prohibit outsourcing where appropriate.

6. Establish a business-continuity plan to address disaster recovery or periodic disruptions of the financial markets.
    A basic business-continuity plan should consider:

    - Data maintenance (backup), preferably off-site, for all required client information.
    - Systems for analyzing, trading, and monitoring investments if primary systems fail.
    - Communication protocols with critical vendors and suppliers.
    - Employee communication protocols and coverage of critical operations.
    - Client communication protocols in the event of extended outages.
    - Periodic testing of contingency plans should be conducted on a firm-wide basis.

7   Establish a **firm-wide** risk management process that identifies, measures, and manages the risk position of the manager and its investments, including the sources, nature, and degree of risk exposure.
    Managers face market risk, credit risk, liquidity risk, counterparty risk, concentration risk, and various types of operational risk. These risks should be analyzed as part of a comprehensive risk management process for portfolios, investment strategies, and the firm. Managers should perform stress tests, scenario tests, and backtests as part of developing risk models that comprehensively capture the full range of their actual and contingent risk exposures. The goal of such models is to determine how various changes in market and investment conditions could affect investments and be explained to clients.

Performance and Valuation

Managers must:

1. Present performance information that is fair, accurate, relevant, timely, and complete. Managers must not misrepresent the performance of individual portfolios or of their firm. Managers must not misrepresent their track record, especially by using historical performance that they did not personally achieve or by selectively picking periods of superior performance. Managers must clearly identify hypothetical or modeled results. Managers should provide as much additional information as is feasible to clarify performance results.
2. Use fair-market prices to value client holdings and apply, in good faith, methods to determine the fair value of any securities for which no independent, third-party market quotation is readily available.
    Pooled funds with independent members on the board of directors should give such members the responsibility to review end of period valuations. If pooled funds have no independent members, they should delegate the valuation review to an independent third party. Managers should use widely accepted valuation methods, consistently applied, to value portfolio holdings.

Disclosures

Managers must:

1. Communicate with clients on an ongoing and timely basis. Managers must select appropriate methods of communicating with clients so that they can evaluate their financial status.
2. Ensure that disclosures are truthful, accurate, complete, and understandable and are presented in a format that communicates the information effectively. Managers must ensure that they do not misrepresent information in any way. Managers must make disclosures in plain language that effectively communicate with clients and prospects. Managers must determine the manner, frequency, and circumstances of disclosures.

3. Include any material facts when making disclosures or providing information to clients regarding themselves, their personnel, investments, or the investment process.

   Managers must provide full and complete information, defined as information that reasonable investors would want to know when making the investment decision or choosing whether to continue using the manager.

4. Disclose the following:
   a. Conflicts of interests generated by any relationships with brokers or other entities, other client accounts, fee structures, or other matters.

      Managers should avoid all conflicts, if possible. Where they cannot be avoided, managers must disclose conflicts in enough detail so that clients can make reasonable judgments about the manager's objectivity.

   b. Regulatory or disciplinary action taken against the manager or its personnel related to professional conduct.

      Managers must disclose situations in which firm personnel have been disciplined for violating standards related to integrity, ethics, or competence.

   c. The investment process, including information regarding lock-up periods, strategies, risk factors, and use of derivatives and leverage.

      Managers must disclose how investment decisions are made and implemented, including identification and discussion of the relevant risk factors.

   d. Management fees and other investment costs charged to investors, including what costs are included in the fees and the methodologies for determining fees and costs.

      Return information provided to clients should include both before- and after-fee returns, as well as any unusual expenses. Managers must clearly explain, in plain language, the methodology of determining all costs charged to investors and when they apply. All fees charged to clients should be listed retrospectively and broken down in a meaningful way (commissions, management fee, incentive fee, and so forth) so that clients can determine how much, and for what, they have actually been charged. Prospective clients should be provided with an estimate of the fees they would be expected to incur.

   e. The amount of any soft or bundled commissions, the goods and/or services received in return, and how those goods and/or services benefit the client.

      Client commissions used in soft dollar arrangements must be disclosed. Disclosures must describe the amount of commissions spent, the products or services received, and how the client benefited.

   f. The performance of clients' investments on a regular and timely basis.

      Managers must provide regular, ongoing performance reporting. Such reporting should occur at least quarterly and, when possible, within 30 days after the end of the quarter.

   g. Valuation methods used to make investment decisions and value client holdings.

      Managers should disclose the valuation methods used to determine account balances by asset class (market close, internal models, third-party valuations, and so forth). Such disclosures should be specific and communicated in a way that clients can understand.

   h. Shareholder voting policies.

      Managers who exercise voting authority must exercise it in an informed and responsible manner for the benefit of the client. Managers must disclose such policies and procedures to clients. Proxy voting policies should specify guidelines for instituting regular review for material issues, methods of reviewing them, guidance about additional actions required when votes are against management, and a system to delegate share-voting responsibilities. Clients should be able to obtain information from the manager about how their shares were voted.

i. Trade allocation policies.
    Managers must disclose how trades are allocated and the priority a client can expect to receive in the allocation process. Managers must disclose any changes in this trading policy.

j. Results of the review or audit of the fund or account. Managers must disclose audit results to clients if the fund or account has been subject to an audit.

k. Significant personnel or organizational changes that have occurred at the manager level. Managers should make clients aware of any significant managerial changes in a timely manner. These might include staff changes or merger and acquisition activities of the manager.

l. Risk management processes.
    Managers must disclose their risk management processes, any material changes, and specific risk information to each client. Relevant risk metrics at the individual product/portfolio level should also be provided.

OVERVIEW OF THE GLOBAL INVESTMENT PERFORMANCE STANDARDS
Cross-Reference to CFA Institute Assigned Reading #6

Purpose and Objectives of GIPS
Goals of the Global Investment Performance Standards (GIPS) Executive Committee:

- Establish industry-wide best practices for calculating and presenting performance information.
- Obtain worldwide acceptance of a common performance measurement and presentation standard based on principles of **fair representation** and **full disclosure**.
- Promote use of accurate and consistent performance information.
- Encourage fair, global competition for all markets without creating barriers to entry for new firms.
- Foster industry self-regulation on a global basis.

Objectives:

- Establish best practices for calculating and presenting performance information.
- Promote confidence that performance information has been prepared using globally common valuation principles and methods.
- Promote asset manager quality assessment by discussing how historical results were achieved.

Key characteristics:

- Voluntary ethical standards.
- Intended to ensure fair representation and full disclosure; firms may have responsibility to include information not required by GIPS.

Scope:

- Apply to investment management firms and not to individuals.
- All actual fee-paying discretionary portfolio composites are defined by investment mandate, objective, or strategy.

> **IMPORTANT:** Where GIPS conflicts with local law, firms should follow local law and make appropriate disclosures.

GIPS has **requirements** that must be followed, and **recommendations** that lead to best practices. Firms do not violate GIPS standards by following requirements but not recommendations.

Provisions of the GIPS Standards

Fundamentals of Compliance
GIPS standards apply on a firm-wide basis rather than only for a specific composite, asset class, strategy, or other.

Firms must comply with *all* requirements of the GIPS standards as well as provide any additional information required for fair representation and full disclosure.

- No compliance "except for"
- No partial compliance

- No characterizing as being "in accordance with," "in compliance with," or "consistent with the GIPS standards"

In addition to GIPS standards, firms must also comply with requirements and clarifications presented in:

- Guidance statements
- Interpretations
- Question-and-answer publications
- Clarifications published by GIPS Executive Committee and CFA Institute

> **IMPORTANT:**
> Only an investment management firm may claim compliance; software providers and third-party performance measurement vendors cannot.

Firms must establish, maintain, and consistently apply policies and procedures related to GIPS standards.

The firm may not refer to an individual account as having been calculated in compliance with the GIPS standards, except when presenting to the individual client.

Firms must not present false or misleading information.

Firms are defined for GIPS compliance as an investment management firm, subsidiary, or division presented as a distinct business entity. A **distinct business entity** has:

> **IMPORTANT:**
> Even if not organizationally separate, functional separation may qualify a unit as a distinct business entity.

- Organizational and functional segregation from other business entities
- Autonomy over the investment decision-making process
- Discretion over assets under management

Total firm assets: Fair value of *all* firm assets under investment management responsibility (even if not discretionary or fee-paying). Firms with discretion over subadvisors must include those results in firm composites. (Market value of all firm assets was used prior to January 1, 2011.)

Changes in firm definition must not alter composite performance history. In joint marketing, compliant performance must be segregated from noncompliant performance, and the compliant firm must be easily distinguished from other participating firms.

Recommendations:

- Comply with recommendations.
- Compliant performance should undergo third-party verification.
- Adopt the broadest, most meaningful definition of the firm.
- Annually provide a compliant presentation to each client.

Input Data

Firms must capture and maintain all information required to produce compliant presentations:

- Use fair value data (i.e., not market value) beginning January 1, 2011:
  - Use market value (not cost or book value) prior to January 1, 2011.
  - Only use cost or book value for calculations requiring after-tax performance.
- Use trade data (rather than settlement date) accounting beginning January 1, 2005.
- Use accrual accounting for assets earning interest income:
  - It is recommended to accrue dividends as of ex-dividend date.

External cash flows describe capital that enters or leaves a portfolio. After January 1, 2010, portfolios must be revalued at each **large external cash flow** and end of each calendar month-end or last business day.

- Beginning January 1, 2001—at least monthly
- Prior to January 1, 2001—at least quarterly

GIPS standards do not specify "large" with respect to cash flows; firms must individually define it.

Firms must use the same beginning and ending annual dates (calendar or last business day) unless the composite reports on a non-calendar fiscal year.

> **IMPORTANT:** Firms must not opportunistically value portfolios at other times (i.e., to improve reported returns).

Recommendations:

- Perform valuation at all (rather than just large) external cash flows.
- Obtain valuation from qualified independent third party; no source shopping to secure highest valuation.
- Accrue investment management fees for net-of-fee performance presentation.

Methodology and Return Calculations

Total return provides the best measure of portfolio return because it considers income and unrealized gain. In the case of no external cash flows:

$$r_t = \frac{V_t - V_0}{V_0}$$

If there are external cash flows, the inter-flow returns should be geometrically linked through the reporting period:

$$r_{twr} = (1 + r_1) \times (1 + r_2) \times \ldots \times (1 + r_t) - 1$$

GIPS standards require such time-weighted return linking at large external cash flows (although such linking at all cash flows is recommended).

Prior to January 1, 2005, GIPS allows midpoint return calculations (Dietz method) based on net external cash flow (*CF*):

$$r_{Dietz} = \frac{V_1 - V_0 - CF}{V_0 + 0.5CF}$$

Beginning January 1, 2005, GIPS requires daily weighted cash flows (modified Dietz method):

$$r_{Mod\ Dietz} = \frac{V_1 - V_0 - CF}{V_0 + \sum_{i=1}^{n} w_i CF_i}$$

The proportion of days the cash flow is in the portfolio is calendar days (*CD*) less the number of calendar days *before* the cash flow occurs (*D_i*):

$$w_i = \frac{CD - D_i}{CD}$$

If cash flows are assumed to occur at the beginning of the day, add 1 to the numerator.

The **modified IRR method** calculates the internal rate of return (IRR) for the period adjusted for cash flows:

$$V_1 = \sum_{i=1}^{n} [CF_1(1+r)^{w_i}] + V_0(1+r)$$

The equation is solved for the value of r that equates the weighted cash flows equal to the ending value. Because this is weighted by w_i, it qualifies as time-weighted. The original IRR would be money-weighted.

The portfolio manager's return must be included in portfolio composite returns even if a different manager earned the cash return.

Actual, not estimated, **trading expenses** (e.g., brokerage commissions, spreads from internal or external brokers, exchange fees and taxes) must be considered in the return calculation. **Custody fees** are not considered for return calculations.

> **IMPORTANT:** When calculating gross-of-fee returns where fees are bundled, the portion with the trading expense must be deducted, or, if not separable, the entire bundled fee must be deducted.

Recommendations:

- Accrue withholding taxes subject to reclamation.
- Deduct non-reclaimable taxes when calculating return.

Composite Return Calculations

A **composite** involves proportion-aggregated returns from portfolios similar in investment mandate, objective, or strategy. The composite return is the sum of individual portfolio returns weighted by the proportion of beginning portfolio assets in the composite:

$$r_C = \sum_{i=1}^{n} \left[r_i \times \frac{V_{0,i}}{\sum_{i=1}^{n} V_{0,i}} \right]$$

The method involving weighted external cash flows is:

$$V_P = V_0 + \sum_{i=1}^{n} (CF_i \times w_i)$$

> **IMPORTANT:** The GIPS standards require weighting at least monthly beginning January 1, 2010. Weighting less frequently reduces the composite's ability to reflect aggregate portfolio performance.

Each V_P across i portfolios can be substituted into the equation for composite return:

$$r_C = \sum_{i=1}^{n} \left[r_{P,i} \times \frac{V_{P,i}}{\sum_{i=1}^{n} V_{P,i}} \right]$$

Another method considers all the portfolio values and external cash flows during the period as one portfolio, and uses the modified Dietz method for the return calculation.

Inclusion in Composites
All actual, fee-paying, discretionary accounts must be included in at least one portfolio.

- Firms must not link simulated or model portfolio performance with actual performance; such performance can be shown as **supplemental information**.
- Non-fee-paying discretionary portfolios may be included with appropriate disclosure.
- Nondiscretionary portfolios may not be included; they do not reflect management skill at managing to the mandate, objective, or strategy.

A **discretionary portfolio** is one for which the investment manager has discretion necessary to implement the intended strategy:

- Investment policy statement (IPS)–mandated restrictions do not necessarily render a portfolio nondiscretionary.
- Frequent withdrawals may be sufficient to make strategy implementation impossible.

> IMPORTANT:
> The GIPS standards recommend that firms disclose when proprietary assets—which are usually non-fee-paying—are included in a composite.

Defining Investment Strategies
Firms are not allowed to include portfolios managed to different mandates, objectives, or strategies in the same composite.

The hierarchy for composite definition includes:

- Investment mandate: Summary or product description (e.g., large-cap global equities).
- Asset classes: Firms may further define by country or region (e.g., equity, European equity).
- Style or strategy (e.g., growth, value, active, indexed, telecommunications).
- Benchmark: Often used where the benchmark describes the investment universe (e.g., S&P 500 Index, BM&FBOVESPA).
- Risk/return characteristics: Based on targeted excess return, tracking error from index, or benchmark.

Entering and Exiting Composites
New portfolios should ideally be included in the first full month after the firm receives control over the funds. However, delays investing the funds may result from asset redeployment, purchase of relatively illiquid assets, and so on.

GIPS allows flexibility in investing the funds, but firms must define a policy for each composite.

Firms must keep portfolios in a composite through the last full period in which the firm managed the funds or maintained discretion over the portfolio.

Portfolios should not change composite unless:

- The composite definition changes and the portfolio no longer fits.
- The portfolio's mandate, objectives, or strategy changes and the composite no longer fits.

> **IMPORTANT:**
> The portfolio's performance must remain with the original composite.

Firms should use **temporary new accounts** to accommodate significant external cash flows rather than remove entire portfolios from a composite.

- A large cash inflow would be held in a temporary new account until it could be deployed in the client's strategy.
- Cash and securities to fund a large cash outflow would be held in a temporary new account until liquidation.

Firms must not include new portfolios with less than the minimum asset level set for a composite, and must establish standards when portfolios already in a composite fall below minimum asset levels.

> **IMPORTANT:**
> A minimum asset level can be changed prospectively, but not retroactively.

Guidance recommends establishing a corridor (e.g., +/– 5%) around the minimum asset threshold. If the portfolio falls below the corridor value for two consecutive periods, it would be excluded from the composite. Conversely, the portfolio must remain above the corridor for two months before it would be included.

GIPS recommends that firms do not present to a client materials about a composite that does not meet the minimum requirements.

Carve-Out Segments

A **carve-out segment** identifies a group of portfolios within a composite that could represent a stand-alone composite (e.g., an investment mandate, asset class, etc.):

> **IMPORTANT:**
> A carve-out must not be included in a composite unless it is managed separately with its own cash balance.

- Prior to January 1, 2010: Identify and disclose the policy used to allocate cash to the carve-out.
- Between January 1, 2006, and prior to January 1, 2011: Include percentage of composite represented by carve-out portfolios.

Disclosure

A firm may claim compliance only with respect to the entire firm; it does not claim compliance "except for" anything. Claims used in advertising appear later.

Firms verified by third-party verification may use the following statement:

> [Insert name of firm] claims compliance with the Global Investment Performance Standards (GIPS®) and has prepared and presented this report in compliance with the GIPS standards. [Insert name of firm] has been independently verified for the periods [insert dates]. The verification report(s) is/are available upon request.

> Verification assesses whether (1) the firm has complied with all the composite construction requirements of the GIPS standards on a firm-wide basis, and (2) the firm's policies and procedures are designed to calculate and present performance in compliance with the GIPS standards. Verification does not ensure the accuracy of any specific composite presentation.

Unverified firms must use the following statement:

> [Insert name of firm] claims compliance with the Global Investment Performance Standards (GIPS®) and has prepared and presented this report in compliance with the GIPS standards. [Insert name of firm] has not been independently verified.

In addition, firms may obtain third-party verification for a specific composite, which is called an examination.:

> [Insert name of firm] claims compliance with the Global Investment Performance Standards (GIPS®) and has prepared and presented this report in compliance with the GIPS standards. [Insert name of firm] has been independently verified for the periods [insert dates].

> Verification assesses whether (1) the firm has complied with all the composite construction requirements of the GIPS standards on a firm-wide basis, and (2) the firm's processes and procedures are designed to calculate and present performance in compliance with the GIPS standards. The [insert name of composite] composite has been examined for the periods [insert dates]. The verification and examination reports are available upon request.

Other required disclosures (unless noted as recommended):

- Definition of the firm:
    - Redefinition requires disclosure of redefinition, date, and reason.
    - List other firms within same parent company (recommended).
- Management events that would help clients interpret presentation:
    - Results achieved by portfolio manager or research group no longer with the firm
    - Any past results achieved by other firms or affiliations
    - Use and dates for subadvisors (after January 1, 2006; recommended for prior periods)
- Valuation events:
    - Policies for portfolio valuation, return calculation, and compliant performance presentation are available on request.
    - Portfolios not valued as of last business day or calendar month end (prior to January 1, 2010)
    - Use of subjective unobservable inputs that materially affect valuation (after January 1, 2011)
    - Material differences in GIPS valuation hierarchy
    - Recommended:
        - Key valuation principles and dates, description, and reason for any changes
        - Use of subjective unobservable inputs that materially affect valuation (prior to January 1, 2011)
        - Disclosure of material changes to calculation methods
- List of firm composites available on request; includes those discontinued within prior five years:
    - Description sufficient to understand investment mandate, objective, or strategy
    - **Composite creation date**—Date when accounts were first grouped into the composite
    - Composite redefinition date, description, and reason
    - Minimum asset levels and any changes to minimums

- ○ Policy used to allocate cash to carve-outs (periods prior to January 1, 2010)
  - ○ Definition of significant cash flows and applicable periods for definition
  - ○ If composite contains proprietary asset portfolio(s) (recommended)
- Currency used to present performance:
  - ○ Differences in exchange rates and valuation resources between portfolios
  - ○ Differences in exchange rates and valuation resources between composites and the benchmark (after January 1, 2011)
- Treatment of withholding tax on dividends, interest, and capital gains, and whether benchmark is net of withholding tax
- Benchmark description:
  - ○ If a custom benchmark, state the components, weights, and rebalancing process.
  - ○ If no applicable benchmark, disclose why.
  - ○ If benchmark changes, describe date, change, and reason.
  - ○ Describe differences between the composite and the benchmark (recommended).
- Treatment of fees:
  - ○ Gross-of-fee returns are investment returns less trading expenses.
  - ○ Disclose any fees deducted in addition to trading expenses.
  - ○ Net-of-fee returns are gross-of-fee returns reduced for management fees (including performance-based fees and carried interest):
    - ■ Disclose any fees deducted in addition to trading expenses and investment management fee.
    - ■ Disclose whether fees are model or actual investment management fees.
    - ■ Disclose deduction of performance-based fees.
- Disclose fee schedule appropriate to compliant performance presentation:
  - ○ Bundled fees: Types of fees included
  - ○ Management fees
- Internal dispersion measure used/presented
- Derivatives: Description of material use, presence, and extent sufficient to understand risk
- Local laws/regulations/GIPS standards: If the performance presentation conforms and, if not, type and reason for nonconformance:
  - ○ List periods of GIPS noncompliance prior to January 1, 2000
  - ○ Only compliant periods may be shown after January 1, 2000
- Annualized three-year *ex post* standard deviation for monthly composite returns and benchmark returns:
  - ○ Firms must disclose if that measure is unavailable.
  - ○ Firms must disclose if an alternative method is used:
    - ■ Describe why standard measure is not appropriate or relevant.
    - ■ Describe alternative method and why selected.

> **IMPORTANT:**
> Distinguish between *carried interest*, an allocation of an investment vehicle's profits, and *performance-based fees*, which are a percentage applied after exceeding a minimum return.

Presentation and Reporting

GIPS-compliant performance presentations embody the ideals of full disclosure and fair representation. The core elements of a GIPS-compliant presentation for all periods include:

- Composite and benchmark annual performance for all years
- The number of portfolios in the composite (if greater than five)
- Assets represented in the composite for all years:
  - ○ Dollar value
  - ○ Percentage of total firm assets represented by the composite *or* total firm assets
- Measure of **internal dispersion** if composite includes more than five portfolios (i.e., dispersion of returns for portfolios included in the composite)

Each GIPS-compliant composite performance presentation requires:

- Annual performance:
    - Since inception or a minimum of five years
    - Building to 10 years of performance
- Nonannualized partial period returns (if 10-year period includes inception/termination dates on or after January 1, 2011):
    - Composite inception through initial annual period end
    - Annual period start through composite termination
- Benchmark total return for each annual period presented
- Method of dispersion including but not limited to:
    - High-low values
    - Range
    - Interquartile range (i.e., the middle 50% of observations; excludes outliers)
    - Standard deviation:
        - Equal-weighted standard deviation
        - Asset-weighted standard deviation
- For both composite and benchmark (identical periodicity of measures):
    - Three-year annualized *ex post* standard deviation using monthly returns (for periods beginning January 1, 2011)
    - Additional *ex post* measure, with appropriate disclosures, if standard deviation is inappropriate (e.g., asymmetric returns distribution)
- Carve-outs: Percentage of total composite assets represented in the composite (periods beginning January 1, 2006, and before January 1, 2011); no requirement to disclose outside that period
- Non-fee-paying portfolios: Percentage of non-fee-paying portfolios represented in the composite (end of annual period)
- Past-performance linking (composite-specific basis):
    - New firm employs substantially all the previous investment decision makers.
    - Decision-making process remains independent and substantially intact within the new firm.
    - Reported performance can be supported and documented.

Additional recommendations for firms to present:

- Gross-of-fee returns (i.e., best representation of attaining strategy indicated by the benchmark)
- Returns without deduction for administrative expenses (i.e., they are outside manager control)
- Cumulative benchmark and composite returns over the presentation period
- Equal-weighted mean and median returns (in addition to required asset-weighted returns)
- Quarterly performance presentation updating, including monthly or quarterly returns
- Annualized composite and benchmark returns for periods longer than one year (e.g., 10-year cumulative return geometrically decomposed into annual return)
- Annualized three-year standard deviation of returns (and other measures) for periods prior to January 1, 2011:
    - Corresponding benchmark and composite returns presented for same periods
    - Additional relevant *ex post* dispersion measures
    - Any other additional quantitative information that clients will find useful for evaluating strategy risk

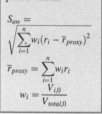

- Compliant reporting for all historical periods (rather than noncompliant performance presentation as allowed prior to January 1, 2000)
- More than 10 years of compliant performance

Real Estate

Real estate as an asset class includes:

- Partially or wholly owned properties
- Insurance company separate accounts, commingled funds, and property unit trusts
- Private placement securities of real estate investment trusts (REITs) and real estate operating companies (REOCs)
- Participating mortgage loans or other instruments that participate in operating results

Certain real estate–related instruments are excluded from the special real estate provisions:

- REITs and other publicly traded real estate securities
- Mortgage-backed securities
- Commercial and residential loans and other private debt investments having no participation in property performance

> **IMPORTANT:**
> Firms must not link periods of noncompliant performance with compliant performance. Noncompliant performance prior to January 1, 2006, must be disclosed. No noncompliant performance may be presented after January 1, 2006.

Requirements and recommendations are considered effective for periods beginning January 1, 2011, unless otherwise noted.

- Valuation:
    - Principles:
        - Fair value beginning January 1, 2011
        - Market value prior to January 1, 2011 (2005 GIPS market value conventions)
    - Internal frequency (i.e., may be performed by in-house valuators):
        - End-of-quarter beginning January 1, 2010
        - Quarterly beginning January 1, 2008
        - Every 12 months prior to January 1, 2008
    - External frequency (i.e., must be performed by unrelated third-party valuators):
        - Every 36 months prior to January 1, 2012
        - Every 12 months beginning January 1, 2012, unless client agreements specify otherwise; then, at least every 36 months unless client agreement specifies more frequently (e.g., 24 months)
    - Third-party valuators must be:
        - External, independently licensed, certified, professionally designated appraisers/valuators
        - If credentials are unavailable, must be well-qualified with experience in type of property being valued
    - Firms must present the percentage of assets receiving external valuation as of each reporting period end.
- Return calculations after transaction costs (i.e., gross-of-fee returns) must be made at least quarterly beginning January 1, 2006.
- Includes trading expenses (i.e., commissions, closing costs, etc.) and advisory, legal, financial, and investment banking costs incident to buying, selling, restructuring, or recapitalizing.
- Annual component returns (i.e., capital returns and income returns) must be calculated separately using geometrically linked time-weighted rates of return beginning January 1, 2011.

- Quarterly component and composite returns must be calculated by asset-weighting individual portfolio returns.
- Component return presentations must clearly identify whether composite and component returns are gross of fee or net of fee:
  - Should present gross-of-fee component returns if only gross-of-fee composite return is presented.
  - Should present net-of-fee component returns if only net-of-fee composite return is presented.
  - Should present at least gross-of-fee component returns if both gross- and net-of-fee composites are presented.
  - Firms using monthly component return calculation may use a quarterly aggregation method that fairly and accurately reports results across all portfolios in a composite (i.e., they are not limited to geometrically link monthly results that will not properly cumulate).
- Disclosures:
  - Definition of discretion
  - Valuation method(s), including method of comparables, income capitalization, and so on
  - Changes to valuation methods beginning January 1, 2011
  - Valuation frequency
  - Linked noncompliant periods prior to 2006
  - Dispersion method (high and low annual time-weighted return

> **IMPORTANT:**
> Core real estate strategies focus on income returns, opportunistic strategies focus on capital returns, and total return strategies attempt both income and capital returns.

Recommendations include:

- Annual period-end independent valuation for all assets prior to January 1, 2012 (i.e., not just beginning on that date)
- Both gross-of-fee and net-of-fee composite and composite component returns
- Disclosure of:
  - Accounting principles (i.e., U.S. GAAP, IFRS, etc.)
  - Differences between performance reporting and financial reporting at the end of each annual period
  - Material changes to valuation policies for periods prior to January 1, 2011
  - Non–real estate percentage in composites at the annual period end

GIPS standards specify additional requirements for closed-end real estate funds:

- Since-inception internal rate of return (SI-IRR) items:
  - Net-of-fees SI-IRR (i.e., since-inception IRR) presented in addition to time-weighted return
  - Nonannualized partial period net-of-fees SI-IRR (if 10-year period includes inception/termination dates on or after January 1, 2011):
    - Composite inception through initial annual period end
    - Annual period start through final liquidation date
  - If gross-of-fees SI-IRR is presented, must be for same periods as net-of-fees SI-IRR
  - SI-IRR for benchmark as of each annual period end
- Composite definition based on **vintage year** as well as investment mandate, strategy, or objective:
  - Year of first drawdown or capital call from investors, or
  - Year first committed capital from outside investors is closed and legally binding

- Financial history and status must include:
  - Committed capital: Amount of capital that has been promised
  - Since-inception paid-in capital: Amount of capital that has been drawn down
  - Since-inception distributions
- Ratios:
  - PIC multiple: Paid-in capital to committed capital
  - TVPI (**investment multiple**): Total value to since-inception paid-in capital
  - DPI (realization multiple): Since-inception distribution to since-inception paid-in capital
  - RVPI (unrealized multiple): Residual value to since-inception paid-in capital

Private Equity

Private equity includes fixed-life, fixed-commitment vehicles (i.e., not open for subscriptions or redemptions):

> **IMPORTANT:**
> The financial history and ratios are the same for real estate and private equity presentation.

- **Primary fund vehicles** make direct investments in companies.
- **Funds of funds** invest in other closed-end primary funds but may make direct investments.
- **Secondary funds** invest in other funds of funds.

General partners screen early stage business plans, select potential candidates, conduct due diligence on those potential candidates, structure deals, place capital calls against capital committed by limited partners, and manage the ongoing relationship with the investment. As the investment matures, the general partners take companies public and pay out the limited partners.

Limited partners provide funding, and their loss is limited to their investment.

- Input data: Fair value determination at least annually beginning January 1, 2011
- Return calculations: Must use SI-IRR in addition to return specified by GIPS:
  - Daily or monthly cash flows prior to January 1, 2011.
  - Daily-only cash flows beginning January 1, 2011.
  - Distribution of stock must be valued at distribution and considered a cash flow.
- Presentation:
  - Gross-of-fee returns must be presented using actual transaction costs.
  - Net-of-fee returns must be presented after deduction of actual investment management fees and carried interest.
  - All fund-of-funds returns must be net of underlying fund/partnership fees and expenses, including carried interest.
- Composites:
  - Primary fund vehicles must be included in at least one composite by vintage year *and* investment mandate, objectives, or strategy.
  - Funds of funds must be included in at least one composite by vintage year for the fund of funds and/or investment mandate, objectives, or strategy.
- Disclosure:
  - Vintage year and how determined, and **final liquidation date**
  - Valuation methods, and material changes during periods beginning January 1, 2011
  - Any valuation methods in addition to GIPS
  - Periodicity of cash flows if not daily for periods prior to January 1, 2011
  - Periods of noncompliance prior to January 1, 2006
  - Gross-of-fee returns—any expenses other than transaction costs deducted
  - Net-of-fee returns—any expenses other than transaction costs and management fees

- Benchmark calculation method—method used for calculating public market equivalent (PME) benchmarks
- Presentation:
  - Composite SI-IRR gross-of-fees and net-of-fees returns must be clearly presented.
  - Partial years (inception/termination) must not be annualized.
  - SI-IRR of composite and benchmark as of each year end.
  - Benchmark same vintage year and investment mandate, objectives, or strategy as composite for all periods.
  - No noncompliant performance for periods after January 1, 2006.
  - Percentage of primary fund assets in fund-of-funds vehicles (beginning January 1, 2011).
  - Fund-of-funds composites defined only by investment mandate, objective, or strategy:
    - Must aggregate underlying investments by vintage year and present SI-IRR gross of management fees for those.
    - The benchmark, if presented, must reflect the same vintage year and underlying mandate, objectives, or strategy.
    - Percentage of direct investments included in fund-of-funds composites (beginning January 1, 2011).
- Financial history and status must include:
  - Committed capital: Amount of capital that has been promised
  - Since-inception paid-in capital: Amount of capital that has been drawn down
  - Since-inception distributions
- Ratios:
  - PIC multiple: Paid-in capital to committed capital
  - TVPI (**investment multiple**): Total value to since-inception paid-in capital
  - DPI (realization multiple): Since-inception distribution to since-inception paid-in capital
  - RVPI (unrealized multiple): Residual value to since-inception paid-in capital

Recommendations:

- Value investments at least quarterly.
- SI-IRR calculations use daily cash flows for periods prior to January 1, 2011.
- Material differences between performance and financial reporting should be disclosed and explained.

IMPORTANT: The financial history and ratios are the same for real estate and private equity presentation.

Separately Managed Accounts (SMAs)
Account sponsors often hire subaccount managers, each of which has expenses and fees. The account sponsor then presents them to clients with the sponsor's own fee "wrapped" around the subaccount manager fees. A sponsor may also have separately managed accounts (SMAs) with no wrap fee imposed.

GIPS standards regarding wrap-fee SMAs exist in addition to core GIPS, especially with respect to bundled fees.

IMPORTANT: Combining both wrap-fee SMAs with non-wrap-fee SMAs in the same composite may result in a competitive disadvantage for the non-wrap-fee accounts.

Disclosures:

- A composite containing a wrap-fee SMA must disclose each period that the composite does not contain the wrap-fee SMA.
- Periods of noncompliance prior to January 1, 2006, must be disclosed.

- Firms may not link noncompliant periods on or after January 1, 2006, to compliant periods.
- Style-defined composites that include wrap-fee accounts must include all appropriate accounts.
- Performance must be presented net of the entire wrap fee.
- Firms providing SMA services to a sponsor under a wrap-fee arrangement must disclose the sponsor if presenting results specific to a sponsor.
- Firms may present performance gross of the wrap fee to gain business, but must include disclosure that the presentation is only for use by the prospective sponsor.

GIPS Valuation Principles

Performance reporting should focus on:

- **Fair representation:** Accurate asset values obtained through appropriate policies and procedures
- **Full disclosure:** Providing valuation-related information required by GIPS, as well as documentation of policies and procedures appropriate for valuation

GIPS standards require firms to apply **fair value** (rather than **market value**) beginning January 1, 2011.

Fair value transactions result from knowledgeable and prudent negotiations between unrelated parties acting in their own best interests (i.e., at arm's length). This value must be established by using an objective, observable, unaltered market price from active markets on the valuation date, if available.

Where objective, observable, unaltered market prices are unavailable, firms should use market prices for similar investments in active markets.

IMPORTANT:
Fair value must include accrued income.

If market valuations for similar investments are not available, use (in order):

- Quoted prices for identical or similar investments in inactive markets
- Observable market-based inputs other than quoted price
- Subjective, unobservable inputs (assumptions about assumptions other market participants would use)

Inactive markets are characterized by:

- Thinly traded assets (i.e., few transactions)
- Noncurrent prices
- Substantial price variations from market makers

Real estate valuation:

- Must not use valuation where valuator's compensation depends on value
- Use only single value (rather than range of values)
- Rotate appraisal firms every three to five years (recommended)

Private equity valuation:

- Valuation method selected must be most appropriate for investment characteristics.
- Selection of valuation method should be based on:

- ○ Data quality and reliability
- ○ Data comparability for other transactions and/or firms
- ○ Business development stage
- ○ Considerations unique to the investment

Advertising Guidelines

Advertisement includes any type of communication addressed to or intended for more than one prospective client.

One-on-one presentations, including presentations to the investment committee or board of a plan sponsor or other prospective single client, are not considered advertising.

Firms that choose to claim GIPS compliance in advertising may:

- Include a compliant presentation in the advertisement, or
- Follow the GIPS Advertising Guidelines.

All advertisements are required to disclose:

- Definition of the firm
- How to obtain composite descriptions and performance presentations

Compliance statement for advertisements:

- [Insert name of firm] claims compliance with the Global Investment Performance Standards (GIPS®).

Advertisements that provide performance data are required to derive it from a compliant presentation:

- Noncompliance for periods prior to January 1, 2001
- Composite and benchmark description (same as compliant presentation)
- Currency in which return is presented
- Gross-of-fees, net-of-fees, or both types of performance
- One of the following types of returns:
    - ○ Annualized one-, three-, and five-year composite returns through the most recent period
    - ○ Period-to-date one-, three-, and five-year composite returns through the most recent period (through same period corresponding to the compliant presentation)
    - ○ Period-to-date composite returns in addition to five years of annual composite returns (through same period corresponding to the compliant presentation)
- Presence, frequency of use, characteristics of, and extent of derivatives and short positions sufficient to identify risks

Verification

Verification describes the process of an independent verifier assessing whether the firm has:

- Complied with the GIPS standards on a firm-wide basis
- Implemented policies and procedures designed to calculate and present GIPS-compliant performance

> **IMPORTANT:**
> Firms may include other information as long as it is not given more prominence than the required information.

The minimum initial period for verification is since inception or one year. GIPS standards recommend verification for all periods claimed by the firm as being compliant.

Purpose
Verification supports fair representation and full disclosure principles.

Third-party verification provides greater assurance that GIPS standards were adhered to in presenting performance, but does not guarantee the accuracy of any composite performance presentation.

Scope
Verification applies on a firm-wide basis. The output product from verification is a single report assessing compliance on a firm-wide basis.

A verified firm may request further verification of a specific composite or composites.

A principal verifier may accept the work of another independent verifier if it is reasonably sure the other verifier is qualified. The principal verifier must document the basis for such acceptance.

Sampling is allowed, with sample size based on:

- Number of composites at the firm
- Number of portfolios in each composite
- Types of composites
- Assets under management
- Internal control procedures
- Years under examination
- Computer applications used to construct and/or maintain composites and calculate performance
- Use of external firms to measure performance

Pre-Verification Procedures
GIPS verifiers must make themselves familiar with:

- GIPS
- Relevant laws and regulations
- Corporate structure and operating methods of the firm
- Firm's GIPS-related policies and procedures
- Firm's methods for calculating portfolio value and investment performance

Verification
Verifiers must be able to determine appropriate:

- Firm definition
- Calculation and disclosure of firm assets
- Composite descriptions, membership, and relevant benchmark
- Application of discretion
- Procedures for assuring existence and ownership of client assets
- Inclusion of all actual, fee-paying, discretionary accounts in at least one portfolio
- Treatment of:
    - Income, interest, and dividend accruals
    - Taxes, tax accruals, and tax reclaims

- o Purchase, sale, open/close of positions
- o Investment accounting and valuation

Verifiers must confirm:

- Firms are using a GIPS-compliant return formula:
  - o Recalculate and compare return presented for selected portfolios and composites.
- Accuracy of calculations for composites and benchmarks (from sample):
  - o Consistency with compliant presentation.
- Portfolios are correctly classified as discretionary or nondiscretionary.
- Portfolios are included in the correct composite:
  - o Trace selected composites from management agreement to composite.
  - o Check that movements among composites are appropriate.
- Firm disclosures are consistent with internal policies and verifier findings.

Verifiers must maintain documentation justifying their recommendation. This includes a letter from the firm undergoing verification that it has followed all its policies and procedures and that they are compliant with GIPS standards for the period under verification, and must contain any specific representations to the verifier.

After-Tax Return Calculations
Effective January 1, 2011, all after-tax information is supplemental information and subject to the GIPS Guidance Statement on the Use of Supplemental Information.

Substantial additional information must be captured and maintained when after-tax return calculations have to be made.

- Custom benchmarks are better suited to after-tax portfolio performance comparison, but will not generally be suited to composite performance comparison.
- Shadow portfolios using mutual funds or exchange-traded funds can simulate purchases and sales in client portfolios.
- After-tax benchmarks become problematic because the client's individual asset values and tax situation would drive the tax issues addressed by the benchmark.

The following cases do not necessarily consider the portfolio manager's ability to optimize tax liability via well-timed purchases and sales within the portfolio.

The pre-liquidation method reduces pre-tax income and price-appreciation return by the amount of applicable taxes. The method disregards unrealized gains and losses and may underestimate taxes embedded in the unrealized amount.

The mark-to-liquidation method assumes all investments are sold at the end of the period and taxes become immediately due. This method overstates tax liability by disregarding time value of money effects on future tax liability.

Performance measurement allows comparison of manager skill; firms may wish to eliminate the tax effects of nondiscretionary portfolio flows. The adjustment should assume that all securities are proportionately liquidated in order to avoid management selecting highly appreciated securities for the hypothetical adjustment.

Firms should disclose the percentage return benefit created for a composite by tax-loss harvesting if realized losses exceed realized gains during the period.

BF
CME

THE BEHAVIORAL FINANCE PERSPECTIVE
Cross-Reference to CFA Institute Assigned Reading #7

Traditional Finance Perspective

Utility-Maximizing Decision Making

Utility describes satisfaction from consuming a good or service. Because no direct measurement of satisfaction can be made, economists usually consider the satisfaction of one choice against other choices.

Utility theory recognizes choices people make as a rational judgment between *expected* levels of satisfaction.

Rational judgment involves the ability to:

1. Assign a probability to potential outcomes.
2. Use Bayesian inference to update outcome probabilities based on new information (i.e., conditioned probabilities).
3. Decide a course of action expected to maximize utility (i.e., rational decision making).

Rational decision making involves adhering to the premises (i.e., axioms) of utility theory:

- **Completeness.** There are well-defined preferences over the set of all known choices (i.e., between A and B, A and C, and B and C) and an ability to choose between them.
- **Transitivity.** There is internal consistency of decisions (i.e., if prefer A to B, and B to C, then will prefer A to C).
- **Independence.** Preference order persists with addition of a lesser choice to two existing choices; allows additivity of utility (i.e., given completeness and transitivity, still prefer A to B if C is added in the same amount to both).
- **Continuity.** An unbroken utility curve describes equal utility derived from different combinations of two goods.

Rational economic man (REM) will then determine the highest utility curve (i.e., furthest from the origin) within a budget constraint.

> **IMPORTANT:** Different people will have different utilities and assign different probabilities for each potential outcome, so they are unlikely to all reach the same asset price conclusion.

This gives rise to the idea that security prices contain all available information; that is, each price represents the present value sum of expected future outcomes.

Risk Aversion

Risk aversion describes a rational decision maker's reluctance to equate probability-weighted expected utility $E(U_x)$ with a *known* utility U_x.

A risk-neutral investor will pay the expected value of an investment without any risk premium. Risk averse investors will require a risk premium while risk seeking investors may actually pay more for an investment than they expect to receive on the off chance they'll earn a greater return than expected.

Diminishing Marginal Utility

Marginal utility is the additional utility from each additional unit of consumption.

> **IMPORTANT:**
> Don't confuse marginal utility curves (i.e., representing utility for one good) with indifference curves (i.e., representing trade-off preference of one good for another good). However, the diminishing utility of each good gives shape to the curve representing indifference between the two.

Diminishing marginal utility describes how consuming more and more of the same thing yields less and less additional satisfaction in a **concave** marginal utility curve.

Risk-averse investors exhibit diminishing marginal utility for increases in wealth. Risk-neutral investors have straight-line utility curves, whereas risk-seeking investors have convex (bowl-shaped) curves.

Behavioral Finance Perspectives

Behavioral finance recognizes that psychological variables distort rational decision-making processes assumed for neoclassical economics (i.e., traditional finance).

> **IMPORTANT:**
> If investors are not completely rational, then markets are not always efficient as envisioned in neoclassical economics.

Prospect Theory

Prospect theory relaxes the traditional risk-aversion assumption and makes assumptions consistent with *expected* utility theory.

Prospect theory assigns value (i.e., utility) to *changes* in wealth rather than *levels* of wealth, and replaces probability with decision weights. The value function is concave for gains implying risk aversion, and convex for losses implying risk seeking. Decision weights are less than probabilities.

The concave value function in the **domain of gains** recognizes the risk-averse preference for a smaller certain gain to a slightly larger potential gain. The convex value function in the **domain of losses** recognizes the risk-seeking preference for a slightly larger potential loss to a certain loss.

Prospect theory identifies two phases:

1. Framing/editing: Decision maker decides on heuristics and uses them to rank alternatives:
   - Framing—presenting the choice or options
   - Editing—narrowing options based on constraints and identifying appropriate options for further study
2. Evaluation/choice: Decision maker forms expected value for each choice as the sum of probability-weighted values for expected outcomes.

> **IMPORTANT:**
> Using these heuristics can result in inconsistent choices depending on how the alternative prospects are framed.

Editing simplifies the choice by reformulating and organizing available options using two sets of operations:

1. Operations for each prospect separately:
   - Codification—Perceive outcomes as gains and losses relative to a reference point rather than final states of wealth.
   - Combination—Sum probabilities associated with identical gains or losses.
   - Segregation—Separate the probability of an event not happening from the probability of it happening.
2. Operations applied to two or more prospects:
   - Cancellation—Common outcomes between choices are discarded; the remainder are compared.
   - Simplification—Round the probability for each outcome.
   - Detection of dominance—Discard less likely outcomes without further examination.

> **IMPORTANT:**
> Prospect theory hypothesizes that people are loss averse rather than risk averse; that is, they will have different attitudes toward risk depending on their reference point. (a gain or a loss)

Neuro-Economics

Neuro-economics seeks to describe behavioral decision making in terms of neural events (i.e., blood flow and chemical levels in different parts of the brain). Traditional finance makes simplifying assumptions about the effects of these events.

Scientists have found that dopamine levels rise in expectation of reward as well as receipt of a reward, whereas failed expectations result in low serotonin levels that create impulsiveness, irritability, anxiety, and depression.

Euphoric effects of high dopamine levels could explain overconfidence and risk-taking behavior. Depressive effects of low serotonin levels could explain fear of loss, failure to make needed changes, and use of high-risk, low-probability strategies to escape losses.

The amygdala (part of the inner brain) may be responsible for market panics rather than rational responses to falling prices.

Traditional economists dispute whether neuro-economic theories adequately describe economic reality.

Traditional finance focuses on how decisions *should be* made; behavioral finance focuses on how decisions *are* made.

Cognitive Limitations

Even with computers, people suffer from intellectual, informational, computational, and financial limitations, which they attempt to circumvent:

- **Bounded rationality.** Acting rationally within bounds around decision making:
  - **Parameters**—Deciding how much will be done to aggregate relevant information and reach decisions.
  - **Heuristics**—Rules of thumb to make analysis less burdensome.
- **Satisficing** (satisfy + suffice). Finding adequate rather than optimal solutions:
  - **Adequate solution**—Resolves the situation while meeting the needs of the decision maker.
  - **Optimal solution**—Maximizes utility available from a decision.

Satisficing often occurs as the result of time and cost limitations.

- Means-end analysis: Move toward the goal in stages rather than looking for alternative methods.
- Divide and conquer: Break the problem into subproblems and create solutions for subproblems rather than solving the holistic problem.
- Focus on the situation without regard for the surrounding economic and political environment; limiting alternatives makes this easier.

> **IMPORTANT:**
> Bounded rationality applies to a decision maker who acts rationally, but within a bounded set of goals.

Summary of Effects

- Underweight moderate- and high-probability outcomes (i.e., moderate gains or losses); overweight low-probability outcomes (i.e., extreme gains or losses).
- Risk seeking (i.e., convex value function) below a wealth reference point; risk averse (i.e., concave value function) above a wealth reference point.
- The value function is steeper for losses than for gains (i.e., avoiding loss is more important than achieving gains).

> **IMPORTANT:**
> People are *risk averse* when there is a moderate to high probability of gains with a low probability of losses, but are *risk seeking* when there is a high probability of losses versus a low probability of gains.

BF
CME

Portfolio Construction

Traditional Perspective
The traditional perspective assumes that professional managers can determine from mean-variance efficient portfolios the single portfolio most suitable based on investment objectives, risk tolerance obtained via a questionnaire, and an investor's constraints or other circumstances.

Behavioral models suggest investors and managers do not have perfect information or react perfectly to that information.

No behavioral model has gained acceptance sufficient to replace the traditional perspective.

Consumption and Savings
People classify wealth into current income, currently owned assets, and the present value of future income; replaces life cycle approach, which says people spend and save money to achieve a short-term and long-term spending and saving plan.

> **IMPORTANT:**
> Investors will undersave for future income based on full consumption of current income and much if not all of their current assets.

- **Mental accounting:** Although wealth is fungible, people look at it as coming from different sources.
- **Framing:** People use the source of the wealth as a basis for decisions about how to spend or save; current income has high marginal propensity to consume, while any income saved becomes current assets or future income.
- **Self-control:** Long-term sources are unavailable for current spending.

Asset Pricing
In traditional finance, present value involves a discount factor that includes real required return (assumed to be equal across investors), objectively determined risk premiums, and an inflation premium.

Behavioral stochastic discount factor–based (SDF-based) asset pricing models include an additional premium for sentiment in required return.

- Bullish: Overestimate expected growth; underestimate volatility with great confidence. Sentiment risk decreases required return.
- Bearish: Underestimate expected growth; overestimate volatility with little confidence. Sentiment risk increases required return.

The standard deviation of analyst forecasts serves as a sentiment risk measure; widely dispersed forecasts indicate lower analyst enthusiasm about expected security performance.

> **IMPORTANT:**
> Positive sentiment is a negative risk premium.

Value stocks have greater dispersion of analyst earnings estimates. To compensate the sentiment risk, expected earnings are valued using higher required return. Lower valuation results in lower price-earnings (P/E) ratios.

Sophisticated investors can systematically exploit systematic investor sentiment errors but cannot systematically exploit random errors.

Portfolio Theory
Traditional approaches use mean-variance analysis and consider covariance in establishing an optimal diversified portfolio on the efficient frontier.

Behavioral portfolio theory (BPT) acknowledges five differences in risk aversion in the domain of gains versus risk seeking in the domain of losses:

1. Given equal priority, upside goals receive more funding than minimizing potential losses.
2. Strategic asset allocation depends on the goal assigned to the funding layer; allocation for higher goals includes riskier assets.
3. Lower risk tolerance in the domain of gains results in a greater number of securities there; concavity of utility curve indicates faster satiation of specific security.
4. A perceived information advantage for a security results in overallocation to that security.
5. Loss aversion creates a need for greater cash balances to meet funding needs without liquidating loss positions, and may result in a greater number of potential losing positions.

> **IMPORTANT:**
> A BPT portfolio uses bonds (insurance policy) to fund critical goals in the domain of gains, and uses risky securities (lottery ticket) to fund aspirational goals in the domain of losses.

BF
CME

Adaptive Markets

The **adaptive markets hypothesis (AMH)** holds that market participants must adapt to competition for scarce resources to survive. The AMH updates the **efficient market hypothesis (EMH)** for bounded rationality, satisficing, and evolutionary principles.

Biases toward continuing previously successful behavior rather than adapting as competition shifts are explained by use of heuristics (i.e., rules of thumb) learned to become successful.

Implications:

- The most important goal is survival.
- Market participants must adapt or die.
- Changes in the competitive market and risk preferences cause risk premiums to change over time.
- Successfully exploiting pricing anomalies can yield excess return.
- Any strategy will have periods of higher return and lower return.

THE BEHAVIORAL BIASES OF INDIVIDUALS
Cross-Reference to CFA Institute Assigned Reading #8

**BF
CME**

Categories of Behavioral Bias
The major categories of individual behavioral bias are:

- Behavioral finance micro (BFMI): Individual investor (i.e., biases):
  - **Cognitive errors** (conscious)—Faulty analysis process resulting from memory, information processing, or statistical errors (e.g., using rules of thumb).
  - **Emotional biases** (unconscious)—Faulty reasoning resulting from feelings and impulses.
- Behavioral finance macro (BFMA): Market behavior (e.g., anomalies)

Cognitive errors involve faulty reasoning; emotional biases result from pleasure seeking or pain avoidance.

Emotions include perceptions, beliefs, or feelings that arise spontaneously as a mental state without conscious effort. Emotions may be real or imagined, and individuals experiencing them may only be able to work around them rather than control them.

In some cases, market participants make cognitive errors that justify their emotional biases.

> **IMPORTANT:** Investors can identify the sources of and therefore overcome cognitive errors more easily than emotional biases.

Cognitive Errors
Cognitive errors occur when investors fail to gather appropriate information, consider it carefully, and update probabilities.

Belief Persistence Biases
A **belief persistence bias** involves cognitive errors that reject contradictory new information:

- Selective exposure: Notice only information of interest.
- Selective perception: Ignore or modify contradictory information.
- Selective retention: Remember and consider only confirming information.

Conservatism bias results when financial market participants (FMPs) overweight initial observations or information and then fail to adequately update perceptions when new information arises.

This bias is related to the amount of effort involved in information acquisition, data processing, and updating existing projections (i.e., cognitive costs).

FMPs should consider new information and react decisively when a new conclusion arises.

Confirmation bias results when people only notice belief-confirming information, or disregard or fail to properly weight contradictory information.

FMPs may ignore negative information once they have decided, or may develop screening criteria that bolster positive information about the investment. In the process, good investments may be screened out.

Concentrated positions often result, especially if the investor's own company is involved.

FMPs should attempt to overcome confirmation bias by actively seeking opinions contradictory to their own. Investment ideas should be confirmed via third-party research before confirming the opinion via purchases.

Representativeness bias involves classifying new information based on meaning derived from past information, even if it doesn't fit:

- **Base-rate neglect** ignores the probability that new information matches existing information used for classification.
- **Sample-size neglect** uses isolated cases or small sample sizes to represent the general case.

FMPs may continue to apply existing methods of using information in classifying investment opportunities, or make investments based on small bits of information. Investors will fire their investment manager when supposed results don't occur, or sell a security when they cannot properly classify new information.

FMPs can avoid representativeness bias by proper asset allocation, making changes only when adequate information to support a change has developed, and using longer-term performance data.

To avoid representativeness bias, investors should ask whether an investment belongs to group A or is statistically more likely to belong to group B.

Illusion of control bias occurs when people believe they have more control or influence than they actually have.

Suffering from illusion of control bias leads to overconcentration in portfolio positions and frequent trading that increases costs and drives down returns compared to buy-and-hold strategies.

Detection of illusion of control bias requires understanding the complexity of capital markets with little prospect for control. Success depends on systematic factors (e.g., economic growth, market sentiment, etc.) rather than any investor skill.

FMPs should seek contrary opinions. Investors can remind themselves of their own fallibility by keeping transaction records, including the rationale for any trade.

Hindsight bias involves remembering only information that reinforces existing beliefs. This stems from a viewpoint that results in the past were inevitable rather than risky at the time. In part, this follows from filling in memory gaps with preferential information.

Suffering from hindsight bias leads to a false sense of confidence, and can lead investors to believe money manager performance should have been better than it was.

FMPs should keep transaction records, including the rationale for any trade. They should remind themselves that managers should invest according to their strategy and that this will result in ups and downs over time. Educating investors and measuring managers against benchmarks can help toward this end.

Information-Processing Biases

This category of cognitive biases results from irrational information use.

BF
CME

Anchoring and adjustment bias involves people developing an initial estimate (the anchor) and subsequently adjusting that estimate up or down.

Consequences of this bias are that people weight the anchor too heavily and then make insufficient adjustments that bias the final estimate regardless of the new information's importance.

Overcoming this bias involves discovery of whether the investor is sticking to the original anchor for legitimate reasons.

Investors should be advised that past prices contain little information about the future expectations for their investments.

Mental accounting bias occurs when people treat money differently depending on its source or expected use. Although money is inherently fungible (i.e., each currency unit is interchangeable with other units), people segregate these pools of funds from other uses, with some pools believed more important to protect than others.

Consequences of mental accounting bias include failing to consider correlation of returns among various pools. This can result in inefficient diversification. People may also chase income in their mental accounting scheme without considering potential losses, resulting in principal erosion.

Effective education about the drawbacks of engaging in this behavior can help overcome mental accounting bias. Combining all their assets can surprise investors about how much they have and what they can accomplish by allocating across all the pools. Using total return rather than pool-focused returns will also help them understand how wealth can grow while maintaining moderate income withdrawals.

IMPORTANT: Investors may engage in offsetting positions (i.e., buying and selling the same security) as well as concentrated positions that move together with high correlation.

Framing bias occurs when people decide differently based on how the decision maker views the risks and returns of the choice as well as how the choice is formulated. This involves risk seeking in the domain of losses versus risk aversion in the domain of gains.

Narrow framing results when people decide a subset of the big picture such as return potential without due consideration of the risks.

Consequences of framing bias include identifying the same opportunity differently depending on whether it is stated in the domain of losses (e.g., probability of not achieving goal is 25%) or is the complementary statement in the domain of gains (e.g., probability of achieving goal is 75%).

Investors may also choose suboptimal investments depending on how they are framed, even with properly identified risk tolerances.

Excessive trading may also occur with short-term price fluctuations.

Investors should try to be neutral when analyzing investments (i.e., without loss or gain framing). This bias can be mitigated by determining whether a riskier investment was selected in the domain of losses rather than the domain of gains.

IMPORTANT: Investors should always focus on expected risks and returns rather than past performance.

Availability bias uses shortcuts (i.e., heuristics) to investment outcomes based on how readily information comes to mind.

- Retrievability: The first thing to be recalled is considered the most likely.
- Categorization: Searches take place within perceived relevant sets of information.

- Narrow range of experience: More weight is attached to experiential observation.
- Resonance: People project their preferences onto others, and believe there is a higher probability of believing/liking what they do.

Consequences include being overly swayed by advertising, or restricting investments to familiar categories (e.g., domestic equities). Failure to diversify may result from retrievability and categorization, and will tend to cause inadequate diversification. Improper asset allocation can result from investments or companies that don't resonate.

Detection should focus on determining whether the investment selection results from what FMPs have heard recently or what they like, or whether it results from a disciplined approach—that is, a long-term focus, a proper strategic asset allocation, and thorough research and analysis of investment options.

Investors can also keep in mind the ultimate outcome of asset bubbles when other investors are caught up in a new bubble.

Emotional Biases

Fewer **emotional biases** have been identified, but they are harder to control for than cognitive errors because people are often invested in their feelings more than in cognitive processes. Individuals will often become defensive when faced with their own emotional biases.

Loss Aversion Bias

Loss aversion results from the declining marginal utility of wealth. People strongly prefer avoiding losses to scoring gains, and people will incur additional risk to avoid losses.

FMPs suffering from loss aversion bias may also trade excessively when selling winners, which results in higher costs and lower returns.

> **IMPORTANT:**
> The *disposition effect* describes how people will dispose of winners quickly, which limits upside potential, but will hold losing positions in hopes of avoiding losses on a position, which increases position risk.

Loss aversion bias combines with framing bias to attract those in loss positions to attempt recoupment.

Myopic loss aversion is a special case in which people tend to use bonds for long-term funding (rather than a properly diversified portfolio) in the domain of gains, and use equities with an outsized risk profile for short-term gains in the domain of losses. Over time, this results in unjustifiably high equity risk premiums.

> **IMPORTANT:**
> The *house-money effect* describes investors with gains—especially unexpected gains—in an investment as believing that money to be different from other money, and engaging in more risk-seeking behavior with it.

Loss aversion bias can be mitigated by a disciplined approach; it is impossible to completely eliminate the pain of an investment loss.

Overconfidence Bias

Overconfidence bias results when people overestimate their analytical abilities and judgment, as well as the usefulness of information they possess. Although showing aspects of both cognitive and emotional biases, it is included as an emotional bias because it is difficult to get people to revise self-perceptions:

- **Prediction overconfidence.** Assigning unrealistically narrow confidence intervals to predictions, resulting in poorly diversified portfolios.
- **Certainty overconfidence.** Assigning unrealistically high probabilities to outcomes for which the investor is responsible, often resulting in excessive trading when investments fail to meet return predictions.

> **IMPORTANT:**
> A long-term investor will be more likely to accept portfolio risk than a short-term investor, so investments should be reviewed regularly but infrequently.

Overconfidence becomes intensified when combined with **self-attribution bias**, which is related to investor self-esteem:

- Self-enhancing—claiming responsibility for success
- Self-protecting—denial of responsibility of failure

FMPs with overconfidence bias:

- Underestimate risks and returns.
- Hold concentrated portfolio positions.
- Engage in excessive trading.
- Underperform the market.

To detect and mitigate overconfidence, traders should review trading records, understand the reasons for winners and losers, and calculate portfolio performance over at least a two-year period. This process disciplines the FMP against too much risk and excessive trading.

Self-Control Bias

Self-control bias results when people fail to act in their long-term interests and instead succumb to short-term satisfaction. This outcome may result from **hyperbolic discounting** in which people prefer smaller payoffs now to larger future payoffs.

Self-control bias can result in undersaving for the future. FMPs then attempt to make up the shortfall by accepting too much portfolio risk, which puts the asset base in jeopardy.

When combined with mental accounting, FMPs will overallocate to bonds for income. This further stretches the portfolios' ability to meet long-term goals due to lack of reinvested earnings as well as lack of capital appreciation. Risk-seeking FMPs are likely to invest in risky equity securities to make up the difference.

FMPs should integrate a written personal budget and investment plan.

Status Quo Bias

Status quo bias occurs when people prefer to do nothing rather than make a change (i.e., they maintain the status quo). While regret-aversion bias and endowment bias involve a reason not to change (although it may be emotional rather than rational), status quo bias requires no conscious decision. Try not to confuse the status quo bias (do nothing) with conservatism (slow to update new information).

FMPs with status quo bias—especially when paired with regret-aversion bias and endowment bias—will maintain inappropriate risk profiles and fail to explore outcome-improving alternatives.

Detection and mitigation involve educating FMPs on risk-reducing and return-enhancing diversification.

Endowment Bias

Endowment bias occurs when FMPs value an asset in their possession more than if they were to buy it. This contrasts with rational economic man (REM), who would purchase a good for the same price at which he sells it.

> **IMPORTANT:**
> FMPs with concentrated holdings in company stock should examine how they would fare if a simultaneous force reduction and falling share price occurred.

The "endowment" of special importance to a security or an investment may result from inheritance from a loved one or simply from making the effort to buy it. On occasion, people cite disloyalty as the reason for not wishing to sell at an appropriate price.

FMPs suffering from endowment bias will continue to maintain an inadvisable asset allocation, refusing to diversify and preferring not to make changes (i.e., elements of status quo bias).

> **IMPORTANT:** Emotional attachment that threatens financial goals must be moderated rather than accepted and worked around. Advisors should learn emotional intelligence to deal with such issues.

Detection and mitigation of endowment bias might include asking investors what they would invest in if they received the same amount of cash rather than the investment. It may be appropriate to ask the former owner's intention for the investment.

It may be appropriate to ease into a new investment before cashing out the endowed investment and risking investor disaffection.

Regret-Aversion Bias

Regret-aversion bias occurs when people avoid making decisions for fear they will be unsuccessful. While similar to status quo bias, regret aversion differs in that there is a reason (i.e., regret) they prefer not to decide rather than simply a lack of initiative as with status quo bias.

Regret aversion can cause FMPs to hold losing positions for fear they might rebound after the sale, or to exit and remain out of a market in which they just lost money when the prudent action would be to remain invested:

> **IMPORTANT:** Fear of regret may cause herding action, where people sell or purchase securities with the market to avoid regretting a decision that runs counter to prevailing opinion.

- Errors of commission—actions people take
- Errors of omission—actions people could have taken but did not

Consequences involve underperforming portfolios of low-risk securities and failing to reach investment goals. Well-known or popular companies are chosen rather than those equally likely to succeed.

FMPs can detect and mitigate the effects of regret-aversion bias by understanding diversification benefits. Advisors should illustrate how everyone makes mistakes and why bubbles can be as bad as downturns.

Asset Allocation and Investment Policy

Behavioral portfolio theory employs goals-based investing in which an optimized portfolio considers each goal separately as a layer of the composite asset structure. Risk management for the portfolio considers the probability and likelihood of losses.

> **IMPORTANT:** Where traditional theory suggests people are risk averse, behavioral portfolio theory suggests they are loss averse.

This approach helps investors understand the appropriate level of risk for their goals, as well as satisfying loss aversion preferences.

In this approach, the base of the investments pyramid assigns low-risk investments to the client's obligations and needs. Moderate-risk investments fund priorities and desires, while higher-risk or speculative investments fund aspirational goals.

> **IMPORTANT:** A behavioral portfolio may not be efficient from a mean-variance optimization standpoint because each layer has been optimized separately, but will be easily understood and followed by investors.

Behaviorally Modified Asset Allocation

Rational portfolio allocation involves selecting from efficient portfolios that optimize risk and return identified via questionnaire and goal setting.

Behaviorally modified asset allocation distinguishes between cognitive biases and emotional biases to determine which preferences can be modified and which must be followed, and establishes a portfolio based on a modified asset allocation the investor will follow.

Two considerations determine whether an advisor should adapt to or moderate client biases:

BF
CME

1. Level of wealth: Greater wealth compared with needs allows greater adaptation because only high-impact events jeopardize the client's standard of living (i.e., standard of living risk [SLR]).
2. Type of behavioral bias:
   - Moderate cognitive biases with a high SLR.
   - Adapt to emotional biases with a low SLR.

As much as +/− 10% adaptation will be required for the high-SLR emotional bias situations, while low-SLR cognitive bias adjustments will be closer to +/− 2%.

BEHAVIORAL FINANCE AND INVESTMENT PROCESSES
Cross-Reference to CFA Institute Assigned Reading #9

Classification by Investor Type

Uses and Limitations
Investor types are a heuristic that is useful for establishing the type and degree of behavioral adjustments that should be made in client interactions and portfolio construction.

Limitations include:

- Investors don't approach different aspects of their lives with equal confidence or care.
- Bottom-up approaches in which the advisor tests for all potential biases may be too time-consuming for some advisors.
- Quantitative measures work better to moderate cognitive biases (i.e., middle of the active–passive scale).
- The same individual may exhibit both cognitive errors and emotional biases.
- The same individual may exhibit multiple investor-type characteristics.
- Aging results in behavioral changes.
- Individuals act irrationally and unpredictably.

Behavioral Advisor–Client Relations

Successful Relationship Characteristics
- Advisor understands client goals, constraints, and behavioral characteristics, and integrates these into the investment policy statement (IPS).
- Advisor has a consistent, systematic approach with the client.
- Advisor effectively communicates progress toward goals.
- Advisor and client both benefit.

> IMPORTANT: All categorization schemes exhibit the limitation that investor changes may invalidate advisor-selected types.

Limitations of Risk Questionnaires
Risk tolerance appears to change with question framing.

Questionnaires supply information for only broad risk tolerance parameters; other assessment tools are helpful.

Risk tolerance is a cognitive process for institutional investors but an emotional process for individual investors.

> IMPORTANT: A behavioral finance approach helps clients and advisors build stronger bonds, which are important in maintaining a long-term relationship.

Behavioral Portfolio Construction
Behavioral biases influence how investors use securities in constructing portfolios.

Inertia and Default
Even with no transaction charges, most investors decide not to change an asset allocation (i.e., status quo bias).

> IMPORTANT: Risk tolerance questionnaires may fail to properly assess emotional biases.

Some plans now offer target date funds that become more conservative as investors approach retirement. However, such plans may be unable to adapt to individual situations.

Naive Diversification and Framing

Naive diversification describes asset allocation that exhibits cognitive errors resulting from framing or using simple heuristics (i.e., rules of thumb).

For example, with simple heuristics investors may allocate equally to a stock and a balanced fund (i.e., $1/n$ diversification), although the balanced fund also includes equities.

With framing different funds as different choices (rather than asset classes to choose from), the same investor may allocate equally across many funds where equity funds predominate and equally across many funds in another case where bond funds predominate, resulting in dramatically different allocations to equities and to bonds in the two cases.

Company Stock Investment

Plan participants overallocate funds to shares of their company's stock. This could be due to financial incentives, but it also occurs in the absence of incentives. Other explanations:

- Employees have familiarity with the company and overconfidence in its stock.
- Employees expect that future returns will be like those in the past.
- Framing and status quo effects: Employees look at the company's matching contributions of stock as investment advice and allocate more of their own money to company stock.
- Loyalty effects: Employees believe they are helping the company.

Overconfidence

Overconfidence results in excessive trading, as investors believe they have superior outlooks on the market or security.

Overconfident investors have not only higher trading costs, but higher opportunity costs for sold assets (i.e., **disposition effect**).

Home Bias

Although information costs can result in investor preference for their own country's assets, other explanations include status quo, availability, confirmation, endowment, and illusion of control biases.

Mental Accounting

Traditional asset allocation considers the entirety of the investor's assets in an allocation designed to optimize return for the expressed risk tolerance, taking into consideration the asset class covariances.

Behavioral asset allocation considers each goal as a separate layer of a pyramid, with an asset allocation appropriate for the risk tolerance associated to each goal. Low-risk investments fund obligations and needs on the pyramid bottom (i.e., most important), moderate-risk investments fund priorities and desires, and higher-risk and speculative investments fund aspirational goals at the top of the pyramid.

Analyst Forecasts

Biases in Research

Too much structured information can lead to **representativeness bias** in which available data matches analyst expectations. Adequate data is important to successful forecasts, but may exceed what is necessary.

A **story** explains evidence with a fitting scenario. Analysts who use a story to fit extraneous evidence and then reach a conclusion may be showing representativeness bias.

Analysts who reach a conclusion and then accept or seek only supporting evidence engage in **confirmation bias**. Research should include contrary opinions.

In the **conjunction fallacy**, analysts use probabilities additively rather than in conjunction as a method of supporting their conclusions.

Analysts engage in the **gambler's fallacy** when they overweight probability of mean reversion, and the **hot hand fallacy** when they overweight the probability of continued similar returns rather than some reversion.

Studies suggest that analysts estimate the values of growth companies using too little risk and estimate the values of value companies using too much risk. The continued trajectory of each may be representativeness bias combined with confirmation bias.

Analysts can guard against anchoring and adjustment bias by carefully evaluating previous forecasts, but constructing a base scenario for a new forecast that uses the current environment. Systematically collecting and evaluating information, including contrary data or opinion, can help avoid emotional biases as well as cognitive biases.

Assigning probabilities can help avoid assuming absolutely likely or totally unlikely scenarios. Updating scenarios using a Bayesian conditioning process will speed the process and maintain structure, while enforcing review of previous work to assess its validity.

> **IMPORTANT:** Look for the term "however" to indicate a potential contrary data point or opinion, and the term "moreover" to indicate a potential confirming data point or opinion.

BF CME

Biases in Management-Supplied Information

Anchoring and adjustment bias describes the process of putting undue weight on a starting value (i.e., the anchor) and adjusting the forecast for new data based on the starting value rather than a new objective value. The management of an analysis target that frames the business as successful can create an anchor position for the analyst against which further results and achievements merely provide an adjustment.

Overconfidence bias and **illusion of control bias** may influence company management's optimism. **Self-attribution bias** to attract management incentives may create an expression of responsibility for success, and work together with other biases to underestimate the probability of failure.

Pro forma and other reframing situations usually result in better outcomes than actual results. Analysts should view these reframing situations for possible anchoring concerns.

> **IMPORTANT:** Analysts should gather all relevant information before reaching a conclusion, and ensure that information is assessed relative to the current environment.

Biases in Forecasting

Analysts are subject to behavioral biases, and in some cases their expertise and an **illusion of knowledge bias** combine to create **overconfidence bias**. The illusion of knowledge bias may arise from having a great deal of data, although adding more information doesn't increase forecast accuracy. Instead, it can simply increase confidence.

Representativeness bias occurs when available data matches the forecast. **Availability bias** involves giving more weight to readily available information. These two biases reinforce each other and provide a basis for overconfidence.

The **illusion of control bias** can make people believe there is less forecast risk, even though having more and representative information will not remove forecast risk. Using complex

> **IMPORTANT:** Analysts guard against management influence by maintaining a systematic approach.

models can reinforce the illusion of control bias, although more complex models may be less robust (i.e., have lower forecasting accuracy) outside the narrow range of the forecast.

Confidence increases still further with self-attribution bias—that is, analysts believing they cause success and only others are responsible for failure. Skewed forecasts (i.e., nonsymmetrical confidence intervals) and misdirected performance incentives may be signs of self-attribution bias.

Analysts can be especially overconfident when holding a contrarian viewpoint.

Hindsight bias further feeds the illusion of control bias and overconfidence bias by allowing analysts to misremember actual situations or remember only positive outcomes (i.e., selective recall) in further ego enhancement.

Including additional data that cannot be analyzed in the same way as other data may increase overconfidence via the illusion of knowledge bias, but will add little accuracy. Ensuring a large enough sample size using comparable data will reduce inaccuracy and unjustified confidence.

Analysts can avoid or compensate for overconfidence via accurate, timely, and well-structured feedback (i.e., based on analytical review of the base assumptions versus actual results).

Peer and supervisor review help to properly attribute success and failure. Rewards for accuracy are also important.

Analyst conclusions should be as straightforward and specific as possible to avoid hindsight bias. If the forecast can be objectively reviewed via the data, assumptions, and model, the analyst has less opportunity to impose a subjective viewpoint attributing success.

Investment Committee Decision Biases

Applying many sets of skills to a research report or asset allocation decision can result in superior outcomes. Individual biases, however, can creep into committee decisions. Social proof bias results when analysts accept the judgment of others rather than using it as another decision point.

People often support a leader's position, regardless of whether it results in success, or moderate their own positions to better fit with the committee consensus.

Feedback for past committee decisions is slow and inaccurate. Good work becomes more likely when:

- Diverse member cultures, experiences, and skills are present (i.e., less prone to social proof bias).
- The committee's environment encourages dissent.
- Members have adhered to an agenda.
- They have reached a clear decision.

Market Behavioral Biases

The efficient market hypothesis (EMH) describes markets in which participants cannot earn excess returns after fees and expenses (i.e., small excess returns before fees and expenses may be obtainable).

A market anomaly describes persistent excess returns with predictable direction. However, persistent excess returns may also indicate shortcomings in the underlying asset pricing model:

- Rational behavior not captured by the model (e.g., investor response to taxes)
- Reward for excess risk not perceived for the model

Momentum Effects

Momentum describes correlation between past and future price behavior when it should be random. Upward momentum lasts for about two years; return to trend takes between two and five years.

Herding behavior involves trading on the same side of a trade as other investors to capture private information, or acting as other investors do when their own private information would tell them otherwise. Herding reflects cognitive dissonance or regret avoidance when designed to reassure and comfort investors.

Anchoring on the purchase price and a belief that risk has increased (although an increase in fundamental values may also be indicated) explain willingness to sell. **Availability bias** (i.e., recency effect) causes investors to believe a trend should continue because it has continued.

Hindsight bias causes investors to believe they should have known a trend would continue, and may buy into a heavily appreciated security simply to avoid regret at not owning it. This creates a **trend-chasing effect**.

Reversion to the mean may take longer than the original trend, as those who purchased the security want to avoid regret (**disposition effect** of loss aversion) and hold on to it with the hope it will go back up (**gambler's fallacy**).

> **IMPORTANT:** Publishing an anomaly will typically cause arbitrage that removes the anomaly.

Bubbles and Crashes

Asset bubbles occur when an asset class price index trades more than two standard deviations above or below the long-term trend. Traditional finance theory indicates that bubbles should not occur more than 5% of the time, but occur 10% of the time for some asset classes in some markets.

Crashes involve a price collapse of 30% or more over several months.

During bubbles, investors may exhibit the following biases:

- Overconfidence: An investor rejects contradictory information, underestimates risks, overtrades, and fails to diversify.
- Self-attribution bias: Even if an FMP sells positions too soon, profits lead to self-attribution.
- Confirmation bias: Selling for a gain tends to confirm decisions for an original purchase and reinforce self-attribution bias.
- Hindsight bias: An investor misremembers justifications for an investment to better attribute personal success.

> **IMPORTANT:** Market trending patterns result from emotional biases and belief in mean reversion.

> **IMPORTANT:** It is not a behavioral bias if rational investors hold a position during an asset bubble if they are unsure of when the market will break.

Noise trading involves trading on irrelevant information rather than new relevant information. Part of the overconfidence bias results from an **illusion of knowledge bias** created through market noise (i.e., unjustified price increases, high trading volume, etc.).

Anchoring occurs when FMPs fail to sufficiently update beliefs and instead engage in self-attribution bias to rationalize losses and flawed decisions as someone else's fault and any continued gains as personal success.

The **disposition effect** encourages FMPs to hold on to losing positions.

Value and Growth

Value stocks include companies with low P/E ratios, low ratios of price to cash flow (P/CF), low ratios of price to dividends (P/D), and high ratios of equity book value to market value (BV/MV). Growth stocks are the opposite.

Value stocks have outperformed growth stocks; small-cap stocks have outperformed large-cap stocks.

Fama and French believe book-market ratios and size effects could be rational given expectation of greater risk exposure, less ability to weather economic downtrends, and so on.

Other studies recognize mispricing:

- Halo effect: Good growth record may overshadow pricing risk.
- Overconfidence: Growth rates are predicted with more confidence than is justified.
- Home bias: Attraction of a stock is influenced by personal experience.

BF
CME

> **IMPORTANT:** Writing put options can reflect the additional return required to compensate investors for excess risk perceived in nongrowth equities.

STUDY SESSION 4: CAPITAL MARKET EXPECTATIONS

CAPITAL MARKET EXPECTATIONS, PART 1
Framework and Macro Considerations: Cross-Reference to CFA Institute Assigned Reading #10

Framework

The following approach helps to ensure internal consistency across asset classes (cross-sectional consistency) and over time (intertemporal consistency):

1. Specify the expectations set (i.e., asset classes) and time horizons.
2. Research the historical record to develop some possible ranges for future results.
3. Specify the methods/models and their required inputs.
4. Determine the best information sources.
5. Implement the research and investment process. Apply experience and judgment to interpret the current investment environment. Make sure to apply consistent assumptions, compatible methods, and consistent judgments to ensure cross-sectional and inter-temporal consistency.
6. Provide the necessary expectations set along with documented conclusions.
7. Use actual outcomes as feedback to the expectations setting process. While several cycles may be necessary to validate longer-term conclusions, the actual data may inform the current expectations-setting cycle.

Longer time horizons generally suggest using a discounted cash flow approach. Analysts should make sure to seamlessly integrate shorter-period estimates with longer timeframe projections in order to maintain inter-temporal consistency.

Forecasts generally are subject to three kinds of uncertainty:

- **Model uncertainty**—Related to choosing the wrong conceptual or structural model.
- **Input uncertainty**—Related to errors in the underlying data.
- **Parameter uncertainty**—Related to errors in estimated parameters.

Analysts need to understand the limitations of the data they use with respect to accuracy, timeliness, variable definition, and series construction. In some cases, transcription errors or willful misreporting can limit data accuracy.

Data may also be subject to survivorship bias in which only successful entities are included in the reporting or smoothed data, as with reporting appraised values rather than actual market values.

Data that has undergone regime change suffers from different data definitions in the distinct parts of the series. This gives rise to nonstationarity in which the distinct parts have different variances and result in inaccurate models.

Using more frequent observations tends to improve variance, covariance, and correlation estimates. It does not necessarily result in greater forecast accuracy for the sample mean.

Analysts should be wary of inventing a story to describe a relationship that exists in the data but not in reality (data mining), as well as selecting starting and ending dates that correspond to a convenient measurement period (time-period bias) but don't fit with different data regimes.

Forecasts should reflect conditioning information; that is, information expected to change the direction, amount, rate, timing, or duration of a variable over the forecast period.

A few behavioral biases that could lead to forecast errors include:

- **Anchoring bias**—Giving too much weight to initial information with insufficient adjustment when new information is received.
- **Availability bias**—Overemphasizing recent events because they have a stronger impression than other possible outcomes.
- **Confirmation bias**—Seeking and overweighting evidence that confirms existing or preferred beliefs.
- **Status quo bias**—Perpetuating initial information through a desire to avoid errors involved with change.
- **Overconfidence bias**—Overestimating the ability to understand and use information, which often results in failing to consider possible outcomes especially in the "unknown unknowns" category.
- **Prudence bias**—Avoiding forecasts that appear extreme so that they might be more believable, even when evidence points toward a high probability of the extreme outcome.

Economic and Market Analysis (Part 1)

Trends

Trends are related to long-term rates of change; cycles are shorter-term fluctuations around the longer-run trend. Exogenous shocks involve changes to trend from outside the existing system such as policy changes, geopolitics, natural disasters, or financial crises.

Financial crises may be grouped into three types:

- Type 1—A permanent, one-time decline with resumption of the trend rate after the initial shock.
- Type 2—No persistent one-time decline, but continuation at a lower trend rate.
- Type 3—Both a permanent, one-time decline and continuation at a lower trend rate.

Trend analysis is generally decomposed based on inputs to economic growth:

- Labor input growth
  - Increases in hours worked
  - Labor force size increase (population growth)
  - Labor force participation rate increase
- Labor productivity growth
  - Increasing capital inputs
  - Total factor productivity (TFP) increase (i.e., technology improvement)

Default-free bond rates (e.g., U.S. Treasuries) tend to be linked to the trend rate of GDP growth and should serve as a guiding factor in forecasts. Similarly, aggregate equity market value is related to GDP growth:

$$V_t^e = GDP_t \times S_t^k \times PE_t = GDP_t \times \frac{E_t}{GDP_t} \times \frac{P_t}{E_t}$$

In this formula, S^k equals capital's share of income (i.e, corporate earnings as a percent of GDP).

The following approaches can help forecast changes to trend:

Strengths and Weaknesses of Economic Forecasting Approaches

Forecast Type	Strengths	Weaknesses
Econometric	• Many factors help represent reality; robust (valid statistical relationship). • Quickly updated using new data. • Provides quantitative estimates. • Imposes analytical discipline/consistency.	• Complex, time-consuming to formulate. • Forecasting inputs difficult. • Model may be misspecified due to changing relationships. • False precision impression. • Turning points hard to forecast.

Leading indicators	• Intuitive and simple
	• Focuses on turning points
	• Available from third parties
	• Easy to track
		• Can provide false signals
		• Binary (yes/no) directional guidance
		• Subject to frequent revision
		    ○ Historical data may not be appropriate for forecasting current data.
		    ○ Overstates accuracy due to "over-fitting" in sample.

Checklist approach	• Not overly complex
	• Can include a wide variety of checkpoints (breadth)
	• Flexible
	    ○ Easily incorporates structural changes
	    ○ Items easily added/dropped
		• Arbitrary, judgmental, and subjective
		• Manual process that limits ability to combine different types of information
		• Time consuming

Cycles

Business cycles represent differences between expectations underlying business decisions and what really happens that affects investment outcomes. The business cycle is not well defined; it varies in both intensity and duration and thus turning points become difficult to forecast.

Phases of the Business Cycle

Phase	Economic Features	Capital Market Features
Initial recovery (a few months)	• After the low point, the output gap is large, inflation is decelerating, stimulative policies remain in place, and the economy starts to grow.	• S-T and L-T government bond yields are likely to be bottoming but may still decrease. • Stock markets may begin to rise quickly as recession fears subside. • Riskier small-cap stocks, high-yield bonds, and emerging market securities start to do well.
Early expansion	• Output gap remains negative, but unemployment starts to fall. • Consumers start to borrow to spend; housing and consumer durable demand increases. • Businesses step up production; profits begin to expand rapidly. • Central bank begins to remove stimulus.	• Short rates begin to increase; long rates remain stable or increase slightly. • Flattening yield curve. • Stock prices trend upward.
Late expansion	• Positive output gap and danger of inflation; capacity pressures boost investment spending. • Low unemployment, strong profits, rising wages and prices (inflation). • Debt coverage ratios may deteriorate as business borrows to fund growth. • Monetary policy becomes more restrictive.	• Private sector borrowing causes rates to rise. • Yield curve continues to flatten as short rates rise faster than long rates. • Stocks volatile as investors watch for deceleration. • Inflation hedges (e.g., commodities) may begin to outperform other cyclical assets.
Slowdown	• Fewer viable investment projects and overleveraging cause slowing growth; business confidence waivers. • Inflation continues to rise as business pricing attempts to outpace rising input costs. • The economy is vulnerable to shocks.	• L-T bonds may top but S-T rates continue to rise or may peak; yield curve may invert. • Credit spread widens, depressing bond prices for lower credit issues. • Stocks may fall; utilities and quality stocks likely to outperform.

Contraction (12 to 18 months)	• Firms cut investment spending, then decrease production and unemployment can rise quickly (which hinders household formation).
	• Profits drop sharply; credit markets tighten, accounting transgressions are uncovered, and bankruptcies can result.
		• S-T and L-T rates begin to fall; yield curve steepens.
		• Credits spread widens; remains wide until trough.
		• Stock market
		  ○ Early phase—Declining
		  ○ Late phase—Begins to rise

Beyond one to three years of an expansion or contraction phase, returns increasingly average in expectation of a turning point.

Inflation

Deflation damages the economy because repayment of a loan becomes more expensive to the debtor and results in less available capital for continued economic growth. In contrast, moderate inflation imposes only small costs while allowing the flexibility for the economy to grow.

Analysts should assess both the discount rates and cash flows of investments to determine the effects of inflation:

- Cash equivalents (does not include currency or zero-interest deposits)—Relatively attractive when rates rise and unattractive when rates fall (due to its short duration).
- Bonds—Persistent deflation can benefit higher-credit issues because cash flows become worth more. Lower-credit issues, however, may find additional financing hard to find and this can damage business opportunities. Due to fixed nominal cash flows, inflation effects are transmitted to yield via price changes:
    - Within the expected inflation range—Shorter-term yields rise or fall more than longer-term yields, but the price impact is less due to duration.
    - Outside the expected inflation range—Longer-term yields may rise more quickly.
- Stocks—The valuation process considers inflation in the discount rate applied to cash flows; inflation within an expectation range will have little impact on stock prices. Higher inflation raises the discount rate and decreases valuations.
- Real estate—Lease rates include an inflation expectation that, like stocks, have little impact on asset prices when within an expectation range.

Economic and Market Analysis (Part 2)

Fiscal and Monetary Policy

A government's fiscal policy development and implementation may involve very long lags which, as with monetary policy, reinforces the cycle rather than mediating it. Fiscal policy is more often used to achieve long-term objectives. Central banks, then, usually use monetary policy to smooth short-term cycles, although they may also suffer from lags.

Central banks may use a variant of the Taylor rule to establish an interest rate target that maintains stable growth:

$$i^* = r_{Neutral} + \pi_e + 0.5(Y_e - Y_{Trend}) + 0.5(\pi_e - \pi_{Target})$$

where

$$i^* = r_{Neutral} + \pi_e + 0.5(Y_e - Y_{Trend}) + 0.5(\pi_e - \pi_{Target})$$
i^* = target nominal policy rate
$r_{Neutral}$ = *real* policy rate targeted with trend growth and target inflation
Y_e, Y_{Trend} = expected and trend *real* GDP growth rates
π_e, π_{Target} = expected and target inflation rates

The Taylor rule leaves considerable judgment in the choice of targets and measurement of inputs, and the variables cannot be directly observed.

Under a scenario of negative interest rates (which may be implemented in times of financial crisis), analysts may use the long-run equilibrium *short-term* rate in place of an observed negative interest rate. Estimating this rate involves the Taylor rule $r_{neutral}$ adjusted for the difference between policy rates and default-free rates available to investors.

Monetary and fiscal policy should be viewed as affecting either (1) the interest rate *level* or (2) yield curve *shape*. In general, fiscal policy affects real rates while monetary policy affects nominal rates. Their interaction results in various outcomes.

Effects of Persistent Monetary-Fiscal Policy Mixes

		Fiscal Policy	
		Loose	**Tight**
Monetary Policy	**Loose**	High real rates + High expected inflation = High nominal rates	Low real rates + High expected inflation = Mid nominal rates
	Tight	High real rates + Low expected inflation = Mid nominal rates	Low real rates + Low expected inflation = Low nominal rates

The Yield Curve as a Predictor

The business cycle and fiscal/monetary policy mixes also affect the yield curve *slope*, which depends on:

- Expected short-term rates—The business cycle and government policies drive short-term rates and cause the yield curve to flatten or steepen.
- A risk premium that increases with maturity—The risk premium explains the normally upward slope.

The bond supply at various maturities—Government debt issued at specific maturities (due to demand/funding costs) may affect the yield curve *shape*.

Policy, Rates, and the Yield Curve over the Business Cycle

Phase	Money Market Rates	Bond Yield and Curve Effects
Initial recovery	• Low/bottoming due to stimulative transition to tightening	• Steep yield curve initially • Shortest yields rise first • Longer yields bottom
Early expansion	• Rising, starting to accelerate	• Rising; longer may be stable • Short maturities steepen; longer maturities flatten
Late expansion	• Change to restrictive monetary policy; automatic stabilizers • Above average; rising	• Rising at a slower pace • Curve flattening inward from longest maturities
Slowdown	• Approaching peak under tight monetary policy	• Peak; may decline sharply • Flat to inverted curve
Contraction	• Declining as policy becomes more stimulative	• Declining • Curve steepening

International Interactions

A country's **current account** reflects exports and imports of goods and services, investment income flows, and unilateral transfers. Its **capital account** reflects foreign direct investment (FDI), involving productive asset purchases and sales, and portfolio investment (PI) involving financial asset transactions.

Changes in the current account must be offset by changes to the capital account to balance the two accounts. Financial markets react more quickly to change than the real markets for goods and services via short-term interest rates, exchange rates, and financial asset prices.

Net exports, usually the largest current account component, link directly to the demand for a country's output:

$$Y = C + I + G + (X - M)$$
$$\text{where} \qquad Y - T - C = S$$
$$(X - M) = (S - I) + (T - G)$$

Global investment must be linked to global savings, and each country's savings or investment decisions are determined via its current account.

Empirical evidence suggests that real interest rate differences are not exploitable with regularity across currencies; however, nominal differences may be exploitable. When looking at a non-domestic asset, investors care about 1) nominal return, and 2) any change in exchange rates. In a floating currency regime, interest rates must be higher in a currency expected to depreciate because investors will seek more compensation for the greater risk of loss in currency value. Thus, the interest rates in two countries should then be the same when their currencies are exactly pegged to each other. This must assume unrestricted capital flows to equalize risk-adjusted returns and, a more difficult condition, credible exchange rate equilibrium forever.

BF
CME

CAPITAL MARKET EXPECTATIONS, PART 2
Forecasting Asset Class Returns: Cross-Reference to CFA Institute Assigned Reading #11

Fixed Income Returns

Discounted Cash Flow

Only the DCF approach is precise enough to support trades in individual fixed income securities and attribute source of return with specificity. Asset allocation may not require that level of granularity, however, and other valuation approaches may be appropriate.

Yield to maturity (YTM), the single discount rate equating the present value of cash flows to the bond's price, represents the return on the bond's cash flows. An average of YTMs for individual securities conveniently approximates the portfolio YTM.

Realized return, however, may be different than YTM:

1. Changes in interest rates affect bond prices that result in gains/losses prior to maturity.
2. Cash flow reinvestment may occur at rates above/below the YTM when the bond was purchased.

These variations work in opposite directions. When investment horizon relative to Macaulay duration of the bond or portfolio is:

- **Equal**—capital losses are offset by increases in reinvestment income.
- **Shorter**—the capital gain/loss effects dominate the reinvestment effects such that rising rates result in falling returns.
- **Longer**—the reinvestment effects dominate the capital gain/loss effects such that rising rates result in rising returns.

The easiest way to remember this is to consider that changes in reinvestment earnings need time to offset a capital gain/loss.

The Building Block Approach

The building block approach to expected return for a fixed income security separately recognizes the risk-free rate and premiums for different types of risk:

- **Short-term, nominal default-free rate**—The only observable characteristic; usually the government zero-coupon bill with shortest maturity (e.g., three months)
- **Term premium (duration risk)**—Based on the instrument horizon or holding period; positive, increase with maturity, and vary over time
- **Credit premium (default risk)**—Based on issuer credit worthiness; includes both expected losses and additional risk of unexpected losses
- **Liquidity premium (illiquidity risk)**—Based on ability to sell the security with little market impact and cost

The short-term default-free rate is closely tied to the central bank's policy rate. In a negative interest rate environment, other risk premiums may increase to reflect elevated willingness to pay for safety.

Using a bond with the investment horizon as the basis for a default-free rate ignores the importance of the term premium. Periods longer than the shortest-term maturity may be forecast by combining the short-term rate along an expected path with the expected term premium.

Factors affecting the term premium include:

- **Supply and demand**—The path of future short-term rates should remain unaffected by term structure, but does show the influence of aggregate demand for and supply of maturities.
- **Cyclical effects**—Yield curve slope varies based on expected policy changes.
- **Level-dependent inflation uncertainty**—Recognizes both the change in inflation and the change in expectation.
- **Ability to hedge recession risk**—Demand-driven growth and inflation result in low to negative add-ons to the term premium; supply-driven growth merits a higher term premium to recognize the higher risk of oversupply and subsequent risk of recession during a pullback.

Downgrade bias for AAA and AA bonds (because downgrades are more likely than default) and default risk for below-investment-grade bonds drive credit risk premiums. A and BBB bonds are more sensitive to cyclical change than AAA and AA bonds and spreads/premiums vary more countercyclically. Default rates and the magnitude of default losses tend to rise/fall together, implying accelerating premiums during a falling economy.

The following factors reduce a dealer's risk in holding the bond and thereby decrease liquidity risk:

- High quality
- Relatively new and from a large issue
- Priced near par/reflective of current market levels
- Issued by a well-known company with frequent issues
- Simple structure/standard covenants

Analysts can estimate the pure liquidity premium as the yield spread of option-free bonds from a sovereign or highest-quality issuer over the next highest-quality issuer of similar bonds (e.g., government agency).

Emerging Market Fixed Income
Emerging market debt has similar risks, but analysts should also consider willingness to pay:

- Ability to pay
    - Less diverse tax base due to greater wealth disparity; wealthy more likely to remove capital during a crisis (i.e., capital flight)
    - Less educated/skilled work force; limited infrastructure; less technological sophistication
    - Greater dependence on commodities and agriculture (i.e., cyclical) with low pricing power
    - Small, less sophisticated financial institutions and markets
    - Restrictions on trade, capital flows, and exchange rates
    - Poor monetary discipline and fiscal control
    - Reliance on foreign borrowing, especially from developed countries with hard currency
- Willingness to pay (i.e., political/legal risks)

    ○ Unstable coalition governments unwilling to honor promises by previous/current regimes

    ○ Sovereign immunity making it difficult or impossible to get the government to pay debt

    ○ Weak property rights laws and enforcement leading to inability to enforce claims or recover capital

Warning signs of potential inability or unwillingness to pay:

- Fiscal deficit/GDP greater than 70–80%
- Foreign debt/GDP greater than 50%
- Current account deficit/GDP greater than 200%
- Annual real growth less than 4%
- Falling per capita income
- Persistent current account deficits greater than 4%
- Foreign exchange reserves less than 100% of short-term debt

Equity Returns

Historical Statistics

Equity returns generally have high variance and historical mean performance does not provide a good estimate of future returns. Equity returns in local terms do not vary significantly from country to country. Most noise in historical stock returns comes from changes in the price-to-earnings ratio (P/E) and earnings-to-GDP (E/GDP) ratio.

Discounted Cash Flow

GDP growth is relatively stable and provides a good starting point for forecasting equity returns using the Grinold-Kroner model.

$$E(R_e) \approx \frac{D}{P} + (\%\Delta E - \%\Delta S) + \%\Delta P/E$$

where :

$$E(R_e) = \text{Expected equity return}$$

$$\frac{D}{P} = \text{Dividend yield}$$

$$\%\Delta E - \%\Delta S = \text{Growth rate of earnings per share}$$

$$\%\Delta P/E = \text{Growth rate of the P/E ratio}$$

Nominal growth and expected repricing return constitute capital gain. Share repurchases can result in faster EPS growth. The only long-run assumptions that make sense for this model are $\%\Delta P/E$ = Nominal GDP growth rate, $\%\Delta E = 0$, and $\%\Delta S = 0$.

The Building Block Approach

The equity premium may start from a base that takes either of two forms:

1. Premium over default-free S-T bills
2. Premium over default-free bonds of the horizon maturity

The latter includes both the nominal risk-free rate and a term premium. Finding these values has the same problems with variance of the series.

Equilibrium Approaches

In the Singer-Terhaar approach, the risk premium equals the product of asset standard deviation and the Sharpe ratio. The fully segmented, fully integrated, and partially integrated equations are:

$$RP_i = \sigma_i \times SR_i$$
$$RP_i^G = RP_i \times \rho_{i,GM}$$
$$RP_i^{E(G)} = RP_i^G \varphi_{i,GM} + RP_i^S (1 - \varphi_{i,GM})$$

G indicates that the risk premium reflects the global market, S indicates the segmented market, and *GM* indicates the global market and φ is the degree of a market's global integration. Highly integrated markets will have a range of 0.75–0.90 degree of global integration while emerging markets will have a range of 0.50–0.75. A liquidity premium would then be added to the equity risk premium; less integrated markets are less liquid and would therefore require a greater liquidity premium.

Emerging Market Equity

Emerging market debt analysis considers ability and willingness to pay, but also considers how the value of ownership claims might be expropriated by government, corporate insiders, or dominant shareholders. Country effects tend to outweigh industry effects.

Real Estate Returns

Supply and Demand

Real estate supply remains fixed in the short run and cyclical swings will tend to affect rental revenue and, thus, return. Rental revenues from high quality properties with long-term leases will likely be affected less than lower quality properties or day-lease properties like hotels and motels.

Capitalization Rates

The capitalization rate equals net operating income (NOI) divided by property value. The capitalization rate is like dividend yield for equities and may be used in a similar way.

$$E(R_e) = \text{DIV YLD} + g_{DIV}$$
$$E(R_{re}) = \text{Cap rate} + g_{NOI}$$

Changes to the cap rate should be made to recognize cyclical impact:

$$E(R_{re}) = \text{Cap rate}(1 + \%\Delta\text{Cap rate}) + g_{NOI}$$
$$= \text{Cap rate} + \Delta\text{Cap rate} + g_{NOI}$$

Property values rise when interest rates fall and the economy begins an upswing, and values fall when long-term rates rise as the economy reaches a cyclical peak. However, the countercyclical nature of credit spreads tends to mitigate the procyclical nature of cap rates.

The Building Block Approach
Real estate earns a large term premium based on its high duration. Income-earning properties earn a credit risk premium that depends on its tenants' credit worthiness. Properties earn an equity risk premium for uncertainties related to changes in property value, rent growth, lease rollover/termination, and vacancy rates.

Therefore, the risk premium should be between bonds and stocks to account for both fixed income and equity-like characteristics.

The Equilibrium Approach
Singer-Terhaar may be used in international portfolios, but should:

- Unsmooth returns based on appraisal data to avoid distorting relationships for all asset classes.
- Add a liquidity premium to offset the equilibrium model assumptions of perfect liquidity.
- Consider location factors rather than global financial markets.

REITs tend to act more like stocks in the short run and more like real properties in the long run after adjusting for comparable data, de-levering levered returns, and unsmoothing appraisal data.

Exchange Rate Returns

Goods and Services, Trade, and the Current Account
A country with a trade deficit (i.e., negative exports less imports) can avoid currency devaluation if financed by offsetting capital inflows from abroad. The monetary approach to exchange rate forecasting holds that the real exchange rate for imports will stay the same, but will experience nominal price inflation where a trade deficit persists.

Short-term trade imbalances result from business cycles. Long-term imbalances result from structural issues:

- Persistent fiscal imbalances
- Profitable investment opportunities for innovation and capital deepening
- Institutional characteristics affecting savings decisions (e.g., demographics and preferences)
- Availability of important natural resources
- Prevailing terms of trade

Capital Flows
Exchange rate differences will reflect differences in the short-term interest rates, term premiums, credit premiums, equity premiums, and liquidity premiums between two countries:

$$E\left(\%\Delta S_{d/f}\right) = \left(r^d - r^f\right) + \left(\text{Term}^d - \text{Term}^f\right) + \left(\text{Credit}^d - \text{Credit}^f\right) + \left(\text{Equity}^d - \text{Equity}^f\right) + \left(\text{Liquidity}^d - \text{Liquidity}^f\right)$$

Terms of the equation respectively relate to various parts of the diversified portfolio:

- Money market (nominal short-term rates)
- Government bonds (add term premium)

- Corporate bonds (add credit premium)
- Public equities (add equity premium)
- Private assets including PP&E investment (add liquidity premium)

A more attractive country can suffer from a currency that, ultimately, when investors attempting to capture economic returns overshoot the actual differences in premiums to be captured, ends up rushing out of assets. The overshooting mechanism suggests these stages:

1. The exchange rate will appreciate ($S_{d/f}$ declines) as capital rushes in.
2. Investors question the sustainability of the opportunity and form expectations of reversal.
3. Retracement of some or all gain depending on the degree of asset price adjustment to the underlying opportunity.

Carry trades earn meaningful profits on average, so the risk premiums in the previous equation must also be meaningful despite uncovered interest rate parity (UIP), which would suggest that exchange rate differences only relate to nominal interest rates (i.e., the first term in the earlier equation).

Hot money flows, the first stage of the overshooting mechanism, make it hard for central bankers to implement monetary policy. They may try to buy or sell currency to stabilize the exchange rate or may try to sterilize the impact of inflows by selling government securities to limit bank reserve growth.

Portfolio Balance, Portfolio Comparability, and Sustainability Issues
Relative sizes of currency portfolios do not adjust much over short-to-intermediate horizons, so investors don't need to make long-run strategic changes. Investors may desire tactical adjustments to recognize opportunities brought about by relative economic strength and policy mixes in various countries.

Longer-term currency portfolio allocation depends on a country's relative trend growth rate and current account balance. A currency with persistently high current account deficits will experience downward exchange rate pressure, although the source of the deficit (e.g., profitable investment spending versus lack of fiscal discipline) and whether the deficit country represents a reserve currency are important.

Forecasting Volatility

Variance-Covariance (VCV) Matrix
There are three problems with a variance-covariance (VCV) matrix using historical data:

1. **Sample size**—Some portfolios appear riskless when the number of assets correlated is less than the number of periods in the sample.
2. **Sampling error**—Substantial, given typical sample sizes.
3. **Cross-sectional consistency**—Each pair is correlated without regard to the other pairs.

The first two problems may be resolved by using 10 times the number of periods in a sample as the number of assets.

Multi-Factor Models

The estimated value from a multi-factor model will not equal the true, unobservable VCV matrix value and the matrix does not become less biased (i.e., does not converge to the true value) as the number of observations increases.

Shrinkage Estimation

The VCV matrix can become more efficient in terms of lower mean-squared error (MSE) by developing a weighted average of the sample VCV matrix and an estimated target VCV matrix such as that developed using a factor model: biased, but more plausible than a VCV matrix.

Estimating Volatility from Smoothed Returns

Using estimated price data and returns (e.g., real estate and private equity) distorts variance estimates and correlations with other assets. A simple, widely used model assumes the current true return R_t is a weighted average of the current, unobservable true return r_t and the previous observed true return R_{t-1}:

$$R_t = (1-\lambda)r_t + \lambda R_{t-1}$$
$$0 < \lambda < 1$$
$$var(r) = \left(\frac{1+\lambda}{1-\lambda}\right) var(R) > var(R)$$

R_t is unobservable but can be estimated using a relationship between the unobservable return and one or more observable variables (e.g., REIT index for real estate or a similar public equity index for private equity).

Time-Varying Volatility: ARCH Models

Autoregressive conditional heteroskedasticity (ARCH) models can be used when volatility clusters over time, as with financial crises:

$$\sigma_t^2 = \gamma + \alpha\sigma_{t-1}^2 + \beta\eta_t^2$$
$$= \gamma + (\alpha+\beta)\sigma_{t-1}^2 + \beta(\eta_t^2 - \sigma_{t-1}^2)$$

where

η_t = unexpected component of return in period t
$(\eta_t^2 - \sigma_{t-1}^2)$ = shock to the variance in period t
β = how much shock feeds into current variance
$(\alpha+\beta)$ = extent current volatility influences future volatility

The assumption is that some portion of prior period return carries into current period return.

Adjusting a Global Portfolio

Looking at inter-related factors can help analysts determine validity of a current SAA:

1. Estimate the VCV matrix for all asset classes.
2. Estimate asset class returns using the VCV matrix and Singer-Terhaar model.
3. Estimate equity market returns using the Grinold-Kroner model and assumptions about economic growth, earnings growth, valuation models, dividends, and net share repurchases.
4. Estimate fixed income returns using the building block approach and assumptions regarding economic cycle and monetary/fiscal policy.
5. Estimate moderate currency movements using relative investment opportunities and potential for overshooting.

6. Incorporate potential currency movements into expected stock and bond returns.
7. Combine equilibrium expected returns from the Singer-Terhaar model with expected returns from the remaining steps using the Black-Litterman framework.

Analysts should address the extent to which expectations are already included.

Trend Growth
Equities benefit when productivity growth is high and new technologies begin providing benefits. Interest rates, however, may increase to slow growth to more manageable rates. Country specific changes suggest reallocation to the country with the best opportunities, which may require moving assets from developed to emerging markets. Assets will tend to move toward emerging markets as the risk premium for lack of liquidity disappears (i.e., due to global integration).

Cyclical Phase
Buy low; sell high. At the bottom, movement toward equity purchase causes bond prices to fall. At the top, equity growth likely slows and expected return falls while the higher rates make bonds more attractive.

Monetary and Fiscal Policy
Tightening monetary policy is bad for bonds because rates will rise, and not very good for stocks because it will slow expansion. If these expectations are already reflected in prices, looking for structural change may yield more gains.

Current Accounts, Capital Accounts, and Currencies
Focus on longer-term trends in the current account balance. Currencies initially appreciate in a country with more opportunities and then depreciate as financial markets question whether the currency has become overvalued (i.e., overshooting). Analysts should consider reallocation decisions not on the opportunities alone, but the opportunities in relationship to current valuation.

Study Session 5: Asset Allocation and Related Decisions in Portfolio Management

AA
CM

AA
CM

OVERVIEW OF ASSET ALLOCATION
Cross-Reference to CFA Institute Assigned Reading #12

Investment Governance

Those responsible for investment governance organize decision-making responsibilities and oversight activities. The investment committee typically obtains approval for the strategic asset allocation and then oversees portfolio decisions. Effective investment governance ensures that the strategic asset allocation decision achieves an asset owner's return objectives within acceptable constraints and in compliance with applicable laws and regulations.

Governance establishes and clarifies the mission, creates a plan, and reviews progress toward objectives. Management executes the plan.

Common elements of effective governance include:

- Articulate the long- and short-term objectives.
- Allocate decision rights and responsibilities based on knowledge.
- Establish processes related to the investment policy statement and strategic asset allocation.
- Establish processes related to portfolio monitoring.
- Undertake a periodic governance audit.

An important consideration involves whether to delegate a duty of effective governance to staff or outside parties. This generally depends on the knowledge, expertise, and capacity (e.g., time) to effectively administer a responsibility. The following summarizes a normal governance plan:

- Approve
    - Mission
    - Investment policy statement
    - Asset allocation
    - Risk management principles
- Delegate
    - Investment manager and service provider selection—Staff
    - Portfolio construction (asset selection)—Portfolio manager
    - Asset price monitoring and rebalancing—Staff
- Oversee
    - Investment manager monitoring, performance evaluation, and reporting
    - Governance audit

Key elements of the reporting framework include:

- Benchmarking
    - Portfolio managers—Purpose for which they were hired
    - Portfolio governance—Policy versus actual portfolio
- Investment manager reporting
    - Performance relative to mandate
    - Performance relative to objective
- Governance reporting—Good governance structures reduce the need for emergency meetings and instead focus on periodic reporting.

Good governance seeks to avoid decision-reversal risk—the risk of reversing a chosen course of action at exactly the wrong time, the point of maximum loss. The governance audit ensures that the governing body's structure, policies, and procedures produce the desired result. It should include consideration of structures for onboarding those within the structure, succession, and release from employment. Good governance also seeks to eliminate or reduce blame avoidance (i.e., failing to accept responsibility for errors).

The Economic Balance Sheet

An **economic balance sheet** includes assets and liabilities as well as extended assets and liabilities not on conventional balance sheets.

For individual investors, extended assets include human capital, the economic present value of an investor's future labor income, pension income, and expected inheritances. The present value of future consumption is an extended portfolio liability.

For institutional investors, extended portfolio assets include underground mineral resources or the present value of future intellectual property royalties. Extended portfolio liabilities include the present value of prospective payouts.

Asset allocation considers the full range of assets and liabilities to arrive at an appropriate asset allocation choice. For example, including the sensitivity of an individual investor's earnings to equity market risk results in a more appropriate allocation to equities.

At age 25, most of an individual's working life is ahead of him or her. Therefore, human capital dominates the economic balance sheet. As the individual ages, the present value of human capital decreases as human capital is converted into earnings. Earnings saved and invested accumulate financial capital. By a retirement age of 65, the conversion of human capital to earnings and financial capital is complete.

Human capital is roughly 30% equity-like and 70% bond-like. In this case, the asset allocation chosen for financial capital should reflect an increasing allocation to bonds as human capital declines to age 65.

Asset Allocation Approaches

There are three broad approaches to asset allocation: (1) asset-only, (2) liability-relative, and (3) goals-based.

1. **Asset-only approach** focuses on the asset side of the investor's balance sheet, and liabilities are not explicitly modeled. For example, mean-variance optimization (MVO) is an asset-only approach that considers only the expected returns, risks, and correlations of the asset classes in the opportunity set.
2. **Liability-relative approach** or **liability-driven investing (LDI)** explicitly accounts for the liabilities side of the economic balance sheet, dedicating assets to meet legal liabilities and quasi-liabilities. The liability-relative approach aims at an asset allocation that provides for the money to pay liabilities when they come due. When constructing a liability-hedging portfolio, the remaining balance of assets can be invested in a riskier-assets portfolio.
3. **Goals-based approach** or **goals-based investing (GBI)** specifies sub-portfolios aligned with each of an individual investor's specific goals ranging from supporting lifestyle needs to aspirational goals. For example, retirees might specify a goal of maintaining their current lifestyle and a goal of leaving a bequest to their children.

The sum of all sub-portfolio asset allocations results in an overall strategic asset allocation for the total portfolio.

Asset-only approaches use volatility (standard deviation) and the correlations of asset class returns to minimize risk at a given level of return. Other risk measures include risk relative to a benchmark (e.g., tracking risk) and downside risk (i.e., semivariance, VaR). Monte Carlo simulation also provides information about how an asset allocation performs when one or more variables are changed.

Liability-relative approaches focus on the risk of not having enough assets to pay obligations when due, and uses shortfall risk as a measure of risk.

Goals-based approaches are concerned with the risk of failing to achieve goals and can be quantified as the maximum acceptable probability of not achieving a goal.

Asset Classes

An asset class can be defined as a set of assets that have economic similarities to each other, and that have characteristics that make them distinct from other assets. Asset classes reflect systematic risks with varying degrees of overlap.

The listing of asset classes often includes the following:

1. **Global public equity**—developed, emerging, and frontier markets and large-, mid-, and small-cap asset classes.
2. **Global private equity**—venture capital, growth capital, and leveraged buyouts.
3. **Global fixed income**—developed and emerging market debt.
4. **Real assets**—private real estate equity, private infrastructure, and commodities.

The following are five criteria in specifying asset classes:

1. Assets within an asset class should be homogeneous.
2. Asset classes should be mutually exclusive.
3. Asset classes should be diversifying.
4. The asset classes as a group should make up most of the world's investable wealth.
5. A selected asset class should absorb a large proportion of an investor's portfolio.

Traditional asset allocation uses asset classes as the unit of analysis, which obscures the portfolio's sensitivity to overlapping risk factors such as inflation risk. As a result, controlling risk exposures may be problematic.

Factor-based approaches assign investments to the investor's desired exposures to specified risk factors. Multifactor risk models can control the systematic risk exposures in asset allocation by specifying risk factors and the desired exposure to each factor. Asset classes can be described with respect to their sensitivities to each of the factors.

Policy Portfolio

The **policy portfolio** is the strategic asset allocation expected to achieve investment objectives given risk tolerance and investment constraints. Determining the asset allocation for the policy portfolio depends in part on the type of allocation specified by the strategy.

Asset-only approaches establish portfolios based on efficient use of asset risk. Given a set of asset classes and assumptions concerning their expected returns, volatilities, and correlations, the mean-variance optimization approach delineates an efficient frontier of portfolios expected to offer the greatest return at each level of portfolio return volatility, hence the highest Sharpe ratio among portfolios with the same volatility of return.

Liability-relative approaches explicitly consider liabilities, implementing a liability-hedging portfolio based on liabilities and a return-seeking portfolio.

Goals-based approaches split the portfolio into three components: a component called "lifestyle—minimum" intended to provide protection for lifestyle in a disaster scenario, a component called "lifestyle—baseline" to address needs outside of worst cases, and a component called "lifestyle—aspirational" that reflects a desire for a chance at a markedly higher lifestyle. Goals-based approaches set the strategic asset allocation in a bottom-up fashion.

Global Market Portfolio

The global market portfolio represents a highly diversified asset allocation that can serve as a baseline asset allocation in an asset-only approach. It is the portfolio that minimizes nondiversifiable risk, which is uncompensated. Therefore, it is the available portfolio that makes the most efficient use of the risk budget.

Other arguments for using it as a baseline include its position as a reference point for a highly diversified portfolio and the discipline it provides in relation to mitigating any investment biases, such as home-country bias.

Strategic Implementation Choices

After establishing the strategic asset allocation policy, the asset owner must address the strategic passive/active choice before moving on to implementation.

The first consideration of the passive/active choice is whether to tactically deviate from strategic asset allocation. **Tactical asset allocation (TAA)** deliberately under- or overweights asset classes relative to their target weights in the policy portfolio to add value. TAA is active management at the asset-class level.

The second consideration relates to passive and active implementation choices in investing the allocation to a given asset class. At the broadest level, the choice is among passive investing, active investing, or a mix of both active and passive suballocations.

Passive investing can be implemented through an index-tracking portfolio, such as an exchange-traded fund or a mutual fund. Indexing is the lowest-cost approach to investing but still involves transaction costs as the fund purchases and sells securities that move in and out of the index.

Active investing can be implemented through a portfolio of securities that reflects the investor's perceived special insights and skill and makes no attempt to track an asset-class index's performance. The objective of active management is to achieve, after expenses, positive excess risk-adjusted returns relative to a passive benchmark.

- The range of implementation choices can be viewed as falling along a passive/active spectrum, because some strategies use both passive and active elements. For example, an investor who indexes to a value equity index is active with regard to *value* tilting but passive in implementation because the strategy involves indexing.

Rebalancing

Rebalancing is the discipline of adjusting portfolio weights to the strategic asset allocation and serves to control portfolio risks that have become different from what the investor originally intended.

Rebalancing approaches include:

- Calendar-based approach rebalances the portfolio to target weights on a periodic basis, such as quarterly.
- Range-based approach sets rebalancing thresholds (trigger points) around target weights. The ranges may be fixed width, percentage based, or volatility based. Range-based rebalancing permits tighter control of the asset mix compared with calendar rebalancing.

AA
CM

PRINCIPLES OF ASSET ALLOCATION
Cross-Reference to CFA Institute Assigned Reading #13

The traditional mean-variance optimization (MVO) approach is often used in asset-only asset allocations. The MVO produces an efficient frontier based on three sets of inputs:

1. Returns, R_m.
2. Standard deviations of returns, σ_m.
3. Pairwise correlations between all available asset classes, ρ_{ij}.

Any asset allocation mix on the efficient frontier has the minimum level of risk for a given level of return or the maximum return for a given level or risk. When we incorporate a client's utility function, we are able to find an optimal asset allocation mix that maximizes the client's utility. A utility function is often in the form of:

$$U_m = E(R_m) - 0.005\lambda\sigma_m^2$$

where :

m = Asset allocation mix
U = Client's utility function
λ = Client's coefficient of risk aversion

MVO exhibits seven major weaknesses and limitations:

1. Resulting optimal asset allocations are highly sensitive to small changes in input variables (expected returns, standard deviations, and pairwise correlations).
2. Asset allocations tend to be highly concentrated in a subset of the available asset classes.
3. MVO focuses on only mean and variance of asset returns. However, clients may be concerned about more than just mean and variance of asset returns. For example, clients may exhibit a preference for skewness in returns when buying lottery tickets.
4. Even though asset allocation may appear diversified across assets, the sources of risk may not be well diversified.
5. MVOs are asset-only strategies. They do not allow liabilities or consumptions.
6. MVO is a single-period framework and does not consider trading and rebalancing costs and taxes.
7. MVO does not address evolving asset allocation strategies, path-dependent decisions, and non-normal distributions.

To improve the quality of MVO asset allocation, we have the following three approaches:

1. Use reverse optimization to compute implied returns associated with a portfolio. The goal is improving the quality of inputs. The Black-Litterman model enables clients to combine their forecasts of expected returns with reverse optimization. This way, the resulting optimized portfolio is more consistent with input variables.
2. Adding constraints beyond budget constraints in optimization allows advisors to incorporate real-world restrictions (such as short-selling restrictions, weight upper/lower bounds in asset classes) into optimization and to achieve more meaningful optimization outcomes for clients.

3. The resample MVO technique treats the efficient frontier as a statistical construct. Resampling is a large-scale sensitivity analysis to seek the most efficient and consistent optimization combining MVO and Monte Carlo approaches.

There are multiple other approaches that address non-normal optimizations, where preferences of skewness and/or excess kurtosis, among other factors, are incorporated into the analysis and optimization.

Traditional asset allocation decisions focus on only clients' financial capital and ignore their human capital, other non-traded assets, and liabilities. Human capital is the present value of the client's expected future labor income. An asset allocation decision achieves incremental improvements if it takes into consideration four additional factors outside the scope of the traditional MVO:

1. Size of human capital relative to the total wealth of the client.
2. Correlation between the rate of increase in human capital and financial market return.
3. Size of non-traded assets and correlation between non-traded assets and financial assets.
4. Degree of liquidity of financial assets, human capital, and non-tradable assets.

High-net-worth clients may often have the ability and willingness to invest in less liquid asset classes, including direct real estate, infrastructure, and private equity, to seek higher return and better diversification at the overall portfolio level.

Illiquid assets differ from liquid assets in many different dimensions. Unlike liquid assets, illiquid assets often carry significant idiosyncratic risk that is difficult to diversify. Due to the illiquid nature of these assets, the volatility of an index of these illiquid assets does not reflect the true return volatility of the index. Additionally, capital market assumptions that may well fit liquid assets may not apply easily to illiquid assets. Finally, there are no low-cost passive investment vehicles to track the performance of an illiquid asset class.

In practice, the following three approaches are often used:

1. Replace illiquid asset classes (such as direct real estate) by liquid implementation vehicles (such as real estate funds) whose returns are highly correlated with the performance of the illiquid asset classes in an asset allocation.
2. Include illiquid asset classes in an asset allocation, but use the return and risk characteristics of their implementation vehicles to proxy the return and risk characteristics of the illiquid asset classes in optimization calculations and decisions.
3. Include illiquid asset classes (such as direct real estate) in an asset allocation, but model the inputs to represent highly diversified characteristics (returns and risks of a real estate index) associated with the illiquid asset classes.

Monte Carlo simulation addresses some weaknesses and limitations of MVO. Four benefits of Monte Carlo simulation are:

1. It can be used in a multiple-period framework and it improves upon the single-period model of MVO.
2. It provides a realistic picture of the distribution of potential future outcomes, based on which we can infer the likelihood of meeting various financial goals, the expected value of the assets' future value across time, and the potential maximum drawdowns.
3. It can incorporate trading costs and costs of rebalancing a portfolio. It may also incorporate taxes.

4. It can model non-normal multivariate return distributions, serial and cross-sectional correlations, distribution requirements, an evolving asset allocation strategy, path-dependent decisions, nontraditional investments, non-tradable assets, and human capital.

A risk budget is a particular allocation of portfolio risk. An optimal risk budget is one to satisfy portfolio optimization. Our goal is to seek an optimal risk budget. Portfolio risk can be total risk, market risk, active risk, or residual risk. Here are three statements that are directly related to the risk budget process:

1. The risk budget identifies the total amount of risk and allocates the risk to different asset classes in a portfolio.
2. An optimal risk budget allocates risk efficiently, which is to maximize return per unit of risk taken.
3. The process of finding the optimal risk budget is risk budgeting.

The concept of marginal contribution to portfolio risk is an important one because it allows us to (1) track the change in portfolio risk due to a change in portfolio holding, (2) determine which positions are optimal, and (3) create a risk budget.

In a risk budget setting, we have the following relations:

> Marginal contribution to total risk (MCTR)
> = Asset beta × Portfolio standard deviation
>
> Absolute contribution to total risk (ACTR)
> = Asset weight × MCTR
>
> Ratio of excess return to MCTR
> = (Expected return − Risk-free rate)/MCTR

An asset allocation is optimal when the ratio of excess return (over the risk-free rate) to MCTR is the same for all assets.

Factor-based asset allocation utilizes investment risk factors instead of asset classes to make asset allocation decisions. These factors are fundamental factors that historically have produced return premiums or anomalies to investors. These factors include, but not limited to:

1. Size (small cap versus large cap).
2. Valuation (value stock versus growth stock).
3. Momentum (winners versus losers).
4. Liquidity (low liquidity versus high liquidity).
5. Duration (long term versus short term).
6. Credit (low-rated bonds versus high-rated bonds).
7. Volatility (low-volatility stocks versus high-volatility stocks).

Note that these seven factors are implemented as a zero-cost investment or self-financing investment, in which the underperformer is short-sold and outperformer is bought. By construction, they are often market neutral and carry low correlations with the market and with other factors.

Liability-relative asset allocation is an asset allocation process with the presence of the client's liabilities within the investment horizon. In this context, assets are viewed as an inventory of capital, with potential additions due to new investments, to be made available to satisfy future consumption and liability needs. Considerations are likelihood of having sufficient capital to meet future liabilities, financial management of the capital surplus (net of future liabilities), and restatement of tradition risk metrics in relation to liabilities, among others.

Here are seven characteristics of liabilities that can affect asset allocation decisions:

1. Fixed versus contingent cash flows.
2. Legal liabilities versus quasi-liabilities.
3. Duration and convexity of liability cash flows.
4. Value of liabilities as compared with the size of the sponsoring organization.
5. Factors driving future liability cash flows (inflation, economic conditions, interest rates, risk premium).
6. Timing considerations, such as longevity risk.
7. Regulations affecting liability cash flow calculations.

These factors affect liability-relative asset allocation in multiple ways. For example, it's critically important to select appropriate discount rates to compute the present value of the liabilities, which directly determines the funding status of a pension plan. Liability characteristics also determine the composition of the liability matching portfolio and the tracking error (called basis risk in this context), which measures the degree of mismatch between the liabilities and its corresponding hedging portfolio.

As an example, the surplus of a pension plan is computed with the following five steps:

1. Calculate the market value of assets.
2. Project future liability cash flows.
3. Determine an appropriate discount rate for liability cash flows.
4. Compute the present value of liabilities.
5. Surplus = Market value (assets) − Present value (liabilities). Funding ratio = Market value (assets) ÷ Present value (liabilities).

There are three main approaches in liability-relative asset allocation:

1. The surplus optimization approach uses the traditional MVO approach based on the volatility of the surplus volatility as the measure of risk. It is similar to MVO for asset-only optimization. The difference is that risk measure in surplus optimization is the volatility of the surplus. The following steps summarize the surplus optimization approach.
   a. Select asset categories and determine the planning horizon.
   b. Estimate expected returns and volatilities for the asset categories, and estimate liability returns.
   c. Determine any constraints on the investment mix.
   d. Estimate the expanded correlation matrix (asset categories and liabilities) and the volatilities.
   e. Compute the surplus efficient frontier and compare it with the asset-only efficient frontier.
   f. Select a recommended portfolio mix.
2. The two-portfolio approach or hedging/return-seeking portfolio approach partitions assets into two groups: a hedging portfolio and a return-seeking portfolio. The hedging

portfolio is managed so that its assets are expected to produce a good hedge to cover required cash outflows from the liabilities. The return-seeking portfolio can be managed independently of the hedging portfolio. Portfolio managers and investment advisors can potentially treat the return-seeking portfolio as an asset-only portfolio and apply traditional MVO in the asset allocation process. The two-portfolio approach is most appropriate for conservative investors who wish to reduce or eliminate the risk of not being able to pay future liabilities. Variants of the two-portfolio approach include:

a. Partial hedge: Capital allocated to the hedging portfolio is reduced in order to generate higher expected returns from the return-seeking portfolio.
b. Dynamic hedge: The investor increases the allocation to the hedging portfolio as the funding ratio increases.

The two-portfolio approach has its limitations.

a. It cannot be used when the funding ratio is less than 1.
b. It cannot be use when a true hedging portfolio is unavailable; for example, the liabilities are related to payments for damages due to hurricanes or earthquakes.

3. The integrated asset-liability approach is used by some institutional investors to jointly optimize asset and liability decisions. Banks, long/short hedge funds, insurance companies, and reinsurance companies often must render decisions regarding the composition of liabilities in conjunction with their asset allocation. The process is called asset-liability management (ALM) for banks and dynamic financial analysis (DFA) for insurance companies. The approach is often implemented in the context of multiperiod models via a set of projected scenarios. The integrated asset-liability approach provides a mechanism to discover the optimal mix of assets and liabilities. It is the most comprehensive approach among the three liability-relative asset allocation approaches.

Characteristics of liability-relative asset allocation approaches are summarized in the following table.

Surplus Optimization	Two-Portfolio	Integrated Asset-Liability
Simplicity	Simplicity	Increased complexity
Linear correlation	Linear or nonlinear correlation	Linear or nonlinear correlation
All levels of risk	Conservative level of risk	All levels of risk
Any funding ratio	Positive funding ratio for basic approach	Any funding ratio
Single period	Single period	Multiple periods

It's important to examine the robustness of asset allocation strategies. Four commonly used robustness tests are:

1. Simulation based on historical return and risk data.
2. Sensitivity analysis where the level of one underlying risk factor is changed and the resulting asset allocation outcomes are investigated.
3. Scenario analysis where the levels of multiple risk factors are changed in a correlated manner and the resulting asset allocation outcomes are investigated. Stress testing is one such case.
4. Multistage simulation analysis where a comprehensive examination of impact of uncertainty in all risk factors is conducted. Market risk factors include but are not limited to inflation, interest rates, credit spreads, currency prices, and GDP growth rates.

Firm risk factors include asset mix, product mix, capital structure, insurance and reinsurance, and hedging.

It's important to recognize that individual clients are different from financial institutions in multiple ways in terms of goals, time horizon, risk measure, return determination, risk determination, and tax status. Individual clients have different needs from those of institutions. Consequently, asset allocation processes should address individual clients' multiple goals, multiple time horizons, and various level of priorities over different goals.

	Institutions	Individuals
Goals	Single	Multiple
Time horizon	Single	Multiple
Risk measure	Volatility	Probability of missing goal
Return determination	Mathematical expectations	Minimum expectations
Risk determination	Top-down/bottom-up	Bottom-up
Tax status	Single, often tax-exempt	Mostly taxable

There are three implications from the characteristics of individuals' goals:

1. The overall portfolio needs to be divided into sub-portfolios to allow each goal to be addressed individually by a specific sub-portfolio.
2. Both taxable and tax-exempt investments are important.
3. Probability-adjusted and horizon-adjusted expectations (called "minimum expectations") replace mathematical expected returns to determine the funding cost for a goal. The minimum expectations are the minimum return expected to be earned over the investment horizon to achieve a given probability of success (in meeting a goal).

Goal-based asset allocations have two fundamental parts:

1. Creation of portfolio modules: The model portfolio modules are created based on capital market assumptions. The portfolio modules should cover a wide spectrum of the investment universe, across essentially all asset classes and risk factors. The portfolio modules should be sufficiently differentiated so that they are individually different from other modules to create effective choices to address clients' needs. Modules should be reviewed and revisited on a periodic basis to ensure they deliver intended functions.
2. Identifying clients' goals and matching the goals to appropriate sub-portfolios and modules: The urgency and/or priority can be described by "needs, wants, wishes, and dreams," or in terms to avoidance, "nightmares, fears, worries, and concerns." Considerations are placed on time horizon, success probability, liquidity, intra-asset class allocation, and risk/return trade-off. For a client's given time horizon and success probability, the module is chosen that delivers the highest annualized minimum expected after-tax returns, after taking liquidity of the module into consideration.

In this context, the MVO is performed with various constraints, making the efficient portfolios only conditionally efficient subject to the constraints. They may not be globally unconditionally efficient. Additionally, different levels of liquidity of various asset classes, non-normal distribution of module returns, and drawdown control all affect the goal-based asset allocation decision making. Finally, goal-based asset allocation must be reviewed regularly.

Here are five commonly applied reasonable asset allocation schemes that may not be fully optimal. However, they often appear in the literature and they are popular as simple rules of thumb.

1. The "120 minus your age" rule recommends the percentage of stocks in a client's portfolio. It considers the client's age, her ability to take risk, time horizon, and diversification. The rule motivates creation of target-date funds, which systematically rebalance stock/bond weights over time.

2. The "60/40 stock/bond" rule states that clients should skip asset allocation optimization and simply hold 60% stocks and 40% bonds.

3. The endowment model or Yale model is an asset allocation approach that emphasizes large allocation to nontraditional investments, including private equities and other alternative investments. It's widely used among U.S. university endowment funds. The strategy combines high allocations in nontraditional investments and active asset management. Additionally, the strategy also seeks to earn an illiquidity premium over long time horizons that characterize endowment funds.

4. In a risk-parity asset allocation, each asset class or risk factor contributes equally to the total risk of the portfolio in order to well diversify the portfolio. A major weakness of the model is that it ignores expected returns. It focuses on only risk without addressing return enhancement in an asset allocation.

5. The 1/N rule is a simple and naive rule where an equal weight is assigned to each asset or asset class. Empirical studies have found that the 1/N rule performs better in terms of Sharpe ratios and certainty equivalents than theory might suggest.

Market price movements and the passage of time alter portfolio weights from their target levels. Rebalancing is the process of adjusting portfolio weights to align with the original scheme based on a strategic asset allocation.

The traditional MVO is a one-period model that assumes a buy-and-hold strategy over the investment horizon. Consequently, the need for rebalancing is not addressed. However, in practice, clients' goals often expand over multiple periods with multiple investment horizons. Consequently, portfolio rebalancing becomes an important element in implementations of an asset allocation process.

An appropriate rebalancing policy considers both the benefits and the costs of rebalancing. The benefits include reduction of expected loss due to tracking error (basis risk) from the optimum asset allocation. Additionally:

- Rebalancing earns a diversification return. The compound growth rate of a portfolio is greater than the weighted average compound growth rates of the component portfolio holdings.
- Rebalancing earns a return from being short volatility.

Here are the factors affecting the optimal corridor width of an asset class in the portfolio rebalancing process.

Factor	Effect
Transaction costs ↑	Wider corridor
Risk tolerance ↑	Wider corridor
Correlation with the rest of portfolio ↑	Wider corridor
Volatility of the rest of the portfolio ↑	Narrower corridor

Analysis suggests that fixed transaction costs favor rebalancing to the target weights, and variable transaction costs favor rebalancing to the nearest corridor border.

AA
CM

ASSET ALLOCATION WITH REAL-WORLD CONSTRAINTS
Cross-Reference to CFA Institute Assigned Reading #14

Theories in asset allocation ignore many real-life constraints in implementation of asset allocation schemes. In practice, an asset manager must consider important factors such as asset size, liquidity needs, taxes, regulatory considerations, and time horizon when the asset manager carries out an asset allocation scheme for an asset owner.

- **Asset size:** The impact on asset allocation due to asset size differs across different asset classes. Cash equivalents and money market funds generally have no size constraints. Large-cap and small-cap developed market equity funds, emerging market equity funds, developed market sovereign bond funds, investment-grade bond funds, non-investment-grade bond funds, and private real estate equity funds are accessible to both small and large asset owners. Alternative investments, including hedge funds, private debt, private equity, infrastructure, and timberland and farmland may be accessible to large and small asset owners. Some vehicles may have legal minimum qualifications that exclude small asset owners. Additionally, small investors may achieve diversification by using a commingled vehicle such as a fund of funds or an alternative exchange-traded fund (ETF). For very large funds, the allocation may be constrained by the number of funds available.

    a. The size of an asset owner's portfolio affects asset allocation. For example, a small portfolio limits the asset owner's available opportunity set, and a large asset size makes it difficult to fully capture investment opportunities and benefits in smaller niche markets.

    b. Economies of scale and diseconomies of scale are key factors that affect implementation of asset allocation. As assets under management (AUM) increase, scale and resources provide a competitive edge. However, as fund AUM increases, trade size must increase to avoid a transaction cost disadvantage. Larger trades trigger a greater price impact. It becomes difficult to deploy capital effectively in some actively managed funds with a large AUM.

    c. Fund managers with a large AUM may also need to pursue investment ideas outside their core areas of investment expertise.

    d. Different asset classes are constrained to a different degree due to asset sizes. Liquidity, trading costs, and sizes of the underlying asset classes (e.g., large-cap developed market equity versus private equity) all play a role to the degree asset size impacts investment decisions.

    e. Regulatory restrictions can impose a size constraint.

    f. Smaller portfolios are constrained by size. They may be too small to be adequately diversified. They may be constrained in their ability to access private equity, hedge funds, and infrastructure investments.

    g. When the asset size is sufficiently large, an asset owner may have to invest the assets in multiple active funds. Performances in these funds may tend to offset one another, resulting in an index-like portfolio with high management fees to the asset owner.

    h. Asset size as a constraint is often a more acute issue for individual investors than for institutional asset owners. High-net-worth families may pool assets through vehicles such as family limited partnerships, investment companies, funds of funds, or other forms of commingled vehicles to hold their assets, which allow them to access investment opportunities that may not be available to these families individually due to small asset size.

- **Liquidity:** There are two dimensions of liquidity in asset allocation decisions: the liquidity needs of the asset owner and the liquidity characteristics of the asset classes in the investment opportunity set.
  a. Different asset owners' assets allocated for different goals are set to achieve an investor's liquidity needs. For example, long-term investors such as endowment funds can exploit any illiquidity premium associated with real estate, private equity, and other illiquid asset classes. An individual investor's ability and willingness to take on liquidity risk play an important role in asset allocation in investment portfolios.
  b. Asset managers need to consider the intersection of asset class and investor liquidity in the context of an asset owner's governance capacity. Asset liquidity changes with market conditions. During a financial crisis when liquidity dries up, asset owners should avoid acting irrationally, such as selling assets at steep discounts and locking in permanent losses.
  c. A successful asset allocation effort will stress the proposed allocation; it will anticipate, where possible, the likely behavior of other facets of the saving/spending equation during times of stress. Also, liquidity needs must consider the circumstances and financial strength of the asset owner and what resources the owner may have beyond those held in the investment portfolio. For example, an automobile insurance company that manages its risk exposure using the law of large numbers may have a stronger ability to take liquidity risk than an insurance company whose risk exposure is related to natural disasters.
- **Time horizon:** An asset owner's time horizon is a key element in any asset allocation decision. Sizes and timing of liabilities and funding goals directly determine choices of asset classes in an investment portfolio.
  a. As time progresses, the characteristics of both assets and liabilities change. Considerations include an asset owner's utility function and human capital. Allocation of financial capital should be optimally determined in conjunction with the beneficiary's utility function and human capital, both of which change over time.
  b. Asset allocation decisions need to consider changing characteristics of liabilities over time. When the asset owner is young with a long investment horizon, potentially risky and less liquid investments can be included in the portfolio to hedge the long-term bond nature of liabilities. However, as time elapses and the asset owner approaches retirement age, the asset allocation should be concentrated on short-term bonds or other cash-like investments to match the cash-like nature of pending liabilities.
  c. Asset allocation decisions evolve with changes in time horizon, human capital, utility function, financial market conditions, and the asset owner's priorities.
- **Regulatory and other external constraints:** Financial markets and regulatory entities often impose additional constraints that affect investment decisions and asset allocation.
  a. **Insurance companies:** Fixed-income products are typically the largest component of insurance companies' asset base so that the assets are closely matched with liabilities. Additionally, allocation to certain asset classes are often constrained by regulators.
  b. **Pension funds:** Asset allocation decisions of pension funds are often constrained by tax rules and regulations, including upper and lower bounds in proportion of assets that can be allocated to particular sectors or asset classes. For example, Brazil limits pension funds to invest no more than 8% of assets in real estate. Pension funds are also subject to a wide range of funding, accounting, reporting, and tax constraints that may affect asset allocation decisions.

c. **Endowments and foundations:** Endowments and foundations generally have a long investment horizon and often have more flexibility over payments from the fund than pension funds and insurance companies. They have two major asset allocation constrains: tax incentives and creditworthiness considerations.

   i. Tax incentives: Endowments and foundations keep their tax-exemption benefits if they satisfy certain minimum spending requirements or meet socially responsible investment minimums.

   ii. Credit considerations: External factors may restrict the level of risk taking in the portfolio despite its long investment horizon.

d. **Sovereign wealth funds:** The governing entities often adopt regulations that constrain the opportunity set for sovereign wealth funds. Additionally, asset size, liquidity, time horizon, regulations, and even cultural and religious factors as well as environmental, social, and governance (ESG) considerations may all affect asset allocation decisions of sovereign wealth funds.

Taxes are an important consideration in any investment and asset allocation decisions. Owing to differences in tax treatments (e.g., capital gains versus income), some asset classes are more tax efficient than others. The generally accepted rule is to place less tax-efficient assets in tax-advantaged accounts to achieve after-tax portfolio optimization for a given tax environment.

- **After-tax portfolio optimization:** Note the following intuitive equation:

$$r_{at} = P_d r_{pt}(1 - t_d) + P_{cg} r_{pt}(1 - t_{cg})$$

where :

$$
\begin{aligned}
r_{at} &= \text{Expected after-tax rate of return} \\
r_{pt} &= \text{Expected before-tax rate of return} \\
P_d &= \text{Proportion of } r_{pt} \text{ attributed to dividend income} \\
P_{cg} &= \text{Proportion of } r_{pt} \text{ attributed to capital gains} \\
t_d &= \text{Dividend tax rate} \\
t_{cg} &= \text{Capital gains tax rate}
\end{aligned}
$$

Many approaches adjust a portfolio's current value by reducing its embedded tax liabilities (assets), as if all assets were liquidated and tax impact is realized.

For entities with tax-exempted status, such as charities, goal-based asset allocations allow more precise tax adjustments.

A key concept is that expected after-tax return standard deviation (σ_{at}) is smaller than pre-tax return standard deviation (σ_{pt}). They are related by the following equation, where t is the marginal tax rate.

$$\sigma_{at} = \sigma_{pt}(1 - t)$$

Taxes alter the distribution of returns by reducing both the expected mean return and return standard deviation.

The optimal after-tax asset allocation depends on the interaction of after-tax rates of returns, after-tax standard deviations, and correlations.

Asset allocation decisions should be made on an after-tax basis.

- **Taxes and portfolio rebalancing:** As market conditions change over time, asset class weights in a portfolio change and tend to move away from previously set target levels. Portfolio rebalancing is needed to return actual allocation to the strategic asset allocation (SAA). However, discretionary portfolio rebalancing can trigger realized capital gains and losses and the associated tax liabilities that could have been otherwise deferred or even avoided.

  Taxable asset owners should consider the trade-off between the benefits of tax minimization and the merits of maintaining the targeted asset allocation by rebalancing.

  Because after-tax volatility is smaller than pre-tax volatility, it takes a larger movement in a taxable portfolio to change the risk profile of the portfolio. Consequently, rebalancing ranges for a taxable portfolio (R_{Taxable}) can be wider than those of an otherwise identical tax-exempt portfolio ($R_{\text{TaxExempt}}$).

  $$R_{\text{Taxable}} = R_{\text{TaxExempt}}/(1 - t)$$

  Tax loss harvesting is another commonly used strategy related to portfolio rebalancing and taxes.

  Strategic asset location refers to placing less tax-efficient assets into tax-deferred or tax-exempt accounts such as pension and retirement accounts. For example, equities should generally be held in taxable accounts, and taxable bonds and high-turnover trading assets should be placed in tax-exempt or tax-deferred accounts to maximize the tax benefits of those accounts.

Asset allocation decisions are a dynamically changing and adjusting process. Market conditions and asset owner circumstances often require revising an original asset allocation decision. There are basically three elements that may trigger a review of an existing asset allocation policy:

1. **Changes in goals:**
   a. As a result of changes in business conditions and changes in expected future cash flows over time, a mismatch may arise between the original intended goal and the current goal of the fund to best serve the fund's needs.
   b. Changes in an asset owner's personal circumstances may alter risk appetite or risk capacity. Life events such as marriage, having children, and becoming ill may all have an impact on the needs and goals of an individual benefiting from an investment portfolio.
2. **Changes in constraints:** Any material change in constrains, including asset size, liquidity, time horizon, regulatory, or other external constraints, should trigger a reexamination of existing asset allocation decisions.
3. **Changes in beliefs:** Investment beliefs change with market conditions, among many other factors. They are a set of guiding principles that govern the asset owner's investment decisions. Investment beliefs include expected returns, volatilities, and correlations among asset classes in the opportunity set.

Long-term asset allocation decisions are strategic asset allocation (SAA), also known as policy asset allocation. Short-term asset allocation decisions are tactical asset allocation (TAA). TAA takes advantage of short-term investment opportunities and allows short-term deviations from SAA target portfolio weights.

TAA seeks to earn additional return by underweighting or overweighting asset classes relative to the policy portfolio to take advantage of expected market conditions. TAA builds on the assumption that short-term asset returns are at least partially predictable. TAA is an asset-only approach. It is not based on successful selection of individual stocks or sectors. Instead, TAA attempts to generate alpha using timing of market or risk factors.

TAA performance can be evaluated using the following three methods:

1. Comparing the Sharpe ratio realized under the TAA relative to the Sharpe ratio that would have been realized using the SAA.
2. Evaluating the information ratio or the t-statistics of the average excess return of the TAA portfolio relative to those of the SAA portfolio.
3. Plotting the realized return and risk of the TAA portfolio versus the realized return and risk of portfolios along the SAA's efficient frontier.

Additionally, performance attribution analysis can be used to decompose excess returns from TAA.

TAA investment decisions may trigger additional costs, including trading fees and taxes for taxable investors. TAA may also increase the concentration of risk relative to the policy portfolio. Benefits from TAA should be evaluated against any additional costs.

There are two broad approaches to TAA:

1. Discretionary TAA assumes that skills in predicting and timing short-term market movements yield abnormal positive returns. In practice, discretionary TAA attempts to avoid or hedge away negative returns in down markets and enhance positive returns in up markets. Market and risk factors that affect discretionary TAA decisions include valuations (price-to-earnings ratios, price-to-book ratios, and dividend yield), term and credit spreads, central bank policy, GDP growth, earnings expectations, inflation expectations, and leading economic indicators. Additionally, TAA considers market sentiment—indicators of optimism or pessimism of financial market participants. These indicators include margin borrowing, short interest, and a volatility index.
2. Systematic TAA uses signals to capture asset-class-level return anomalies that have been empirically demonstrated as producing abnormal returns. Value and momentum are examples of such factors. Valuation ratios, such as dividend yield, cash flow yield, and Shiller's earnings yield (the inverse of Shiller's P/E ratio) have been shown to have some explanatory power in predicting future equity returns.

Investors may not act according to capital market theories. Human behavior can be less rational than theories assume. We list six biases in asset allocation and recommend ways to overcome these biases.

1. **Loss aversion:** Loss aversion is the tendency of avoiding losses as opposed to achieving gains. The investor's utility function decreases significantly more for a loss than it increases for an equal amount of gain. Loss aversion can be mitigated by framing

risk in terms of shortfall probability or by funding high-priority goals with low-risk assets.

2. **The illusion of control:** The tendency to overestimate one's ability to control events leads to more frequent trading, greater concentration of portfolio positions, or a greater willingness to employ tactical shifts in asset allocation. The illusion of control is a cognitive bias. It can be mitigated by using the global market portfolio as a starting point in asset allocation and using a formal asset allocation process based on long-term return and risk forecasts, optimization constraints anchored around asset class weights in the global market portfolio, and strict policy ranges.

3. **Mental accounting:** Mental accounting is an information procession bias in which investors treat one sum of money differently from another sum of money based solely on the mental account the funds are assigned to. Goal-based investing incorporates the mental accounting bias directly into the asset allocation solution by aligning each goal with a discrete sub-portfolio.

4. **Recency or representativeness bias:** This is the tendency to overweight the importance of the most recent observations and information rather than longer-dated or more comprehensive information. Return chasing is an example of recency bias. It leads to overweighting stocks with good recent performance. A formal asset allocation policy with prespecified allowable ranges may constrain recency bias.

5. **Framing bias:** Framing bias is an information processing bias in which an investor may answer a question differently based solely on the way in which the question is asked. For example, an investor's asset allocation may be influenced merely by the way the risk/return trade-off is presented. Framing bias can be mitigated by presenting the possible asset allocation choices with multiple perspectives on the risk/reward trade-off.

6. **Familiarity or availability bias:** This is an information processing bias in which an investor takes a mental shortcut when estimating the probability of an outcome based on how easily the outcome comes to mind. Familiarity bias involves a preference for the familiar, and commonly appears as home bias. Familiarity bias can be mitigated by using the global market portfolio as the starting point in asset allocation and by carefully evaluating any potential deviations from this baseline portfolio.

AA
CM

AA
CM

OPTION STRATEGIES
Cross-Reference to CFA Institute Assigned Reading #15

Replicating Asset Returns

Put-call parity identifies the equivalence between a call and a risk-free bond to a put and the underlying security. This leads to a relationship between put and call prices:

$$S_0 + p_0 = c_0 + \frac{X}{(1+r)^T}$$
$$S_0 = c_0 + \frac{X}{(1+r)^T} - p_0$$

Reverse the signs in the formula above to create a short position rather than the long position.

Put call parity from the formula above may also be used to develop put and call prices:

$$p_0 = \frac{X}{(1+r)^T} - S_0 + c_0$$
$$c_0 = S_0 - \frac{X}{(1+r)^T} + p_0$$

The relationship between the stock and present value of the exercise price helps to understand the possible outcomes from an option position and represents the intrinsic value of the option. The relationship for an American option that can be exercised any time until expiration can be summarized as:

$$\text{Option premium} = \text{Intrinsic value} + \text{Time value}$$
$$c_0 = \text{Max}(0, S - X) + \text{Time value}$$
$$p_0 = \text{Max}(0, X - S) + \text{Time value}$$

Time value can only be calculated as option premium less the intrinsic value; that is, it cannot be directly observed.

The present value of a forward contract for the underlying that expires at the same time as the put and call can be substituted for the underlying in the above equation, leading to the calculation of a synthetic forward position:

$$\frac{F_0(T)}{(1+r)^T} = c_0 + \frac{X}{(1+r)^T} - p_0$$

Covered Calls and Protective Puts

The combination of a long security and a short call is called a **covered call** because the security "covers" potential exercise of the short option by the holder. The combination of a short security and a long put is called a **protective put** because the put "protects" against falling prices.

Covered call writers may have one of the following motives:

- **Yield enhancement**—Potentially increasing portfolio return by the amount of the option premium. This strategy is justified in a flat market.
- **Reducing a position**—Appropriate for a manager who wishes to reduce a position at a known price.
- **Target price realization**—This involves writing a covered call at or near the security's target price.

A short call decreases portfolio **delta** (i.e., the option price change when underlying price changes) and shorts **gamma** (i.e., the rate of change in delta). This, in turn, reduces potential upside when the underlying value increases. Gamma is highest at the strike price and increases rapidly as the option nears maturity or price volatility of the underlying increases. Gamma decreases as the underlying moves away in either direction from the exercise price.

At expiration, only the intrinsic value will apply (i.e., there is no time value). The easiest way to remember the formulas is to consider how intrinsic value is calculated and whether the profit will be zero, positive, or negative under the circumstances.

The profit/(loss) of a **short call** at expiration is the call premium received and (1) any loss from having the security called, or (2) zero if the option expires worthless to the holder:

$$\Pi_c = c_0 - \text{Max}[(S_T - X), 0]$$

Profit at expiration of a **covered call position** is the capital gain/(loss) on the underlying plus profit/(loss) from the short call position:

$$\Pi_{CC} = (S_T - S_0) + \Pi_c$$
$$= (S_T - S_0) + c_0 - \text{Max}[(S_T - X), 0]$$

The breakeven price for the underlying at expiration must occur when the option is out of the money for the capital loss to offset receipt of the option premium. Setting profit to zero for the case where the call is out of the money, the breakeven price is:

$$0 = (S_T - S_0) + c_0 - \text{Max}[(S_T - X), 0]$$
$$S_T^* = S_0 - c_0 + \text{Max}[(S_T - X), 0]$$
$$= S_0 - c_0$$

The maximum loss occurs when the underlying price goes to 0 at expiration because the capital loss will be so much higher than the received option premium. Setting S_T to 0, the maximum loss is:

$$\text{Maximum loss} = (0 - S_0) + c_0 - \text{Max}[(0 - X), 0]$$
$$= c - S_0$$

[Note that the maximum loss formula is different from that in the CFA Institute text because that formulation stated losses in positive terms.]

The maximum profit occurs when the price of the underlying at expiration exceeds the exercise price and the option is exercised, but the capital gain plus option premium more than offsets the loss due to exercise by the holder:

$$\text{Maximum } \Pi_{CC} = (S_T - S_0) + c_0 - \text{Max}[(S_T - X),0]$$
$$= (S_T - S_0) + c_0 + X - S_T$$
$$= X - S_0 + c_0$$

Again, these calculations include only the intrinsic value and not the time value for the positions because they apply to expiration. The Black-Scholes-Merton (BSM) model does consider time, but assumes stationary volatility while, in practice, volatility varies across time and strike prices. **Theta** measures sensitivity of an option price to daily time decay. **Vega** measures sensitivity of the option price to changes in volatility. Differences in time and the term structure of volatility explain the difference in the cost of options with different expirations.

A put protects against declining prices for its underlying security with an option premium, a face value equal to the exercise price, and a deductible equal to the difference in the exercise price and the initial value. An option also has a term similar to that of term life insurance. Based on this comparison, protective puts may also be known as **portfolio insurance**.

Protective put buyers may be motivated to protect themselves against losses in portfolio value or to preserve a capital gain.

The value of the protective put position (long stock and long put) is:

$$V_{PP} = S_T + \text{Max}[(X - S_T),0]$$

The profit/(loss) of a put option at expiration equals the benefit from the put less its cost:

$$\Pi_p = \text{Max}[(X - S_T),0] - p$$

The profit/(loss) of a **protective put position** at expiration equals the gain/(loss) on the underlying security less the profit from the put position:

$$\Pi_{PP} = (S_T - S_0) + \text{Max}[(X - S_T)] - p_0$$

To break even, the underlying asset price must rise by enough to offset the put premium; therefore, the breakeven point equals the initial stock price plus the option premium:

$$0 = (S_T - S_0) + \text{Max}[(X - S_T),0] - p_0$$
$$S_T^* = S_0 + p_0$$

The maximum gain is unlimited because the capital gain is only reduced by the put premium paid because there is no profit contribution from the put:

$$\text{Maximum } \Pi_{PP} = (S_T - S_0) + \text{Max}[(X - S_T),0] - p_0$$
$$= (S_T - S_0) - p_0$$

AA
CM

The maximum loss is capped at the capital loss less the put premium:

$$
\begin{aligned}
\text{Maximum Loss} &= (S_T - S_0) + \text{Max}[(X - S_T),0] - p_0 \\
&= (S_T - S_0) + X - S_T - p_0 \\
&= X - S_0 - p_0
\end{aligned}
$$

Equivalence to a Long Asset/Short Forward Position

Call deltas range from 0 to 1 because the option price increases as the underlying asset price increases (i.e., direct relationship). Put deltas range from 0 to –1 because the option price decreases as the underlying asset price increases (i.e., inverse relationship). A long ATM call option will have a delta of about 0.5 and a long ATM put option will have a delta of about – 0.5.

Forwards are proxies for the underlying; long forwards have delta from 0 to 1 and short forwards have delta from 0 to –1.

Portfolios also have delta and adding options to cover or protect that will affect portfolio delta. This hedged portfolio can be compared to a long asset and short forward position.

Risk Reduction Using Puts and Calls

Covered calls reduce the price uncertainty for price increases. Protective puts eliminate the price uncertainty for price decreases.

Long call positions have positive delta; short call positions have negative delta. A long put position will have negative delta as described previously; a short put position will have positive delta (i.e., negative negative delta). A **cash-secured put** (also known as a **fiduciary put**) involves writing a put option and backing the short put with enough **cash** to purchase the face value represented. This is different from writing a covered call in that the option writer owns the underlying securities.

Position Delta

A portfolio (position) delta equals the net of the individual position deltas:

$$
\begin{aligned}
\Delta_{\text{Position}} = &\ \text{Underlying} \times Sign \times \Delta_{\text{Underlying}} \\
&+ \text{Options} \times Sign \times \Delta_{\text{Option}}
\end{aligned}
$$

Long positions will have positive signs and short positions will have negative signs. The option delta depends on whether the option is a put (negative delta) or a call (positive delta). Therefore, a short call position will have a negative sign to indicate a short position and a positive delta.

The two positions (asset and option) can be set on opposite sides of the equation to calculate the number of options necessary to completely or partially hedge the portfolio delta:

$$
\begin{aligned}
\Delta_{\text{Position}} = &\ \text{Underlying} \times Sign_{UP} \times \Delta_{\text{Underlying}} \\
&+ \text{Options} \times Sign_{OP} \times \Delta_{\text{Option}} \\[2mm]
\text{Options} = &\ \frac{\text{Underlying} \times Sign_{UP} \times \Delta_{\text{Underlying}}}{Sign_{OP} \times \Delta_{\text{Option}}}
\end{aligned}
$$

Buying Calls and Writing Puts on a Short Position

An investor with a short position in the underlying security profits when the underlying price increases and loses money when the underlying price falls.

To protect a portfolio from losses as the price of the short underlying rises, an investor can **buy** a call option rather than sell a call option, as would be appropriate to earn option premium and lessen the effect of a long position declining in value. If the price of the underlying increases, the short underlying position will decrease in value and the long call will increase in value.

Investors wishing to protect a portfolio from losses as the price of the short underlying rises (and earn option premium) may also **sell** a put option, rather than buy a put option as would be appropriate to protect against a falling long position. However, writing a put does not protect against losses as effectively as selling the call because the short stock position can have unlimited losses.

Spreads and Combinations

Money spreads involve two like options on the same asset that differ only by exercise price. These are called **spreads** because the payoff depends on the difference in the exercise prices. A **butterfly spread** is slightly different because it depends on the difference between the payoffs from two spreads.

Bull Spreads and Bear Spreads

Bull spreads become more valuable when the underlying price increases; **bear spreads** become more valuable when the underlying price decreases. **Debit spreads** result in a net cash **outflow** from the spread; **credit spreads** result in a net cash **inflow**.

Bull Spread Dynamics

A bull spread using **calls** involves a long call at the lower strike price, offset by a short call at the higher strike price. Call bull spreads are debit spreads because the cash outflow from the more expensive long position in the lower strike price call is greater than the cash inflow from the less expensive short position in the higher strike price call. The cost of the call spread is the net premium difference:

$$\text{Call spread net outlay} = (c_L - c_H)$$

The value of the spread at expiration is the net value of the options, which revolves around the price of the underlying:

$$\text{Spread } V_T = \text{Max}[S_T - X_L, 0] - \text{Max}[S_T - X_H, 0]$$

The profit from the spread at expiration equals the spread value—the value of the low-strike call less the value of the high-strike call—less the outlay:

$$
\begin{aligned}
\text{Spread } \Pi \quad &= \text{Spread } V_T - \text{Spread net outlay} \\
&= \text{Max}[S_T - X_L, 0] - \text{Max}[S_T - X_H, 0] - (c_L - c_H) \\
\text{For } S_T \leq X_L: \text{Spread } \Pi \quad &= 0 - 0 - (c_L - c_H) = -(c_L - c_H) \\
\text{For } X_L < S_T < X_H: \text{Spread } \Pi &= S_T - X_L - (c_L - c_H) \\
\text{For } S_T \geq X_H: \text{Spread } \Pi \quad &= X_H - X_L - (c_L - c_H)
\end{aligned}
$$

The breakeven price for the call spread occurs between the exercise prices where the spread value is equal to its net cost:

$$
\begin{aligned}
0 &= \text{Max}[S_T - X_L, 0] - \text{Max}[S_T - X_H, 0] - (c_L - c_H) \\
&= (S_T^* - X_L) - 0 - (c_L - c_H) \\
S_T^* &= X_L + (c_L - c_H)
\end{aligned}
$$

Because the breakeven point occurs between the exercise prices and the stock will be called away above X_H, the maximum profit is capped when $S_T = X_H$:

$$
\begin{aligned}
\text{Max } \Pi &= \text{Max}[S_T - X_L, 0] - \text{Max}[S_T - X_H, 0] - (c_L - c_H) \\
&= X_H - X_L - (c_L - c_H)
\end{aligned}
$$

Below X_L, both call options expire worthless and the investor loses the net premium:

$$
\begin{aligned}
\text{Max Loss} &= \text{Max}[S_T - X_L, 0] - \text{Max}[S_T - X_H, 0] - (c_L - c_H) \\
&= 0 - 0 - (c_L - c_H)
\end{aligned}
$$

A bull spread using **puts** involves a short position in the higher strike price put and a long position in the lower strike price put. Put bull spreads are credit spreads because the cash outflow from the more expensive long position in the lower strike price put is less than the cash inflow from the less expensive short position in the higher strike price put.

Bear Spread Dynamics

A bear spread using **puts** involves a long put at the higher strike price offset by a short put at the lower strike price. Put bear spreads are debit spreads because the cash outflow from the more expensive long put position in the higher strike put is greater than the cash inflow from the less expensive short position in the lower strike put. The cost of the put spread is the net premium difference:

$$
\text{Put spread net outlay} = (p_H - p_L)
$$

The value of the put bear spread at expiration is the net value of the options, which revolves around the price of the underlying:

$$
\text{Spread } V_T = \text{Max}[X_H - S_T, 0] - \text{Max}[X_L - S_T, 0]
$$

The profit from the put bear spread at expiration equals the spread value—the value of the low-strike call less the value of the high-strike call—less the outlay:

$$
\begin{aligned}
\text{Spread } \Pi &= \text{Spread } V_T - \text{Spread net outlay} \\
&= \text{Max}[X_H - S_T, 0] - \text{Max}[X_L - S_T, 0] - (p_H - p_L) \\
\text{For } S_T \leq X_L : \text{Spread } \Pi &= X_H - X_L - (p_H - p_L) \\
\text{For } X_L < S_T < X_H : \text{Spread } \Pi &= X_H - S_T - (p_H - p_L) \\
\text{For } S_T \geq X_H : \text{Spread } \Pi &= -(p_H - p_L)
\end{aligned}
$$

The breakeven price for the put bear spread occurs between the exercise prices where the spread value is equal to its net cost:

$$
\begin{aligned}
0 &= \text{Max}[X_H - S_T, 0] - \text{Max}[X_L - S_T, 0] - (p_H - p_L) \\
&= (X_H - S_T^*) - 0 - (p_H - p_L) \\
S_T^* &= X_H - (p_H - p_L)
\end{aligned}
$$

The maximum gain for the put bear spread occurs where the short put holder exercises the put at X_L, capping the position profits:

$$
\begin{aligned}
\text{Max } \Pi &= \text{Max}[X_H - S_T, 0] - \text{Max}[X_L - S_T, 0] - (p_H - p_L) \\
&= (X_H - S_T) - (X_L - S_T) - (p_H - p_L) \\
&= X_H - X_L - (p_H - p_L)
\end{aligned}
$$

The maximum loss for the put bear spread is capped at the net premium outlay when price rises to X_H or higher and both puts expire worthless:

$$
\begin{aligned}
\text{Max loss} &= \text{Max}[X_H - S_T, 0] - \text{Max}[X_L - S_T, 0] - (p_H - p_L) \\
&= 0 - 0 - (p_H - p_L) \\
&= -(p_H - p_L)
\end{aligned}
$$

A bear spread using **calls** involves buying the higher strike price call and selling the lower strike price call. Call bear spreads are credit spreads because the cash outflow from buying the higher strike price call is less than the inflow from selling the lower strike price call.

The following table summarizes the relationships between the type of spread and options used:

	Calls	Puts
Bull	Debit	Credit
Bear	Credit	Debit

Straddles

A **long straddle** involves buying a put and a call at the same underlying price; a **short straddle** involves selling a put and a call at the same underlying price. A long straddle buys volatility to take advantage of a certain price move in an uncertain direction, but the underlying asset price must move above or below the strike price by at least the total amount spent on the straddle. A short straddle sells volatility to take advantage of a market expected to stagnate.

When the strike price is near the money, straddle delta is close to zero and the strategy is neither bullish nor bearish. Call deltas approach +1 and put deltas approach 0 as the underlying price rises; call deltas approach 0 and put deltas approach −1 as the underlying price falls.

Straddle value at expiration equals the combined value of the long call and the long put:

$$
\text{Straddle } V_T = \text{Max}[S_T - X, 0] + \text{Max}[X - S_T, 0]
$$

Net outlay for the options is:

$$\text{Net Outlay} = (c_0 + p_0)$$

Straddle profits equal the straddle value at expiration less the net outlay for the options:

$$\Pi = \text{Max}[S_T - X, 0] + \text{Max}[X - S_T, 0] - (c_0 + p_0)$$

Maximum loss occurs if the underlying price stagnates at the exercise price, in which case the loss equals the cost of the options. Breakeven occurs at two prices; that is, when $X - S_T$ equals the cost of the options or when $S_T - X$ equals the cost of the options.

Maximum profit is unlimited with a long call but the maximum profit on a long put occurs if the underlying price falls to 0. Profits occur when prices rise more than the position costs or fall more than the position costs:

$$\begin{aligned} \text{Spread } \Pi &= \text{Spread } V_T - \text{Spread net outlay} \\ &= \text{Max}[S_T - X, 0] + \text{Max}[X - S_T, 0] - (c_0 + p_0) \\ \text{For } S_T < X : \text{Spread } \Pi &= X - S_T - (c_0 + p_0) \\ \text{For } S_T > X_H : \text{Spread } \Pi &= S_T - X - (c_0 + p_0) \end{aligned}$$

While long collars benefit from price movement, short collars benefit from the erosion of theta (i.e., time value).

Collars

A collar involves a long position in the underlying, a long put to protect the downside, and a short call to offset the cost of the put. Ideally, the options will have the same strike price. A zero-cost collar involves a long put and a short call with the same premium, but these usually involve a lower exercise price for the put than for the call.

Assuming the zero-cost long collar situation with a long asset, a long put having a strike price of X_L and a short call having a strike price of X_H, position value is:

$$V_T = S_T + \text{Max}[(X_L - S_T), 0] - \text{Max}[(S_T - X_H), 0]$$

The net outlay for the long put and the short call can be represented as:

$$\text{Collar net outlay} = (p_0 - c_0)$$

The profit on the positions include the gain/loss in the underlying asset plus the profit from the options less their cost:

$$\begin{aligned} \text{Position } \Pi &= S_T - S_0 + \text{Max}[X_L - S_T, 0] - \text{Max}[S_T - X_H, 0] - (p_0 - c_0) \\ \text{For } S_T \le X_L : \text{Position } \Pi &= X_L - S_0 - (p_0 - c_0) \\ \text{For } X_L < S_T < X_H : \text{Position } \Pi &= S_T - S_0 - (p_0 - c_0) \\ \text{For } S_T \ge X_H : \text{Position } \Pi &= X_H - S_0 - (p_0 - c_0) \end{aligned}$$

Maximum profit on the zero cost collar is capped at $X_H - S_0$ because it will be called away at any price greater than X_H. The maximum loss is capped at $S_0 - X_L$ because the put will be covered at X_L. Breakeven for a zero-cost collar obviously occurs at S_0.

The put option protects investors much like the fixed value of a bond while the short call removes the benefits of equity ownership in a company. The collar position is economically intermediate between fixed-income exposure and equity exposure.

Calendar Spreads
Calendar spreads sell an option at one date and buy an option at another date. In a long calendar spread, an investor buys the far expiry call and sells the near expiry call. A short calendar spread sells the far expiry call and buys the near expiry call.

The investor is long or short the time value of the option with far expiry options decaying at a slower rate than near expiry options. The investor in a long calendar spread expects a relatively stagnant market or an increase in volatility. The investor in a short calendar spread expects a big move in the underlying or a decrease in volatility.

Volatility Skew

Realized volatility (i.e., historical volatility) measures the range of past price outcomes for an underlying asset and equals the square root of the realized variance of returns. Implied volatility is the value that equates the model price of an option to its market price and is not observable directly. When option prices are compared within or across asset classes or relative to their historical values, they are assessed by their implied volatility.

One-month annualized volatility can be determined from the BSM model generalized for the time left until the option expires and based on a 252-day trading year:

$$\sigma_{Monthly}(\%) = \frac{\sigma_{Annual}(\%)}{\sqrt{\frac{252}{n}}}$$

The simplest way to measure the prevailing volatility level involves using the BSM to calculate implied volatility from ATM option prices in the market. The BSM, however, assumes constant volatility but option-implied volatilities differ with moneyness relative to the exercise price, the type of option (i.e., put or call), and time to expiration. As the market price diverges from the strike price, implied volatility most commonly increases for OTM puts and in-the-money calls and decreases for OTM calls and in-the money puts. The most common graphing for that volatility skew function looks like a *smirk*. When OTM put and call option-implied volatility are both greater than ATM option-implied volatility, the graph looks like a *smile*.

Figure 1: Volatility Smile and Smirk

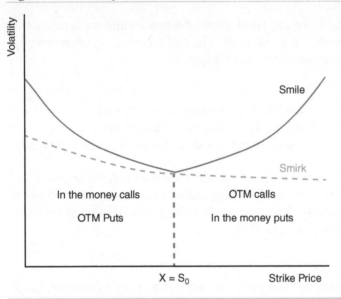

The smirk tends to be more common because investors use OTM puts for portfolio insurance but have less interest in OTM calls. Investor sentiment along with relative demand for puts or calls determines the shape of the smirk. A sharp increase in skew, accompanied by an increase in the absolute level of implied volatility, indicates bearish market sentiment.

Strategy Selection

Investors should consider both the expected underlying asset's price direction and expected volatility change to decide how to establish a position.

		Underlying Asset Outlook		
		Bearish	**Neutral Range**	**Bullish**
Expected volatility change	**Decrease**	Write calls	Write straddle	Write puts
	No change	Write calls/Buy puts	Calendar spread	Buy calls/Write puts
	Increase	Buy Puts	Buy straddle	Buy calls

SWAPS, FORWARDS, AND FUTURES STRATEGIES
Cross-Reference to CFA Institute Assigned Reading #16

The following describes uses for non-option derivatives:

Common Uses	Typical Derivatives
Hedging and directional bets (modifying portfolio returns and risk exposures)	Interest rate, currency, and equity swaps/ futures
Creating desired exposures to an underlying	Forwards, futures, total return swaps
Asset allocation and portfolio rebalancing	Equity index futures, government bond futures, index swaps
Inferring various market expectations	Fed funds futures, inflation swaps, VIX futures

Changing Risk Exposures

Interest Rate Exposures

A portfolio manager can use swaps to change cash flows from a fixed-rate instrument to a floating rate instrument if the investor expects rates to rise. Conversely, the investor can use swaps to change cash flows from floating to fixed if they expect rates to fall. These different purposes could arise in a company with a liability, an investor's interest-bearing asset, or a financial institution wishing to hedge interest rate exposures.

For example, a firm expecting falling interest rates may issue floating rate bonds. If their view on interest rate direction changes to a rising rate scenario, the firm may want to change its floating rate payments to fixed rates to avoid payments to bondholders that increase with rates. Only the fixed- or floating-rate counterparty will make a payment to the other (i.e., a net payment).

Interest rate swaps may also be used to manage target duration for a bond portfolio. In that case, the portfolio manager expecting rates to rise will decrease duration of the portfolio and the manager expecting rates to fall will increase target duration. Duration for the swap is the net duration between the two cash flow streams exchanged. For a pay-fixed, receive-floating swap the duration could be expressed as the long floating-rate duration less the short fixed-rate duration:

$$MDUR_S = MDUR_{\text{Floating}} - MDUR_{\text{Fixed}}$$

This leads to the insight that the swap notional amount can adjust portfolio duration to a target duration:

$$N_S = MV_P \times \left(\frac{MDUR_T - MDUR_P}{MDUR_S} \right)$$

where
MV_P = portfolio market value
$MDUR$ = modified duration target, portfolio, and swap

Interest Rate Forwards and Futures

A forward rate agreement (FRA) is used mainly to hedge a loan expected to be taken out in the future or to hedge against changes in the level of interest rates in the future. FRAs are advance-settled, meaning that the net payment among counterparties equals the interest rate agreed in the contract and the actual rate at settlement, applied on the notional amount and discounted to present.

The same may be accomplished using exchange-traded futures, although this involves less customization but eliminates the counterparty risk. These may be settled based on some index value; for example, Eurodollar futures are cash settled based on a principal value of $1 million and three-month maturity and are quoted in terms of the IMM index equal to 100 less the annualized yield. The basis point value (BPV) shows the dollar movement for a 0.01% (i.e., 1 bp or 0.0001) change in futures contract value:

$$BPV = \text{Face value} \times 0.01\% \times \frac{\text{Days}}{360}$$

$$BPV_{IMM} = \$1,000,000 \times 0.01\% \times \frac{90}{360} = \$25$$

Fixed Income Futures

Eurodollar futures are commonly used to hedge remaining maturities of up to three years. Fixed income (bond) futures rather than interest rate futures may be more appropriate to hedge longer-term exposure.

A contract seller usually chooses to close the contract prior to delivery, but may choose which security to deliver if necessary. Bond futures permit the seller to satisfy delivery obligations with bonds maturing within a window after the delivery date. The seller will, of course, choose the cheapest-to-deliver (CTD) bond meeting the criteria and the invoice to the buyer (i.e., principal invoice amount) must be adjusted by a conversion factor (CF) reflecting specific characteristics of the security tendered by the seller:

$$\text{Principal invoice amount} = \text{Contract size} \times (\text{Futures settlement price}/100) \times CF$$

The principal invoice amount would add any accrued interest.

The basis for the futures contract equals the spot cash price for the seller's tendered security less the fixed-income futures price multiplied by the CF. The basis of the CTD bond will be close to zero. Arbitrageurs can profit by purchasing the lesser-valued of other bonds and the futures contract.

BPV for the CTD, the target, and the portfolio are calculated using a formula presented earlier:

$$BPV = \text{Face value} \times 0.01\% \times \frac{\text{Days}}{360}$$

Duration of the bond futures contract will depend on the CTD bond adjusted for the conversion factor:

$$BPV_F = \frac{BPV_{CTD}}{CF}$$

Hedge ratio BPV, also based on a previous formula relationship is:

$$BPVHR = \frac{BPV_T - BPV_P}{BPV_F}$$
$$= \frac{BPV_T - BPV_P}{BPV_{CTD}} \times CF$$

Currency Exposures

Exchange rates change over time, creating **currency risk** for those exposed to the two currencies. These risks can be managed by using swaps, forwards, and futures.

Currency Swaps

A firm may be able to obtain lower-cost financing for a foreign project in its local currency. It could then use a cross-currency basis swap to exchange the local currency for the foreign currency. A currency swap is different from an interest rate swap by (1) using primarily floating rates on both sides, (2) associating the interest rates to different currencies, and (3) potentially exchanging the notional amounts at inception of the swap.

The relationship necessary for covered interest rate parity is:

$$(1 + r_d) = S_{f/d}(1 + r_f)F_{d/f}$$
$$F_{f/d} = S_{f/d}\frac{(1 + r_f)}{(1 + r_d)}$$
$$\% \text{ Forward premium} = \frac{r_f - r_d}{1 + r_d} \approx r_f - r_d$$

Covered interest parity generally does not hold, however, creating a basis in the swap equal to the swap interest rate *difference* less the interest rate *difference* used to determine the forward exchange rate (i.e., %forward premium).

The basis, then, is:

$$\text{Basis} = r_f - r_d - \% \text{Forward premium}$$

Note that the first two rates are the foreign and domestic rates used in the swap. This basis will generally be included along with the local currency reference floating rate. Cross-currency basis spreads vary over time and are driven by supply/demand for cross-currency financing as well as credit and liquidity factors.

The same idea may be used to implement a carry trade in which a trader borrows in one currency, uses a currency swap for a country where the interest rate difference is greater than implied by the forward rate, and converts back at the end of the swap. Negative basis indicates borrowing the domestic currency to lend in a foreign currency.

Currency Forwards and Futures

Corporations may use forward contracts to manage risk of foreign currency cash flows because they can be customized. Dealers and investors often use standardized futures contracts to manage currency risk in a portfolio.

For example, a firm expecting to receive foreign cash at a future time and wanting to fix the value in local currency terms would sell the foreign currency forward:

$$\text{Contracts} = \frac{E(CF_T)}{\text{Contract size}}$$

If the changes in futures and spot prices are equal during the life of the futures contract, the hedge will be fully effective.

Equity Exposures

Equity Swaps

Equity swaps involve one party exchanging an equity return for a fixed payment, a floating payment, or another equity return. The equity return may be based on a single security, a basket of securities, or an index. They are preferred by investors with limited access to a desired market, when taxes apply to stocks but not to swaps, or when corporate actions (e.g., distributions, splits, etc.) increase monitoring costs on the equity position.

Equity swaps are usually collateralized to reduce counterparty risk; swaps involving a single security are usually cash settled.

The equity party agrees to pay returns on the underlying equity position to the other party; that party receives cash flow when the underlying return is negative. That party also receives the fixed, floating, or other equity leg return. If the other equity leg return is negative, they pay that cash flow to the counterparty. The return on the underlying includes the dividend. The net payment can be represented symbolically for a long or short equity swap as:

$$\text{Net swap payment} = \text{Sign} \times V_{\text{Notional}} \times (r_1 - r_2)\left(\frac{n}{m}\right)$$

where

$$
\begin{aligned}
\text{Sign } +/- &= \text{Long position/short position in leg 1} \\
V_{\text{Notional}} &= \text{Notional value of the swap position} \\
r_1, r_2 &= \text{Return on leg 1 and 2, respectively} \\
\frac{n}{m} &= \text{Partial year adjustment factor}
\end{aligned}
$$

If leg 1 represents an equity position and leg 2 represents a reference rate plus spread, a positive sign is long the equity return and pays the floating rate plus spread. The equity return may include both a capital gain return and dividend yield. The other leg will specify the criteria for that return. If returns are annualized and the actual period is partial year, make sure to adjust returns by the last term.

[Note that there are a variety of ways n/m might be expressed.]

Equity Forwards and Futures

Investors in equity forwards or futures may desire to achieve portfolio diversification, implement tactical allocation decisions, or gain international exposure. The instrument may be based on an underlying index or an individual stock. Settlement generally involves a net payment on an index underlying or delivery of the stock on a single stock underlying.

The number of contracts required on a position requires acknowledging not only the contract price, but the number of shares represented by the contract:

$$\text{Contracts} = \frac{V_{\text{Notional}}}{V_F} = \frac{V_{\text{Notional}}}{P_F \times \text{Multiplier}}$$

Portfolio or position beta may adjusted by using the following relationship:

$$N_f = \frac{V_{\text{Portfolio}}}{V_F}\left(\frac{\beta_T - \beta_{\text{Portfolio}}}{\beta_F}\right)$$

The sign of the resulting calculation will be positive if target beta exceeds portfolio beta, indicating a long futures position. Complete hedging involves target beta of 0. Equitizing a cash position involves target beta of 1 and portfolio beta of 0.

Derivatives on Volatility

Investors wishing to hedge a portfolio against declining asset values can do so by selling volatility.

Volatility Futures and Options

Volatility is the standard deviation of returns and volatility indexes measure the market's volatility expectation implied in option prices. To hedge equity values in a downturn, the stock market's implied volatility must increase by more than volatility expectations reflected in the VIX at inception of the volatility index futures contract.

The term structure for volatility futures reflects current volatility, expected future volatility, and supply and demand conditions by participants in the VIX futures market. The term structure is flat if investors expect a stable market over the near to long term. A futures market in **backwardation** indicates that investors expect declining volatility; a market in **contango** indicates that investors expect rising volatility. Backwardation is the normal condition because investors typically believe volatility will be higher in the short term.

Figure 2: Futures Backwardation and Contango over Time

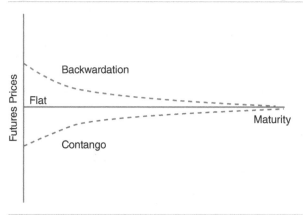

Longer-maturity contracts are less sensitive to short-term VIX movements such that futures prices may not reflect short-term changes in the volatility index, especially when it experiences large spikes. Long-term contracts become more costly due to roll-down when the short-term part of the term structure is steep.

VIX options are European-style contracts that provide asymmetrical exposure to potential increases or decreases in anticipated volatility. Traders purchase call options when they expect increased volatility (due to falling asset prices) and purchase put options when they expect decreased volatility (due to stable market conditions).

Variance Swaps

Investors can make directional bets on variance or can hedge portfolio variance with a variance swap. A swap buyer pays the difference between the fixed variance strike and annualized realized variance on the underlying over the period specified and applied to notional variance. No cash changes hands at swap inception or during the life of the swap, only at maturity.

A long variance position receives a cash settlement from the seller when realized variance is greater than the swap strike and makes a payment when realized variance is less than strike.

Traders think in terms of volatility rather than variance, so variance swaps are agreed by the parties in terms of **vega notional** rather than variance notional. Vega notional relates to average profit or loss for a 1% change in volatility from the strike; that is, a 1% increase in volatility on a $50,000 vega notional will result in a payoff by $50,000.

Swap payoffs increase as volatility increases (due to convexity in the position). The swaps become particularly effective at hedging long equity portfolios during periods of extreme market volatility. Swap sellers believe such tail risk will not materialize and are said to be short volatility.

Although put and call options for all strike prices are not available, a long variance swap can be simulated by a short futures contract on the asset and the sum of static positions in puts and calls over many maturities. A long variance swap is long gamma and has a convex payoff. Thus, the strike level set for a variance swap corresponds to the implied volatility of a put with a strike price equal to 90% of the current asset price.

The variance swap value at any time t relies on the realized variance in the underlying at the measurement date less the variance implied in the options for the new tenor, both adjusted for periodicity:

$$V_{t,VS} = N_{VAR} \times PV_t(T) \times \left\{ [VOL_{\text{Realized}}(0,t)]^2 \frac{t}{T} + [VOL_{\text{Implied}}(0,t)]^2 \frac{T-t}{T} - \text{Strike}^2 \right\}$$

where

$$N_{VAR} = \frac{N_{\text{Vega}}}{2 \times \text{Strike}}$$

$PV_t(T) = PVIF$, the present value of $1 received at time T

The settlement payment at maturity depends on the notional variance multiplied by the difference between realized variance and strike variance:

$$\begin{aligned} \text{Settlement}_T &= \frac{N_{\text{Vega}}}{2 \times \text{Strike}} \left(\sigma^2 - X^2 \right) \\ &= N_{VAR} \left(\sigma^2 - X^2 \right) \end{aligned}$$

CURRENCY MANAGEMENT: AN INTRODUCTION
Cross-Reference to CFA Institute Assigned Reading #17

Currency Effects on Portfolio Risk and Return

Notation, Terminology, and Convention

Although **foreign exchange**, **FX**, or **forex** markets identify currency exchange markets, the terms "foreign" and "domestic" are not used except from a trader's perspective.

Base currency (B) identifies the subject of the quote in the denominator; **price currency** (P) identifies the currency used against the base in the numerator:

- Quoting format: P/B (i.e., units of price currency per unit of base currency):
  - For example, 0.9800 USD/CHF means 0.9800 U.S. dollars per Swiss franc; alternatively, the price of a Swiss franc is 0.9800 U.S. dollars.
  - Foreign exchange markets may show this as CHF/USD 0.9800, although only the previous description will be used here.
- The exam often indicates currency exchange by completely describing it: "0.98 U.S. dollars per Swiss franc."

Pricing conventions:

- Usually there are four decimals, with the rightmost decimal known as a "pip."
- Forward quotes may have five or six decimals.
- Currencies requiring many units (e.g., JPY) may be carried out to only two decimals.

Dealer quotes:

- **Bid quote**: Price at which the trader will buy and market participant may sell the base currency.
- **Ask quote (offer)**: Price at which the trader will sell (offer) and market participant may buy the base currency.
- **Bid–ask spread (bid–offer spread or market width)**: The ask less the bid (i.e., **market width**).

Ask (offer) prices are almost always higher than bid prices so that the dealer earns a spread.

Forward contracts describe any agreement for settlement past spot closing. Spot closing takes place with T+2 two-day settlement for most and T+1 for U.S./Canadian dollars.

> **IMPORTANT:** ABC/ XYZ bid–ask spreads can be converted to XYZ/ABC bid–ask spreads via reciprocals, but the positions switch place (i.e., the new ask quote will be the higher of the new reciprocal values).

- Points over/under spot: Difference between forward rate quote and spot quote:
  - Scaled to the number of decimal points in the quote
  - Relevant to the maturity (i.e., not annualized)
- Forward premium: Points above spot
- Forward discount: Points below spot

Forward premium/discount for various maturities may be listed as a spot bid–ask in P/B terms, plus/minus the points over/under spot; divide by 10,000 for four-decimal quotes and by 100 for two-digit quotes (JPY).

For example, 1.0168 bid for CHF/USD at −58.94 is converted as:

$$1.0168 + \left(\frac{-58.94}{10,000}\right) = 1.0168 - 0.005894 = 1.010906$$

Forward **maturity** describes the time from spot settlement to forward settlement.

Portfolio managers use forwards to hedge currency risk of assets denominated in a foreign currency. To roll over a hedge position, they swap a maturing forward position into a later-maturity forward.

- Matched swaps have equal amount and maturity.
- Swaps with the same maturities are priced using the bid–ask midpoint.

Return Decomposition
Decomposition describes the process of attributing a portfolio outcome (i.e., risk, return, etc.) to the asset classes or securities that make up the portfolio:

- **Foreign currency return, r_{FC}** — Return in the asset's home currency
- **Foreign exchange return, r_{FX}** — Return attributable to change in value of the P/B relationship
- **Domestic currency return, r_{DC}** — Foreign currency return in terms of the investor's home currency

For each asset **i**, weighted based on **domestic** currency asset values:

$$r_{DC,p} = \sum_{i=1}^{n} \omega_i[(1 + r_{FC,i})(1 + r_{FX,i})\text{-}1]$$

Negative weights can represent short positions, but all weights must sum to 100%.

Foreign exchange return must be priced using the investor's reporting (domestic) currency:

$$r_{FX} = \frac{S_{DC/FC,T}}{S_{DC/FC,t}} - 1$$

Volatility Decomposition
Domestic return variance σ^2_{DC} depends on variances for asset return in domestic currency terms and for foreign exchange return, as well as the correlation of asset return in domestic currency terms and foreign exchange returns:

$$\sigma^2_{DC} = \omega_{FC}\sigma^2_{FC} + \omega_{FX}\sigma^2_{FX} + 2\omega_{FC}\sigma_{FC}\omega_{FX}\sigma_{FX}\rho_{FC,FX}$$

With no exchange rate risk, $\sigma^2_{DC} = \sigma^2_{FC}$. Diversification of uncorrelated assets and currencies lowers domestic return risk for the portfolio, as does short selling one of two correlated assets.

Reliability of volatility-related variables may be compromised due to:

- Computational challenges of using multiple assets
- Varying historical volatility relationships

IMPORTANT: Reporting generally favors use of standard deviation (i.e., the square root of the variance) to ensure comparability with percentage return.

- Dependence on measurement period
- Consensus forecast limitations:
  - Sensitive to sample size and composition
  - Not always available with a consistent starting point
  - Not always immediately reported

Historical volatility may also differ from **implied volatility** (i.e., risk priced into option contracts).

Strategic Decisions for FX Risk

Strategic decisions involve the degree of active management (i.e., exposure to exchange rate risk).

The investment policy statement (IPS) specifies:

- Target percentage of currency exposure passively hedged
- Active management corridor around the target exposure
- Hedge rebalancing frequency
- Benchmark to assess hedging performance
- Permitted hedging instruments (e.g., types of forwards/options)

Optimization

Portfolios circumvent the calculation problem of simultaneously solving all possible asset/exchange return combinations along with their correlations by:

1. Optimizing the portfolio of fully hedged returns
2. Selecting desired active currency exposures

Portfolio optimization for foreign assets follows the same basic steps as for domestic assets, resulting in a set of efficient portfolios along a risk/return frontier.

Selecting Currency Exposures

Some studies indicate that FX hedging benefits for global bond and fixed-income portfolios depend on the domestic currency. Other studies indicate that longer-term trends and current market conditions determine hedging benefits.

Reserve currencies (e.g., U.S. dollar) tend to appreciate in a global currency crisis as investors seek safety.

Active viewpoints cite potential alpha from currency exposure:

- Market inefficiencies
- Short-term relationship changes

Hedging costs include:

- Trading costs:
  - Trading infrastructure costs (i.e., **administrative costs** such as technology costs, costs of banking in different currencies, personnel and training costs of front-, middle-, and back-office operations, etc.)
  - Monitoring costs
  - Unrecoverable costs of expired options

- ○ **Churning** (i.e., paying away the dealer spread, especially to remain fully hedged)
        - ○ Potential losses in rolling forward hedges
    - Opportunity costs: Giving up potential FX returns

Hedging viewpoints include:

- Partial hedging: Leave some of the FX risk unhedged.
    - ○ Global equity—Diversification benefits of uncorrelated assets/currencies
    - ○ Fixed income—Less or no hedging:
        - Bonds and FX returns both highly correlated with interest rates
        - Little or no diversification benefit
- Unhedged: Remain unhedged and reduce costs.
    - ○ Purchasing power parity (PPP) and other parity links drive long-term %Δs to 0.
    - ○ There are no long-term benefits to FX hedging.
    - ○ Use an unhedged portfolio benchmark.

Hedge more fully as:

- Risk preference decreases.
- *Ex post* (i.e., lost opportunity) regret decreases.
- Income/liquidity needs increase.
- Time horizon contracts.
- Fixed-income assets in portfolio decrease.
- Cost of hedging decreases.
- Perception of currency exposure benefit decreases.

Hedging Strategies
From risk averse to risk seeking:

- Passive hedging: Protects portfolio with full hedging; removes manager opinions on FX.
    - ○ Reflects lack of adequate currency return for additional risk.
    - ○ Performance mirrors asset-only return benchmark (i.e., no currency return).
- Discretionary hedging: Manager protects portfolio with hedging; adds alpha.
    - ○ Percentage deviation of actual MV_{FC} from target value in FC terms
    - ○ Performance measured against hedged asset benchmark
- Active currency management: Manager seeks alpha.
    - ○ Mandated risk limits
    - ○ Performance measured against hedged asset benchmark
- Currency overlay portfolio: Separate FX account or separate manager:
    - ○ May be restricted to FX exposure
    - ○ May be FX as an asset class:
        - Not limited to asset portfolio exposures
        - Alpha-seeking active management

Tactical Decisions

Tactical decisions involve manager choices for active currency management.

Economic Fundamentals
An emphasis on economic fundamentals assumes that exchange rate determination in free markets is based on underlying economic relationships (i.e., purchasing power parity).

IMPORTANT:
Currency alpha mandate for FX as an asset class should have minimum correlation with other sources of alpha—especially currency exposures—as well as other asset classes.

AA
CM

Simple model:

- The real exchange rate is determined by the ratio of real purchasing power.
- Short-term variations reflect changes in differential:
  - Inflation
  - Country risk premiums

The base currency in a P/B quote pair appreciates (i.e., more P units are required to purchase each B unit) if there is an increase in:

- B's long-run real purchasing power
- Interest rates (real or nominal), which increases demand for B's currency to lend
- Expected foreign inflation (P and all other countries)
- Foreign risk premiums (P and all other countries)

Technical Analysis
Underlying assumptions of technical analysis are:

- Underlying economic fundamentals are discounted in favor of supply and demand cues.
- Analysts can forecast future prices using past price data.
- Repetitions in past price data provide opportunities.

A **resistance level** occurs where assets are overbought; a **support level** occurs where assets are oversold. As an asset value approaches a support or resistance level, sell or buy stops are triggered that resist further gain or support the price from further loss.

> IMPORTANT: Technical analysis is less useful in nontrending markets.

Momentum carries prices through resistance or support levels.

Carry Trade
The **carry trade** involves:

- Funding currency: Lower interest rate currencies (borrow)
- Investment currency: Higher interest rate currencies (lend)

$$\%\Delta S_{P/B} \approx i_P - i_B$$

Where base currency is the low interest rate currency in the P/B relationship:

Uncovered interest rate parity suggests that positive %Δs should result in future *price* currency depreciation to offset the yield advantage. Currencies may, however, vary from expected value for long periods, creating a return opportunity in forward rates (i.e., **forward rate bias**).

Covered interest rate parity suggests that covering the eventual currency repatriation with a forward contract (i.e., buying the *base* currency) should eliminate the forward rate bias (i.e., low interest rate currencies trade at a forward premium to spot):

$$\frac{F_{P/B} - S_{P/B}}{S_{P/B}} = \frac{(i_P - i_B)\left(\frac{t}{360}\right)}{1 + i_B\left(\frac{t}{360}\right)}$$

> IMPORTANT: Lower-volatility carry trades have greater opportunity for success.

Carry trade portfolios need not have the same number of funding and investment currencies; managers can weight exposures for r_{FX} and σ_{FX} viewpoints.

Volatility Trading

Delta hedging involves using an offsetting spot transaction to completely offset currency risk, or forward contracts in a hedge ratio that completely offsets FX movements.

Volatility trading involves hedging all or part of the volatility risk (i.e., sensitivity of option price to changes in price volatility of the underlying) using option *vega*: Note that the currency trader is not long the base currency. Instead, the trader has a strong view about the volatility of the base currency.

- **Straddle**: Offsetting at-the-money put and call; makes money when either put or call goes in-the-money more than option premiums.
- **Strangle**: Offsetting out-of-the-money put and call; makes money when either goes in-the-money more than (less expensive) option premiums.

Managers use delta hedging and volatility trading together to offset price risk while making bets on price volatility (but not direction of price movement).

Volatility will remain low for long periods, but extreme volatility will be brief and result from unexpected market stress. Speculative volatility traders use net-short positions to capture premium from options expiring out-of-the-money.

Currency Management Tools

Strategic management focuses on long-term benchmark-related decisions, whether passive or in the active management spectrum. Tactical management focuses on shorter-term decisions around the benchmark. Both strategic and tactical approaches use forwards, options, and FX swaps.

Forward Contracts

Managers use both forward and futures contracts to manage currency exposures. They prefer forwards because:

- Flexible contracts conform more readily to specific portfolio needs; futures are standardized as to amount and maturity date.
- Forwards can be written in any currency pair (i.e., two futures contracts would have to be written to cross-hedge if one of the currency pairs is not readily paired with the other).
- Forwards require no initial margin; futures contracts require initial margin and mark-to-market maintenance.
- Forwards trade in a more liquid market than do futures.

The underlying asset value changes over time, and the hedge ratio may drift from the desired exposure:

- **Static hedge**: No hedge resetting is performed. While less costly, this will increase currency exposure as the underlying drifts.
- **Dynamic hedge**: Size, maturity, and ratio of forwards are adjusted in accordance with the direction/amount of underlying asset change and the degree of active management permitted.

Mismatched swaps (i.e., from changes in the underlying or change in desired exposure) consist of:

- Initiation: Sell foreign currency (equal to initial portfolio value) forward for domestic currency.
- Near leg (i.e., expiring forward):
  - Settle near leg by buying foreign currency for domestic currency in spot market.
  - Receive initial domestic currency value of portfolio.
  - Portfolio profit (or loss) in domestic currency terms results from asset return and FX return; the latter is offset by profit (or loss) in domestic currency terms on the forward.
- Far leg (i.e., new forward):
  - Sell foreign currency (equal to new portfolio value) forward for domestic currency.

Roll yield is the spot exchange rate at any given time plus the points for a given maturity (i.e., the implicit cost of the hedge). Roll yield equals the absolute value of the forward premium or discount with a sign corresponding to gain or loss:

$$\left| \frac{F_{P/B} - S_{P/B}}{S_{P/B}} \right|$$

- Positive roll yield (i.e., gain): Trading the **forward rate bias** (i.e., equivalent to a **carry trade**):
  - Buying the base currency at a forward discount
  - Selling the base currency at a forward premium
- Negative roll yield (i.e., loss): Trading against the forward rate bias (i.e., equivalent to a negative carry trade):
  - Selling the base currency at a forward discount
  - Buying the base currency at a forward premium

A risk-averse manager will still accept a negative net value hedged position if the risk of a higher FX loss outweighs the certain hedging cost. A risk-neutral manager will **not** implement that hedge.

Risk-averse managers may go unhedged if the negative net value hedged position is so great as to outweigh the unhedged alternative.

Currency Options
Currency options are European exercise (i.e., exercisable at expiration) instruments that offer the right but not the obligation to buy the underlying currency (calls) or sell the underlying currency (puts) at a preagreed price.

Protective puts match put options to a long currency position:

- Depreciation: Manager has the right to exercise the put option for a strike price better than the spot price.
- Appreciation: Manager allows the put to expire unexercised.

IMPORTANT: Negative roll yield weighs against using a fully hedged position; trading the forward bias weighs toward complete hedging (or overhedging).

IMPORTANT: The advantage of options is avoiding the loss of future currency gains (the same as with forward hedging).

Option value drivers include:

- Intrinsic value: Difference between the strike price of the option and the spot exchange rate; at-the money (ATM) options are more expensive than out-of-the-money (OTM) options.
- Time value: Premium for time to expiration:
  - Greater as volatility increases
  - Decays toward expiry

Hedging Cost-Reduction Strategies

Cost-reduction measures involve:

- Less upside potential
- Less downside protection

Over-/Underhedging Using Forwards

Less downside protection moves from 100% hedged to more discretionary positions.

- **Overhedged** (expect depreciation): Sell more than 100% of the base position.
- **Fully hedged** (neutral expectation): Sell 100% of the base position.
- **Underhedged** (expect appreciation): Sell less than 100% of the base position.

Dynamic hedging with forwards:

- Base currency depreciates: Increase hedge ratio back to 100% cover.
- Base currency appreciates: Decrease hedge ratio back to 100% cover.

Forwards give upside potential away for lower cost.

Protective Puts Using OTM Options

Options are used to:

- Limit downside risk while maintaining upside potential.
- Earn option writing premiums.

OTM options are less expensive than ATM options, but introduce downside risk.

Reduce premium on protection with:

- **Short risk reversal** (i.e., collar): Buy OTM put and sell OTM call.
- **Long risk reversal**: Buy OTM call and sell OTM put.

Put Spread

> IMPORTANT: Short and long positions in risk reversals depend on selling or buying the call, respectively.

Put spreads involve buying an OTM put and funding it by writing a deeper OTM put with the same maturity. Cheaper or zero-cost methods are used by altering:

- Notional amounts: Increase in OTM notional:
  - Greater exposure if expiry with price lower than furthest price from ATM
  - More appropriate for expressing manager view than for hedge
- Strike prices: Moving strike prices closer together; decreases hedge protection.

To profit from modest depreciation, fully hedge with forwards and overlay with a put spread as a tactical position.

Seagull Spread

A **short seagull spread** involves a put spread and a short call; that is, long a protective put to sell the base currency, short a deep OTM put, and short a call. The short positions in a put and a call are the "wings," and the long put closer to the money is the "body."

The long position comprising a short seagull spread may allow a more expensive ATM option because the manager sold two options.

A **long seagull spread** involves a short put closer to or at-the-money and long call and long put in the wings. This provides inexpensive downside protection.

Exotic Options

Vanilla options are simple European put and call options used by corporations and investment funds.

> **IMPORTANT:** "Long" and "short" spread designations are determined by the option positions in the wings of the spread.

Exotic options are more complex options with special features used by currency overlay managers and speculators.

While they are a high-profit-margin item for dealers, exotic options have disadvantages:

- They are difficult to value for regulatory and accounting purposes.
- It is difficult to obtain more favorable hedge treatment for financial reporting.
- There is a lack of familiarity among smaller potential users.

> **IMPORTANT:** Exotic options allow low-price-risk customization at the expense of less downside protection or upside potential.

Vanilla options may be modified to exotic with the addition of special features:

- **Knock-in**: A vanilla option is created when the spot price reaches a predetermined price.
- **Knock-out**: The option is extinguished when the spot price reaches a predetermined price.

Binary options (also known as **digital options** or **all-or-nothing options**) pay a fixed amount when the spot price reaches a predetermined price. They:

> **IMPORTANT:** Knock-in and knock-out options create less costly, but more restrictive risk protection.

- Leverage bets on FX direction.
- Have a specified extreme payoff if successful.
- Are more expensive.

Hedging Process

For a price/base (P/B) pair:

- **Price currency**: The portfolio currency, also known as the exposure, transaction, or foreign currency
- **Base currency**: The counter currency, also known as the investor's domestic currency

Return is calculated in terms of the investor's domestic currency, but includes both an asset return component and a foreign exchange component.

Investors may choose to hedge the value of the portfolio in terms of B (i.e., keep it the same relative to P):

- **Appreciation of B**: P units increase per unit of B (i.e., B is worth more).
- **Depreciation of B**: P units decrease per unit of B (i.e., B is worth less).

Considerations in the hedging process, especially with active management, are:

> **IMPORTANT:** For a portfolio of assets with no gains, losses, or expenses, a complete hedge (i.e., the manager has an uncertain viewpoint or is risk averse) would allow conversion into the same amount of originally invested currency.

1. Identify currency to hedge (i.e., maintain or increase value of) as the base in the P/B pair.
2. Determine price movement expectation.
3. Active management: Directional bias applied to express market viewpoint:
   - Appreciation—Less hedging (or buy); involves long base currency instrument:
     - Long call option or long forward contract (i.e., buying the base currency forward)
     - Writing options or buying OTM call to reduce costs
     - Bullish exotic strategies that pay off if the base currency appreciates
   - Depreciation—More/complete hedging (or selling) involves:
     - Long put option or short forward contract (i.e., selling the currency forward)
     - Writing options or buying OTM put to reduce costs
     - Bearish exotic strategies that pay off if the base currency depreciates

Multiple Foreign Currencies

Although the basic tools are the same as for a single currency, hedging multiple foreign currencies requires considering correlations.

Cross Hedge

A **cross hedge** describes using one asset or derivative to offset risk on another asset. Cross-hedging two assets using negatively correlated currency exposures can avoid the expense of directly hedging the assets.

Macro Hedge

A macro hedge occurs when risk exposures for the entire portfolio are hedged rather than hedging individual asset risk exposures:

- Gold limits risk from extreme market stress.
- Asset index derivatives.
- Fixed-weight basket of currency derivatives.

Minimum-Variance Hedge Ratio

A **minimum-variance hedge ratio** describes an optimal cross-hedging ratio (**b**) determined by regression analysis to minimize the error term:

$$\epsilon = y - (a + bx)$$

Both the percentage change in value of the asset to be hedged (**y**) and the percentage change in value of the hedging instrument (**x**) are measured in terms of the investor's domestic currency.

> **IMPORTANT:** This is not used for direct hedging via forwards, but is useful for cross-hedging and macro hedges.

Basis risk occurs due to imperfect correlation between currency price movement and the hedging instrument. This can require reestimating minimum variance hedge ratios.

Managing Emerging Market Currencies

Emerging market currencies are subject to:

- Normal conditions: Higher transaction costs (i.e., wider bid–ask spreads)
- Extreme conditions: Severe loss of liquidity

Cross-hedging in thinly traded currencies can become expensive. For example, one trade may go through one bank and another trade through another bank, or liquidity for the first leg may be fine but liquidity for the second leg has been impaired by market conditions.

Positions in an illiquid currency asset may be easy to enter gradually, but difficult to exit quickly. This can especially occur with popular carry trades or fad investment regions.

Currencies subject to these extreme illiquidity events have return distributions with fatter tails and negative skewness. This makes comparing Sharpe ratios difficult.

Central banks support a declining currency by increasing the policy interest rate. Hedging costs increase due to negative roll yield as forward prices for the emerging market currency fall in response to the new higher rate and demand for the currency.

Portfolios become more correlated and less diversified when contagion occurs and one country suffers from another country's currency woes. Haven currencies (e.g., USD, GBP, EUR, etc.) become popular, and a large basket of emerging market currencies becomes unpopular.

Extreme market events can occur when pegged currencies break or governments intervene in markets or currencies.

Nondeliverable Forwards (NDFs)

A **nondeliverable forward (NDF)** circumvents currency controls by going long the controlled currency, but cash delivery is made in the noncontrolled currency of a pair (i.e., in the P/B notation, B is cash delivered rather than physical delivery of P).

Forward pricing in NDFs for countries with capital controls may reflect supply-and-demand conditions rather than official pricing of the controlled currency.

AA
CM

IMPORTANT: NDFs will often seek to profit by appreciation of the noncontrolled currency of a pair.

FI
EPM

FI
EPM

OVERVIEW OF FIXED-INCOME PORTFOLIO MANAGEMENT
Cross-Reference to CFA Institute Assigned Reading #18

Roles of Fixed-Income Securities in Portfolios

Diversification Benefits

Diversification benefits are possible by combining U.S. and international investment-grade bonds, high-yield bonds, emerging market bonds, and equities:

- High-yield bonds, emerging market bonds, and equities have high correlation with each other.
- U.S. investment-grade bond subgroups have low correlation with equities.
- International investment-grade bonds have low correlation with equities and U.S. high-yield bonds, but moderate correlation with emerging market bonds.

Additional diversification benefits are possible by combining fixed-income asset classes with real estate and commodities.

A flight to higher quality is observed during times of market stress.

Correlations increase during times of market stress as investors simultaneously avoid all risk assets.

Regular Cash Flow Benefits

Cash flows can be structured to meet needs, such as the need for payment of some currency amount.

Laddering (i.e., staggering) fixed-income maturities can help reduce interest rate risk and bond price risk.

Credit events (e.g., failure to make scheduled payments, change in issuer credit status, etc.) or market events—such as reduction in interest rates resulting in early repayment of underlying mortgages in MBS securities—can change cash flow patterns, which in turn can require portfolio adjustments.

Table 1:Inflation Protection Features

	Coupon	Principal
Fixed-coupon vanilla bonds	Unprotected	Unprotected
Floating-rate securities	Protected	Unprotected
Inflation-linked securities	Protected	Protected

Inflation-linked bonds can effectively be considered a separate asset class, and provide diversification benefits against other types of fixed-income securities.

Fixed-Income Mandates

Fixed-income securities are structured based on objectives:

- Liability-based mandates: Offset or match future liabilities with expected payments.
- Total return mandates: Attempt to outperform a benchmark.

Liability-Based Mandates

- Individuals: Planning for college education or new home purchase.
- Institutions: Planning for pension payouts, life insurance payouts, and so on.

Immunization reduces or eliminates the risks to liability funding arising from interest rate volatility over the planning horizon. Types are:

- Cash flow matching: Exactly matching coupon and maturity inflows with expected payouts.
- Duration matching: Changes in interest rates affect asset values similarly to liability values whether increasing or decreasing:
  - Present value (PV) of assets matches PV of liabilities, *and*
  - Duration of liabilities matches duration of assets.

Disadvantages of cash flow matching:

- Purchase of proper maturities/amounts may cause timing mismatches that require reinvesting matured issues (reinvestment risk) or other exposure.
- High transaction costs exist even with quantitative optimization approaches.
- Rebalancing may be desirable to maintain lowest cost mix of securities (changes in available issues and market conditions).

Disadvantages of duration matching:

- Does not protect against issuer-specific events or default.
- Does not protect against changes in yield curve shape (i.e., slope, curvature, etc.); protects only against *parallel* yield curve changes.
- Frequent rebalancing is required as market conditions (and thus durations and PVs) change.

Exam hint: Only cash flow matching with zero-coupon bonds at exact maturity perfectly immunizes the portfolio. Interest rate change effects are irrelevant because the bonds are held to maturity. Reinvestment risk doesn't exist because the cash flows all occur at the point needed to defease the liability.

Contingent immunization involves active management for portfolio surplus (assets less liabilities greater than zero). If surplus falls to predetermined level, only immunization.

Horizon matching uses cash flow matching for short-term liabilities (i.e., maturing in less than 5 years) and duration matching for long-term liabilities.

Total Return Mandates

Key metrics measure portfolio performance relative to a benchmark:

- Active return: Portfolio return less benchmark return.
- Active risk (aka tracking risk, tracking error): Annualized standard deviation of active returns.

Total return mandates are classified based on active return-risk levels.

FI
EPM

- Pure indexing:
  - Match the benchmark weights as closely as possible.
  - Match risk factors.
  - Low turnover, generally with index or tiny variations from benchmark.
- Enhanced indexing:
  - Slight mismatch with benchmark weights to achieve 20–30 bps outperformance.
  - Primary risk factors (especially duration) are matched; other factors may have slight mismatch (usually 50 bps or less).
  - Slightly higher turnover than benchmark.
- Active management:
  - Mismatch with benchmark weights to achieve 50 bps or greater outperformance.
  - Primary risk factor mismatch; higher active risk level.
  - Higher turnover.

Equities and bonds tend to underperform benchmarks. Even pure bond indexing underperforms the benchmark, but underperforms less than equity indexing due to lower fees and management costs.

Bond Market Liquidity

Liquidity expresses the price impact of a quick liquidation. Liquid securities trade at narrower bid-ask spreads, in larger quantities, and more frequently, which results in lower yield. Illiquid securities need a higher yield to compensate investors.

Fixed-income markets are less liquid than equity markets due to unique:

- Coupon rates
- Maturity dates
- Special features
- Embedded options

Bond markets may not show all available securities at best prices (i.e., lower transparency).

Finding a fixed-income dealer holding securities with desired features at best prices generates search costs.

Lower liquidity with:

- Time since issuance (because dealers have supply right after issuance, but buyers of those bonds may hold them to maturity).
- Lower credit quality.
- Lower acceptance as collateral in repo market (sovereigns are more liquid than lower-quality corporates).
- Smaller issue size (because smaller issues will not be included in index/benchmark).

Using exchange-traded options (e.g., futures and options on futures) may provide a more liquid alternative. Using over-the-counter (OTC)-traded instruments (e.g., interest rate and credit default swaps) may also help reduce risk.

Exchange-traded funds (ETFs) may provide a liquid option. Portfolio managers may purchase ETF shares and then redeem them for the underlying bonds using authorized participants (e.g., qualified banks and other institutions) as intermediaries with ETF sponsors.

Fixed-Income Returns Model

Portfolio managers use *expected* returns to position assets for risk and return properties desired for the portfolio:

$$
\begin{aligned}
E(R) \approx \ &\text{Yield income} \\
&+ \text{Rolldown return} \\
&+ E(\Delta\text{Price due to yields and spreads}) \\
&- E(\text{Credit losses}) \\
&+ E(\text{Currency gains and losses})
\end{aligned}
$$

Assuming no reinvestment income, **yield income** (aka **current yield**) is computed as:

$$
\text{Current yield} = \frac{\text{Annual coupon payment}}{\text{Bond price}}
$$

Rolldown return recognizes the value change as a bond approaches maturity ("pull to par") under an assumption of zero rate volatility (i.e., unchanged yield curve).

$$
\text{Rolling return} = \text{Yield income} + \text{Rolldown return}
$$

Expected price change due to change in the yield or spread depends on the bond's modified duration and convexity, or effective duration and convexity in the case of bonds with options:

$$
E(\%\Delta P) = (-D_{\text{Mod}} \times \Delta Y) + (C \times 0.5\Delta Y^2)
$$

Expected credit losses represent the loss probability (i.e., expected default rate) multiplied by the expected loss severity (i.e., loss given default):

$$
E(\text{Credit losses}) = E(\text{Default rate}) \times E(\text{Loss severity})
$$

Expected currency gains or losses in reporting currency terms must also be considered. Currency losses occur when the asset currency depreciates against the reporting currency.

Limitations of the model include:

- Reinvestment at bond yield to maturity (YTM).
- Duration: Considers only parallel yield curve shifts.
- Excludes richness/cheapness effects: Deviations from the fitted yield curve at certain maturities.

Leverage

Leverage involves using borrowed capital to enhance return. Leverage improves return when portfolio return is greater than borrowing cost. Portfolio return using leverage is calculated as:

$$
\begin{aligned}
r_P &= \left(\frac{\text{Portfolio return}}{\text{Portfolio equity}}\right) = \frac{r_I(V_E + V_B) - r_B V_B}{V_E} \\
&= r_I + \frac{V_B}{V_E}(r_I - r_B)
\end{aligned}
$$

where r_I = investment asset return, r_B is the cost of funds, and V_E and V_B are the values of equity and borrowing, respectively. Therefore, the numerator in the first line of the equation represents the return on portfolio assets less borrowing costs.

Methods of Leverage

Futures contracts allow large positions to be controlled with little margin (i.e., equity). Leverage is the exposure (i.e., position size greater than margin) normalized for the margin amount:

$$L_{Futures} = \frac{Notional\ amount - Margin}{Margin}$$

Swaps allow conversion to a long/short portfolio for minimal collateral required by the counterparties or, increasingly since the financial crisis of 2008, a clearinghouse. A manager can swap a position in long bonds to avoid rising rates by paying the fixed rate and receiving a floating rate. This effectively results in a long/short portfolio.

Structured financial instruments, such as **floating-rate notes** (**floaters**) and their inverse add more leverage to the swap. Inverse floaters add leverage to the inverse relationship between bond prices and interest rates and are ideal for expressing a strong expectation of falling interest rates:

$$Coupon\ rate = Fixed\ reference - (Multiplier \times Floating\ reference)$$

where the floating reference is usually the London Interbank Offered Rate (LIBOR), and the contract usually specifies that the coupon rate cannot be less than 0.

Repurchase agreements essentially involve a collateralized loan where a security seller agrees to repurchase the security later (often after one day) at a stated price. **Reverse repo** indicates the opposite side of the transaction.

- Bilateral—borrower and lender only
- Trilateral—borrower and lender through an intermediary

The price difference over the period indicates the repo rate. Underlying collateral protects the lender in a repo. The haircut involves the value of collateral over the amount borrowed, multiplied by the annual interest rate scaled for the time interval.

- Cash-driven: Borrower needs cash, and collateralizes using Treasuries or other high-quality debt. Trilateral is common.
- Security-driven: Lender seeks a specific security for speculation, arbitrage, or hedging. Bilateral is common.

In **securities lending** transactions with cash collateral, the borrower pays a fee that decreases as investment liquidity increases (i.e., you pay more to borrow infrequently available securities). In financing transactions, the lender pays a slight fee to borrow the money.

The securities borrower gets a **rebate** on coupon payments received by the lender during the loan term:

FI
EPM

$$\boxed{\text{Rebate rate} = \text{Collateral earning rate} - \text{Securities lending rate}}$$

The rebate rate may be negative for difficult-to-borrow securities.

Risks of Leverage

Moderate portfolio losses can be multiplied due to leverage. This can lead to forced liquidation when margin falls to unacceptably low levels. This may be especially true when asset values have fallen substantially, and the manager must liquidate at fire-sale prices.

Lenders may withdraw financing during crisis periods, even though a particular portfolio may not experience extreme value deterioration.

Fixed-Income Portfolio Taxation

Taxes are typically applied to:

- Coupon earnings: Generally a higher rate.
- Capital gains: Generally a lower rate; may be only for longer-term gains in some jurisdictions.
- Capital losses: May be disallowed as offset against other income and applied only against capital gains in some jurisdictions; carry-forward and carry-back provisions may apply.

Zero-coupon bonds represent an interest rate earned over time, and taxes will usually be imputed as if the bond earns a coupon.

Tax-loss harvesting involves selling losing positions to offset gaining positions. Losses are often taken earlier, whereas gains are deferred.

Lower turnover helps defer capital gains.

Investment Vehicle Taxation

Mutual funds and other pooled investment vehicles are assumed to generate taxable return when received by the fund rather than when paid to investors as dividends.

The United States also uses pass-through capital gains taxable based on investment gains in the fund, rather than gains in investor share value as in some other countries.

LIABILITY-DRIVEN AND INDEX-BASED STRATEGIES
Cross-Reference to CFA Institute Assigned Reading #19

Liability-Driven Investing

Asset–liability management (ALM) strategies consider both rate-sensitive assets and liabilities in the portfolio decision-making process. Liability-driven investing (LDI) and asset-driven liabilities (ADL) are special cases of ALM.

Liability-driven investing (LDI) takes the liabilities as given and builds the asset portfolio in accordance with the interest rate risk characteristics of the liabilities. The present value of those liabilities depends on current interest rates. The estimated interest rate sensitivity of liabilities is used as a starting point when making investment portfolio decisions. An LDI strategy starts with analyzing the size and timing of the entity's liabilities.

Exhibit 1: Liabilities Classification Scheme

Liability Type	Cash Amount	Timing
I	Known	Known
II	Known	Uncertain
III	Uncertain	Known
IV	Uncertain	Uncertain

Type I liabilities, such as traditional fixed-rate bonds with no embedded options, have known amounts and payment dates. For type I liabilities, yield duration statistics such as Macaulay, modified, and money duration apply.

Type II, III, and IV liabilities have uncertain amounts and/or uncertain timing of payment. For these types of liabilities, curve duration statistics such as effective duration are needed. A model is used to obtain the estimated values when the yield curve shifts up and down by the same amount.

Asset-driven liabilities (ADLs) take the assets as given and structure debt liabilities in accordance with the interest rate characteristics of the assets. Assets can be categorized by the degree of certainty surrounding the amount and timing of cash flows, just like the liabilities.

Managing a Single Liability

Immunization is the process of managing a fixed-income portfolio to minimize the variance in the realized rate of return over a known investment horizon.

For a single liability, immunization is achieved by matching the Macaulay duration of the bond portfolio to the horizon date. As time passes and bond yields change, the duration of the bond portfolio changes and needs to be rebalanced. An immunization strategy aims to lock in the cash flow yield on the portfolio, which is the internal rate of return on the cash flows.

The requirements of a bond portfolio to immunize a single liability are that it (1) has an initial market value that equals or exceeds the present value of the liability, (2) has a portfolio Macaulay duration that matches the liability's due date, and (3) minimizes the portfolio convexity statistic.

Immunization can be interpreted as a "zero replication" strategy in that the performance of the bond portfolio over the investment horizon replicates the zero-coupon bond that provides for perfect immunization. This zero-coupon bond has a maturity that matches the date of the single liability. There is no coupon reinvestment risk or price risk, because the bond is held to maturity.

A sufficient condition for immunization is a parallel shift. If the change in the cash flow yield is the same as that on the zero-coupon bond being replicated, immunization can be achieved even with a non-parallel shift to the yield curve.

The risk to immunization is that the yield curve twists, causing the cash flow yield on the bond portfolio not to match the change in the yield on the zero-coupon bond that would provide for perfect immunization.

This risk is reduced by minimizing the dispersion of cash flows in the portfolio. Concentrating the cash flows around the horizon date makes the immunizing portfolio closely track the zero-coupon bond that provides for near-perfect immunization.

Managing Multiple Liabilities

The immunization approaches to manage multiple liabilities include cash flow matching, duration matching, derivatives overlay, and contingent immunization.

Cash flow matching involves a portfolio of fixed-income bonds with cash flow matching the amount and timing of the liabilities.

Duration matching involves a portfolio of fixed-income bonds structured to track the performance of the zero-coupon bonds that would perfectly lock in the rates of return needed to pay off the liabilities. The strategy is to match the money duration.

The requirements to immunize multiple liabilities are that (1) the market value of assets is greater than or equal to the market value of the liabilities, (2) the asset basis point value (BPV) equals the liability BPV, and (3) the dispersion of cash flows and the convexity of assets are greater than those of the liabilities.

Derivatives overlay uses futures contracts on government bonds to immunize liabilities. The number of futures contracts needed to immunize is:

$$N_f = \frac{\text{Liability portfolio BPV} - \text{Asset portfolio BPV}}{\text{Futures BPV}}$$

$$\text{Futures BPV} = \frac{\text{BPV}_{\text{CTD}}}{CF_{\text{CTD}}}$$

Contingent immunization pursues active investment strategies if the surplus is above a designated threshold. If the surplus erodes, the mandate reverts to a purely passive strategy of building a duration-matching portfolio. The objective is to attain gains on the actively managed funds in order to reduce the cost of retiring the debt obligations.

Liability-Based Strategies

Liability-driven investing (LDI) can be used for interest rate–sensitive liabilities, such as those for a defined benefit pension plan. There often is a large duration gap with pensions because pension funds hold sizable asset positions in equities that have low effective durations and their liability durations are high. Interest rate swap overlays can be used to reduce the duration gap as measured by the asset and liability BPVs.

The interest rate swap can be looked at as the same as a combination of bonds. From the pension fund's perspective, the swap is viewed as buying a fixed-rate bond from the swap dealer and financing that purchase by issuing a floating-rate note (FRN). The swap's duration is taken to be the high duration of the fixed-rate bond minus the low duration of the FRN, explaining why a receive-fixed swap has positive duration.

The notional principal (NP) on the interest rate swap needed to close the duration gap to zero can be determined from the following relationship:

$$\text{Asset BPV} + \left[\text{NP} \times \frac{\text{Swap BPV}}{100} \right] = \text{Liability BPV}$$

The hedging ratio is the percentage of the duration gap that is closed with the derivatives. Because asset BPVs are less than liability BPVs in typical pension funds, the derivatives overlay requires the use of receive-fixed interest rate swaps. Because receive-fixed swaps gain value as current swap market rates fall, the fund manager could choose to raise the hedging ratio when lower rates are anticipated. If rates are expected to go up, the manager could strategically reduce the hedging ratio.

An alternative to the receive-fixed interest rate swap is a purchased receiver swaption. This swaption confers to the buyer the right to enter the swap as the fixed-rate receiver. Because of its negative duration gap (asset BPV is less than liability BPV), the typical pension plan suffers when interest rates fall and could become underfunded. The gain on the receiver swaption as rates decline offsets the losses on the balance sheet.

Another alternative is a swaption collar, the combination of buying the receiver swaption and writing a payer swaption. The premium received on the payer swaption that is written offsets the premium needed to buy the receiver swaption.

The choice to hedge with the receive-fixed swap, the purchased receiver swaption, or the swaption collar depends in part on the pension fund manager's view on future interest rates. If rates are expected to be low, the receive-fixed swap typically is the preferred derivative. If rates are expected to go up, the swaption collar becomes attractive. And if rates are projected to reach a certain threshold that depends on the option costs and the strike rates, the purchased receiver swaption can become the favored choice.

Liability Structure Risks

Model risks arise in LDI strategies because of the many assumptions in the models and approximations used to measure key parameters. For example, the liability BPV for the defined benefit pension plan depends on the choice of measure (accumulated benefit obligation [ABO] or projected benefit obligation [PBO]) and the assumptions that go into the model regarding future events (e.g., wage levels, time of retirement, and time of death).

Spread risk in LDI strategies arises because it is common to assume equal changes in asset, liability, and hedging instrument yields when calculating the number of futures contracts, or the notional principal on an interest rate swap. The assets and liabilities are often on corporate securities, however, and their spreads to benchmark yields can vary over time.

Counterparty credit risk is a concern if the interest rate swap overlays are uncollateralized. Over-the-counter derivatives increasingly include a Credit Support Annex (CSA) to mitigate counterparty credit risk. A typical CSA calls for a zero threshold, meaning that only the counterparty for which the swap has negative market value posts collateral.

Bond Index Investing

Investing in a fund that tracks a bond market index offers the benefits of both diversification and low administrative costs. Tracking risk is the deviation of the returns between the index and the fund and arises when the fund manager chooses to buy only a subset of the index.

Full replication is producing a portfolio that is a perfect match to the benchmark portfolio. The approach attempts to duplicate the index by owning all the bonds in the index in the same percentage as the index. Full replication is difficult and expensive to implement in the case of bond indexes because issues are illiquid and infrequently traded.

Enhanced indexing uses a sampling approach in an attempt to match the primary index risk factors and achieve a higher return than under full replication. By investing in a sample of bonds rather than the whole index, the manager reduces the construction and maintenance costs of the portfolio.

Active management involves aggressive mismatches on duration, sector weights, and other factors. Primary risk factors are typically major influences on the pricing of bonds, such as changes in the level of interest rates, twists in the yield curve, and changes in the spread between Treasuries and non-Treasuries.

Alternative Passive Bond Investing

Investing indirectly for a passive index-based exposure includes a bond mutual fund, an exchange-traded fund (ETF), and an index-based total return swap.

An asset manager must weigh the ongoing fees associated with mutual funds and ETFs against the bid–offer cost of direct investment in the underlying securities in the index.

A total return swap (TRS) has some advantages over a bond mutual fund or an ETF. As a derivative, it requires less initial cash outlay than direct investment in the bond portfolio for similar performance. However, a TRS carries counterparty credit risk. As a customized over-the-counter product, a TRS can offer exposure to assets that are difficult to access directly, such as some high-yield and commercial loan investments.

Liability Benchmarks

The manager should consider the duration preferences when choosing a fixed-income benchmark. Benchmark selection must factor in the broad range of issuers and characteristics available in the fixed-income markets.

The use of an index as a widely accepted benchmark requires clear, transparent rules for security inclusion and weighting, investability, daily valuation and availability of past returns, and turnover.

Fixed-income market dynamics can drive deviation from a stable benchmark. First, given that bonds have finite maturities, the duration of the index drifts down over time. Second, the composition of the index changes over time with the business cycle and maturity preferences of issuers. Third, value-weighted indexes assign larger shares to borrowers having more debt,

FI
EPM

leading to the "bums problem" that bond index investors can become overly exposed to leveraged firms.

Laddered Bond Portfolio

A laddered portfolio spreads the bonds' maturities and par values evenly along the yield curve. A laddered portfolio offers the advantage of protection from shifts and twists in the yield curve through cash flow diversification by balancing the position between the two sources of interest rate risk—cash flow reinvestment and market price volatility.

The strategy is superior to that of bullet or barbell portfolios. This structure works well in stable, upwardly sloped yield curve environments as maturing short-term debt is replaced with higher-yielding long-term debt at the back of the ladder. A laddered portfolio also offers an increase in convexity because the cash flows have greater dispersions than those of a more concentrated bullet portfolio. A laddered portfolio also provides liquidity in that it always contains a soon-to-mature bond that could provide high-quality, low-duration collateral on a repo contract if needed.

STUDY SESSION 8: FIXED INCOME PORTFOLIO MANAGEMENT (2)

YIELD CURVE STRATEGIES
Cross-Reference to CFA Institute Assigned Reading #20

Foundational Concepts for Yield Curve Strategies

A **yield curve** represents yields theoretically available to investors at various maturities. There are three types:

1. **Par:** The yield to maturity represented by bonds at each maturity; may be interpolated for missing or desired maturities.
2. **Spot:** The yield curve showing discount rates for various bond maturities assuming they have a single cash flow at maturity.
3. **Forward:** The implied yields if investors were indifferent to holding a bond with a certain maturity or a combination of the one-year bond with a forward maturity making up the difference.

Yield Curve Dynamics

Three basic yield curve movements are:

1. **Parallel shift:** Yields at all represented maturities change by the same number of basis points.
2. **Slope:** Flattening or steepening of the curve; the difference between near-maturity low interest rate and far-maturity high interest rate.
3. **Curvature:** The degree of bulge in the yield curve.

A parallel shift may also be called a change in "level." A change in slope and curvature may be bundled together and called a change in "shape."

The **butterfly spread** measures curvature for a yield curve:

$$\text{Butterfly spread} = 2Y_{MT} - (Y_{ST} + Y_{LT})$$

where the subscripts indicate short-term, medium-term, or long-term yields. Larger positive values indicate more curvature.

A yield level increase will tend to occur along with flattening slope and decreasing curvature. This occurs because the short end of the curve reacts more to a yield level increase than does the long end of the curve.

Duration and Convexity

Duration (types of):

- **Macaulay duration:** Reflects effective maturity. Linear relationship with maturity; a 20-year zero-coupon bond has $2 \times$ duration of 10-year zero-coupon bond.
- **Modified duration:** Estimates "full" price (including accrued interest) sensitivity for a 1% change in the reference rate.
- **Effective duration:** Estimates price sensitivity for changes in a benchmark yield (rather than the bond's own yield). Used for bonds with embedded options, due to poorly defined cash flows for such bonds.

FI
EPM

- **Key rate duration (partial duration):** Estimates price sensitivity to changes in rates at key maturities.
- **Money duration:** Related to modified duration, but estimates price sensitivity in currency units to a 1% change in reference rate.
- **Price value of a basis point (PVBP):** Measures sensitivity in currency terms to one basis point change.

Convexity:

- Describes price deviation from the linear price-yield relationship expressed by duration.
- Convexity is the second-order percentage change in price for a given change in yield such that a 20-year zero-coupon bond has $4 \times$ duration of a 10-year zero-coupon bond.
- Longer maturity also results in greater convexity, so long bonds become more valuable as yields decrease.
- Positive convexity means the price will change more as yields decrease, which is a valuable attribute and leads to lower yields on such bonds.
- Convexity depends on dispersion of cash flows around the duration point.
- For bonds of a given duration, zero-coupon bonds have the lowest convexity.
- Coupon-paying bonds have greater convexity than zero-coupon bonds of the same duration.
- Convexity is not as important as duration (it is a second-order effect).

Yield curve inversion occurs when investors bid up prices for longer-maturity bonds in expectation that yields will decrease or volatility will increase. This can lead to negative slope or to greater curvature (if mid-maturity bond yields don't decline commensurately).

Portfolio managers buy convexity when they expect returns from falling yields to exceed costs (in lower yield) of high-convexity bonds.

Major Yield-Curve Strategies

Portfolio managers can add value to benchmark returns using active strategies. Duration management is the most powerful active strategy.

Stable Yield Curve

Buy and Hold
Although "buy and hold" sounds passive, managers make active bets against the benchmark by choosing parts of the curve where yield changes won't affect return, or by purchasing longer-duration/higher-yield securities. These are held for some period that optimizes the return.

Rolldown Strategies
Rolldown strategies:

- Ride the yield curve as longer-maturity, lower-priced securities become shorter-maturity, higher-priced securities.
- Differ from buy-and-hold strategies because the manager earns a capital gain by selling the shorter-maturity securities at appreciated prices, as well as earning the coupon.
- Require an upward-sloping yield curve.
- Maximize rolldown return by targeting especially steep portions of the upward-sloping curve.

FI EPM

Selling Convexity

Managers receive less yield on higher-convexity bonds. If the manager expects low volatility, the higher-convexity bonds are of little value and can be profitably traded to managers expecting higher volatility.

To save transaction costs and portfolio disruption, the manager can sell convexity by selling:

- Puts on bonds the manager would consider owning if the put is exercised, or
- Covered calls (on bonds in the portfolio).

Manager earns option premium, and lowers portfolio convexity. However, investment constraints may prevent option writing.

Callable bonds integrate a call option with the bond upon issuance in return for a lower price/ higher yield to the buyer. The price-yield difference reflects the buyer's option premium received.

Mortgage-backed securities (MBSs) involve selling an option for the borrower to repay early.

Carry Trade

A carry trade involves buying a security with higher return than the cost to finance the purchase. A common carry trade involves borrowing in a country with a low interest rate, converting the currency into that of a country with a higher interest rate, and investing the converted currency at the higher interest rate. The trade is unwound at the end of the period by converting the principal and interest back to the initial currency.

Evidence indicates exchange rates may not appropriately adjust to remove this interest rate differential, but managers should remain aware of exchange rate risk.

This can also be accomplished through securities in the same currency. Opportunity may exist to buy longer-maturity, higher-yielding securities and financing them with shorter-maturity, lower-yielding securities.

Changes in Level, Slope, or Curvature

Managers cannot typically make consistent calls about the level and shape of the yield curve, and are often constrained closely to benchmark duration. Where room exists for active management, however, managers can earn superior returns from strategic bets that materialize.

Managing Duration

Portfolio managers:

- Shorten duration if they expect yield increases (minimize losses).
- Lengthen duration if they expect yield decreases (maximize gains).

Duration management offers better opportunity for active return gains than most strategies.

Duration management applies to parallel yield curve shifts.

Earning returns from duration management requires positioning securities based on expected shape changes in the yield curve. For example, a portfolio may miss the yield change in one part of the curve while a properly positioned portfolio with equal duration will participate.

Methods:

- **Buy/sell securities:** It is easy to increase a cash position by selling, but harder to increase duration if fully invested (manager must sell and then buy).
- **Simple interest rate derivatives:** Interest rate futures, puts and calls on bonds, caps and floors, options on swaps (swaptions).
  - Overlay derivatives portfolio keeps hedging decision separate from security selection.
  - Futures have the advantage of easy leverage.
- **Complex derivatives:** Interest-only or principal-only strips, collateralized mortgage obligations (CMOs), structured notes, and others.
- **Leverage only:** Borrowing against the portfolio to increase position size.

Buy futures to increase duration; sell futures to decrease duration.

$$\text{Contracts required} = \frac{\text{PVBP}_T - \text{PVBP}_P}{\text{PVBP}_F}$$

where the subscripts on PVBP indicate the target value T, actual portfolio value P, and futures value F.

A negative result indicates the manager should sell contracts.

Exam hint: This formula is like the formula used when you know the duration of the futures contract.

Leverage rather than futures may also be used to change duration. The amount to purchase using leverage equals the number of contracts required (from the preceding formula) times the value of each futures contract. Alternatively:

$$\frac{V_N}{V_P} = \frac{D_N}{D_P}$$

$$V_N = V_P \times \frac{D_N}{D_P}$$

where the subscripts indicate the value and duration of the notional portfolio N (including equity and debt) and the actual portfolio P.

The amount to purchase using leverage equals VN – VP, the value of the notional portfolio less the value of the actual portfolio.

Duration refers to asset-only duration without regard to liabilities required to achieve the notional duration.

Longer-duration bonds are not required to affect the duration of the actual portfolio. Using bonds with longer or shorter duration adds *curve risk* to the portfolio (i.e., exposure at different maturities on the yield curve).

Leverage increases duration and interest rate risk. Use of leverage in a portfolio with credit risk increases *both* credit risk and liquidity risk.

Receive-fixed, pay-floating *swaps*, like leverage, represent a long position in a bond and a short position in a short-term security:

- Increase duration.
- Undefined in terms of duration:
    - Both have zero value at initiation.
    - PVBP identifies the value change with rate changes.
- Swaps are less flexible in the short term, and less liquid than futures.

Pay-fixed, receive-floating swaps reduce duration.

The process for determining the swap size is like determining the number of futures contracts, but depends on scaling: For million-unit currency increments, multiply the contract number from the formula by one million to determine the total swap size in currency units.

Exam hint: The multiplier from the formula will be smaller for futures when the cheapest-to-deliver (CTD) bond has maturity less than the 10-year note on which it is benchmarked.

Buying Convexity

Portfolio managers with tight duration constraints can actively manage through convexity:

- **Falling yields:** Portfolios with greater convexity will increase more in value than portfolios with less convexity.
- **Rising yields:** Portfolios with greater convexity will decrease less in value than portfolios with less convexity.

Methods:

- Shifting bonds in a portfolio:
    - Modest improvements may result.
    - Difficult to implement with large portfolios of credit securities.
- Call options:
    - Faster price increase than bond when yields fall; rate of increase slows to 1:1 with bond.
    - Slower price decline than bond when yields rise; rate of decrease slows.
    - Loss is limited to option value decline.

Yield decline should occur quickly to avoid drag on returns.

Using convexity as a method to assess portfolio value changes applies only for parallel yield curve shifts.

FI
EPM

Bullet and Barbell Structures

For bullet structures:

- Maturities are concentrated near the midpoint of a range.
- Generally are used to avoid steepening yield curve.

For barbell structures:

- Maturities are concentrated at either ends of a range.
- Generally are used to avoid flattening yield curve.
- Falling long rates: Long maturities capture larger gains.
- Rising short rates: Short maturities have smaller losses.

Barbells outperform bullets in a downward parallel shift scenario.

Barbells outperform bullets in a flattening yield curve scenario.

Bullets outperform barbells in a steepening yield curve scenario.

Managers use **key rate duration** (i.e., **partial duration**) to calculate cash flows that result when a key maturity yield changes, thereby changing the interpolated forward rates. Price sensitivity to the change at each key maturity is determined in terms of price value of a basis point using the formula:

$$E(\Delta V_P) = V_{P,K} \times PVBP_K \times (-\text{Curve shift in bp})$$

where the expected change in portfolio value equals the portfolio value at the key maturity multiplied by the price value of a basis point at the key maturity multiplied by the negative of the curve shift in basis points.

Relative Outperformance Given Scenario

Yield Curve Scenarios		Structure
Level change	Parallel shift	Barbell
Slope change	Flattening	Barbell
	Steepening	Bullet
Curvature change	Less curvature	Bullet
	More curvature	Barbell
Volatility change	Decreased volatility	Bullet
	increased volatility	Barbell

Formulating a Portfolio Positioning Strategy for a Market View

Parallel Upward Shift
Bonds with forward implied yield change greater than forecast yield change will enjoy higher return in a magnitude based on duration as they roll down the yield curve.

$$r_{Total} = Y_0 - D_1(Y_1 - Y_0)$$

where subscripts indicate beginning or end of the period.

A portfolio facing no constraints can position to maximize r_{Total}.

Parallel Yield Changes of Uncertain Direction

Increase convexity by using a barbell strategy when a yield change is certain, but the direction of the change is not. Current portfolio duration is maintained by weighting the best bonds at either end by:

$$D_P = w_s D_s + w_L D_L$$
$$= w_s D_s + (1 - w_s)D_L$$

where the subscripts indicate duration for the portfolio P, the short-maturity security S, and the long-maturity security L.

Using Butterflies

The appropriate long position depends on whether the manager expects flattening (i.e., long barbell) or steepening (i.e., long bullet), just as it is outside the butterfly structure:

- Long the wings (barbell structure) and short the body (bullet structure):
    - Flattening curve *or* volatile interest rates
    - Buying convexity in exchange for lower yield
    - Parallel yield curve increase
- Short the wings and long the body:
    - Steepening curve *or* stable interest rates
    - Selling convexity in exchange for higher yield

Exam hint: Long wings require *excess* volatility (more than market has priced in) for added profit, not volatility itself.

Structures include:

- **Duration neutral:** Wings and body have both equal duration and equal money weight (aka money duration neutral).
- **50/50 (used by dealer firms):** Short 50% of duration in the body and long 50% in the wings:
    - Long wings have ½ duration value (market value × modified duration) in each wing.
    - Manager may believe body is rich relative to wings, but not know how that will resolve.
- **Regression weighting:** Regression analysis of recent market data (30–45 days) used to weight short and long wings.

Condors are like butterflies but with longer wings and bigger bodies; that is, 2-year and 30-year wings and *both* 5 years and 10 years in the body.

Using Options
Sell convexity bonds (30-year maturity) and purchase call options:

- **Rising rate scenario:** Outperforms because options may expire worthless but still be less than loss on 30-year bonds.
- **Falling rate scenario:** Outperforms because option value accelerates faster than 30-year bonds until delta reaches 1:1.

Buying MBSs is equivalent to selling prepayment option to homeowners (selling convexity):

- **Rising rate scenario:** More sensitive than non-option bond; rising rates reduce prepayments.
- **Falling rate scenario:** Less sensitive than non-option bond; falling rates induce prepayments.

Structured Notes
Structured notes provide customized exposure to various maturities, especially the front end of the yield curve, but may lack liquidity.

Types:

- **Deleveraged floaters:** Coupon floats with indexed interest rates, but less than 1:1.
- **Leveraged floaters:** Coupon floats with indexed interest rates, but greater than 1:1.
- **Ratchet floaters:** Coupon floats upward, but ratchets to each higher level (i.e., sets new minimum coupon paid).
- **Range accrual notes:** Daily interest accrual occurs only if reference rate is within a range.
- **Extinguishing accrual notes:** All future accruals cease if reference rate goes outside a range (compensated with higher floor than range accrual notes).
- **Interest rate differential notes:** Payment of difference between rate at two different maturities.
- **Dual-currency notes:** Denominated in one currency but the coupon is paid in a second currency.

FIXED-INCOME ACTIVE MANAGEMENT: CREDIT STRATEGIES
Cross-Reference to CFA Institute Assigned Reading #21

Investment-Grade and High-Yield Corporate Bond Portfolios

The four Cs of credit analysis are capacity, character, collateral, and covenants.

Investment-grade securities have higher credit ratings that reflect lower credit and default risk, and generally pay a lower yield. **Speculative securities** have lower credit ratings that reflect higher credit and default risk, and generally pay higher yield. The latter are also known as **high-yield securities**.

The most important considerations for portfolio managers (PMs) are:

- **High yield:** Credit risk.
- **Investment grade:** Interest rate risk, credit migration risk, spread risk.

Credit Risk
Credit risk includes:

- **Default risk:** Probability an issuer will fail to make full and timely payments.
- **Loss severity:** Amount of loss given that the issuer has defaulted.

$$\text{Credit loss rate} = \text{P(Default)} \times \text{Loss severity}$$

Credit Migration Risk and Spread Risk
Credit migration risk: The risk that a credit issuer will experience credit quality deterioration.

Spread risk: The risk that the spread between the credit security and the reference security will change adversely.

- Measured by spread duration, the percentage increase in bond price for a 1% decrease in spread.
- Spread duration is approximately equal to modified duration for non-callable fixed-rate corporates, and different for floaters.

Interest Rate Risk
Investment-grade portfolios have more exposure to interest rate risk than high-yield portfolios:

- A strong economy can cause credit spreads to narrow more for high-yield securities than for investment-grade securities.
- Higher interest rates often accompany a strong economy due to competition for funds.
- Greater credit spread narrowing in high-yield securities offsets adverse interest rate movement.

Exam hint: High-yield bond prices behave more like equity security prices than investment-grade bond prices and could be considered correlated with equity.

With lower interest rates and tight credit spreads, high-yield securities act more like investment-grade debt and less like equity.

FI
EPM

Different yield spread sensitivities result in different quoting conventions:

- **Investment grade:** Spread over benchmark.
- **High yield:** Price.

Empirical duration captures price-interest behavior by regressing market prices for bonds against benchmark interest rate movements. Empirical duration is lower than effective duration for high-yield debt.

Liquidity and Trading
Liquidity, represented by the bid-ask spread, describes how quickly and easily a security can be bought or sold without affecting market price:

- Liquid securities have narrower bid-ask spreads.
- Individual bond liquidity depends on the size of:
  - The initial offering of the bond.
  - The market.

Initial offering and market size are bigger for investment-grade bonds, and therefore they are more liquid than high-yield securities.

Dealers generally hold smaller inventory of high-yield bonds, therefore adding to illiquidity.

Turnover in high-yield portfolios is more expensive due to the greater bid-ask spreads.

Credit Spreads

Credit Spread Measures
Credit spread measures help investors understand the return they will receive for assuming:

- The issuer's probability of default.
- The loss given default.
- Credit migration risk.
- Liquidity risk.

Benchmark spread subtracts a reference rate from the bond's yield to maturity (YTM):

- G-spread when the benchmark is an on-the-run government bond:
  - Easy to calculate (or interpolate if credit security maturity is between two government bonds).
  - Different market participants calculate the same way (linear interpolation).
  - Allows selling or short-selling two reference bonds to reduce duration of credit security.
  - Changes in interpolated benchmark yield and duration of credit security can be used to calculate price changes of credit security.

The I-spread process is like the G-spread, but uses swap rates in the same currency as the credit security. The I-spread:

- Has a smoother curve than the government yield curve.
- Is not as affected by demand for specific on-the-run government securities.

Use a hedge instrument based on the spread measure used.

Use **Z-spread** and **option-adjusted spread (OAS)** to compare relative value across different types of credit securities:

- **Z-spread:** Spread added to each yield-curve point so that the present value (PV) of bond cash flows equals price.
- **OAS:** Spread added to one-period forward rates that sets arbitrage-free value equal to price.
  - Useful for bonds with embedded options.
  - Depends on interest rate volatility assumptions.
  - OAS is theoretical comparison tool (i.e., bond is unlikely to experience OAS).
  - Most relevant measure for portfolio level comparison (face-value-weighted OAS of securities in portfolio).

Excess Return

Excess return (XR) is the return of a bond after hedging interest rate risk (i.e., return from assuming credit risk). PMs manage credit risk separately from interest rate risk.

$$XR \approx (s \times t) - (\Delta s \times SD)$$

where XR is holding period return, s is beginning spread, t is the fraction of a year, and SD is spread duration.

This equation assumes no default losses, but can be adjusted to expected XR (including credit losses) by subtracting expected annual credit loss (probability of default multiplied by loss severity). Expected annual credit loss should be multiplied by the period of a year t to adjust for partial years:

$$EXR \approx (s \times t) - (\Delta s \times SD) - (t \times p \times L)$$

Credit Strategy Approaches

A **credit strategy** tries to outperform benchmark performance within certain risk parameters.

Bottom-Up Approach

A bottom-up approach is also called a **security selection strategy** because it assesses relative risk-return trade-offs, generally across similar credit risks (as opposed to investment grade versus high yield). There are four steps:

1. Establish eligible universe and divide into sectors (e.g., capital goods).
2. Further divide sectors to establish similar company-level risks.
3. Weigh credit risks against the expected excess return.
4. For two issuers with similar credit risks, purchase the bond with greater spread to the benchmark rate.

For bonds with an expected holding period less than maturity, also consider the expected credit spread change over the holding period.

Portfolio diversification and liquidity may be additional considerations for estimating the highest expected excess return.

Total return investors may not separate interest rate risk and credit risk, so are less concerned with comparing expected excess return.

Investors may use a **spread curve** of credit spreads plotted against either maturity or duration of a company's outstanding bonds. The spread curve identifies which company has greater a credit spread at a given duration/maturity. If the more creditworthy company has a greater spread at a duration/maturity, then this is a good candidate for purchase.

Other considerations include:

- **Bond structure:** Bond features and priority in the capital structure.
- **Issue date:** Recently issued bonds have more liquidity and narrower bid-offer spreads.
- **Supply:** An issuer's existing bonds may experience spread widening and price declines:
  - Investors sell existing supply for new supply, or
  - Issuer gives price concessions for new bonds, or
  - Debt is signaling an increase in credit risk.
- **Issue size:** Larger issues are held by more investors and may have greater liquidity.

Within each sector allocation of an investor's model portfolio, the PM may purchase equal weights of each issue or overweight the most attractive issues using weights based on:

- Market value.
- Spread duration.

Sometimes purchasing the perfect bond is difficult:

- **Substitution:** Using second- or third-choice issue.
- **Index or derivative exposure:**
  - Benchmark bonds
  - Credit default swap index derivatives
  - Total returns swaps on the benchmark index
  - Exchange-traded funds
- **Maintain cash position:** Useful only if the desired issue is expected to become available quickly.

Top-Down Approach
The top-down or macro approach focuses on:

- Economic growth.
- Interest rates.
- Currency movements.
- Corporate profitability and default rates.
- Industry trends.
- Changes in credit spreads.
- Risk appetite.

Process:

1. Determine which sectors have better relative value.
2. Overweight sectors with better relative value.

Sector definitions typically are broader than for a bottom-up approach; a top-down approach may be "investment grade versus high yield."

PMs must decide the acceptable credit quality for a portfolio based on the desired excess return over the benchmark:

- Credit cycle considerations: Imperfect correlation with economic cycle, although reasonable inverse correlation of default rates with economic growth.
- Expected credit spread changes.

Strong GDP growth forecast beyond one year suggests narrowing credit spreads and potential excess returns.

Approaches to assess portfolio credit quality include:

- **Average credit rating:** Credit rating categories are assigned numerical values, and nonlinear weighting is applied based on duration.
- **Average OAS:** Each issue's OAS is weighted by market value; this does not account for duration of issues and could underestimate risk.
- **Weighted-average spread duration:** Can account for credit spread volatility risk.
- **Duration times spread (DTS):** Duration multiplied by average spread; less intuitive than either measure.

Exam hint: Arithmetic weighting based on ratings categories will underestimate credit risk.

Excess returns in a top-down approach use the same formula as previously:

$$\text{EXR} \approx (s \times t) - (\Delta s \times \text{SD}) - (t \times p \times L)$$

- PMs may also use spread-versus-leverage measures to determine which macro sectors offer better risk-reward opportunities.
- Interest rate management may be an important part of a top-down strategy, although effects of interest rate movements are typically hedged in a bottom-up strategy:
  - ○ **Effective duration:** Important measure for parallel shifts in the yield curve.
  - ○ **Effective convexity:** Measures changes in duration for parallel interest rate shifts.

Exam hint: Don't pay to have convexity in a portfolio when volatility is low. A low-volatility portfolio will perform poorly relative to the benchmark when interest rates change, but additional spread income may more than compensate for that.

Managing interest rate exposures involves selecting appropriate securities for their credit exposure and key rate duration qualities. Disadvantages include:

- Maturity decisions cannot be separated from credit curve management and credit security selection.
- It is difficult to buy bonds for certain key rate durations.
- Only very short-maturity securities or floaters avoid interest rate exposure (without using derivatives).

FI
EPM

Not all investors are willing or able to use derivatives, but they have the advantage of separating key rate duration from credit curve exposures.

Interest rate exposure may be managed with securities such as callable bonds or agency pass-through mortgages, or with derivatives.

Investors can express a currency viewpoint in a top-down environment by purchasing credit securities in countries with yields expected to fall and sell credit securities in countries with yields expected to rise. Forwards and futures may also be used to manage this exposure.

To overweight a potentially strong country without expressing a currency viewpoint, sell currency forwards for that country's currency.

Spread curves introduced in the bottom-up approach can be used to analyze relative value in segments determined for the top-down analysis.

Comparing Bottom-Up and Top-Down
Macro factors result in the majority of credit returns, but these are closely followed and it is difficult to earn an information advantage. Bottom-up analysis allows managers to find an information advantage in a small segment.

Managers may use bottom-up analysis on a segment identified via top-down analysis.

Environmental, Social, and Governance Considerations in Credit Portfolio Management
Environmental, social, and governance (ESG) issues:

- Poor ESG records may highlight potential credit quality issues:
    - Environmental lawsuit costs and fines
    - Strikes, boycotts, and other costs related to poor labor relations
    - Aggressive or fraudulent accounting due to poor governance
- Guideline constraints:
    - Against companies with some percentage of revenues from controversial activities or products
    - Securities of governments with poor human rights records

Portfolio-level risk measures:

- Monitoring exposure to securities of companies with poor ESG records.
- Average ESG score on portfolios: Market value weighting for ESG scores to achieve portfolio exposures.

In addition to avoiding securities of companies with poor ESG records, portfolios may also target securities of companies that make positive ESG contributions:

- Not-for-profit hospitals
- Low-income housing projects
- Green energy

Liquidity Risk and Tail Risk

Corporate bonds are less liquid than sovereign bonds (with few exceptions). Electronic trading platforms (ETPs) improve liquidity, but differences remain.

Measures of Secondary Market Liquidity

Trading volume:

- Trading volumes are lower since the 2008 financial crisis owing to reduced holdings by broker-dealers.
- Reduction in high-yield liquidity was less compared to reduction in liquidity of corporates.
- U.S. government securities also suffered from reduced liquidity.

Spread sensitivity:

$$\text{Spread sensitivity} = \frac{\Delta \text{Spread}}{\%\text{Outflow}} = \frac{\Delta \text{Spread}}{\text{Funds withdrawn}/\text{AUM}}$$

The high-yield market is less liquid by this measure than the investment-grade market. Spread sensitivity increases as the economy declines.

Wider bid-ask spreads indicate less liquidity. Be careful: Spreads often narrow after widening for a brief period of volatility.

Managing liquidity:

- Cash.
- Liquid, non-benchmark bonds: Incremental return higher than cash.
- Credit default swaps (CDSs) index derivatives: Relatively more liquid than credit markets.
- Exchange-traded funds (ETFs): Liquid, but prices may deviate from net asset value of underlying and experience strange movements when credit markets become volatile.

Tail Risk

Tail risk involves a greater number of high or low returns than would be indicated by a normal distribution. It is difficult to model and impossible to predict.

- Model unusual return patterns.
- Scenario analysis: Performance under certain scenarios:
  - Historical—behavior given past unusual circumstances
  - Hypothetical—behavior given potential unusual circumstances
- Correlation risk becomes important under scenario analysis.

Managing tail risk:

- Diversification – Only modest incremental cost
- Hedges – Options and CDSs are most common; however, a hedge lowers the return if a risk fails to materialize. Some portfolios may disallow options.

International Credit Portfolios

Relative Value

Global credit cycles affect all regions, but to different degrees. Portfolio managers can earn excess returns by correctly identifying timing and location of credit cycle weakening.

Regional differences in concentration of ratings may affect investment decisions, such as a greater BB concentration in European high-yield portfolios versus CCC concentration in U.S. portfolios. An improving credit cycle favors U.S. high-yield portfolios versus European high-yield portfolios.

Supply and demand factors may depend on credit cycles and differences in investor type.

Emerging Markets
Emerging markets have a higher concentration of commodities companies and banks.

There is also more government ownership/control.

Emerging markets have a higher concentration of lower investment-grade and higher high-yield securities. This reflects a rating agency cap for sovereign rating in which subject credit security is based.

Global Liquidity Considerations
Liquidity is particularly constrained in emerging markets; investors demand a premium for lack of liquidity.

Currency Risk
Hedge currency risk if cost effective, especially in low interest rate environment.

Legal Risk
Each country may have unique bankruptcy laws. Some countries may allow government or shareholder involvement.

Structured Financial Securities

Structured instruments either repackage risks in some way or have collateral backing the security:

- Asset-backed (including mortgage-backed)
- Collateralized debt obligations (CDOs)
- Covered bonds

Advantages:

- Higher returns than other types of fixed-income securities
- Improved portfolio diversification
- Exposure to different markets and macro exposures (e.g., real estate) than investment grade and high yield

Mortgage-Backed Securities
Residential mortgage-backed securities (RMBSs) have advantages:

- **Liquidity:** Agency RMBSs (backed by Fannie Mae, Freddie Mac, Ginnie Mae) provide comparable return with often greater liquidity.

- **Macro exposure:**
    - ○ Residential and commercial real estate.
    - ○ Interest rate volatility: Less default risk because backed by U.S. government agency or U.S. government-sponsored enterprise.
- **Spread stability:** More stable spreads during volatility spikes relative to corporate bonds.

Asset-Backed Securities

Asset-backed securities (ABSs) include securities with collateral from non-mortgage assets:

- Auto loans and lease receivables
- Credit card receivables
- Student education loans
- Other personal loans, bank loans, and accounts receivable

ABSs offer possible return and diversification benefits.

They express views on commercial and consumer credit.

ABSs have greater liquidity than corporate bonds have in some sectors.

Collateralized Debt Obligations

Collateralized debt obligations (CDOs) are securities collateralized with one or more types of debt obligations (e.g., corporate loans, bonds, etc.). With credit tranching (i.e., subordination of classes), investors can select a risk-return profile:

- Senior
- Mezzanine
- Subordinated (i.e., the residual or equity tranche)

CDOs do not offer much diversification benefit or unique exposure opportunities, but do offer:

- **Relative value opportunities:** In spite of only a few defaults in higher-rated tranches during the global financial crisis, CLO/CDO spreads widened more than corporate spreads in comparable credit categories based on the expected default rate of the underlying collateral.
- **Default correlation exposure:** Mezzanine values increase relative to senior and subordinated tranches when correlations increase.
- **Leveraged exposure:** Mezzanine and residual classes have leveraged exposure.

Covered Bonds

A covered bond is a debt obligation issued by a bank and "covered" via a pool of segregated assets. Both the assets in the cover pool and the general bank assets are available to cover the bond in case of default.

An investor can reduce exposure to the financial sector by selling bank bonds and purchasing covered bonds.

The most common types of covered bonds are euro-denominated **Pfandbriefe**, which are also the largest segment of the private bond market in Europe. (Singular form is **Pfandbrief.**)

FI
EPM

OVERVIEW OF EQUITY PORTFOLIO MANAGEMENT
Cross-Reference to CFA Institute Assigned Reading #22

Roles of Equities in a Portfolio

Capital Appreciation
Long-term returns on equities have historically been highest among all major asset classes primarily due to capital appreciation. Equity returns are often highly correlated with the business cycle. Stocks, especially growth stocks, tend to outperform other asset classes during periods of economic growth. Stocks tend to underperform, however, during weak economic periods.

Dividend Income
Cash dividends represent the primary source of income from a stock portfolio. Firms are not obligated to pay dividends. The firm's board of directors decide dividend policy and payout ratios. Value stocks frequently retain a smaller portion of net income and pay out a greater portion of their earnings as dividends than do growth stocks that must retain a greater portion for reinvestment.

Dividend yields on equity securities typically comprise less of total return than interest yields on bonds. Yet, income returns are significant and important to stock investors. Historically the S&P Index produces a dividend yield between 1% and 3%. Preferred dividends are the main component of total returns on preferred shares with capital appreciation or depreciation dependent more on yield curve movements than on company growth.

Diversification with Other Asset Classes
Equities provide considerable diversification benefits against other asset classes, although correlations among asset class returns change over time. Volatility and correlations among returns of different equity indices tend to increase during financial crises, which reduces the benefits of diversification.

Potential Inflation Hedge
Equity returns can help offset inflation as businesses pass inflationary input cost increases on to customers. A company successfully implementing this approach protects its profit margin and cash flows, which in turn helps stabilize share prices during inflationary periods. Holders of fixed-payment bonds, on the other hand, receive only the contractually obliged interest, and the value of their holding tends to decrease during inflationary periods.

Client Considerations for Equities in a Portfolio
A client's portfolio often includes equities as an integral part of the investment policy statement (IPS).

Equity investments enjoy income generation and growth potential, but also suffer from return volatility and sensitivity to various macroeconomic variables. Consequently, equity investors should understand the underlying tradeoff between equity returns and risk.

FI
EPM

Equity Investment Universe

Analysts frequently group equity securities according to similar characteristics that tend to affect their return.

Segmentation by Size and Style

Size describes market capitalization of the underlying firms. Typical equity size categories include large cap, mid cap, and small cap. These distinctions do not have formal definitions and are categorized differently among financial market participants.

Style may include categories based on multiple metrics such as price-to-book ratios, price-to-earnings ratios, earnings growth rate, dividend yield, and book value growth rate. Typical categories include value styles representing a bargain price for a desired market return factor or yield and growth styles representing increases in revenues, earnings, or some other measure that will hopefully translate to capital appreciation.

Segmentation by size and style provide the following advantages for portfolio managers:

1. Portfolio managers can construct an overall equity portfolio in a relatively manageable way.
2. Segmentation by size/style results in diversification across economic sectors and industries.
3. Active equity fund managers can construct performance benchmarks for specific size/style segments.
4. Segmentation allows a portfolio to reflect a company's maturity and potentially change growth/value orientation.

Disadvantages include (1) different category definitions by different market participants and (2) companies changing category over time.

Segmentation by Geography

Common categories include developed markets, emerging markets, and frontier markets. Geographic segmentation facilitates global diversification but also has drawbacks:

1. Domestic companies, especially in developed countries, may be global in nature and provide less-than-expected international diversification
2. Foreign currency return against the portfolio's base currency that compounds against local returns

Segmentation by Economic Activity

The production-oriented approach classifies companies by type of product or inputs to the production process (e.g., North American Industry Classification System or NAICS and Industrial Classification Benchmark or ICB). The market-oriented approach classifies companies based on the markets they serve, the way revenue is earned, or the way customers use the company's products (e.g., the Global Industry Classification System or GICS).

Segmentation creates useful industry performance benchmarks but may involve classification problems when a firm's business activities span multiple industries.

Finally, some indices reflect specific investment approaches (e.g., environmental, social, and government or ESG concerns).

Income and Costs in an Equity Portfolio

Dividends

Income from an equity portfolio typically derives from dividends. Large cap and value stocks tend to carry the highest dividend yield. Growth firms typically pay little to no dividend because they reinvest a substantial part of cash flow or are still cash flow negative. Other dividend types include special cash dividends, stock dividends, or an option dividend that gives shareholders an option to choose either cash or stock. In some cases, the option can be sold for income.

Securities Lending Income

Shareholders may lend their shares to short-sellers for income. The fee for stock loans ranges from 0.2% to 0.5% on an annualized basis in developed markets. In emerging markets, fees are typically higher, 1% to 2% annualized for large cap stocks. Other than stock loan fees, stock lenders can reinvest cash collateral received against the share loan. Index funds are frequent stock lenders.

Dividend Capture

Dividend capture is a strategy to buy a stock just before its ex-dividend dates and sell it on or after ex-dividend dates to capture cash dividends, in hope that the price drop in stock on the ex-dividend date is less than the size of the cash dividend. If so, dividend capture strategy makes a positive alpha.

Writing Options

Investors may write covered calls and cash-covered puts to generate cash income while holding an equity portfolio. A covered call involves writing a call when holding the underlying stock. A cash-covered put involves writing a put on a stock when holding cash in the amount of the exercise price of the put option. The goals of these strategies are to generate additional cash income for the portfolio.

Management Fees

Managers charge fees as a percentage of assets under management at regular time intervals, such as quarterly. The fees include direct costs of research and portfolio management.

Performance Fees

Performance fees, also called incentive fees, align manager and investor interests by rewarding portfolio managers for good investment returns. A high-water mark may be implemented along with performance fees to prevent performance fees until the fund exceeds a previous high level of value.

Administration Fees

Administration fees may include registration fees, depository fees, and custody fees.

Marketing and Distribution

Marketing and distribution costs include charges related to marketing, sales, advertising, sponsorship, producing and distributing brochures, platform fees, and sales commissions.

Trading Costs

Explicit trading costs include brokerage commissions, taxes, stamp duties, and stock exchange fees. Implicit trading costs include bid-ask spread, market impact, and delay costs. Performance reporting may show some explicit costs but includes implicit costs as part of return without separate disclosure.

FI
EPM

Investment Approach Considerations

Investment strategies that involve frequent trading and demand liquidity are like to have higher trading costs than long-term buy-and-hold investment strategies. Index funds may face hidden costs such as trading ahead of a known constituent change (i.e., predatory trading).

Shareholder Engagement

Shareholder engagement occurs when investors actively vote on corporate actions or otherwise interact with company management to influence:

- Strategies (e.g., synergies, mergers and acquisitions)
- Allocation of capital
- Corporate governance
- Remuneration
- Composition of the board of directors

Voting is the most influential element of shareholder engagement. Shareholders vote on corporate issues, monitor performance of management and the board of directors in general meetings, known as general assemblies. Proxy voting enables shareholders who are unable to attend a meeting to authorize another individual to vote on their behalf. External proxy advisory firms may provide voting recommendations and may highlight potential controversial issues. Loaning shares to someone else transfers voting rights to the borrower. Empty voting refers to the practice of borrowing shares solely to exercise the voting rights.

Engagement activities by portfolio managers include regular meetings with company management or investor relations teams.

Activist investing refers to activist investors who specialize in taking stakes in companies and creating change to generate value on the investment. Activist investing can include letters to and meetings with management, presentations to other investors, and media campaigns.

Shareholder engagement can result in more effective corporate governance and culture, which in turn may lead to better company performance. Shareholders who have ESG or other non-financial concerns may benefit from shareholder engagement. Stakeholders other than shareholders may have an interest in engagement issues.

Disadvantages of shareholder engagement include:

- Time and money costs
- Short-term management capitulation at the expense of long-term shareholder benefits
- Breaching insider trading rules if management shares information with active shareholders at the expense of others

Equity Investment Across the Passive-Active Spectrum

Managers must attract capital to earn fees and incentives and will often position their strategy to attract client funds. Managers of large-cap equity funds typically lack an information advantage because the securities are fully exposed to analyst scrutiny and will reduce expenses through their choice of passive approach. Managers in markets without such scrutiny and confident of their abilities will often exploit their superior knowledge with an active approach to outperform their benchmark on a net-of-fees basis.

Suitable benchmarks should choose constituents with enough liquidity to prevent excessive implicit and explicit trading costs, be broadly based to accurately measure alpha, and be passively managed such that the managers understand the constituents in the investable universe.

Client-specific mandates (e.g., ESG, unique circumstances, etc.) often require active management to meet IPS requirements.

Active asset management typically increases trading costs and management fees over passive management. Active asset management also faces additional risks including reputation risk from potential violations of rules, regulations, client agreements, or ethical principles, and the risk that successful active managers may potentially leave the firm (i.e., key person risk).

Actively managed funds generally have higher turnover, which generates short-term gains and a higher tax burden than passively managed funds.

FI
EPM

PASSIVE EQUITY INVESTING
Cross-Reference to CFA Institute Assigned Reading #23

Passive equity investing seeks to duplicate or replicate the returns of a benchmark index. Passive investing can also include exposure to a changing set of market segments. Passive investment strategies do not engage in security selection and offer low costs, diversification, and higher tax efficiency relative to active management.

Choosing a Benchmark

Benchmarks in general must satisfy three criteria:

1. **Rules-based**—Rules must be objective, consistent, and predictable (e.g., rules for including a stock in an index and frequency of index reconstitution)
2. **Transparent**—Index providers must disclose the rules used in creating an index so that investors can evaluate the suitability of an index for investment benchmarking
3. **Investable**—Portfolio managers must be able to purchase constituent securities without undue cost

Indexes as a Basis for Investment

Investors must be able to replicate an index's performance in the market.

An index provider may "free-float adjust" the outstanding shares of a constituent security to exclude shares that are held by governments and other entities in order to reflect the actual liquidity of the company's shares.

Buffering (using a buffer zone when determining whether a stock should move from one index to another) and packeting (splitting a stock position into two indexes, e.g. small-cap and mid-cap) can be used to enhance investability by smoothing the index migration process.

Considerations When Choosing a Benchmark Index

The three main considerations in choosing an appropriate benchmark for a passively managed equity portfolio are market exposure, risk-factor exposure, and style exposure.

Market exposure involves portfolio beta with the applicable market index based on objectives and constraints as in an investment policy statement (IPS). Exposures may be influenced by market segment (e.g., domestic versus global, sectors versus broad market, etc.), size (i.e., large-cap, mid-cap, small-cap), investment style (growth, value or blended) and other characteristics such as price momentum and stock quality.

Risk-factor exposure relates to risk factors such as size, style, price momentum, and liquidity, and enables evaluation of the benchmark's correlation with risk factors.

Growth versus value style exposure differentiates between growth stocks with high P/E ratios, EPS growth and price momentum and value stocks with low P/E and price-to-book ratios and high dividend yields.

Index Construction Methodologies

A traditional indexing strategy involves tracking the returns of a market-capitalization-weighted benchmark index. Since market-cap-weighted portfolios are based on the efficient market hypothesis, an indexing strategy is often referred to as beta exposure.

A **market-capitalization-weighted index** weights each security's price by using the ratio of its market capitalization to the sum of capitalizations for all constituent securities. This method tends to "weight liquidity" because the largest capitalization securities have the greatest market liquidity. Most market-cap-weighted indexes are adjusted to weights using only shares available for trading (i.e., free-float adjusted).

A **price-weighted index** sums individual stock prices and divides by the number of stocks in the index. The divisor must be adjusted to reflect stock splits and other outstanding share-changing events. Price-weighted index returns are determined as if an investor holds one share of each constituent security in a portfolio, although this tends to be rare in practice.

An **equally-weighted index** is constructed by assigning equal weights to each security, resulting in the least concentrated index portfolio, as measured by the Herfindahl-Hirschman Index (HHI). Equal-weighted index returns are determined as if an investor owns identical cash amounts in each constituent security. This weighting scheme requires periodic rebalancing and over-represents small companies.

Other index weighting schemes do not use market prices but instead use a stock's fundamental characteristics such as sales, cash flow, and book value as a basis for weighting each index constituent.

Factor-Based Strategies

A passive factor-based strategy overweights or underweights risk factors that drive return (i.e., "smart beta" exposure):

- Growth—high P/E ratios, EPS growth, and price momentum
- Value—low P/E and price-to-book ratios, and high dividend yields
- Size—overweighting or underweighting small-, mid-, or large-cap sectors of the market
- Yield—high-dividend-yielding stocks especially with low interest rates
- Momentum—stocks that have outperformed the market over a some period
- Quality—earnings quality, dividend growth, cash flow generation, and degree of leverage
- Volatility—low volatility to reduce downside risk

A passive factor-based strategy can replace or complement a market-cap-weighted indexing strategy. A passive factor-based strategy may also incorporate factor rotation to make active bets on expected changes in market conditions.

Exam Hint: Active strategies decide the factor tilt in advance of implementation where passive strategies use it to tactical advantage.

Key considerations for a passive factor-based strategy are:

- Compared to a broad market-cap-weighted strategy, a passive factor-based strategy tends to concentrate exposure to the desired risk factor, with negative consequences if this risk factor underperforms.
- A passive factor-based strategy aims to outperform the risk/return profile of a market-cap-weighted strategy. Passive factor-based strategies can be:
    - Return-oriented—these include dividend yield, momentum, and fundamentally-weighted strategies.
    - Risk-oriented—these include volatility weighting and minimum-variance weighting strategies which are intended to either minimize downside volatility or overall portfolio volatility.

FI
EPM

   ○   Diversification-oriented—these include equally-weighted and maximum diversification strategies.
- Portfolio managers who implement factor-based strategies tend to use multiple benchmark indexes, e.g. a factor-based index and a broad market-cap-weighted index. This may result in a tracking error from the client's perspective when returns of a passive factor-based strategy are compared against the returns of a broad market-cap-weighted index.
- Passive factor-based strategies are likely to have higher management fees and trading commissions than a broad market-cap-weighted indexing strategy, resulting in lower returns after fees, all else being equal.

Approaches to Passive Equity Investing

Pooled Investments
Open- and closed-end index mutual funds are easy to purchase/sell and offer an inexpensive way for investors to track the performance of indexes. ETFs are similar to index funds with the major exception that they are purchased on an exchange, just like stocks. Managers of such funds rebalance, reconstitute, reinvest dividends, and perform other portfolio-required changes.

Advantages of ETFs over index mutual funds:

- Priced and trade throughout the day like stocks
- Have lower expense ratios
- Allow buying on margin and short positions
- More indexes than index mutual funds
- "In-kind" redemption process that may improve tax efficiency

Disadvantages of using ETFs compared to index mutual funds include:

- Commission costs that may more than offset the lower expense ratios
- Lower market liquidity

Derivatives-Based Approaches
Derivatives-based strategies offer passive equity investors benefits such as low costs, ease of implementation, and leverage. However, options expire, and futures and swap contracts may need to be rolled over to match an investor's time horizon. Derivatives not cleared through a clearinghouse may have counterparty default risk. Small investors may also lack access to some derivatives markets.

Passive equity investors tend to use derivatives-based strategies to align an existing stock portfolio more closely to stated objectives rather than to gain long-term exposure. Derivatives-based overlay strategies include:

- Completion overlays—used to restore the portfolio's beta (which has drifted over time) to its target beta
- Rebalancing overlays—used to buy/sell securities synthetically to achieve rebalancing objectives
- Currency overlays—used to hedge the returns of foreign currency stocks back into the investor's domestic currency
- In addition, equity index derivatives, such as equity index futures contracts, offer passive investors the following benefits compared to cash-based approaches
- Increase or reduce exposure to the index-based portfolio in a single transaction

FI
EPM

- Implement tactical portfolio exposure decisions more efficiently
- Greater liquidity of derivatives markets

Futures prices are not completely aligned with spot prices, so passive investors may use equity index swaps to obtain index exposure rather than expose the portfolio to such **basis risk**. A typical equity index swap may involve an agreement by two parties to exchange the return on a specified equity index for a floating interest rate.

Advantages of equity index swaps include:

- Ability to synthetically create any index.
- Lower cost than buying all the positions.
- They can be used to leverage or hedge a position.

Disadvantages of equity index swaps include:

- Counterparty default risk for swaps not centrally cleared
- Liquidity risk due to customized swap transactions created in the OTC market
- Interest rate risk borne by the floating-rate counterparty
- Tax policy risk due to potentially changing tax laws that currently favor swaps

Separately-Managed Direct Equity Investment
Initial construction requires tools to buy and sell large volumes of stocks at the same time (i.e., **program trading**). The portfolio manager must pay commissions on initial purchases and ongoing maintenance trades.

Portfolio Construction

Full Replication
Full replication requires purchasing **every** security contained in the benchmark index in the **exact** proportion of the index. Full replication should result in **negligible tracking error** but requires a large enough mandate size and liquid index constituents.

Full replication becomes **more** expensive when securities contained in an index trade in illiquid markets. As smaller and more illiquid stocks are subsequently added, trading costs increase tracking error creating a U-shaped tracking error curve.

Stratified Sampling
Stratified sampling carves the index into various cells or strata according to the characteristics of the securities in the index (e.g., industries or equity styles) and **weights each cell in line with index weightings**. Each cell typically includes the most liquid securities representative of the cell or strata. This enables a low-cost approach to closely track the index. Indexes can also be stratified using multiple dimensions; for example, a global equity index can be stratified by country and then by industry within each country.

Optimization
Optimization approaches can be used **in conjunction with stratified sampling or on a stand-alone basis**. An optimization model run without constraints uses security characteristics such as beta and size to construct the mimic portfolio. Additional constraints such as the maximum number of securities and total portfolio risk can also be added.

FI EPM

Optimization approaches enable investors to construct index-based portfolios with **lower** tracking error compared to stratified sampling alone. The optimization model also explicitly considers historical correlations. However, these historical relationships may change over time.

Blended Approach
An index-based portfolio can also use full replication for highly-liquid securities and stratified sampling or optimization for the remaining securities to achieve tracking in a cost-efficient manner.

Tracking Error Management

Excess Return and Tracking Error
Excess return equals the difference between the return on the portfolio (R_p) and the return on the benchmark index (R_B) and can be positive or negative. Excess return indicates how the portfolio has performed relative to its benchmark index.

A portfolio's tracking error is defined as the standard deviation of its excess return.

Passive managers aim to minimize tracking error and avoid negative excess returns.

Potential Causes of Tracking Error
Tracking error in an index-based portfolio can be attributed to:

- Management fees.
- Use of sampling rather than full replication.
- Intra-day trading of index constituents.
- Broker commissions.
- Cash drag—An index-based portfolio with cash balances will dilute returns relative to the benchmark index (i.e., negative tracking error in a bull market and positive in a bear market).

Controlling Tracking Error
Tracking error control involves tradeoffs between benefits and costs of full replication:

- Minimizing trading costs (including broker commissions) that negatively affect the performance of an index-based portfolio.
- Minimizing cash drag by:
  - Investing cash flows from investors and dividends from stocks in the index-based portfolio at the same prices used for index valuation; or
  - Using derivatives such as equity index futures contracts to equitize a cash position.

Sources of Return and Risk in Passive Portfolios

Attribution Analysis
Attribution analysis enables investors to understand sources of return for their portfolios relative to benchmark returns at the sector level. Attribution can also be used to develop portfolio return expectations in different market conditions.

Securities Lending

Index-based portfolio managers can offset portfolio management expenses and improve portfolio returns by loaning portfolio securities to other investors. Borrowers must also provide cash or securities as collateral for the borrowed securities and return any dividends received to the lender.

The lender may also sell loaned securities at any time, and the borrower must return the securities to the lender in time for settlement.

The risks of securities lending include:

- **Credit risk**—this is dependent on the credit quality of the borrower.
- **Market risk**—the value of the collateral, when posted in the form of securities, may fall over time.
- **Liquidity risk**—the liquidity of the collateral, when posted in the form of securities, should be considered by the lender.
- **Operational risk**—this arises from using lending agents to implement the securities lending transaction.
- **Cash collateral investment risk**—this arises when the lender decides to invest cash collateral in risky securities to boost returns.

Investor Engagement and Activism

Passive equity portfolio managers can use voting and engagement with company management to improve corporate governance practices to increase returns. Some companies may not wish to engage with index-based portfolio managers due to their mandate requiring them to hold the shares.

FI
EPM

FI
EPM

ACTIVE EQUITY INVESTING: STRATEGIES
Cross-Reference to CFA Institute Assigned Reading #24

Approaches to Active Management

Differences in the Information Used
Fundamental analysts may approach selection via the following approaches:

- **Top down**—Research focuses on how economic variables such as GDP growth, money supply, and expected inflation will affect various countries, sectors, or industries. The analyst then chooses companies expected to outperform due to superior management and product pipeline.
- **Bottom up**—Research focuses on peer-relative valuation, profitability, leverage, and other historical information, as well as impressions from company visits and statements from management. Analysts review financial statement footnotes, accounting policies, and ESG components.

Fundamental analysis taxes human capability, so analysts may specialize in a specific industry rather than attempt to personally understand every security.

Quantitative analysis usually excludes nonquantifiable variables from the forecasting model.

Differences in the Focus of the Analysis
Fundamental investors tend to focus on a specific group of stocks and take larger positions in fewer securities.

Quantitative investors focus on specific factors rewarded with return by the market and spread these factor bets across a larger number of securities.

Differences in Orientation to the Data
Fundamental investors forecast future performance of the company behind the security. Quantitative investors determine current factors rewarded by the market based on historical relationships.

Quantitative research avoids look-ahead bias and survivorship bias by using historical data on both ongoing concerns and former businesses. Fraudulent data reported by a company should still be used if the market was not aware of the fraud at the time.

Fundamental approaches may use a variety of techniques to normalize company results against fraudulent historical data.

Differences in Portfolio Construction
Fundamental investors determine "high-conviction" stocks based on extensive analysis of their target universe. The following risks apply to this type of analysis:

- Inaccurate forecast of business performance
- Inaccurate fair value assessment
- Market misperceptions of correct analyst assessments

Qualitative managers monitor and rebalance the portfolio more often due to security level risks.

Quantitative managers monitor and rebalance the portfolio periodically as portfolio level risk factor returns differ from the model.

Types of Active Management Strategies

Bottom-Up Strategies

Competitive advantages such as access to natural resources, innovative technology and business processes, barriers to entry, exclusive distribution arrangements, and so on are important because they lead to superior return on capital relative to the firm's peers.

A firm's **business model** represents the company's overall strategy for running the business in a way that creates value for a customer and captures that value in the form of revenues and profits (i.e., the firm's value proposition). Successful business models are scalable; the firm can increase in size up to the limits of its market while retaining profitability at a certain level.

Management determines the firm's business model and a strategy for implementing the model to achieve shareholder return requirements. Qualitative determinations about a company's management influence analyst expectations for market performance of its shares:

- Competence and long-term strategy and plans
- Minimizing agency problems via aligning management and shareholder interests
- Ability to attract and retain high-quality talent
- Opportunities and threats related to the firm's ESG characteristics

Corporate **branding** gives a company an identity within a market and represents its value proposition to customers. Sustainable business models typically generate strong brand loyalty among customers and in many cases allow firms to charge a premium for their products.

Value-Based Approaches

Value-based approaches identify and select stocks trading at a significant discount to intrinsic value:

- **Relative value**—Shares with low P/E, P/B, or other favorable value metric against the firm's industry or other peer group within an industry.
- **High-quality value**—Shares with high earnings quality or other redeeming features.
- **Deep value**—Shares at extreme discounts to their asset value that could be liquidated at a profit if need be or otherwise profitably reorganized, or at discounts resulting from informational inefficiencies arising from lack of general market interest.
- **Restructuring/distressed investing**—Shares of companies finding it difficult to make short-term liability payments where investors seek control with the goal of restructuring to increase value. More common in a weak economy, this is similar to deep-value investing, although companies do not need to be in distress to be part of deep value.
- **Contrarian investing**—Shares recently out of favor purchased with the hope of price recovery when the market rediscovers their true value.
- **Income investing**—Shares with a floor under their value based on relatively high dividend yield and growth potential.
- **Special situations**—Shares of companies that could spin off divisions or assets gained through a merger.

Growth-Based Approaches

Growth-based approaches seek shares of companies with high growth in revenues, earnings, or cash flow. Firms with **earnings momentum** sometimes increase at an increasing rate.

Growth at a reasonable price (GARP) strategies combine elements of growth and value by seeking above-average growth with a price lower than would be suggested by the growth rate.

Top-Down Strategies

Top-down strategies focus first on macro variables that affect the market. Portfolio managers may implement such strategies using ETFs, custom baskets of securities and derivatives.

Country and Geographic Allocation

In addition to looking at relative macro variables, this approach may also analyze volumes of initial and secondary share issuance, share buybacks, and the flows of investment funds.

Sector or Industry Rotation

Sector/industry rotation identifies and invests in potentially outperforming sectors within a country (e.g., locally specific real estate or consumer staples companies) or in potentially outperforming sectors globally (i.e., for globally integrated industries). Sector or industry performance can be determined from the top down or as a bottom-up process via aggregating individual security expectations.

Volatility-Based Strategies

Managers with skill at predicting actual price volatility different from option-implied volatility can successfully trade VIX futures or index swaps or enter into volatility swaps and variance swaps.

Traders expecting a large market move but not having an opinion on the direction of the move can enter a straddle by buying a call and put with the same strike price and expiration date. Losses occur in the amount of the option premiums if the market remains flat, but gains result when the market moves a significant amount.

Thematic Strategies

Innovative technology, demographic, or political drivers as well as economic cycles can create broad macroeconomic or individual company opportunities for investment. Unless the manager wishes to make only short-term investments, analysts should focus on themes with long-run structural effects.

Factor-Based Strategies

Security selection focuses on return factor characteristics (e.g., size, earnings quality and momentum, relative value, etc.) that markets reward with return and selects securities with those characteristics.

Style-rotation strategies recognize that certain factors receive greater rewards at certain times, and "rotate" or invest into securities with rewarded factors for a specific environment. This applies more to quantitative than to fundamental approaches.

Data mining describes a statistical relationship in data that doesn't make economic sense. Models may pass backtesting but fail in an investment setting.

Long-short factor-based portfolios rank securities by expected performance and then go long the expected best-performing quantile and short the expected worst-performing quantile. Shorting may not be possible in some portfolios, the performance of factors may differ between the best-performing and worst-performing quantiles, and concentration tends to occur in specific stocks across managers with this same approach. Exposure to non-modeled factors can significantly affect performance, especially in the leveraged short strategy.

Factor-mimicking portfolios (FMPs) are theoretical long-short, dollar-neutral portfolios with exposure to a specific factor only and no exposure to other factors. FMPs are expensive to implement.

Factor-tilting portfolios, in contrast, track an index, but the PM makes factor-based bets.

Value factors address price less than intrinsic value; that is, price divided by any fundamental factor. The metric may take the reverse form of a fundamental factor divided by price (e.g., dividend yield). High book-to-market ratio may also be used to indicate a value stock. The value premium compensates investors for assuming risk that the firm will not recover from an adverse position or will deteriorate. Some studies instead suggest that behavioral biases cause the premium.

The **price momentum** approach holds that stocks enjoying higher price appreciation during some past period will continue to enjoy price appreciation. Losses from price momentum strategies can suffer high losses (i.e., tail risk) due to gains created by behavioral biases. Sector-neutralized price momentum removes the sector exposure component to reduce extreme sector risk, especially in long-short strategies.

Research indicates that stock prices fail to fully reflect information in accruals and that accrual-to-price relationships may be cyclical. Therefore, *earnings quality* approaches determine dividend sustainability, management efficiency, capital utilization, profitability, and solvency. Analyst sentiment, especially earnings revisions, may be used to reflect potential earnings quality turning points.

Alternative approaches use data such as satellite images, online mentions, credit card processing information, and other unstructured data sources combined with structured data (i.e., earnings reports, etc.) to establish a broader picture of company activities. This "big data" approach can also be applied to supply chain data.

Activist Strategies
Activist investor strategies include:

- Financial reforms that better utilize investor capital, change dividends, or reduce the number of shares outstanding (i.e., share buybacks)
- Realigning management compensation with share price performance
- Unlocking value by spinning off divisions or divesting subsidiaries
- Advancing an ESG cause

Target companies typically have slower revenue and earnings growth than the market average, negative price momentum, or corporate governance structures that benefit management at the expense of shareholders.

Activist investors may seek change via:

- Board representation or nominating board members
- Engaging with management by writing letters, making direct phone calls, and private meetings with members of management
- Attending the annual general meeting with suggestions of change
- Launching "breach of fiduciary" legal proceedings
- Joining with other shareholders to demand action
- Launching a media campaign to reform management practices

Proponents contend that activism improves corporate monitoring and discipline. Opponents contend activism wastes management time and detracts from the mission.

Hedge funds and private equity firms that enjoy lower regulatory standards often pursue activist agendas. Their performance-based fee structure in addition to a fee for AUM makes it lucrative for such financial participants to pursue activist strategies.

Evidence suggests that activist targets have higher financial leverage but enjoy improving fundamentals after an activist event. Activist investors deliver Sharpe ratio results only marginally higher than the S&P 500.

Other Strategies

Statistical Arbitrage and Market Microstructure Strategies

"Stat arb" strategies use stock price, dividend, trading volume, and limit book data in traditional technical analysis, time-series analysis and econometric models, and machine learning processes (artificial intelligence or AI).

In a **pairs trading strategy**, for example, managers use either qualitative or quantitative methods to determine firms with correlation in price movement. The manager shorts the outperforming security with the idea it will return to the correlation with lower price; the manager goes long the underperforming security with the idea it will return to the correlation with higher price.

Microstructure-based trades involve exploiting supply and demand imbalances in the NYSE Trade and Quote (TAQ) book or other data source, observing positions in the limit book, or other anomalies that may be available for only milliseconds.

Event-Driven Strategies

Mergers and acquisitions, restructuring and spinoffs, special dividends and buybacks, and other corporate events can result in temporary mispricing.

Creating a Fundamental Active Investment Strategy

Portfolio managers employ an active investment strategy to outperform a benchmark on a risk-adjusted basis by using special allocation insights, superior security analysis and selection techniques, or via access to proprietary data.

Steps to create an active fundamental strategy:

1. Define the investment universe and market opportunity within the IPS mandate.
2. Screen the investment universe for likely investment opportunities based on the strategy.

3. Obtain additional information about the output from the initial screen via sector/industry analysis and by analyzing financial reports.
4. Forecast cash flow or earnings for target opportunities.
5. Develop valuations from the forecasts and determine undervalued securities.
6. Construct a risk-optimized portfolio that achieves the strategy.
7. Use the buy-sell discipline to take profits and avoid losses, as well as periodically rebalance the portfolio.

The manager's investment thesis involves defining the opportunity and economic, financial, behavioral, or other reasons for those uncovered opportunities. Managers remain neutral to their benchmark in industries where they have no investment thesis for a sector or industry.

Creating a Quantitative Active Investment Strategy

Creating a Quantitative Investment Process
Steps to create a quantitative investment process:

1. Define the market opportunity—Build models using publicly available data to forecast rewarded factors and potential return.
2. Acquire and process data—Understand data availability, map data from sources into their database in a usable format, scrub outliers from the data (where appropriate), and maintain the database.
3. Backtest the strategy.
4. Evaluate the model—Use out-of-sample tests to establish whether the model performs well under different scenarios.

A factor's information coefficient (IC) provides a linear relationship description of effectiveness in generating holding period returns or other target variables.

The Pearson IC examines the factor relationship with current period and next-period performance and, as a correlation measure, ranges from –1 to +1. Outliers influence the coefficient, and judgment must occasionally be used in normalizing the outliers. A monthly IC of 5% to 6% is considered significant.

The Spearman rank IC modifies the Pearson IC to describe the relationship between ranked factor scores and ranked forward returns. Practitioners prefer the Spearman IC because it is not influenced as heavily by outliers and, therefore, provides more robust relationship data.

The following issues become particularly important in quantitative investing:

- Variance-covariance estimation—The large number of securities requires many calculations.
- Trading costs—Limit explicit costs (commissions, fees, and taxes) and implicit costs (trading delays, bid–ask spread, market impact).

FI
EPM

Equity Investment Style Classification

Investment style classification allows investors to evaluate sources of added value from the manager's style and execution. Equity style classifications typically balance pairs of attributes such as growth/value, large/small capitalization, high/low volatility, and so on.

Approaches to Style-Based Classification

Holdings-based approaches aggregate individual security attributes into an indication of the manager's actual investment style. The same portfolio could theoretically be judged differently by different vendors, however, based on different data sources, timing, or method used.

There is no standard for capitalization classification. Large-cap companies generally offer less organic growth with less risk, small-cap companies have more growth potential and greater risk, and mid-cap companies fall somewhere between. Small-cap companies may have limited liquidity and may be less followed by analysts.

Equity style analysis starts by scoring an individual security's style. A simple system ranks stocks by their price-to-book (P/B) ratios. Value stocks fall in the lower half and growth stocks in the upper half, subject to 50% of market capitalization in each half. Other factors may be weighted and continued. Core portfolios mix value and growth stocks.

A returns-based style analysis examines return characteristics:

$$r_t = \alpha + \sum_{s=1}^{m} \beta^S R_t^S + \varepsilon_t$$

where

r_t = fund return for period t

r_t^S = style S return for period t

β^S = fund exposure to style S

    (constrained to $\sum \beta^S = 1$ with $\beta^S > 0$ for a long-only portfolio)

α = value added by the fund manager

ε_t = residual return unexplained by style indexes used

This is especially useful in cases where a manager does not disclose the securities in a portfolio.

The manager's own description of the portfolio's strategy in a fund prospectus may be useful for determining which indexes to test, although periodic management can render self-identification less useful.

Some equity hedge fund styles (e.g., market-neutral, dedicated short bias, or long/short portfolios) don't fit any style category and their strategy may not be determinable by returns-based style analysis. The prospectus becomes the source of defining such strategies.

Strengths and Limitations of Styles-Based Analysis

Holdings-based style analysis provides better identification of portfolio style than returns-based analysis because it uses all holdings as the basis for determination. However, it requires identification of all portfolio stocks and their style attributes. This is a drawback for analysts wishing to understand style drift because some historical data may not be accessible. Data limitations and flaws in the returns-based analysis can limit reliability of that type of style analysis.

ACTIVE EQUITY INVESTING: PORTFOLIO CONSTRUCTION
Cross-Reference to CFA Institute Assigned Reading #25

Building Blocks of Active Equity Portfolio Construction

Fundamentals of Portfolio Construction

Active return represents the portfolio manager's bets against benchmark:

$$R_A = \sum_{i=1}^{n} (w_i - W_i) r_i$$

where

w_i = portfolio weight of asset i

W_i = benchmark weight of asset i

r_i = return on asset i

Managers gain money on average by overweighting outperforming assets and underweighting underperforming assets:

- **Strategically**—Adjusting active weights of the strategy to outperform benchmark weights over a long period.
- **Tactically**—Identifying temporarily mispriced sectors, industries, or securities to achieve returns not explained by long-term exposure to systematic risk.
- **Idiosyncratically**—Random shocks, noise, and so forth.

The first two represent skill, whereas the last results from luck:

$$R_A = \sum (\beta_{pk} - \beta_{bk}) F_k + (\alpha + \varepsilon)$$

where

β_{pk} = portfolio sensitivity to each reward factor k

β_{bk} = benchmark sensitivity to each reward factor k

F_k = rewarded factor return

α = return due to manager skill at security selection and timing

ε = i diosyncratic return (e.g., due to earnings surprises)

It is difficult to separate alpha return from idiosyncratic return.

Building Blocks Used in Portfolio Construction

Market return comprises the biggest component of portfolio return regardless of strategy. Managers should be measured against a benchmark representing the strategy employed.

Managers add value by varying exposure to a specific factor using technical skills or through other skills involved with a fundamental approach.

Assuming a homogeneous market (e.g., U.S. equities) and similar holding period, individual investors perform at the benchmark level of return, and outperformers have made trades with underperformers. Managers measured against a style-tilted benchmark can generate alpha by

FI
EPM

increasing allocation to factors during periods when they are positive and decreasing allocation when returns to those factors are negative.

To generate alpha, the additional performance must be greater than the added costs of active trading.

Concentrated portfolios are less diversified and tend to have greater idiosyncratic risk. Factor-oriented managers attempt to eliminate idiosyncratic risk by holding a diversified portfolio; gifted stock pickers seek the idiosyncratic (and therefore theoretically unrewarded) return in a concentrated portfolio.

A manager's uncorrelated "bets" affect alpha and therefore information coefficient (i.e., how well the manager's forecast excess returns correspond to realized excess returns). This information coefficient can then be combined into a realization of expected active portfolio return:

$$E(R_A) = IC\sqrt{BR}\sigma_{R_A}TC$$

where

IC = Expected information coefficient (correlation between forecast and actual active return)

BR = Breadth (the number of independent, uncorrelated manager decisions)

σ_{R_A} = Active risk (tracking risk of the portfolio against the benchmark)

TC = Transfer coefficient (the degree to which portfolio insights translate to investment decisions)

The transfer coefficient will be 1 for a portfolio allowing the manager to transfer all insights into investment decisions. Based on this formula, the time horizon required to realize excess returns shortens as the number of independent decisions, BR, increases or the percentage of insights allowed to become investment decisions, TC, increases.

Approaches to Portfolio Construction

Implementation: Choice of Management Approaches

Exhibit 1: Building Blocks for Types of Approaches

	Systematic	Discretionary
Top down	Macro factors Factor timing Diversified	Macro factors Factor timing Diversified/concentrated*
Bottom up	Security-specific factors No factor timing Diversified	Firm-specific factors Potential factor timing Diversified/concentrated*

*May be diversified or concentrated depending on the manager's strategy/style.

Either systematic or discretionary approaches provide exposure to rewarded factors. Top-down managers first emphasize macro factors, whereas bottom-up managers first emphasize security-specific managers. Discretionary managers, especially those with a top-down approach, are more likely to implement factor timing. Systematic portfolios will be more diversified; discretionary portfolios will be less diversified.

A benchmark-aware portfolio will tend to more closely resemble its benchmark whereas a benchmark-agnostic portfolio will have more deviation from its benchmark. **Active share** represents the degree of deviation from a benchmark:

$$\text{Active share} = 1/2 \times \sum_{i=1}^{n} |w_i - W_i|$$

where

n = number of securities in the portfolio or the benchmark

w_i = weight of security i in the portfolio

W_i = weight of security i in the benchmark

The two sources of active share include:

1. Portfolio securities not in the benchmark.
2. Portfolio securities in the benchmark at different weights.

Active risk uses a variation of the active return formula and may be either forward looking or historical:

$$\sigma_{R_A} = \sqrt{\sigma^2 \left(\sum (\beta_{PK} - \beta_{BK}) \times F_k \right) + \sigma_\varepsilon^2}$$

The first term under the radical is variance attributed to factor exposure, and the second term is variance of idiosyncratic risk.

Managers can completely control active share but cannot control active risk (due to the correlation with other under- or overweight securities). Overweighting or underweighting stocks with correlated returns (e.g., in the same industry) will result in *less* active risk than the same weight differences in stocks with uncorrelated returns.

Assuming a single-factor exposure model and an unconstrained investor, active risk:

- Increases with the portfolio's net exposure to the factor, regardless of idiosyncratic risk
- Can be attributed entirely to active share when the factor exposure is neutralized
- When idiosyncratic risk is low or diversified
- Increases when factor and idiosyncratic exposure volatilities increase

Reducing the idiosyncratic component is part of the key to reducing unwanted active risk.

Objectives and Constraints

Risk-adjusted return used in portfolio construction should use returns net of implementation costs. The objective function would use these net returns to optimize the portfolio based on the definition of risk; active risk would use the information ratio (active return per unit of active risk), and expected volatility would use the Sharpe ratio (excess return over the risk-free rate per unit of portfolio volatility).

Constraints stated relative to a benchmark would typically use the information ratio; constraints stated in absolute terms would use the Sharpe ratio. The absolute approach may also state position limits as a percentage of the portfolio, whereas the relative approach would state such limits in terms of variance from the benchmark.

Risk Budgeting

Effective risk management requires:

- Determining the appropriate risk measure.
- Budgeting the appropriate risk for the strategy.
- Recognizing each strategic element's contribution to risk.
- Determining the appropriate risk budget for individual positions or factors.

Absolute Versus Relative Risk Measures

Total portfolio risk rises when:

1. Adding an asset with covariance higher than the portfolio.
2. Replacing a lower-covariance asset with a higher-covariance asset.

The reverse will also be true, and the same is true with countries, sectors, and so forth, as for individual assets.

A manager should limit exposure to risks outside his capabilities as reflected in the benchmark:

$$V_p = Var\left(\sum_{i=1}^{n}(\beta_{ip} \times F_i)\right) + Var(\varepsilon_p)$$

Relative risk measures variance of the portfolio's active return:

$$AV_p = \sum_{i=1}^{n}\sum_{j=1}^{n}(w_i - W_i)(w_j - W_j)RC_{ij}$$
$$CAV_i = (w_i - W_i)RC_{ip}$$

where

AV_p = Variance of the portfolio's active return
CAV_i = Contribution of each asset to portfolio active variance
RC_{ij} = correlation of benchmark-relative returns between assets i and j
RC_{ip} = correlation of benchmark-relative returns between asset i and the portfolio

Managers can determine the risk contribution of each position (i.e., whether factor, country, sector, or individual security) based on its weight in the portfolio and covariance with the portfolio. In the relative risk framework, adding a high-volatility asset to a portfolio might *lower* active risk if the asset has high covariance with its benchmark.

Determining an Appropriate Risk Level

Total as well as relative **risk appetite,** as well as subjective risk judgments regarding style and skill level, affect strategy implementation (e.g., portfolio structure, turnover, etc.). For example, a manager without short-selling ability may not be able to cost-effectively raise the portfolio's information ratio as much as a manager with short-selling ability.

FI
EPM

Managers can maintain an optimal Sharpe ratio by leveraging returns and managing absolute risk in a one-period model. Over multiple periods, however, the effects of leverage ultimately diminish compound (i.e., geometric) return. Arithmetic returns from leverage decrease as a function of variance, a squared term, so the degree of leverage at some point becomes sufficient to offset the return benefit. Funding costs (not shown here) further lower the beneficial degree of leverage.

Additional Risk Measures Used in Portfolio Construction and Rebalancing

Heuristic Constraints

Heuristic (i.e., nonformal) constraints may result from experience rather than evidence of usefulness:

- Concentration—Geography, sector, industry, or security
- Exposure to risk factors—Beta, momentum/value, size
- Currency exposure
- Leverage
- Liquidity
- Turnover (higher trading costs)
- ESG concerns

Portfolios with concentrated positions may attempt to limit single position losses:

- Lesser of 2% of portfolio or $5\times$ benchmark weight (to avoid extreme losses)
- $2\times$ average trading volume over previous three months (to avoid liquidity bottlenecks)

Other portfolio constraints might include:

- Weighted average capitalization $< 75\%$ of its benchmark
- Carbon footprint $< 75\%$ of its benchmark

These constraints help reduce potential problems from overconfidence but can limit strategy realization. Also, heuristic approaches make it difficult to measure the potential effect of proposed changes.

Formal Constraints

Statistical measures can increase understanding of potential effects of proposed changes, but depend on the type of portfolio. The manager of an absolute return fund may ignore the benchmark but be concerned with drawdowns that could affect strategy implementation. A manager who neutralizes market risk in a long/short strategy will be likely to target risks within a certain range to lessen the effects of other types of risk.

Discretionary managers with more concentrated portfolios have wider risk tolerance and watch for deviations from historical risk exposures.

Implicit Cost Considerations in Portfolio Construction

Market Impact

A trade's market impact (i.e., security price movement) depends on the trade size and issue liquidity at the time the manager makes the trade. Large-sized position trades can signal the market that something has changed and affect trade price.

Portfolios may be subject to trade-size constraints that limit unfavorable market impact. These trade-size constraints may relate to fund AUM, the security's market capitalization, or average trading in the security. Larger trades may then be implemented over several days or a longer period.

Dark pools, crossing networks, and other venues for "unlit" trading allow larger trades without as much market impact.

Slippage Costs

Slippage costs describe the price change from the bid-ask spread midpoint at order delivery to the price at order execution. Slippage includes both market impact and volatility/trend costs (i.e., costs of buying/selling into a rising or falling trend).

Slippage costs:
- Tend to exceed commissions.
- Are typically higher for small-cap stocks than large-cap stocks.
- Are not necessarily higher for emerging market stocks.
- Are typically higher when market volatility is higher.

A large order may have to be placed over several days and may have the market impact of its own trades as well as trend costs.

Efficient Portfolio Structure

An efficient portfolio delivers return consistent with risk expectations, although it cannot guarantee excess return over the manager's benchmark even over shorter horizons. Efficient portfolios typically start with a clear investment philosophy and consistent investment process, and they implement the process with low operating costs relative to the type of strategy.

Exploiting Research Insights

Examples of portfolios that exploit research insights include:

- **Long extension portfolios**—Combined positions equal to long only (e.g., 130% long and 30% short).
- **Market-neutral portfolios**—Neutralize market factors exposure (i.e., focus on idiosyncratic factors).
- **Long/short portfolios**—Long extension, market neutral, or unconstrained long or short positions.
- **Equal-risk-premium products**—Combining equal risk subportfolios of factor exposure, levered or delevered, to achieve a desired volatility level for each factor.

Considerations for Long-Short Investing Include
- Need to own the long-term risk premium to achieve return
- Capacity of market to absorb trades and ability to add to positions
- Legal liability limitations (i.e., ability to attract excess loss)
- Regulatory constraints
- Transactional complexity—Security borrowing and ability to manage operational risk
- Higher management costs from short selling
- Personal ideology—Moral aversion to short selling, leverage

FI
EPM

Long/Short Portfolio Construction

Long/short portfolios must establish gross and net exposure limits based on their thesis so that investors have meaningful information about strategy and the associated risk exposure. Net exposure greater than 0% implies some exposure to the market factor.

Long Extension Portfolio Construction

Also known as **enhanced active equity strategies**, long positions greater than 100% of capital are funded by offsetting short sales. In a 130/30 extension approach, gross exposure is 160% although net exposure is 100 percent.

Market-Neutral Portfolio Construction

Market-neutral strategies seek to remove the effects of market movements, positive or negative, to focus on the abnormal return of the manager's insights. Managers do not zero out exposure to all rewarded risks, just those for which they have no specific insight. Neutralizing all market exposure risks would likely result in the risk-free rate less costs and fees.

A market-neutral portfolio's lower volatility and lower correlation with other assets can have diversification benefits to unrelated portfolios of risk assets.

Market-neutral strategies are neutral with respect to risk but may involve positions greater than net 0% long. A simple example would be a $100 long investment in an asset with beta equal to 1 and an $80 short sale against an asset with beta equal to 1.25. Net, the portfolio beta equals 0 $[(1 \times 100/180) - (1.25 \times 80/180)]$. The same concept can extend to size, value, and other rewarded factors such that risk exposure equals 0 for each factor pair.

One variation of the market-neutral strategy buys the top contenders and shorts the losers in a universe of stocks, subject to constraints on the long and short positions.

Pairs trading involves going long and short two securities in the same industry. A variant of pairs trading called statistical arbitrage or "stat arb" quantitatively selects securities in the same industry that temporarily deviate from long-term price correlation, going long the underperforming stock and shorting the outperforming stock. As correlation returns and prices converge, both the long and short positions gain.

Benefits and Drawbacks of Long/Short Strategies

Benefits include:

- Better expression of insights on negative performance
- Efficient use of leverage and the benefits of diversification
- Better control of exposure to rewarded factors
- Expansion of rewarded factors available for investment

Drawbacks include:

- Magnifying the potential of leverage
- Costs of security borrowing
- Lack of securities available to implement a strategy
- Potential reduction to the market return premium
- Short squeeze in which a security's price rises and short sellers buy to cover, thereby further increasing prices

STUDY SESSION 11: ALTERNATIVE INVESTMENTS FOR PORTFOLIO MANGEMENT

AI
PM

AI
PM

HEDGE FUND STRATEGIES
Cross-Reference to CFA Institute Reading #26

Classifying Hedge Funds and Strategies

Single-manager funds have a single portfolio manager or a team of portfolio managers who invest in a single strategy or style. **Multi-manager funds** may be either a (1) **multi-strategy fund** with several portfolio managers employing different strategies within the same fund, or (2) **fund-of-funds** with a manager allocating funds to other distinct funds within a single strategy or across several strategies.

Taxonomy within the single-manager, single-strategy classification usually separates into trading philosophy (e.g., systematic, discretionary), asset classes (e.g., equity, convertible bonds, commodities, forex), or risks assumed (e.g., event driven, directional, relative value).

Different data vendors classify hedge funds differently. The framework employed in subsequent lessons describes major classes of hedge funds by their exposure to the above factors.

Table 1: Hedge Fund Categories

Equity	Event Driven	Relative-Value	Opportunistic	Specialist	Multi-Manager
Long-short equity	Merger arbitrage	Fixed-income arbitrage	Global macro	Volatility	Multi-strategy
Dedicated short bias	Distressed securities	Convertible bond arbitrage	Managed futures	Reinsurance	Fund of funds
Equity market neutral					

Equity Strategies

Long-Short Equity
The goal of long-short equity investing is to achieve alpha returns via stock picking and only secondarily through market timing that could be accomplished via less expensive long-only funds. "Beta-tilting" often decreases alpha by remaining overly long during a market downturn.

Quant managers may also attempt to improve returns from high-conviction positions through use of leverage; this is not common among fundamental managers.

Difference in strategy focus, use of leverage, and willingness to hold positions over time determine a manager's risk factor exposures. Excess small-cap exposure, for example, not only provides benefits of size exposure, but gives a growth tilt to the portfolio. Excess large-cap exposure provides negative size exposure and a value tilt.

Rising markets lead to the idea that most long-short managers will be net long over time while some managers maintain short positions to hedge possible market downturns. Opportunistic managers are likely to have extensive short positions in all markets based on their perceptions of company or sector opportunities.

AI
PM

Dedicated Short Selling and Short-Biased

Dedicated short-selling strategies maintain only short positions based on overvaluation relative to fundamentals and vary their allocation by using the cash position. **Short-biased strategies** search for short-selling opportunities but may balance their portfolios with long positions.

Activist short-selling strategies take a position based on overvaluation and then present research to the market with the hope of driving other market participants to sell short.

Equity Market Neutral (EMN)

EMN strategies go long one position and short a similar or related position. Because market-related risks have been eliminated, EMN portfolios often employ massive leverage.

Pairs trading goes long one stock and short another when their relative valuation relationships become unsustainable. **Stub trading** is a subset of pairs trading that invests 100% of the position—long or short—in the parent and invests the other way in the subsidiaries based on the proportion owned by the parent. **Multi-class trading** is another subset in which different classes of stock in the same company have become incorrectly valued.

Quantitative market-neutral managers make daily or hourly position adjustments based on the relative valuation relationships. Quantitative market-neutral trading becomes **statistical arbitrage trading** when adjustments become even more frequent and relative valuation and relative momentum characteristics are emphasized.

Macro-oriented market-neutral allocators, also known as **market-neutral tactical allocators**, are beta-neutral managers that specialize in sector rotation for generating alpha.

Market neutral strategies have comparatively low risk over time but remain subject to alpha risk, liquidity risk, and tail risk (i.e., large losses during market stress).

EMN portfolio construction involves the following four steps:

1. Exclude stocks from the investment universe with insufficient liquidity and no short-selling potential.
2. Use fundamental models and momentum models to determine buy-sell opportunities.
3. Construct the portfolio with market value-weighted neutrality (i.e., beta of 0) and possibly neutral with respect to other risk factors.
4. Consider cost and availability of leverage, especially in the event of a portfolio drawdown.

Event-Driven Strategies

Event-driven strategies attempt to profit from corporate events such as mergers and acquisitions, bankruptcies, buybacks, restructuring, and so on. The **soft-catalyst approach** trades in advance of the event whereas the **hard-catalyst approach** trades after the event has occurred but the effects of which are not fully reflected in market price. Hard-catalyst trades generally involve less volatility.

Merger Arbitrage

In mergers generally, the initial deal announcement causes the acquiring company's stock to fall due to potential dilution of share value or use of cash, and the target company's stock rises to recognize the premium paid by the acquirer. Merger arbs seeking low volatility may invest only in friendly takeovers while those seeking higher volatility and return may invest in hostile takeovers.

Merger arbitrage classifications include stock-for-stock (i.e., if management considers its share price overvalued) or cash-for-stock (i.e., if fairly valued or undervalued).

If the acquisition succeeds (no adverse event), the merger arb gains the risk premium (like the premium paid on an insurance policy). If the acquisition fails (an adverse event), the merger arb loses on both the long and short positions.

Due to use of leverage, merger arbs prefer the limited partnership fund structure, although some low-volatility liquid alt funds exist. Merger arbs have fewer liquidity issues with cash-for-stock acquisition situations but may face liquidity or regulatory hurdles, especially shorting the acquirer's stock in a stock-for-stock acquisition by emerging market companies.

Purchasing the convertible allows participation in price increases and provides a floor under losses. For deals where the target is less credit worthy than the acquirer, merger arbs may sell credit default swap protection on the target with the idea that its credit quality will improve after acquisition.

Distressed Securities

Distressed securities strategies focus on buying securities of companies in financial stress, facing potential bankruptcy, or in bankruptcy where the workout value is greater than the stock price. The long lockup times, redemption gates, and flexible risk mandates make hedge funds the perfect vehicle for this type of investing.

Managers may seek controlling positions in the company's capital structure components in order to gain representation on the board of directors or to exert control over reorganization or liquidation.

Fulcrum securities such as senior debt will likely be repaid proportionately with equity and end up owning the reorganized company. As the financial distress moderates, new equity enters via IPO and the hedge fund manager exits with the value of the new equity position less the deeply discounted debt.

Part of the opportunity in distressed investing occurs when insurance companies and other regulated entities are forced to sell debt that has fallen below a rating threshold. The "rush to the door" sell may overshoot to the downside the actual value of the holding.

Prospects for success are either very good or very bad, but seldom result in complete success or failure. The long workout times and risk generally limit application of excessive leverage, although returns are at the high end of event-driven strategies generally.

Relative Value Strategies

In addition to relative value strategies employed in equity market neutral (EMN) portfolios, relative value opportunities also exist in fixed-income securities and hybrid-convertible debt. Relative valuation opportunities result from disequilibrium of credit quality, liquidity, and volatility (for option securities).

Fixed Income Arbitrage

Credit-relative risk arbitrage can be more volatile and rewarding than exploiting small pricing differences in sovereign securities. Most strategies use duration-neutral immunization unless they involve yield curve exposure. Managers typically employ derivatives strategies to immunize against larger or non-parallel yield curve changes. Managers may also use derivatives to hedge against sovereign risk, currency risk, credit risk, and pre-payment risk.

High leverage may be used to magnify the small gains expected with most strategies. The size of the haircut (i.e., interest rate) charged by prime brokers depends on the degree of leverage and the type of collateral.

Risks of relative-value strategies involving mortgages and structured products built around them can be high, especially during certain parts of the economic cycle. A negative convexity aspect caused by the pre-payment option also complicates analysis and position maintenance.

Liquidity aspects are good for most of the sovereign debt market and can be poor for the rest of the market, especially certain corporate bond and municipal debt markets. This presents relative value opportunities but, of course, credit and liquidity risks.

Based on the market characteristics, yield curve and carry trades are the most common. Calendar spread strategies rely on long and short positions based on mispricing at different points on the yield curve. Investing across securities in the same issuer may be used to exploit curve flattening or steepening offers the best opportunity. Trades in the same issuer likely capture interest rate risk, but hedge most of the liquidity and credit risks.

Carry trades generally involve going long a higher-yielding security and shorting a lower-yielding security with the hope of profit when mispricing reverses. An example here might be buying higher-yield off-the-run government securities and shorting duration-matched, lower-yield, on-the-run government securities. Prices of on-the-run securities will decrease as they age and the government issues new on-the-run securities. The payoff profile for this strategy resembles a short-put option with profit on the carry and spread narrowing as the strategy unfolds. Widening spreads result in losses.

Convertible Bond Arbitrage

Convertible bonds include a straight debt component plus an option value equal to the stock price less the strike price of an embedded option. Convertible bonds behave more like straight bonds when the stock price is lower than the strike price (out of the money) and more like equity when the conversion value (i.e., conversion ratio multiplied by share price) is high.

Credit-oriented convertible managers assume the credit risk on the underlying and hedge the other mentioned risks. **Volatility-oriented convertible managers** overhedge while other managers may underhedge. The strategy works best with high convertible issuance (good liquidity) and moderate volatility. It fairs less well during downturns when credit is weak or when the market is illiquid.

Use of leverage is high to extract gain from small profits in the delta hedge and must occur on multiple legs; that is, the interest rate hedge, CDS transaction, and short sale.

Opportunistic Strategies

Opportunistic strategies invest in different instruments or markets depending on the risk-return potential. Generally, they may be classified based on the types of instruments or markets they trade in, whether they use systematic or discretionary trading, and whether they rely primarily on technical or fundamental analysis.

Global Macro Strategies

Global macro managers express views on various macro shifts through currency or rate curve positions as well as a wide variety of instruments. They tend to be anticipatory, often setting contrarian positions in advance of a reversing trend. Prospective changes may not materialize or be as expected.

These strategies generally employ very high leverage. This may be riskier than other types of strategies because the binary risk-on/-off nature of the trades decreases the diversification benefits of overlapping but different simultaneous positions.

Managed Futures

Managed futures funds may invest in virtually any position using any security. They are primarily attractive to investors desiring diversification owing to the uncorrelated nature of the instruments with traditional fixed-income or equity securities and real estate. Futures markets are among the most actively traded in the world, so liquidity is usually high across a wide range of asset classes.

Returns tend to be highly cyclical, with the greatest gains coming during periods of change or volatility.

Due to greater liquidity and the daily mark-to-market function, clearinghouses demand little margin and managers can take highly leveraged positions.

Managed futures managers tend to use technical analysis, and many of the strategies are based on momentum/trend or volatility signals. Managers may use a combination of more heavily weighted long-term trend indicators and less heavily weighted short-term indicators to determine a net long-short position. Fundamental relationships—especially volatility factors or carry trade relationships—may also be factored into the position.

Managers hold smaller portfolio sizing in positions with greater correlation to other positions and greater volatility.

Time series momentum (TSM) involves following the development of a relevant series and is the most common model type. TSM goes long assets that trend upward and shorts assets with a downward trend … until the trend reverses and the strategy reverses or simply unwinds.

Cross-sectional momentum (CSM) involves going long assets within a class and short assets in the same asset class. These strategies generally have net zero long-short exposure. CSM strategies work best when one market's performance relative to another market in the same asset class remains stable.

Specialist Strategies

Volatility Trading

Relative value volatility arbitrage sells expensive volatility and buys cheap volatility. Cross-market volatility trading occurs between markets. Cross-asset volatility occurs between assets, whether in the same market or different markets.

Volatility on equity has high *negative* correlation with equity securities; therefore, long volatility diversifies against a falling equity market.

Longer-dated options have more exposure to volatility (vega exposure) while shorter-dated options have more exposure to delta changes (gamma exposure). Volatilities may also have a "smile" across different strike prices where out-of-the-money options trade at greater volatility than at-the-money options and a "smirk" (or "skew") where out-of-the-money puts may trade at greater volatility than out-of-the-money calls.

Short-term VIX (volatility index futures) has the most liquidity and isolates volatility, but experiences relatively rapid mean reversion and slides down the volatility yield curve as the futures approach maturity. Therefore, practitioners may prefer exchange-traded call/put options, OTC options, volatility swaps on standard deviation, or variance swaps. Short-term options may experience greater theta decay (option price decay due to time), which reduces the volatility roll-down payoff.

Reinsurance/Life Settlements

In the last several decades, life policyholders could exchange their insurance contract back to the issuer in exchange for payment. Recently, third-party brokers have been purchasing high cash-value life policies who then sell them to hedge funds. Hedge funds may have a different view of life expectancy than that represented by a certain subset of contracts and thereby profit from the actual versus expected outcomes.

Hedge funds may purchase life insurance policies from a broker or other parties with expertise in identifying:

- Relatively low surrender value to the insured.
- Relatively low premium payments.
- An insured in a group likely to die sooner than assumed by the policy.

Payments to the policy owner of such policies are called **life settlements.**

These criteria have almost nothing to do with financial markets, so these hedge funds are likely to have little correlation and high diversification benefits.

Hedge fund capital has also been flowing to reinsurance of catastrophic risk, which has improved liquidity and increased values for existing contracts. In this case, hedge funds must be staffed with those familiar with sophisticated patterns of geographical inputs such as weather. The fund must be geographically diversified to prevent a catastrophic event from wiping out the fund.

Multi-Manager Strategies

Fund of Funds

A fund of funds (FoF) involves a manager who determines the appropriate mix of strategies and engages appropriate managers representing each strategy. FoFs may be desirable in terms of access, diversification, liquidity, and tax reporting purposes (because the investor gets one statement from the FoF manager). The extra layer of management also adds an extra layer of fees and may also result in lower transparency into individual manager processes.

Multi-Strategy Funds

Multi-strategy funds combine several strategies, presumably with different managers, under the same fund structure. This structure allows more efficient capital reallocation than an FoF, and the fund manager retains full transparency into his fund managers' strategies. Correlations between strategies are also easier to monitor and manage.

This fund structure can also solve the problem of having flat or down overall FoF return but still having to pay incentive fees on funds within the FoF that performed well (i.e., netting risk). However, the problem remains in some funds that individually reward successful strategy teams and pass through incentive costs to the fund owner (i.e., the "pass-through" fee model).

Housing all the processes under one manager does expose the fund to more operational risk, but the main risk is that most multi-strategy funds use higher leverage than FoFs.

Analyzing Hedge Fund Strategies

Each of the foregoing strategies has factor exposures, sometimes overlapping and sometimes unique. Regression analysis can provide information on the characteristics and risks of a specific investment:

- L/S equity and event-driven strategies—Beta risk
- Arbitrage strategies—Credit risk and market volatility tail risk
- Opportunistic strategies—Trend risk (directionality)
- Relative value strategies—Risk of not returning to trend

Conditional Risk-Factor Models

Conditional risk-factor models can establish whether strategy returns derive from specific characteristics of a market; that is, whether they have greater risk during market downturns and when returns are most available. A dummy variable of 1 or 0 can be used to turn on or off the crisis, respectively, for the model.

The following factors are common for the Hasanhodzic and Lo model used in practice:

- Equity risk (S&P 500)—Monthly index total return (includes dividends)
- Interest rate risk (BOND)—Bloomberg Barclays Corporate AA Intermediate Bond Index
- Currency risk (USD)—Monthly return of the U.S. dollar index
- Commodity risk (CMDTY)—Goldman Sachs commodity index (GSCI total return)
- Credit risk (CREDIT)—Spread between Moody's Corporate Bond Yield Index for Baa versus Aaa
- Volatility risk (VIX)—First difference for the end-of-month CBOE VIX volatility index

A four-step "stepwise regression" process then establishes the conditional linear factor model that avoids multi-collinearity but maintains the best explanatory power.

Evaluating Equity Hedge Fund Strategies

Using the conditional model developed above, each strategy's factor exposures are calculated during normal conditions and during crisis. This reveals whether funds tend to have homogeneous (i.e., the same) exposures during a market crisis while having more heterogeneous (i.e., different) exposures during normal markets.

In addition to comparing Sharpe and Sortino ratios, the latter being excess return per unit of downside deviation), managers should investigate *rho*, the first order serial autocorrelation. High *rho* may indicate that current period returns relate to the prior period as the result of smoothing.

AI
PM

Evaluating Multi-Manager Hedge Fund Strategies

Multi-strategy funds do not have significant hedging benefits in a crisis. Some individual fund managers, however, are able to add significant value by pre-crisis selling, deleveraging, and short selling.

FoFs in general often have little USD/VIX exposure during normal times but increased exposure during crisis times, presumably due to leverage.

Portfolio Contribution of Hedge Fund Strategies

When a traditional portfolio with an allocation of 60% stocks and 40% bonds is combined with hedge funds to a new allocation of 48% stocks, 32% bonds, and 20% hedge funds (equally-weighted across all hedge fund categories):

- The highest Sharpe ratio included 20% allocation entirely to systematic futures hedge funds.
- Distressed securities, global macro, and equity market-neutral strategies also had high Sharpe ratios.
- The best Sortino ratios (which reflect return per unit of downside deviation) consist of market-neutral (TASS), systematic futures, L/S equity hedge, or event-driven TASS categories.

These same categories of funds tend to have the best diversification benefits in the combined portfolio.

Opportunistic strategies (e.g., global macro, systematic futures, merger arbitrage, and equity market-neutral) tend to have the lowest maximum drawdown because they have low equity or credit exposure during crisis periods. Event-driven and relative value strategies have equity risk exposure and expanding credit exposure during crisis periods that tend to increase the maximum drawdown.

FoF and multi-manager funds do not enhance risk-adjusted performance much or improve diversification substantially.

ASSET ALLOCATION TO ALTERNATIVE INVESTMENTS
Cross-Reference to CFA Institute Reading #27

The Role of Alternative Investments in Multi-Asset Portfolios

"Alternative" investments include private equity, hedge funds, real assets (including energy and commodity investments), commercial real estate, and private credit. Some assets such as gold may help reduce volatility during many types of market shocks.

Table 2: The Role of Asset Classes in a Multi-Asset Portfolio

Asset Class		Role			
		Capital Growth	Income	Diversifies Public Equity	Safety
Equity	Public equity	H	M		
	Private equity	H	M		
Fixed income and credit	Government		M	H	H
	Inflation-linked		M	H	H/M
	Investment grade		M	H	M
	High-yield		H	M	
	Private credit		H	M	
Real estate	Public real estate	M	H	M	
	Private real estate	M	H	M	
Real assets	Public real assets			H	
	Private real assets	H	H	H	
	Gold				H
Hedge funds	Absolute return		M	H	
	Equity long-short			M	

Functional roles in a portfolio include:

- **Capital growth**—Long-term horizon, high return target.
- **Income generation**—Short-term for parking cash, medium-term or longer-term for income generation to meet spending goals.
- **Risk diversification**—Equity portfolios seeking to diversify beta risk; private credit can help diversify fixed-income portfolios against pure yield curve risk.
- **Safety**—Government bonds or gold can help diversify against market crises.

The Role of Private Equity
Although there are limited diversification benefits when added to a portfolio with equity securities, private equity generally pays an additional risk premium for illiquidity. Lack of public trading means a lack of price discovery and unobservable return volatility, although volatility may be estimated from a public equity index appropriately adjusted based on asset type.

The Role of Hedge Funds
Hedge fund strategies involve several different roles:

AI
PM

- Long/short equity strategies—Adds alpha return while reducing exposure to beta returns
- Short-biased strategies—Adds alpha return from shorting individual company stocks based on fundamental insights; also reduces beta return
- Arbitrage and event-driven—Low to no correlation with traditional asset classes; short-volatility risk that may be missed unless the study period includes a market stress period
- Opportunistic strategies (e.g., global macro and managed futures)—Exposure to non-traditional strategies; very volatile if used as standalone investments.

The Role of Real Assets

Real assets are a category of physical assets with relatively high correlation to inflation or some inflation component.

- **Timber**—Investments increase in value as the tree grows as well as with the underlying land value; owners can decide not to harvest if prices are too low.
- **Tradeable commodities**—Physical commodities may include a separate alpha return in addition to an inflation component:
  - Metals (gold, silver, platinum, copper)
  - Energies (crude oil, heating oil, natural gas, gasoline)
  - Agriculture (wheat, corn, rice, soybeans, cocoa, coffee, sugar, cotton)
  - Livestock (hogs, pork bellies, cattle)
- **Farmland investing:**
  - Own the farmland/pay the farmer—Long horizon investments; owner retains execution risk, commodity risk (e.g., risk of natural disaster), and regulatory risk (e.g., trade disputes).
  - Own the farmland/lease to the farmer—More like commercial real estate investing; farmer retains execution risk and commodity risk.

- **Energy investments**—Long-horizon investments; exploration, development, transportation, and delivery of energy-related products; MLPs typically own mineral rights rather than the land.
- **Infrastructure**—Even longer holding periods; construction and maintenance of public use projects (e.g., bridges, toll roads, airports); may be subject to regulatory constraints; stable to moderate income growth with relatively little maintenance.

The Role of Commercial Real Estate

There are two components that contribute to real estate's perceived inflation protection attributes:

1. **Capital gain**—Underlying property value or land increases
2. **Income**—Rental income increases

Private real estate may provide diversification opportunities not present in public real estate, but smaller investors who cannot purchase and manage suitable properties will find more opportunity in the public market.

Real estate investing involves some combination of developing, acquiring, managing, and disposing of commercial real estate. Strategies include:

- Core—Ownership of property to participate in income and capital gains
- Opportunistic—Ground-up property development or purchase and rehabilitation of distressed property

The Role of Private Credit

Lenders that provide credit to borrowers who may not have access to more traditional loans assume default and recovery risks from the loan as well as additional liquidity risk.

Distressed debt generally takes on more equity-like characteristics because the debt is related to the value of the borrower's underlying assets; that is, idiosyncratic risks dominate yield curve and other risks. Distressed debt also carries a premium for a lack of marketability.

Diversifying Equity Risks

Volatility Reduction over a Short Horizon

Short-term investors may add fixed income securities to a portfolio to decrease volatility. However, using alternative assets valued using appraisals can understate volatility and over-represent diversification benefits. The appraisal-based return data must be unsmoothed to be usable.

Additionally, data may be affected by survivorship bias in which only successful firms continue operating and backfill bias in which only firms having good results survive and are included in a series.

Although many hedge funds, private credit, or private equities experience drawdowns correlated to a falling equity market, certain alternative assets (particularly gold, but also many commodities) may rally during a crisis. Government bonds exhibit slightly negative correlation, suggesting they provide a "risk-off" haven during a crisis.

Correlation does not directly identify the sensitivity of one asset to another. For example, although stocks and bonds have positive correlation with each other and with GDP growth, growth surprises are good for equities but are bad for bonds (due to fears of interest rate increases).

Risk of Not Meeting Goals over a Long Horizon

An allocation to government bonds decreases portfolio volatility, but the lower returns associated with the asset class decrease the probability of achieving a blended public equity/ bond portfolio's target return. An allocation to private equity, in contrast, will decrease portfolio volatility but allow a greater probability of achieving the target return.

Private equity, however, exposes the portfolio to drawdowns during a market crisis. The tradeoff of lower volatility for higher drawdown potential must be managed.

Classifying the Investment Opportunity Set

Traditional Approaches to Asset Classification

Approaches to asset classification typically fall into two categories: (1) liquidity, and (2) behavior under specific economic conditions.

The lack of liquidity and long investment horizon—sometimes greater than 10 years—make it difficult to categorize alternative investments. One method of dealing with that problem is to make a first allocation using traditional asset classes (i.e., stocks, bonds, and real estate) and then a second iteration that mixes each traditional class with an alternative counterpart, as in Exhibit 1.

Exhibit 1: Major Asset Categories			
	Equity and Equity-Like	Fixed Income and Fixed Income-Like	Real Estate
Marketable/liquid	Public equity Long-short equity Hedge funds	Fixed income Cash	Public real estate Commodities
Private/illiquid	Private equity	Private credit	Private real estate Private real assets

Investors may instead choose to differentiate asset roles based on performance in different markets:

- **Capital growth**—Public and private equities
- **Inflation-hedging**—Real estate, commodities (including gold), privately held natural resources (timber), and inflation-linked bonds.
- **Deflation-hedging**—Nominal-return government bonds.

Risk Factor-Based Approaches to Asset Classification

Many traditional and alternative asset classes share characteristics that result in high correlations. For example, a recession increases risk for both high-yield public bonds and private credit. Public equity, private equity, and venture capital strategies tend to have similar betas. Hedge fund betas vary significantly from the global equity class, based on strategy; global macro and equity market-neutral strategies have very low beta with changes in the global equity market, while long-short has a long equity bias and significantly higher beta with the global equity market.

The following risk factors apply to alternative investments:

- Equity market return—Global equity market; the best growth proxy
- Size—Excess return of small-cap over large-cap equities
- Value—Excess return of value versus growth stocks; growth bias assets have negative factor sensitivity
- Liquidity—Liquid stocks earn more return than less liquid stocks; Pastor-Stambaugh liquidity model
- Duration—Sensitivity to 10-year government yield changes
- Inflation—Sensitivity to breakeven inflation changes from inflation-linked bond markets
- Credit spread—Sensitivity to changes in credit spread for high-yield bonds
- Currency—Sensitivity to value changes in the subject currency versus a foreign currency basket.

Comparing Risk-Based and Traditional Approaches

Exhibit 2: Traditional vs. Risk Factor-Based Approaches

	Strengths	Weaknesses
Traditional	Easy to communicate. Differentiates by liquidity or behavior under different market conditions. Operational considerations; easier to allocate to various managers.	Obscures risk categories. May under-diversify risk.
Risk factor-based	Identifies common risk factors; allows better risk diversification. Reliable risk-factor framework; allows better risk management at portfolio level.	Sensitive to the look-back period; chosen horizon may distort forward-looking risk. Converting risk-factor targets to mandates involves liquidity planning, rebalancing range selection, and manager selection.

Considerations Relevant to Alternative Asset Investment

Risk Considerations

Normal return distributions are not useful for most alternative asset returns, especially for asymmetric returns with options or unlimited potential losses, as with short strategies. Therefore, standard mean-variance optimization (MVO) techniques cannot be used with confidence.

MVO frameworks also assume full investment in the assets which will not be valid for capital drawn down by MLPs over several years and distributions at the end of an investment's life.

Return Expectations

Although no method of establishing return expectations for alternative investments currently exists, the building block approach offers some insight to one method of estimating returns:

- Begin with the nominal risk-free rate.
- Add return estimates for factor exposures relevant to the asset class and fund strategy (e.g., equity, yield curve level and shape, credit spreads, leverage, and liquidity).
- Apply an assumption for manager alpha.
- Deduct appropriate manager fees, incentive fees, and taxes.

Investment Vehicle

Investors with enough capital may choose direct investment in a **limited partnership (LP)**. Investors lacking specialized selection skills, operational economies, and enough capital to invest in multiple partnerships may instead invest in **funds of funds (FoF)**. FoFs simplify investor accounting, but investors lose customized exposures and pay an added layer of management and incentive fees.

Separately managed accounts (SMAs)/funds of one have several managers and strategies under the same limited partnership umbrella, which can eliminate the multiple layers of

AI
PM

management fees and the problem of paying underlying performance fees to successful funds within a poorly performing FoF.

Smaller investors may access hedge fund strategies via **mutual funds, UCITS, and publicly traded funds.** Many such vehicles, compared to limited partnerships of qualified investors, remain subject to regulations (e.g., allowing daily redemptions and disallowing lockups and liquidity gates) that limit their ability to implement intended strategies.

Liquidity

A private placement memorandum (PPM) describes various liquidity provisions imposed against limited partners (LPs).

Exhibit 3: Liquidity Provisions for Alternative Investment Vehicles

	Subscription	Redemption	Lockup
Hedge Funds	Often accept capital contributions monthly or quarterly.	30- to 90-day notice required on quarterly or annual. Limits on withdrawals at any redemption date (Gates). 10% holdback of redemption amount pending annual audit.	One year in the United States and longer in Europe. Redemptions during the lock-up period, if permitted, often have 10% penalty.
Private Equity, Private Credit, Real Estate, and Real Asset Funds	Multiple closes; final close for new investors usually one year after first close. Committed capital called in stages over 3–5 years.	No redemption; LPs may be sold on the secondary market subject to GP approval. Distributions paid as investments are realized. Unrealized assets may be distributed in kind to LPs at fund termination.	Usually 10-year life with GP option to extend by 1 or 2 years.

Some funds may begin redemptions before the final capital call if investments are realized. Subscriptions and redemptions may occur more slowly or quickly than anticipated. Both situations encourage greater portfolio allocation to cash or other risk-free assets.

Although private market funds rarely offer liquidity, hedge funds may have negotiable liquidity terms depending on the underlying investments held:

- **Equity-oriented**—Short-biased or short-only funds will have less liquidity than long funds. "Side-pocketed" securities may not be subject to a fund's overall liquidity terms or arrangements.
- **Event-driven**—Merger arbitrage strategies invest in liquid securities but realize returns in chunks. Distressed investments suffer illiquidity and an extended horizon for the workout period.

- **Relative value**—Funds investing in credit, derivatives, convertible securities, or equities are likely to restrict liquidity to avoid "running for the exits." Managed futures funds may allow daily liquidity with short notice to its LPs.
- **Leverage**—Levered strategies allow their lenders first claim on the underlying assets with as little as two days' notice (e.g., stocks, bonds, and derivatives). Again, the most liquid positions may be liquidated to meet these margin calls and remaining investors left with failing positions.

Fees and Expenses

Alternative asset managers typically charge an asset management fee and incentive fee. Some fund types (e.g., private equity) charge a fee on committed capital rather than invested capital. Managers slow to deploy capital are receiving a high asset management fee that may result in a j-curve effect (i.e., negative IRRs that eventually reverse but are difficult to overcome).

Most alternative funds pass through operating expenses (e.g., legal, custodial, audit, administration, appraisal) to investors.

Tax Considerations

Funds dominated by tax-exempt investors may not worry about tax efficiency. Other tax considerations include:

- **Tax-favored investments**—Real estate, timber, and energy investments typically have a depletion allowance that reduces taxable income and may be subject to lower capital gains tax rates.
- **Unrelated business income tax (UBIT)**—Such taxes may be levied against income unrelated to a tax-exempt organization's purpose.
- **Tax misestimation and penalties**—Investors that estimate taxable income may underestimate taxes from investments and incur an underpayment penalty.

Other Considerations

Top tier managers may have to turn away investors due to capacity constraints. Managers may also turn away investors who require transparency to avoid giving away a competitive edge.

Investors may have insufficient investment capital or manpower to perform due diligence:

- Only very large organizations can justify the costs of an in-house team.
- Investors may be poorly served by FoFs or consultants that gain economies of scale by providing non-customized solutions fitting a broad category of clients.

Suitability

Investment Horizon

Investments in private assets (private real estate, private real assets, or private equity) may take 5 to 7 years to develop and 10 to 12 years to exit. Investment horizons of less than 15 years should avoid these investments. Other strategies take less time to enter and exit; public equities or managed futures will have short lockups (if at all) and strategies with strong secondary markets may also suit investors with shorter time horizons.

Expertise

Understanding the risks and due diligence aspects of alternative investments requires a considerable degree of expertise. Even so, GPs may still have an information advantage over LPs. Pension funds should typically have dedicated alternative investment staff or individuals should have or have access to talent required to implement a successful alternative investment strategy.

Governance
Information asymmetries require strong fund governance structures:

- Those tasked with deciding critical actions must have the requisite knowledge, capacity, and time.
- A formal investment policy with clearly articulated short- and long-term objectives.
- A reporting framework capable of monitoring progress toward objectives.

Transparency
Investors in a "blind pool" invest prior to knowing the investment. The manager's "process," however, may be secret.

Private real estate funds often report quarterly (albeit with a one-quarter lag for appraisal data) and disclose the fund size, drawdown progress, unrealized investment valuations, and commentary on market factors relevant to the fund's strategy. Reports usually provide qualitative information (submarket health, expected timing of realizations, etc.) as well as property-level details such as square footage, occupancy rates, tenant credit, and borrowing details (leverage ratios, cost of debt, and debt maturity dates).

Investors should ensure that funds have third party administrators (TPAs) that process all cash flows and calculate LP and fund NAV. Having a TPA is more common in liquid strategies than in private strategies with less liquid cash flows.

Asset Allocation Approaches

One method first uses broad, liquid asset classes and incorporates alternative assets in a secondary iteration. Potentially useful approaches include:

- **Optimization techniques**—MVO allocation to alternative investments may be constrained to underestimating correlation due to smooth data and overallocation to alternatives.
- **Monte Carlo approaches**—Involve a heavy calculation load but work well due to the ability to handle non-normal return distributions.
- **Risk factor-based approaches**—Avoid overlapping risks that may occur when asset classes are used. Suffers from implementation problems (e.g., finding strategies or funds with appropriate risk-return profiles).

A sound asset allocation process should:

- Unsmooth a return series with significant autocorrelation.
- Determine return distribution normality.
- Use an approach that considers the tail risk (if fat tails) and skewness (if greater than normal).

Monte Carlo models are constructed as follows:

1. Determine whether output should consist of asset returns or risk factor returns.
2. Establish the model to generate either asset or risk-factor returns.

- ○ Should the model be random walk, autocorrelation, or mean-reverting.
- ○ Determine whether a normal or fat-tailed model will provide a robust representation during shocks.
- ○ Determine whether volatility and correlation are stable over time (i.e., homoscedastic) or heteroskedastic and how they should be considered.
3. If estimating risk-factor returns, convert the results to asset returns using an appropriate factor exposure sensitivity model.
4. Establish a meaningful relationship between the portfolio purpose and the asset allocation information (e.g., whether certain allocation choices provide a better balance between a pension fund's existing lives and future lives, meet asset-liability management parameters, etc.).

One approach to handling fat tails and skewness uses a factor model that combines a normal period and a crisis period. Using such an approach generally suggests tactical allocations favoring equities during normal times and government bonds during flights to safety in an economic crisis.

Conditional value at risk (CVaR) involves the expected value for returns below the degree of confidence and can significantly alter allocation decisions for a strategy with negative or long tails. VaR describes minimum loss over some period while CVaR describes the average loss in the 5% tail. Minimizing CVaR requires many more observations for a distribution with negative skewness or long tails.

Risk factor-based approaches, however, should be concerned with the following:

- **Differing risk-factor descriptions**—Although asset classes may be subject to some technical descriptor differences, investors may have very different definitions of risk factors and different models to determine sensitivity.
- **Return correlations**—Changing market conditions can dramatically affect return correlations.
- **Sensitivity stability**—Nominal interest rate sensitivity of government bonds tends to be stable, while inflation sensitivity of commodities tends to change with market conditions.

Liquidity Planning

A long-term plan should consider alternative investment liquidity:

- Fulfilling capital calls from the GP in a private investment fund
- Periodic pension payments, endowment funding commitments, a family office's operating expenses, or unexpected expenses by any entity
- Rebalancing an existing portfolio or funding asset manager changes

AI
PM

Capital calls can be estimated with the formula:

$$C_t = RC_t \times (CC - PIC_t)$$

where

C_t = Capital contribution
RC_t = Rate of contribution (%)
CC = Capital commitment
PIC_t = Paid-in capital

Capital calls are outflows to the investor; distributions are inflows to the investor:

$$D_t = RD_t \times NAV_t$$

where

$$NAV_t = (NAV_{t-1} - D_{t-1} + C_{t-1}) \times (1 + G)$$

The above formula assumes NAV_{t-1} is calculated before distributions and current period contributions, both of which are then made after calculating NAV_{t-1}.

Spreading capital commitments over a multi-year schedule will result in lower NAV volatility due to diversification across vintage years as well as to dollar cost averaging.

In the absence of Monte Carlo modeling, investors should establish a base scenario and then produce alternative scenarios to better understand the potential distributions provided and contributions required as well as to stress test the model assumptions.

Monitoring an Alternative Assets Program

Alternative Asset Performance Evaluation

Because strategies depend to a great extent on a manager's specific insights, using custom index proxies for private investments (static return over cash or equity index) or using peer group comparisons is unlikely to capture return, risk, or liquidity characteristics of the fund.

While frequently traded assets can effectively use time-weighted rate of return (TWR), private investments with calldown, drawdown, and application of funds approaches will typically use internal rate of return (IRR). Practitioners often use metrics such as multiple of invested capital (MOIC) to avoid gaming IRR by using calldown and distribution schedules.

Evaluation must also compare investment returns from the same vintage year to avoid cyclical effects.

Comparing strategies and manager expectations may lead to better performance. Evaluators can see whether managers were right for the wrong reasons, wrong for the right reasons, or just wrong.

Monitoring the Manager's Process

Investors should monitor a manager's:

- Key person risk—"Key persons" contribute to a fund's history of success or failure. Investors should look close for a fund with key persons, a chief operating officer, or a compliance officer that has resigned or been fired.
- Alignment of interests—Fund interests should be aligned with investors' interests in order to offset the GP's information advantage (information asymmetry) and avoid agency conflicts between fund manager and investor goals.
- Style drift—Investors should understand a fund manager's special skills that resulted in past success or failure and monitor whether the manager strays into areas where he may lack skill.
- Risk management approach—Investors should understand how the fund avoids catastrophic losses, balances risk and return, and so on, and whether they follow specific rules, especially where leverage is involved.
- Client/asset turnover—Decreasing assets under management (AUM) may indicate lack of client satisfaction with some aspect of fund management; increasing AUM may indicate strategy implementation constraints going forward. High asset turnover will likely result in higher tax exposure and trading expenses.
- Client profile—Clients likely to exit may leave longer-term investors holding less attractive investments. Managers who weather the outflows may find themselves less able to attract key talent.
- Fund service providers—Administrators, custodians, and auditors should be able to perform the required services. Investors should understand why a fund changes a service provider.

AI
PM

AI
PM

OVERVIEW OF PRIVATE WEALTH MANAGEMENT
Cross-Reference to CFA Institute Reading #28

Private Clients versus Institutional Clients

Private client and institutional investor concerns may be grouped and compared as follows:

Table 1: Individual Concerns versus Institutional Concerns

	Individuals	Institutions
Objectives	Broad; diverse	Specific; clearly defined
Constraints	Shorter horizons	Longer horizons
	Significant tax considerations	Few tax considerations
	Portfolios lack scale (i.e., small size)	Economies of scale (i.e., large size)
Other	Less sophistication	Greater sophistication
	Significant behavioral issues	Less impact from behavioral issues
	Less formal governance—wealth manager implements	Investment committees—CIO or delegated to wealth manager

Understanding Private Clients

Information Needed in Advising Private Clients

Advisors gather information from clients through conversations and by reviewing their financial documents. They can then use client information to develop a governance model (IPS).

Personal Information

Advisors gather information via conversations with clients to understand how the client achieved their current level of assets as well as what the client would like to accomplish and the parameters for building and deploying the assets.

Such information includes:

- Sources of client wealth
- Family situation, including marital status, the number of children and grandchildren, and the ages and special needs of family members
- Career, business, or retirement aspirations
- Emotional reactions to previous market events
- Goals

Financial Information

Clients provide information about their assets and liabilities to wealth managers through banking, brokerage, and other statements. This can then be simplified into a balance sheet format.

AI
PM

Table 2: Sample Personal Balance Sheet

Assets	Liabilities
Cash and Equivalents	
Checking and savings accounts	
Money market accounts	
Investment Accounts	**Consumer Debt**
Brokerage accounts	
Alternative investments	
IRAs	
Real Estate owned	**Real Estate Loans**
Personal dwelling	Personal dwelling
Investment real estate	Investment real estate
Personal Property	**Other Debt**
Automobile	
Other personal assets	
Total Assets	**Total Liabilities**
	Net Worth

Cash flows may come from employment income, business profit distributions, government income benefits, annuity income, pensions, and portfolio income/distributions. Individual taxes may apply to income, wealth, and consumption. The accumulation of income over taxes and expenses will add to assets available for later distribution.

Wealth managers may add a great deal of value by helping clients with tax strategies that avoid, reduce, or defer taxes.

Private Client Goals

Planned goals typically include retirement, purchases they want to make, covering child or grandchild education or event expenses (e.g., wedding), wealth transfer and giving (i.e., philanthropy). Unplanned goals may include expenditure on repairs, medical issues, etc.

Wealth managers quantify planned goals, how much to set aside for unplanned goals, and the priorities clients place on each goal. Regularly updating a client's IPS helps wealth managers identify when goals or priorities change.

Private Client Risk Tolerance

Risk tolerance describes a set of risk-related assessments:

- **Risk perception**—How clients subjectively frame the risk of outcomes from an investment decision.
- **Risk capacity**—An objective measure of ability to accept risk that considers the client's wealth, income, liquidity, time horizon, and so on.
- **Risk tolerance**—The willingness to engage in risk behavior (i.e., willingness and perceived ability).

Insights from a risk tolerance conversation with a client may involve:

- Risk-shaping influences in the past
- Investment successes and failures
- Nature and degree of outside influences

- Method of accumulating wealth (e.g., inheritance, sale of business, etc.)
- How the client thinks about risk (e.g., dollar or percentage terms)

Managers must use judgment in translating the results of a risk tolerance questionnaire and the risk conversation into client guidance. Thus, the manager's own views on risk often influence interpretation of client answers. How questions are phrased (i.e., dollar terms versus percentage terms) may influence the outcome.

Technical versus Soft Skills
Technical skills include:

- Quantitative and technology skills
- Understanding capital market dynamics
- Portfolio construction proficiency
- Financial planning knowledge
- Language fluency

Soft skills include:

- Social skills
- Business development and sales skills
- Education and coaching skills
- Communication skills

Investment Planning

Capital Sufficiency Analysis
Capital sufficiency analysis (i.e., capital needs analysis) is the process of determining if a client has or will have enough capital to meet stated objectives.

Deterministic approaches forecast an expected portfolio return and assume that return over the forecast horizon. Such approaches require cash inflows and outflows from the portfolio and a return assumption. This method is unrealistic with respect to the variability of potential outcomes.

Monte Carlo (MC) approaches model variability in key variables and consider the uncertainty of outcomes. Wealth managers can draw conclusions about the probability of funding an objective based on outcomes of numerous MC simulations and the resulting distribution of results. With MC simulation, the wealth manager uses a forward-looking average annual return along with standard deviation of returns rather than relying solely on average return.

More complicated MC approaches identify when the probability of successfully reaching a goal falls below an acceptable range. When that happens, clients can:

- Reduce the goal amount
- Increase contributions toward the goal
- Delay disbursement of funds for the goal (e.g., delay retirement)
- Adopt a strategic allocation with greater expected returns while staying within acceptable risk tolerance

AI
PM

Retirement Planning

First, **human capital** represents the net present value of an investor's future expected income from labor while **financial capital** identifies the value of tangible and intangible assets (excluding human capital).

Throughout the financial stages of life, people turn their human capital into financial capital.

- Education
- Early career
- Career development
- Peak accumulation
- Pre-retirement
- Early retirement—Begin drawing down retirement capital
- Late retirement—Generally reduce expenses related to travel and leisure

However, clients may have competing needs like housing costs, family needs, education expenses, and so on.

Wealth managers must determine and regularly update a suitable distribution rate. A simple approach invests assets into an annuity which periodically distributes income to the individual based on a minimum return assumption for the assets and the longevity of the individual or, in the case of a survivor annuity, the individuals.

Clients assume longevity risk when a stream of income is distributed from assets owned in their portfolio. The insurance company assumes this risk, for a price, when the assets have been deposited in an annuity product.

In retirement planning, clients can use MC models to consider the success of high-priority goals in the face of alternative strategies for gifts, planned purchases, and other cash events.

The following are some relevant behavioral considerations:

- Heightened loss aversion.
- Lower consumption that may be related to greater fear of having enough money should losses occur.
- The "annuity puzzle"—Retirees tend not to invest in annuities although they can increase the probability of meeting objectives. Explanations include reluctance to give up capital that could improve their lifestyle if successfully invested, dislike of losing control over the assets, and high insurance and administration costs.
- Preference for income over capital appreciation—Investors prefer dividend income rather than selling stock and spending the proceeds. Not spending capital may seem like a self-control mechanism.

Investment Policy Statement

Background and Investment Objectives

Background items include relevant personal and financial information. One-time objectives include significant travel expenses, purchase of a second home or boat, or other non-recurring expenditures. Recurring objectives include funding for lifestyle needs and philanthropic or other ongoing objectives.

Investment objectives should be detailed enough to quantify; "growth" is not enough.

Wealth managers should consider cash inflows and outflows, accounts with other managers, and so on, in setting a capital objective. Managers should help clients revise objectives that cannot be met with existing capital and expected contributions and growth.

Investment Parameters

Wealth managers should consider time horizon and how it will affect risk parameters, keeping in mind a client's **risk tolerance**. Understand, however, that the **time horizon** for an ongoing funding requirement does not stop when cash outflows from the portfolio begin.

Managers can address **asset class preferences** by including a statement of how important asset allocation is to success and the process used to inform clients of the risk and return of various asset classes. Managers then either include client-approved asset classes or those classes considered unacceptable.

A section on **liquidity preferences** is appropriate if not already discussed in earlier sections. Investors may decide to sell portfolio assets to meet liquidity needs or may keep a cash buffer to avoid a need to quickly sell assets, potentially at unfavorable prices.

Some investors may have **other investment preferences** that could include a "legacy holding" (i.e., shares that they have an emotional need to keep) or wish to invest in ESG-friendly companies (e.g., avoid high-carbon footprint firms, those engaging in the sale of certain products, or companies using child labor).

Investors may have **constraints** related to using types of assets such as derivatives or limited by investments available in accounts such as a 401(k). They may have constraints against selling assets with a high embedded-capital gain. ESG constraints may also be included here rather than in the other investment preferences section.

Asset Allocation

This section describes a range for the percentage of the portfolio invested in each asset class.

Portfolio Management

This section describes monitoring, implementation and discretionary authority, tactical changes, and rebalancing. Implementation should include the types of investment vehicle (e.g., mutual funds, ETFs, individual assets, etc.) and who will manage them (e.g., proprietary products or processes versus third-party managers).

Duties and Responsibilities

The wealth manager might be responsible for:

- Drafting and maintaining the IPS as well as the schedule for subsequent IPS review
- Developing the asset allocation
- Recommending or selecting investment options
- Assisting with preparing or completing agreements associated with investment offerings
- Monitoring and rebalancing the asset allocation
- Use of derivatives, short selling, and repos
- Monitoring and controlling implementation costs
- Selecting and monitoring asset managers, custodians, and other third parties
- Performance reporting
- Voting proxies

Managers may also provide specific responsibilities associated with each third-party provider.

AI
PM

IPS Appendix

Frequently changing items may be presented in an appendix:

- Modeled portfolio behavior such as a modeled distribution of returns at various percentile ranges, the volatility, and the risks to portfolio success
- Capital market expectations, including expected return and risk for each asset class as well as modeled correlations

Portfolio Construction and Modeling

Allocation and Investments

In **traditional portfolio construction**, asset managers:

- Identify asset classes appropriate for the portfolio.
- Develop capital market expectations.
- Determine allocations to asset classes and, if appropriate, asset location.
- Assess constraints.
- Implement the portfolio.

In the **goals-based approach** to portfolio construction, a manager identifies client goals and assigns funds required for each goal to its own portfolio "bucket." Portfolios for each goal are then optimized for a specific level of volatility or to a specific probability of success. The remainder of the steps are the same as in traditional asset allocation, although the resulting combination of buckets will likely result in a suboptimal allocation for the overall portfolio.

Portfolio Reporting and Review

Portfolio reporting involves communicating portfolio performance while **portfolio review** describes meetings or conversations in which a portfolio manager discusses client situations and investment strategy.

A portfolio report usually includes:

- Performance summary
- Asset allocation, perhaps comparing strategic allocation with actual allocation
- Historical performance since inception of the strategy
- Asset class summary performance (perhaps for individual securities)
- A currency exposure report detailing exchange rate effects on portfolio or asset return
- Purchases and sales for the period
- Contributions and withdrawals for the period

Wealth managers may send a letter with commentary on recent economic and financial events to provide context for any tactical decisions during the period and for the portfolio's performance. The wealth manager may also use that commentary as a platform to encourage wavering clients to stay the course after a period of bad short-term performance.

A **portfolio review** allows managers to ask clients about changes in objectives and constraints, changes in personal or financial information, and differences in expected cash flow. A manager can engage clients on needed changes to allocation, investment vehicles, or managers, or can restate the need to remain focused on the current strategy.

Evaluating Investment Program Success

A successful investment program achieves client objectives with an appropriate amount of risk. However, investment managers should reach agreement with clients on whether their objectives are absolute return, relative return, or meeting a cash flow or financial obligation.

Successful programs also meet objectives on purpose rather than by accident and meet the standards described by the IPS. Third party managers should perform in line with their benchmarks, and their benchmarks should remain stable over time. Managers should determine the benefits of tactical allocations and the costs of deviating from the strategy.

Portfolio performance should be compared to an appropriate benchmark or, for some strategies, against an absolute target (i.e., usually for relatively long holding periods such as over five years).

Ethical and Compliance Considerations

Ethical Considerations

CFA Institute Code of Ethics and Standards of Professional Conduct (Code and Standards) should serve as the starting point for discussing ethical considerations.

Managers have a fiduciary responsibility to exercise a high standard of care when dealing with client assets. Suitability depends on client knowledge, financial situation, and investing experience. In order to provide a suitable investment and a high standard of care, managers must understand their customer (called "know your customer—KYC"). In order to KYC, managers will obtain a variety of confidential information. That confidentiality must not be violated except in certain circumstances (e.g., legal request or sharing for internal implementation purposes).

Wealth managers must recognize and indicate any conflicts of interest such as recommending commission products with the highest commission to the advisor or encouraging clients not to withdraw money simply to maintain AUM-based fees.

Compliance Considerations

Some regulations affecting a wealth manager-client relationship include:

- Markets in Financial Instruments Directive (MiFID II)—Advisors must demonstrate advice suitability, including how it will meet client objectives.
- Common Reporting Standard (OECD Council/G20)—Institutional exchange of financial information on an annual basis.
- The Foreign Account Tax Compliance Act (FATCA, United States)—Requires non-U.S. financial institutions to report account information for U.S. taxpayers and non-U.S. entities in which U.S. taxpayers hold a substantial ownership interest. This is to prevent tax evasion through offshore accounts.

The U.S. Department of Labor's "Fiduciary Rule" is likely dead while the Security Exchange Commission's "Regulation Best Interest" requires broker-dealers to act in the best interest of the retail customer at the time the recommendation is made, without placing the financial or other interest of the broker-dealer ahead of the interests of the retail customer.

AI
PM

Private Client Segments

Mass Affluent Segment

This segment applies primarily to individuals with financial planning needs and substantial assets, but who need financial planning and investment services (e.g., cash flow management, education funding, and risk management). This segment has a higher client-to-manager ratio and services are less customized than other private client segments.

High-Net-Worth (HNW) Segment

Wealth managers in this segment focus on customized investment management, tax planning, and wealth transfer (e.g., bequests and estate planning) for individuals with greater wealth than the mass affluent segment.

Ultra-HNW Segment

Wealth managers coordinate a team of professionals with specialized skills to provide complex solutions. In addition, they may coordinate additional concierge services. A *family office* may hire a wealth manager in this segment for which they are the only client.

Robo Advisors

Robo advisors provide a less expensive service via digital interface through which they gather information, create algorithmic assessments, and make and implement recommendations.

TAXES AND PRIVATE WEALTH MANAGEMENT IN A GLOBAL CONTEXT
Cross-Reference to CFA Institute Assigned Reading #29

Tax Types

Major tax revenue sources are:

- Income:
  - Ordinary income—Salaries
  - Investment income (also known as capital income)—Interest, dividends, realized and unrealized capital gains
- Consumption:
  - Sales—Collected in one step, usually at the point of sale
  - Value added—Collected at various production stages but passed on to the ultimate consumer
- Wealth:
  - Accumulated—Taxes on real estate and other property
  - Transfers—Intergenerational and other transfers (e.g., gifts) of accumulated property

Taxes on Income

Common Elements

Most countries have a **progressive tax structure** (i.e., increasingly higher-percentage tax rates) applied against ordinary income bands.

Exhibit 1: Income Tax Regimes

Regime	Ordinary Income	Interest Income	Dividends	Capital Gains
Common progressive	Progressive	Some favorable or exempt	Some favorable or exempt	Some favorable or exempt
Heavy interest	Progressive	Ordinary rates	Some favorable or exempt	Some favorable or exempt
Heavy dividend	Progressive	Some favorable or exempt	Ordinary rates	Some favorable or exempt
Heavy capital gain	Progressive	Some favorable or exempt	Some favorable or exempt	Ordinary rates
Light capital gain	Progressive	Ordinary rates	Ordinary rates	Some favorable or exempt
Flat and light	Flat	Some favorable or exempt	Some favorable or exempt	Some favorable or exempt
Flat and heavy	Flat	Some favorable or exempt	Ordinary rates	Ordinary rates

In general, "heavy" refers to ordinary income tax rates applicable to one or more categories; "light" refers to favorable or exempt taxation on one or more categories.

Common progressive is most common. **Light capital gain** is second most common. **Heavy capital gain** is least common.

After-Tax Returns and Accumulations

Accrual taxes are imposed annually as opposed to **deferred taxes**, which are imposed after some time.

Accrual Taxes

A **future value** factor applied to a starting amount of capital results in the terminal value at the end of n accumulation periods given return r and tax rate t. The subscript i represents a scenario for interest income or preferred equity income, which most countries tax on an accrual basis.

The future value factor for a currency unit given return on an investment periodically taxed is:

$$FV_i = [1 + r(1 - t_i)]^n$$

Tax drag describes the effect of the tax on final accumulation. Additional tax drag is the difference between nominal and effective tax rates.

For an accrual tax:

- Nominal tax rate is less than effective tax rate.
- The difference between nominal and effective tax rate grows as interest rate increases.
- The difference between nominal and effective tax rate grows as time horizon increases.
- The effect of higher interest rate and longer accumulation is multiplicative.

Deferred Taxation

The future value factor when deferring taxes until the end of an investment horizon is:

$$\begin{aligned} FV_g &= (1 + r)^n - [(1 + r)^n - 1]t_g \\ &= (1 + r)^n(1 - t_g) + t_g \end{aligned}$$

Assuming the same nominal tax rate, deferring taxes increases investment return over the horizon. The advantage of deferral grows as return and time horizon increase.

Some jurisdictions offer lower deferred tax rates for gains earned over long horizons (i.e., one year or greater as with long-term capital gains) to encourage longer-term investing.

> **IMPORTANT:** The value of deferral over a long horizon can more than offset a higher tax rate compared to a lower accrual tax rate.

Deferred Capital Gain

Capital gain indicates the difference between market value and cost basis (i.e., purchase price). Newly invested capital has no embedded gain, but a security with market value greater than its cost basis will have an embedded capital gain. In some cases, the embedded gain is transferred from another taxpayer. A lower cost basis increases embedded gain. For B equal to basis as a percentage of the market value, the future value factor is:

$$\begin{aligned} FV_{gb} &= (1 + r)^n(1 + t_g) + t_g - (1 + B)t_g \\ &= (1 + r)^n(1 - t_g) + t_g B \end{aligned}$$

The t_gB term in the second equivalence adds back the nontaxable basis. If basis equals market value (as with a new purchase), then B equals 1 and the equation here is the same as in the deferred taxation section.

Wealth Taxes
A **wealth tax** is levied periodically against a capital base at a lower rate than income- or gains-based taxes.

$$FV_w = [(1 + r)(1 - t_w)]^n$$

Wealth taxes are different from returns-based and gains-based taxes:

- For $r > t$, decreased proportion of investment growth is taxed.
- For $r = t$, all of investment growth is taxed.
- For $0 < r < t$, increased proportion of investment growth is taxed.
- For $r < 0$, tax reduces principal (i.e., not just growth).

Blended Tax Environment
Pre-tax portfolio return r is a function of the component returns (i.e., dividends, interest, realized capital gain) in percentage proportion p. The deferred (i.e., unrealized) gain is not considered here. After-tax portfolio realized return $r*$ is:

$$r* = r(1 - p_dt_d - p_it_i - p_gt_g)$$

Effective tax rate describes actual tax as a proportion of taxable income. Assuming the same tax rate applies to realized and deferred gains:

$$T* = \frac{t_g(1 - p_i - p_d - p_g)}{(1 - p_it_i - p_dt_d - p_gt_g)}$$

The after-tax future value for each currency unit with both realized and unrealized gains is:

$$FV_{after-tax} = (1 + r*)^n(1 - T*) + T* - (1 - B)t_g$$

Accrual Equivalent Return
Accrual equivalent after-tax return describes the annual return r_{AE} at which a portfolio with value V_0 would grow to result in the same future value V_t as the pre-tax return after all taxes have been levied.

$$r_{AE} = \sqrt[n]{\frac{V_t}{V_0}} - 1$$

Alternatively stated, accrual equivalent return can be stated as:

$$R_{AE} = r(1 - T_{AE})$$

The **tax drag** is accrual equivalent after-tax return less actual return for the portfolio.

IMPORTANT: Wealth taxes are like returns-based and gains-based taxes in that increasing investment horizon results in tax consuming a greater share of growth (i.e, increases tax drag).

Exam hint: As less of the total return results from realized capital gain, more will result from unrealized capital gain.

IMPORTANT: The proportion of gain, p_g, subject to immediate tax does not include unrealized gain.

IMPORTANT: This formula can replace all future versions, assuming the variables are known. It considers taxes against the realized and unrealized portions of blended return.

Accrual equivalent returns are useful for standardizing results of different portfolio strategies for comparison.

Tax-Advantaged Accounts

Tax-Deferred Accounts (TDAs)

Tax-deferred accounts (TDAs) involve contributions from untaxed ordinary income (i.e., tax-deductible contributions) and tax-free growth during the holding period. Withdrawals are usually taxed at the account owner's current ordinary income rate at the time of withdrawal.

$$FV_{TDA} = (1 + r)^n (1 - t)$$

Tax-Exempt Accounts

Tax-exempt accounts (TEAs) involve after-tax contributions that grow tax free through the investment horizon and remain untaxed when withdrawn; that is, they have no future tax liabilities.

$$FV_{TEA} = (1 + r)^n$$

Taxes and Investment Risk

An investor's share of investment risk on a taxed return is $\sigma(1 - t)$ where σ is pre-tax risk.

Maximizing After-Tax Wealth

Investors may have multiple types of accounts due to contribution limits for TEAs and TDAs. **Tax alpha** concerns the value created from properly using asset and account types that maximize an investor's after-tax wealth.

Asset Location

The **asset location decision** involves choices among taxable, TDA, and TEA accounts (where available) based on the tax profile of assets but allocated across each to optimize risk/return decisions.

- Tax-advantaged: Higher-taxed asset types
- Taxable: Lower-taxed asset types

Offsetting short positions in the taxable account can be used to offset overallocation to the highly taxed asset in the tax-advantaged account.

Active management or options-overlay strategies may not lend themselves to deferred-tax portfolios; that is, trading and active management have to earn higher pre-tax alpha than passive management.

Asset allocation should be appropriate not only to asset class, but to holding period. Choice of asset location cannot overcome investment strategies that generate negative alpha or extreme tax inefficiency.

Tax-Loss Harvesting

Tax-loss harvesting involves offsetting gains in one security by realizing losses in other securities. Selling a security at a loss and reinvesting in another lower-value security essentially resets the potential gain (i.e., deferral).

Unrealized tax losses at death of the owner will generally not be transferable. The asset basis is often stepped up to market value at death, and the embedded loss is not transferred.

If part of a position with different entry prices must be sold, it often makes sense to sell the highest-basis portion of the assets first and defer taxes on the lowest-basis portion. This is called highest in, first out (HIFO).

Such strategies may not be useful where tax rates are lower now than they will be in the future. Higher future tax rates would suggest that gains be taken now (i.e., under the lower tax rate environment).

> IMPORTANT: These strategies become more important as the tax rate on capital gains increases.

Holding Period Management

Short-term trading may not offer the same active management advantages when a lower tax is available on long-term gains.

After-Tax Mean Variance Optimization (MVO)

The same asset held in different types of accounts (i.e., taxable, TDA, TEA) is a different asset for mean variance optimization (MVO) because it results in different after-tax holding period returns.

> IMPORTANT: Compare accrual equivalent returns across diverse tax structures.

After-tax accrual equivalent returns and after-tax standard deviations can be substituted in the optimization process.

The optimization model should constrain allocations as required to avoid overallocating to the TDA/TEA types of accounts.

ESTATE PLANNING IN A GLOBAL CONTEXT
Cross-Reference to CFA Institute Assigned Reading #30

Basic Estate Planning Concepts

Estates, Wills, and Probate

Estate describes all the assets a person owns or controls. **Estate planning** describes the process of transferring assets during life and at death.

A **will** specifies the rights others have over the **testator's** property at death. **Probate** is the legal process that establishes the validity of a will.

Intestacy is the state of dying without a will; the court decides disposition of assets based on local law.

Property may be passed by joint ownership, living trusts, retirement plans, and other structures that avoid the expense, public nature, and contestability of the probate process.

Assets transferred to an **irrevocable trust** are not considered part of an estate because the grantor of assets funding the trust no longer owns or controls them.

Structures of Civil Law, Common Law, and Shari'a Law

Civil law countries apply abstract principles established by law to cases. Civil law is the most widely used system.

Common law countries use court cases to establish abstract principles. Common law primarily derives from the British system and includes U.S. courts.

Courts following the law of Islam (i.e., **Shari'a**) are like civil law systems regarding estate planning. Shari'a law can usually be followed in non-Islamic countries by using a will, except where the instructions conflict with local law.

A **trust**, unique to common law, allows the **settlor** to entrust assets to management by a **trustee**. France, Germany, and other civil law countries do not recognize trusts.

Spouses and Other Heirs

Forced heirship rules limit an owner's discretion regarding the share of property transferred to children and spouses.

Clawback provisions allow heirs to gain back their rightful share of property disposed during the owner's lifetime for the purpose of avoiding forced heirship.

Spouses also have marital property rights in most jurisdictions:

- Separate property regimes (civil law): Individual may own property and dispose of it subject to remaining spouse's other rights; may have choice of separate or community property rights.
- Community property regimes: Indivisible 50% interest in income earned during marriage:
  - Gifts and inheritances received outside of marriage remain separate property.
  - 50% of decedent's assets transfer directly to spouse; remainder transfers via provisions of the will.

Tax Considerations

Where wealth-based taxes are levied annually, transfer taxes are levied only during gifting or inheritance:

- Inter vivos transfers (i.e., lifetime gratuitous transfers):
  - Without intent of anything in exchange
  - Taxed against transferor's estate
- Inheritance (i.e., testamentary gratuitous transfers):
  - Received from decedent (at death)
  - Taxed against recipient

There may be an untaxed allowance on both inter vivos and testamentary transfers.

Transfers to spouses are tax exempt in most jurisdictions.

Tax status depends on:

- Location of asset (i.e., domestic or foreign)
- Donor's residence or domicile
- Recipient's residence
- Type of asset (e.g., movable versus immovable)

Core and Excess Capital

Core capital describes assets designated for maintaining a given lifestyle, funding additional desired spending goals, and providing an emergency reserve for unexpected spending requirements.

Excess capital is assets greater than liabilities and the emergency reserve (i.e., excess of assets above core capital).

The present value of spending needs can be calculated as:

> IMPORTANT: Excess capital can be safely transferred to beneficiaries without causing failure to meet lifestyle needs.

- Nominal spending needs discounted at a nominal discount rate, or
- Real spending needs discounted at a real discount rate (i.e., without inflation)

Core capital requirement can be calculated as:

- The present value of spending needs through life expectancy, or
- Each expected future cash flow multiplied by the joint survival probability

Survival Probability Approach

Joint survival probability for a couple is:

$$p(\text{Survival}_J) = p(\text{Survival}_H) + p(\text{Survival}_W) - p(\text{Survival}_H) \times p(\text{Survival}_W)$$

AI
PM

Based on joint survival probability, present value of joint spending needs is:

$$PV(\text{Spending}_J) = \sum_{t=1}^{N} \frac{p(\text{Survival}_J) \times (\text{Spending}_J)}{(1+r)^t}$$

The survival probability approach discounts each period's spending needs by the real risk-free rate because the spending cash flows are nonsystematic (i.e., unrelated to market-based risk inherent in the assets). However, the survivor's spending can be hedged using life insurance.

The emergency reserve incorporated into liabilities considers the shortfall risk of funding assets. A two-year emergency reserve is designed to satisfy anxiety about market cycles and is usually sufficient for planning.

Monte Carlo Approach

The Monte Carlo approach examines many paths, with outcomes based on random values within ranges for each variable (i.e., portfolio return, mortality, emergency experiences, tax changes, etc.). Combining the many potential outcomes gives a feeling of the portfolio's risk as a funding portfolio.

Transferring Excess Capital

Inter vivos gifting bypasses the estate tax on a bequest at death. Local jurisdictions have implemented gift and donation taxes to minimize the revenue loss from inter vivos gifting.

Tax-Free Gifting

Relative value describes the relative benefit of an inter vivos gift to the value of a bequest at death. In this scenario, the relative value of the tax-free gift equals return on investments purchased with a gift r_g less tax on the gift's return t_{ig}, divided by return on estate investments r_e less tax on the estate investment return t_{ie} and tax on the estate bequest T_e at death.

$$RV_{\text{Tax-Free Gift}} = \frac{FV_{\text{Gift}}}{FV_{\text{Bequest}}} = \frac{[1 + r_g(1 - t_{ig})]^n}{[1 + r_e(1 - t_{ie})]^n(1 - T_e)}$$

Gifts Taxable to the Recipient

For a gift taxable to the recipient:

$$RV_{\text{taxable Gift}} = \frac{FV_{\text{Gift}}}{FV_{\text{Bequest}}} = \frac{[1 + r_g(1 - t_{ig})]^n(1 - T_g)}{[1 + r_e(1 - t_{ie})]^n(1 - T_e)}$$

It is also tax efficient to gift assets with higher expected returns to the second generation and keep lower-expected-return assets with the first generation to be passed at death.

In some jurisdictions the authorities may confiscate a gift if the recipient is unable to liquidate the investment to satisfy the gift tax.

Gifts Taxable to the Donor

Cross-border gifts could result in tax against proceeds given and received.

The value of the gift increases if it is taxable to donor's estate rather than to recipient. Assuming $r_g = r_e$ and $t_{ig} = t_{ie}$:

AI
PM

$$RV_{TG,D} = \frac{FV_R}{FV_D} = \frac{[1 + r_R(1 - t_{I,R})]^n[1 - t_{G,D} + t_{G,D}t_{E,D}]}{[1 + r_D(1 - t_{I,D})]^n(1 - t_{E,D})}$$

$T_g T_e$ represents the tax benefit to the recipient of reducing the estate with the gift rather than paying estate tax on the gift.

The value of the gift multiplied by the tax benefit of reducing the estate could be considered a credit for making the gift.

Generation Skipping

Gifting assets to the third generation avoids tax on first- and second-generation bequests. The value of skipping the first and second generations relative to making the two bequests depends on the first-generation estate tax rate:

$$RV_{\text{Generation Skipping Gift}} = \frac{1}{(1 - T_e)}$$

Some jurisdictions levy a generation-skipping transfer tax to recover the amount that would have been lost as tax revenue.

Spousal Exemptions

Spouses in most jurisdictions may make unlimited gifts or bequests to the other spouse without tax, or bequests taxable only above some threshold.

Because there are exclusions for each spouse, it may be efficient to gift the excludable amount to a third party so as not to lose the exclusion from the taxable estate.

Valuation Discounts

Valuation discounts for lack of liquidity and minority interest may be applied to privately held family businesses. Assets subject to valuation discounts will have lower transfer taxes than comparable assets not subject to such discounts.

Assets may be placed in a **family limited partnership (FLP)** to create valuation discounts for transfer purposes. Even cash and marketable securities placed in an FLP may be eligible, although the assigned discount will be less than for privately held companies.

> **IMPORTANT:** Discounts for lack of liquidity are not additive with discounts for minority interest; the combination of the two will tend to be less than their sum.

FLPs are also used to accumulate family member shares to reduce commission costs and gain access to investments requiring a threshold investment.

Deemed Disposition

Bequests in some jurisdictions may result in tax only on the amount over basis, much like a capital gains tax. This **deemed disposition** of the asset treats the bequest as if it were a sale.

Charitable Gifts

Charitable gratuitous transfers involve gifts to charities and result in tax advantages:

- Very few jurisdictions levy a tax against gifts to charitable organizations.
- Most jurisdictions provide a tax deduction for such gifts.
- Charities may be exempt from tax on investment gains.

AI
PM

For planned charitable giving, gifting early makes more sense than a bequest at death:

$$RV_{\text{Charitable Gift}} = \frac{FV_{\text{Charitable Gift}}}{FV_{\text{Bequest}}} = \frac{(1 + r_g)^n + T_{oi}[1 + r_e(1 - t_{ie})]^n(1 - T_e)}{[1 + r_e(1 - t_{ie})]^n(1 - T_e)}$$

In the numerator:

- First term: No tax on investment returns associated with the gift amount
- Second term: Tax deduction against ordinary income (T_{oi}) for amount of gift

Donor can:

- Increase amount of gift with same effect on estate, or
- Use less estate capital to achieve a charitable goal.

Estate Planning Structures

Trusts

In a **trust**, a **settlor** (i.e., **grantor**) transfers assets to a **trustee**, who manages the assets for beneficiaries. Beneficiaries have beneficial ownership of trust assets.

- Revocable trust: Owner retains right to assets and may revoke the trust relationship:
  - Reports and pays taxes on investment returns.
  - Claims against the settlor may be satisfied using trust assets.
- Irrevocable trust: Owner forfeits right to assets and may not revoke trust relationship:
  - Trustee reports and pays taxes (if any).
  - Claims against the settlor cannot be satisfied from trust assets.

Trust distributions to beneficiaries:

- Fixed: Certain amounts and times as specified in the trust document.
- Discretionary: Trustee makes payments to beneficiaries with discretion uncontrolled by the trust document or the grantor.

Trusts are legal relationships in common law and may not be recognized by civil law jurisdictions, although many do. The irrevocable trust offers the most asset protection for the settlor while the discretionary trust offers the most asset protection for the beneficiaries.

Foundations

A foundation is set up to promote education, philanthropy, and so on. A public foundation is set up by public entities (e.g., corporations); a private foundation is set up by an individual or a family and has its own board.

A foundation is a legal person set up in civil law.

Life Insurance

Life insurance can be a useful tool in jurisdictions where trusts are not recognized (i.e., civil law jurisdictions) or where tax outcomes are uncertain:

- Death benefits are not taxed.
- There are minimal or no reporting requirements.

- Premiums are not includable in estates or as gifts taxable to beneficiaries.
- Cash values may accumulate inside the policy value without tax.
- Loans against or withdrawals from cash value may be made by the owner without tax consequences.
- Policy passes directly to beneficiaries (i.e., avoids probate).
- Creditors cannot attach premiums in settlement of claims.

Life insurance is valuable in:

- Providing liquidity to pay taxes on bequests (if any).
- Funding trusts in the case of minors, spendthrifts, or disabled persons.

> **IMPORTANT:** Jurisdictions require a minimum risk before allowing the benefits listed.

Cross-Border Planning

Residence and Source of Income
- **Source jurisdiction** countries (i.e., also known as territorial tax systems):
  - Tax income earned within their borders.
  - Tax noncitizen residents, but not nonresident citizens.
- **Residence jurisdiction** countries tax residents' worldwide income.

The United States taxes its citizens (regardless of residence) and noncitizen residents on worldwide income.

The United Kingdom taxes residents living abroad (resident nondomiciliaries or RNDs) only on income remitted in the United Kingdom. UK RNDs may locate in residence jurisdiction countries where they are not taxed on earnings.

Tax on Wealth and Wealth Transfers
The United States levies taxes on:

- Worldwide wealth transfers of citizens and residents.
- Estate transfers of U.S. assets held by noncitizens and nonresidents:
  - Real estate
  - Movable property
  - Financial assets

Generally, the principles are:

- Source jurisdiction: Tax transfers of assets within a country.
- Residence jurisdiction: Tax all assets transferred by resident.

Disputes among jurisdictions are handled by treaty or other agreement.

Exit Taxes
Countries may impose an **exit tax** in an attempt to reduce taxes lost when high net worth individuals (HNWIs) renounce citizenship and expatriate to another country. The exit tax will often create a deemed disposition for assets leaving the country, which then creates a tax on the gain over basis.

Expatriated citizens may also owe tax on income earned during a "shadow period" after renunciation.

AI
PM

Double Taxation

Conflicts may lead to taxation for the same income or assets across multiple jurisdictions:

- Residence-source conflict (most common): A resident of a residence jurisdiction country earns income in a source jurisdiction country.
- Source-source conflict: Two source jurisdiction countries disagree about where the money was earned.
- Residence-residence conflict: Two residence jurisdiction countries disagree about the residence of an income earner.

The residence jurisdiction country in a source-residence conflict will generally be expected to provide relief from taxation for its resident:

- Credit: Residence jurisdiction country provides a tax credit for taxes paid in the source jurisdiction country; tax is limited to maximum of residence country or source country.
- Exemption: Residence jurisdiction country exempts foreign source income from taxation; tax is limited to source country tax.
- Deduction: Residence jurisdiction country allows deduction for tax paid in the source jurisdiction country; this results in highest tax.

$$\begin{aligned} T_{\text{Deduction Method}} &= T_R + T_S(1 - R_R) \\ &= T_R + T_S - T_R T_S \end{aligned}$$

The Organization for Economic Cooperation and Development (OECD) Model Treaty specifies source-residence conflict resolution:

- Credit or exemption methods are endorsed.
- Interest/dividend income are sourced in the paying entity's country (withheld in source country).
- Capital gains on movable property and financial assets are taxed in seller's residence country.
- Capital gains on immovable property are taxed in asset's source country.

Double tax treaty (DTT) residence-residence conflict resolution considers:

- Permanent home
- Center of vital interests
- Habitual dwelling
- Citizenship

DTTs typically do not resolve source-source conflicts.

Transparency and Avoidance

Financial advisors should attempt to legally minimize client taxes:

- Avoidance (legal minimization) conforms to the law.
- Evasion is misrepresenting or misreporting relevant information to circumvent tax obligations.

Jurisdictions with banking secrecy laws are not appropriate for helping clients evade tax. They are appropriate only for avoiding public scrutiny of transactions.

Most banks have become qualified intermediaries (QIs) to provide beneficial ownership information on U.S. securities while avoiding disclosure for non-U.S. clients.

The European Union Savings Directive requires EU members (except Austria, Belgium, and Luxembourg) to exchange information with one another. The three excluded members apply tax at the source and provide that information to the client's country of residence.

AI
. PM

CONCENTRATED SINGLE-ASSET POSITIONS
Cross-Reference to CFA Institute Assigned Reading #31

The Concentration Problem

Concentrated single-asset positions are those positions in which a client has 25% or more of assets. These positions are often made up of highly appreciated real estate, private companies, or public stock presenting liquidity and tax issues.

Highly concentrated public stock positions may result from:

- Incentive awards to executives
- Private companies going public via an initial public offering (IPO)
- Buy-and-hold investment strategy

Going from a position in private company shares to public company shares may have tax-favored aspects and may solve the liquidity problem, but may not solve the problem of low basis (and high tax liability).

Investment Risks
Concentrated positions may not earn fair risk-adjusted returns due to nonsystematic risk.

- Systematic risk: The capital asset pricing model (CAPM) identifies equity market risk, but other models include:
    - Business cycle risk
    - Inflation risk
    - Other macroeconomic factors
- Nonsystematic risk (i.e., company-specific risk): Exposure to events that affect the company but not the industry or market:
    - Business environment
    - Operations
    - Reputation

> **IMPORTANT:**
> A diversified portfolio has a much lower chance of suffering large losses.

Property-specific risks are the nonsystematic component of real property—that is, risks that affect the property but not the general real estate market:

- Environmental liability
- Credit risk of replacing investment-grade tenants with lower-quality tenants

Managing Concentrated Positions

Objectives for Concentrated Positions
Typical financial objectives and considerations include:

- Risk reduction: Obtain diversification; owners tend to overestimate value and underestimate volatility.
- Monetization: Generate liquidity to satisfy cash flow needs and diversification objectives.
- Optimization (i.e., tax efficiency):
    - Minimize immediate tax consequences of monetization.
    - Defer tax recognition.

Other objectives and considerations are:

- Concentrated stock positions:
    - Maintain control of voting shares.
    - Retain upside potential while increasing current income.
- Privately owned businesses:
    - Maintain overall control.
    - Business phase not optimal for sale (e.g., just entering growth phase, new product under development, etc.).
    - Desire to cede control to loyal management team.
    - Pass control to the next generation.
- Investment real estate:
    - Maintain operating control for property used in another business.
    - Benefit from price appreciation of recent purchase or value-added development.
    - Pass control to next generation.

Liquidity and Tax Considerations
Concentrated positions are generally illiquid, except for public stock. Public stock may be illiquid if:

- The position represents a large percentage of float.
- Applicable securities laws restrict liquidity (e.g., insider rules).

Privately held companies and real estate may suffer from:

- Lack of a public market for ownership shares.
- Different classes of buyers calculating different ownership values.

If sellable, the appreciated asset may trigger substantial taxable gains.

Legal and Other Constraints
Legal, regulatory, and company-specific constraints are often country specific, but generally result in restrictions on:

- Amount and timing of share sales:
    - Blackout periods (i.e., period around earnings and other announcements when insiders cannot sell)
    - Lockup periods (i.e., period after IPO when shareholders cannot sell)
- Avoidance of insider trading
- Compliance with notice, disclosure, and reporting requirements

Margin rules determine how much equity an investor must maintain relative to the portfolio value:

- Rules-based: Substantial margin required for additional investment in same security
- Risk-based: Completely marginable if portfolio insurance (i.e., protective put)

Off-balance-sheet debt such as a **prepaid variable forward** (i.e., collar plus a loan) is not considered a sale for tax purposes but also is not subject to margin requirements.

Short sales to lock in a position may be construed as constructive sales if the owner offers own shares for the short.

Liquidity should be considered because any hedge will be subject to adjustment as market conditions change.

It is difficult to hedge a recent IPO, because the stock has no trading history (i.e., the dealer wants to avoid sharp spikes).

Psychological Considerations
Advisors need to consider cognitive and emotional biases to determine the best approach:

- Emotional biases (difficult to overcome and may need to be worked around):
  - Status quo bias:
    - General bias against change
    - Husband/wife saying never to sell
    - Duty to pass to heirs
    - Coworkers looking down on selling
    - Loyalty/gratitude to employer
  - Overconfidence and familiarity
  - Extrapolation of past returns
  - Endowment effects—Demanding higher selling price than client would pay to purchase shares
- Cognitive biases (may be easier to overcome if pointed out):
  - Confirmation bias—Information that confirms beliefs
  - Conservatism bias—Unwillingness to update for new information
  - Availability heuristic—Probabilities influenced by ability to recall
  - Anchoring and adjustment—Adjustments from an original viewpoint rather than fresh viewpoint
  - Illusion of control—Overestimating personal control

Goal-Based Planning Considerations
Rather than managing the total portfolio as an integrated tool for obtaining multiple goals, financial planning often works with investors' behaviors by segregating assets into risk buckets:

- Personal risk: Prevention of poverty (i.e., emergency funds); low-volatility investments (e.g., Treasuries)
- Market risk: Maintaining current lifestyle; average risk-adjusted returns
- Aspirational risk: Enhancing lifestyle; above-average or speculative returns

> **IMPORTANT:** Personal and market risk are combined in a core portfolio or primary capital described elsewhere. Aspirational risk is described elsewhere as appropriate for surplus capital.

When deciding to sell a concentrated position, clients should consider whether the assets will be needed to maintain the current lifestyle or to prevent poverty.

Asset Location and Wealth Transfers
The type of tax on asset earnings often relates to the asset class of the security, which may be altered by the account type. **Asset location** refers to whether the funds are in a taxable or a tax-deferred/tax-exempt account.

Planning before appreciation allows simple strategies such as gifts to family members or trusts, and **estate freeze strategies** (i.e., transferring future appreciation to heirs to minimize estate and gift taxes).

Estate freeze strategies involve passing assets through closely held family corporations that avoid constructive transfer that triggers a tax event. Classic family-owned corporations may have two classes of stock: the voting preferred shares held by the current generation and a junior common equity class with no voting privileges. The low-value common stock is passed with little current tax consequence.

Postappreciation strategies include gifting highly concentrated positions to a **family limited partnership (FLP)**. The current generation becomes the general partner and retains control over underlying assets. The limited partnership interest available to heirs reduces the value of the underlying assets by a lack of liquidity discount and a lack of marketability discount.

The asset owner can also make charitable contributions of the appreciated assets that allow them to bypass taxes on all the gain.

Five-Step Process
A consistent method of delivering services to each client will help assure that objectives are met:

1. Identify objectives and constraints—elements of the investment policy statement (IPS).
2. Identify tools and strategies to satisfy objectives and meet client needs.
3. Compare tax advantages and disadvantages.
4. Compare nontax advantages and disadvantages.
5. Formulate and document an optimal strategy.

Managing Risk in Concentrated Positions

Tax Considerations
Different tools can result in different tax outcomes, although the diversification outcome is the same. Advisors can add value by optimizing the outcome within the realm of after-tax results.

Non-Tax Considerations
Hedging instruments and other tools have various advantages and drawbacks other than tax outcome:

- Price discovery: Over-the-counter (OTC) instruments transpire via a dealer whereas exchange-traded instruments have active price discovery in an open market.
- Fee transparency: Exchange-traded instruments have transparent fees and expenses whereas OTC pricing masks these.
- Flexible terms: OTC derivatives have more flexible terms and may be completely customizable; exchange-traded securities are less flexible and may not be customized.
- Position offset: Exchange-traded derivatives may be offset by taking an exactly opposite position with the same maturity; OTC derivatives are more difficult to find offsetting positions for.
- Counterparty credit risk:
  - Exchange-traded securities are often marked to market, and the counterparty will have less credit risk than in an OTC-traded derivative that is not marked to market.
  - Investors incur less risk working with intermediaries on an exchange versus counterparties in an OTC transaction.
- Minimum size: Exchange-traded derivatives have lower minimums than OTC derivatives.

Concentrated Public Shares

Monetization involves converting the concentrated positions in publicly traded equity to cash by hedging the position (i.e., removing both the upside and downside) and then borrowing against the hedged position. This results in:

- A hedged, essentially riskless position
- Money market return on the value of the long position
- High loan-to-value (LTV) ratio against the long position

In addition:

- Income generated by the hedged position offsets borrowing costs.
- Borrowed proceeds can be reinvested in a diversified portfolio.

Removing risk from the position can be accomplished by:

1. Short sale against the box (least expensive): Selling short using the same position held long as collateral; may not be allowed in some jurisdictions.
2. Total return equity swap: Owner exchanges returns from concentrated position for fixed or floating payments.
3. Forward sale contract or single-stock futures contract: short forward contract against the asset.
4. Options (i.e., forward conversion): Synthetic short forward position (i.e., long put and short call).

Tax considerations:

- Are potential losses available for offset against current income, or are they added to the basis of the concentrated position?
- Are carrying costs deductible or added to the basis of the hedge?
- Does a contract requiring physical settlement ultimately result in short- or long-term gain?
- Is any gain from the hedge taxed at short- or long-term gains rates?
- Does the hedge affect tax on income and dividends from the underlying? (No tax impact is preferred.)

Investors may also buy **puts** to protect against downside risk while participating in upside potential and deferring capital gains tax. Reduce costs by:

- Lowering the exercise price (i.e., investor self-insures for price loss between at- and out-of-the-money)
- Purchasing shorter-maturity puts
- Purchasing at-the-money puts and selling out-of-the-money puts (put spread)
- Using knock-out puts (which expire when the stock price reaches a certain level)

Zero-premium collars accomplish the same goals as the put strategies (i.e., protect, participate at least to some extent, and defer tax) at a lower cost:

- Buy a put that is at- or just out-of-the-money, and simultaneously sell a call at a price high enough for the premium income to offset the put price.
- If the share price remains above the put price and below the call price, both puts and calls expire worthless.
- The call buyer will exercise if the share price goes above the call price.
- The client may exercise if the share price goes below the put price.

Clients can increase their upside potential by selling a higher-priced call and:

- Lowering the put price (self-insured against greater downside risk)
- Using a put spread (self-insured below the short put)
- Financing part of the put price out-of-pocket

> IMPORTANT: A margin loan against the collared position can then be used to purchase diversifying assets.

AI
PM

A **prepaid variable forward (PVF)** combines the hedge and margin loan in the same instrument to obtain the same result as the zero-premium or zero-cost collar. The number of shares delivered at maturity varies with the share price at maturity:

- Less than put price: All shares are delivered and put strike price is received.
- Between put and call price: Investor delivers put strike price worth of shares.
- Above call price: Investor delivers put strike price worth of shares and pays price difference between market price and call strike price.

A **mismatch in character** occurs when the derivative used to hedge the underlying concentrated position has a different tax treatment (e.g., options received as compensation are taxed as ordinary income whereas options purchased may ultimately be taxed at capital gains tax rates).

A **yield enhancement strategy**, such as writing covered calls, allows the investor greater income on the underlying concentrated position but does not reduce risk on the underlying:

- Investor sells calls at a strike price and earns premium income.
- This is attractive if investor believes shares will trade in a range.
- Investor retains downside risk.
- This prepares the investor for an eventual sale at a predetermined liquidation value.

A tax-optimized equity strategy combines investment and tax management; there are two types:

- Index-tracking separately managed portfolio:
  - Tracks benchmark but outperforms it from an investment and tax perspective.
  - Offers opportunistic capital loss harvesting and gain deferral to offset periodic concentrated portfolio liquidations.
- Completeness portfolio: Tracks index given concentrated portfolio characteristics and new investments, with less emphasis on concentrated portfolio liquidations.

An **exchange fund** allows several investors with concentrated positions to contribute those positions for a share of a now more diversified exchange fund. The cost basis of each investor's shares in the exchange fund is the same as that investor's basis in the concentrated position; there is no taxable event to trigger a capital gain.

A **cross hedge** (i.e., hedging instrument against a similar underlying) may be appropriate in jurisdictions where proper derivatives for hedging are unavailable or where laws or costs preclude direct hedging.

Concentrated Private Shares

Additional concerns regarding concentrated positions in private equity include:

- Asset rich but cash poor; that is, net worth is tied up primarily in the firm.
- Liquidity may be limited due to company restrictions on sales outside the firm.
- Owners' shares are often highly appreciated; selling triggers large tax liability.
- Dilution or loss of control occurs at sale.

AI PM

Strategic Buyers

Strategic buyers are often other firms in the industry that view acquisition of other middle market companies as a low-risk way of gaining market share and earnings growth, especially in a slow-growth market.

Financial Buyers

Financial buyers raise funds from institutional investors and acquire companies to be managed under the umbrella of a private equity fund. Financial buyers usually cannot accrue financial and operational synergies the way strategic buyers can, and will not pay as much to acquire the company.

> IMPORTANT: In leveraged recapitalization, the owner owes tax on the portion withdrawn as cash but defers the gain on shares remaining in the recapitalized firm.

Recapitalization

In leveraged recapitalization, owners transfer stock for cash and retain only a minority interest in the recapitalized firm. The private equity firm pays for its purchased equity via debt through senior and mezzanine (i.e., subordinated) lenders.

After a few years, the private equity firm holding majority interest may take the recapitalized company to an initial public offering, sale to a strategic or financial buyer, or another recapitalization. At that stage, the former owner may be substantially cashed out and may or may not continue to run the company.

Management Buyout (MBO)

In a management buyout (MBO), key employees or executives borrow money to purchase the owner's shares. Financing may be difficult to obtain for MBOs because the employees often don't perform as expected when they have the additional burdens of management.

Owners must then take only a partial withdrawal of capital with a promissory note for the remainder, with the final amount contingent on company performance.

Based on financing dynamics and potential effects of a failed MBO, owners should consider this strategy only if a third-party buyer isn't available and the management offer meets or exceeds what a third party would pay.

Divestiture of Noncore Assets

Noncore assets do not directly bear on the growth or success of the business. Owners may liquidate noncore assets while continuing to run the core business, and reinvest proceeds from the divestiture in a more diversified asset pool.

In some cases, assets may play a role in potential growth of the core business but have a higher use for other purposes. These assets may also be repurposed to unlock value, even by selling to a competitor with a different use in mind.

Sale or Gifting to Family

For the same reasons management may have trouble seeking financing in an MBO, family may have trouble assembling financing to purchase the business assets. The owner may carry a substantial portion of the agreed price in a promissory note.

Gifting strategies provide a viable alternative provided the owner has substantial assets outside the concentrated position with which to meet lifestyle and other needs.

AI
PM

Personal Line of Credit Secured by Company Shares

In this strategy, the owner takes a personal loan from the company with the value of shares backing the loan amount. A put travels with the loan amount, which allows the owner to sell shares back to the company in an amount sufficient to extinguish the loan.

While the loan is outstanding, the owner retains control of the company, avoids a taxable sale event, and can use the proceeds of the loan to diversify.

> **IMPORTANT:** Exercising the put triggers a taxable event for the owner.

Initial Public Offering

Initial public offerings (IPOs) offer a method of exchanging ownership in a private company for publicly traded shares. Going public, however, exposes the owner to greater scrutiny. While removing some of the liquidity constraints of private company equity, it leaves the owner with a concentrated public equity position.

Employee Share Ownership Plan Exchanges

Employee share ownership plan (ESOP) exchange is another staged exit strategy in which the company buys the owner's shares for distribution to employees. In a leveraged ESOP exchange, the company borrows money to purchase owner shares. This takes place over time, optimizing the tax burden on the owner as shares are purchased.

U.S. tax rules permit deferral of the gain only on Subchapter C shares purchased by an ESOP (i.e., not Subchapter S shares). The deferral on gain, along with continued control and stepped-up basis to heirs, makes this strategy compelling.

Investment Real Estate

Alternatives to outright sale of investment property include:

- Mortgage the property:
  - Set the LTV ratio at the point where the net rental income equals the mortgage finance cost.
  - There are no tax consequences.
  - Use the proceeds from the new loan to diversify.
  - Nonrecourse loans are a put back to the lender for the mortgage amount.
- Donor-advised funds:
  - Contribute property now for charitable deduction.
  - Endowment purchases diversified portfolio or manages property.
  - Tax-free growth within charity, no recapture of depreciation, no capital gains tax due.
  - Advise funds until disbursements begin.
- Sale and leaseback: Owner sells to another party at market terms and leases back at market terms.
  - Owner retains use of facility.
  - Sale frees up owner's capital for diversifying portfolio, redeploying into core business, and so on.
  - Sale triggers taxable gain for tax purposes.
  - Rental payments on lease are completely deductible.

RISK MANAGEMENT FOR INDIVIDUALS
Cross-Reference to CFA Institute Assigned Reading #32

Human Capital and Financial Capital

The two primary components of an individual's wealth are:

1. **Financial capital:** Includes all tangible assets such as cash in bank accounts, stocks, bonds, and the family home.
2. **Human capital:** The present value of future expected labor income. Human capital is its own asset class and has its own return and risk characteristics. Young people have a lot of human capital compared with financial capital. At retirement, human capital is equal to zero.

Three key assumptions in the calculation of human capital are:

1. **Mortality rates**, which are based on actuarial assumptions on the probability of survival at a given age.
2. **Risk-free rate**, which is the same for everybody.
3. **Income volatility adjustment**, which is a subjective amount added to the risk-free rate. People with riskier occupations with higher income volatility will have a higher overall discount rate. Higher discount rates are associated with lower human capital, all else equal.

The income volatility risk associated with human capital can be diversified by appropriate financial capital. For example, an executive in the oil and gas industry has high income volatility, so human capital will be equity-like. To diversify, the executive will need less risky bonds as financial capital. By contrast, tenured professors' human capital is bond-like, so they will need more higher-risk equities in their financial capital.

A family's need for financial products changes over seven stages of financial life.

Exhibit 1: Seven Financial Stages of Life

Stage Name	Description and Age Range	Key Characteristics	Financial Advisor Can Help With ...
Education phase	Investing in knowledge through formal education or skill development	• Financially dependent on parents • Very little financial capital • Almost no focus on savings or risk management	Those with dependents might need life insurance
Early career	Has completed education and enters workforce (age 18 to 20s or early 30s)	• Gets married, has children, buys home • High family and housing expenses may not allow for retirement savings	Life insurance can supplement lack of sufficient financial and human capital
Career development	Specific skill development within a given field (age 35 to 50)	• Accumulation for children's college education • Large purchases such as vacation home, travel	Retirement saving
Peak accumulation	Moving toward maximum earnings and greatest opportunity for wealth accumulation (age 51 to 60)	• Retirement planning and travel • High career risk as high-paying job might not be replaced	Reducing investment risk Developing retirement income strategies
Preretirement	A few years before planned retirement age	• Income often at career highs	Decrease investment risk Tax planning for retirement distributions
Early retirement (first 10 years)	Period of comfortable income and enough assets to cover living expenses	• Using savings for enjoyment • Most active period of retirement • Less likely to suffer from cognitive or mobility impairments	Still a need for asset growth, as this phase could last 20 years
Late retirement	Unknown duration	• Physical activity declines • Cognitive or physical problems may deplete savings • May be need for long-term health care	Annuities to reduce or eliminate longevity risk

AI PM

Human capital can be added to a family's tangible, marketable financial assets and liabilities to derive the **economic (holistic) balance sheet**.

Exhibit 2: Economic (Holistic) Balance Sheet

Assets		Liabilities	
Financial capital		Debt	
Liquid assets	$275,000	Credit card debt	$15,000
Investment assets	$1,265,000	Car loan	$35,000
Personal property	$2,150,000	Home mortgage	$685,000
Subtotal	$3,690,000	Home equity loan	$60,000
		Subtotal	$795,000
Human capital	$1,800,000	Lifetime consumption needs	$3,500,000
Pension value	$250,000	Bequests	$300,000
Total Assets	**$5,740,000**	**Total Liabilities**	**$4,595,000**
		Net Wealth	**$1,145,000**

The holistic balance sheet also includes the **present value of vested pensions** as an intangible asset. Intangible liabilities include **lifetime consumption needs** and **bequests** (both are covered in more detail in the reading on estate planning). These items are shaded in gray on the holistic balance sheet.

The family's **net wealth** is $1,145,000, which is the difference between economic assets and economic liabilities. This is not to be confused with **net worth**, which is the difference between financial assets and financial liabilities, which is equal to $2,895,000.

There are three items to consider when determining the appropriate discount rate to use for vested employer pensions:

1. Plan's financial health, such as its funded status: We would use a lower discount rate for income from plans with a fund surplus than for plans with a fund deficit.
2. Credit quality of the sponsoring company: If the company has issued long-term bonds, the yield can serve as a proxy for the discount rate.
3. Additional credit support: In some countries, the government offers a guarantee in case a local defined-benefit pension plan becomes insolvent.

Premature Death Risk (Mortality Risk)

Life insurance can be used to protect against premature death (mortality) risk. There are two types of life insurance:

1. **Temporary life insurance** is insurance for a certain period of time specified at purchase, known as a term. If the individual survives for the entire term, say 20 years, then the policy will terminate unless it automatically renews. Premiums can either remain fixed (or level) or increase over the term as the mortality risk increases. **There is no cash value for term life insurance**.
2. **Permanent life insurance** provides lifetime coverage, assuming the premiums are paid over the entire period. Policy premiums are fixed, and there is generally a cash value associated with the policy. There are two basic types of permanent insurance: whole life

and universal life. Whole life insurance remains in force for the entire life of the insured. Universal life insurance has more flexibility than whole life insurance to vary the face amount of insurance, pay higher or lower premiums, and invest the cash value.

Both types of insurance are deemed **noncancelable**; the policy lapses only at the end of the term (for temporary insurance) or upon death (for permanent insurance), provided that the premiums have been paid.

Other general terms, mainly related to permanent insurance, include:

- **Participating/nonparticipating:** Participating allows for the cash value to grow at a higher rate than the guaranteed value based on the profits of the insurance company. Fixed growth values are known as nonparticipating.
- **Nonforfeiture clause:** A policyholder has the option to receive a portion of benefits if premium payments are missed and the policy lapses. There are three options: cash surrender option, where the cash value is paid; paid-up option, where the cash value is used to purchase a single-premium whole life policy; and extended term option, where the cash value is used to purchase a term life policy, usually with the same face value as the previous policy.
- **Riders:** Riders provide protection beyond the basic policy or other modification to a basic policy provision. One example is accidental death or dismemberment (AD&D), which increases the payout if or when the insured dies or is dismembered by an accident. Other common riders include accelerated death benefit, where those who are terminally ill can receive the death benefits while still alive; guaranteed insurability, which allows the policyholder to buy more insurance later at predefined periods; and waiver of premium, where future premiums are waived if the insured becomes disabled.
- **Viatical settlement:** A viatical settlement allows the policyholder to sell the policy to a third party. After buying the policy, the third party is responsible for paying premiums and will receive the death benefit when the insured dies.

The basic elements of a life insurance policy include:

- **Term and type of insurance:** For example, 30-year temporary life policy.
- **Amount of benefits:** For example, $250,000.
- **Limitations under which death benefit could be withheld:** These could include suicide of the insured within two years after purchasing the policy, or material misrepresentations made by the insured during the application process.
- **Contestability period:** The period when the insurance company can investigate and deny claims.
- **Premium schedule:** Specifying the amount and frequency of premiums to be paid to the insurance company.
- **Riders:** Modifications to basic coverage (see previous points).

There are four parties involved in every life insurance policy, which are also considered basic elements:

1. **Insured:** The person whose death triggers the death benefit payment.
2. **Policy owner:** Owns the policy and is responsible for paying premiums. In most policies, the insured and the policy owner are the same person. When the insured is not the policy owner, the owner must have an insurable interest in the life of the insured. Examples of insurable interests include an ex-spouse purchasing insurance on the other

ex-spouse following a divorce to cover future spousal or child-support payments or a company purchasing insurance on a key executive.

3. **Beneficiary (or beneficiaries):** Receives the death benefit, either as a lump sum (more common) or as an annuity (less common).
4. **Insurer:** The insurance company that writes the policy and pays the death benefits to the beneficiary when the insured dies.

Note that the insurance company will require the owner to have a reason for taking out the policy (i.e., **insurable interest**) other than to gamble on the insured's death.

There are three main considerations in pricing a life insurance policy:

1. **Mortality expectations:** Probability that the insured will die during the term of the policy. Actuaries rely on historical data and future mortality expectations based on age, gender, and other significant medical conditions, such as smoking/nonsmoking. During the underwriting process, actuaries make adjustments to the mortality tables to recognize other factors such as family disease history, risky hobbies, and so forth. All else held equal, men live shorter lives than women, and, given the same age, a man is expected to pay more for life insurance.
2. **Discount rate (or interest factor):** Represents the insurance company's assumed rate of return on its investment portfolio.
3. **Loading:** Life insurance company expenses and profits, if any, discussed later.

Mortality expectations and the discount rate are used to calculate the **net premium** that is paid to the life insurance company. The **gross premium** equals the net premium plus a load representing the two types of costs to the life insurance company:

1. **Underwriting costs:** Sales commission to the agent who sold the commission plus the cost of a physical exam, if required.
2. **Ongoing expenses:** Overhead and administration expenses, monitoring the policy, and verifying death claims. Renewal commissions are paid to the selling agent for the first years of the policy as an incentive to provide advice to the policyholder and to discourage the policy owner from terminating the policy.

The load may also include a profit based on the type of life insurance company:

- **Stock companies** are owned by shareholders and have a profit motive, so they add a projected profit to the load.
- **Mutual companies** are owned by the policyholders themselves, so there is no profit motive, although the gross premium is typically higher than the net premium plus expenses. If mortality outcomes and investment returns are more favorable than expected, the policyholders receive a nontaxable return of their premiums equal to the difference between the gross premium and net premium plus expenses.

Policyholders have a choice when deciding the term to purchase. Annual renewable (one-year) policies for a new insured at a particular age have lower annual premiums than longer-term policies, such as 20 years, which must average out the higher mortality charges in later years. Insurance companies offer loss leaders (i.e., low initial rates) on annually renewable insurance, with policyholders switching to other companies at the end of the short term. However, illness or an accident could cause the renewed policy to be much more expensive.

Whole life policies offer level premiums and the prospect of accumulation of cash value within the policy. The cash value can be withdrawn when the policy endows (matures) or when the policy is terminated by the policyholder. The cash value can also be borrowed as a loan while keeping the life insurance component of the policy in force, but the loan remains a liability that must be subtracted from any death benefit paid. Cash values increase slowly in the early years of the whole life policy as the insurance company makes up for its underwriting expenses. The insurance company is required by regulators to maintain a policy reserve, which is a liability for the company, in the amount of the cash value to be paid out to the insureds if they have not died by the time it is due to be paid.

Payment of premiums to the insurance company to assume mortality risks results in lower lifetime wealth.

The premium and the face value of the whole life policy remain constant, and the cash value increases, but the insurance value decreases over time. This tends to follow the typical pattern of requiring less life insurance as a person gets older and the need to protect human capital diminishes. Remember, human capital tends to fall toward zero as an individual reaches retirement.

When thinking about the cost of life insurance, there is more to consider than just choosing the policy with the lowest premium. There are many variables at play, and it is not easy for potential consumers to compare the cost of life insurance policies. However, there are two methods used to compare the prices of whole life insurance policies:

1. The **net payment cost index** assumes that the insured person will die at the end of a specified period, such as 20 years.
2. The **surrender cost index** assumes that the policy will be surrendered at the end of the period and that the policyholder will receive the projected cash value.

Disability Income Insurance

Disability income insurance is designed to reduce earnings risk caused by the insured becoming less than fully employed as a result of injury or disability. Disabilities tend to be for short periods of time rather than for life.

There are three definitions of full disability that address inability to perform the duties of:

1. One's regular occupation
2. Any occupation for which one is suited by education and experience
3. Any occupation

Using the first definition, a surgeon who loses the use of his or her dominant hand is deemed to be disabled. Using the second definition, a surgeon able to perform the duties of a general practitioner would not be deemed disabled. Using the third definition, even if the surgeon could not practice as a doctor but could teach at a medical school (or hold any other occupation), the individual would not be deemed disabled. For professionals with highly specialized skills, insurance contracts that include the first definition provide the most inclusive coverage, though they will have more expensive premiums.

As an extension to the definition of fully disabled, partial disability means that although the insureds cannot perform all of the duties of their profession, they can remain employed at a lower income. Residual disability means that the insured can perform all professional duties but cannot earn as much money after the disability.

ALTERNATIVE INVESTMENTS, PORTFOLIO MANAGEMENT, AND PRIVATE WEALTH MANAGEMENT

Premiums tend to be fixed, are based on the age of the insured, and are underwritten on the health and occupation of the insured. Coverage is through individual policies and through many employers. Disabled individuals will receive a percentage of the difference between their pre- and post-injury income, usually 60% to 80%, because other pre-injury expenses will be lower (such as commuting to work) and to reduce the likelihood of fraudulent claims.

Additional contract terms include:

Benefit period: How long the payments will be made, typically until retirement. Usually, a minimum number of years of benefits is specified, such as five years, to encourage those close to retirement to maintain their policies.

Elimination period (waiting period): The number of days that the insured must be disabled before payments begin. The typical elimination period in the United States is 90 days. The shorter the elimination period, the higher the premium.

Rehabilitation clause: Provides benefits for physical therapy to get the insured back to work as quickly as possible.

Waiver of premium: The policy owner may suspend premiums during a disability period, and premiums paid during the elimination period are returned.

Option to purchase additional insurance rider: The policy owner may increase coverage without further proof of insurability.

Cost of living rider: Benefits will be increased by an accepted cost of living index or some specified percentage each year.

Noncancelable and guaranteed renewable: The insurance company must renew the policy annually provided premiums are paid, and there will be no changes to the premium or promised disability benefits, even if employment income declines.

Noncancelable: The insurance company must renew the policy annually provided that premiums are paid, but premiums can be increased for the entire underwriting class although not for one particular individual. This is less expensive than a guaranteed renewable policy, but insurance companies with historical losses are expected to raise their premiums.

Homeowner's Insurance

A homeowner's policy can be specified as:

- **All risks:** All risks are included except those specified as being excluded.
- **Named risks:** Only risks specifically listed are covered by the policy.

The claims can be settled in one of two ways:

1. **Replacement cost:** The benefit pays the amount required to repair or replace an item with a new item of similar quality based on today's prices.
2. **Actual cash value:** The benefit equals replacement cost less depreciation.

Clearly, the replacement cost policy will have higher premiums than the actual cash value policy.

A key part of the insurance policy is the **deductible**, which is the amount that the policyholder must pay before any money is paid by the insurance company. Insurance companies price their policies to encourage the use of a higher deductible. A higher deductible means a lower insurance premium. Consider two policy alternatives:

- **Alternative 1:** Policy with a $500 deductible with annual premium of $3,000.
- **Alternative 2:** Policy with a $1,000 deductible with an annual premium of $2,900.

The lower deductible costs $100 more in annual premium. The purchaser needs to think whether the additional $100 of premium is worth the $500 difference between deductibles. A higher deductible means that the policyholder retains more risk but increases expected wealth over time by paying lower premiums to the insurance company.

In addition to homeowner's insurance to cover the cost of casualty losses, some mortgage lenders require homeowners to have life insurance sufficient to repay the mortgage should the borrower die. As the mortgage balance declines over time, an insurance policy can be purchased with a declining face value and premiums. By contrast, insurance companies want the house to be insured for its full value (less the value of the land, which cannot be lost or destroyed) so that it will receive larger premiums. If a house is underinsured, say less than 80% of its replacement cost, any losses are reimbursed at a lower rate.

Homeowners' liability is also addressed within the insurance policy to cover visitors injured in an accident in the home, but excludes professional and business liability, which may be covered separately.

Automobile Insurance

Automobile and other vehicle insurance rates are based on the value of vehicle and underwritten on the primary driver's age and driving record.

There are two types of coverage:

1. **Collision insurance** covers damage from an accident.
2. **Comprehensive insurance** covers damage from other causes, such as fire, hail, glass breakage, and theft.

The insurance amount is up to the replacement cost of the automobile with the same make and model in the same condition. If the cost to repair the automobile is greater than its actual cash value, the insurer will most often pay only the cash value. Liability, including injury and property damage, is also included in the policy. Like a homeowner's policy, the automobile policyholder also retains risk through the use of a deductible. Personal watercraft (boats) and trailers might require a separate insurance policy or an endorsement, which is coverage added to an existing policy.

Health/Medical Insurance

In the United States, there are three kinds of health insurance:

1. **Indemnity plan:** Allows the insured to go to any medical service provider, but the insured must pay a specified percentage of "reasonable and customary" fees.
2. **Preferred provider organization (PPO):** Allows the insured to go to a network of physicians who charge lower prices to individuals within the plan than to individuals who obtain health care on their own.
3. **Health maintenance organization (HMO):** Allows office visits at no or low cost to encourage individuals to seek treatment for minor medical issues before they become serious.

Comprehensive major medical insurance covers most health care expenses, including physician's fees, surgical fees, hospitalization, lab fees, X-rays, and other "reasonable and customary" diagnostic and treatment expenses.

Other key terms and features that could affect the premium of health insurance include:

- **Deductible:** The amount that the insured pays before the insurance company pays any benefit.
- **Coinsurance:** The percentage of any expense that the insurance company will pay, typically 80%.
- **Copayments:** Fixed payments that the insured must make for a particular service, such as $250 per doctor office visit.
- **Maximum out-of-pocket expense (stop-loss limit):** Individual and family maximum amount of expenses incurred beyond which the insurance company will pay 100%.
- **Maximum yearly and lifetime benefits:** Maximum amounts that the insurance company will pay within the respective time periods.
- **Preexisting conditions:** Health conditions that the insured had when applying for insurance that the policy may or may not cover.
- **Preadmission certificate:** An approval from the insurance company before a scheduled (nonemergency) hospital visit or treatment.

Liability Insurance

The liability coverage in the homeowner's and automobile policy may be inadequate to cover a significant accident. In this case, a separate **personal umbrella liability** insurance policy can be purchased. Consider a situation where an automobile policy provides $300,000 of liability coverage but the insured driver causes $650,000 worth of damage. The umbrella policy would pay the additional $350,000 beyond the automobile policy coverage. Such umbrella policies are relatively inexpensive.

Other forms of insurance include title insurance, which ensures that the ownership of property and real estate is not in doubt. Pseudo-insurance contracts (also known as service contracts) are sold when purchasing an automobile, home appliance, or other costly product to avoid repair costs. They are offered at the time of purchase, so sellers can charge a high rate because buyers have limited opportunity to compare insurance prices. Such contracts often include a deductible.

Annuities

Annuities are designed to protect against longevity risk. In other words, individuals will live for an unknown number of years after retirement and need to even out their spending over an uncertain time frame. Private annuities can be purchased from insurance companies. Life insurance provides financial protection for beneficiaries if policyholders die too young, whereas annuities protect people financially who live longer than expected.

Similar to life insurance, there are four parties to an annuity:

1. **Annuitant:** The annuitant is the person who receives the benefits while alive.
2. **Contract owner:** In most cases, the annuitant owns the contract. However, an employer can purchase an annuity for a retiring employee.
3. **Beneficiary (or beneficiaries):** Beneficiaries receive benefits when the annuitant dies provided that the annuity is purchased with a "period certain," which is a minimum guaranteed payment period.
4. **Insurer:** The insurer is the insurance company that is licensed to sell the annuity.

There are five annuity types, depending on whether the annuity is paid out immediately (single-premium immediate annuity or SPIA) or is deferred, and whether the underlying investments in the annuity are more bond-like (fixed) or equity-like (variable).

1. **Immediate fixed annuity:** This is the most common type of annuity, in which the annuitant trades a single lump sum of money at retirement in exchange for a regular promised payment for as long as the annuitant is alive. Payments are expressed as a percentage of the initial payment, which is also known as the *income yield.* So, if an insurance company quotes a 6% income yield, then in exchange for every $100,000 in lump-sum premium, the annuitant will receive $6,000 per year.

   Women live longer than men on average, so women will receive lower income yields. Payments increase with age because of the higher likelihood of death. Annuity pricing also depends on prevailing market yields on bonds because insurance companies tend to invest conservatively. When current yields on bonds are lower than historical bond yields, annuity payments will be low compared with historical averages. If life expectancy is rising at the same time, then payouts will be even lower.

2. **Immediate variable annuity:** The annuitant trades a single lump sum of money today in exchange for a promised income benefit for as long as the annuitant is alive. The income benefit varies over time, depending on the investment performance of the portfolio's underlying assets. During up markets, the payment will go up. During down markets, the payment will go down. The annuitant can purchase an income floor that provides protection during down markets. Without the floor, it is possible that payments could stop if the underlying asset values fall to zero.

3. **Deferred fixed annuity:** The annuitant pays premiums on an ongoing basis prior to retirement and receives an annuity payout at some future date. At any time prior to retirement, the investor can cash out the accumulated funds, which may be subject to a surrender charge. At retirement, the annuitant can either cash out or annuitize the accumulated funds with a periodic fixed payment, with most investors choosing to annuitize.

4. **Deferred variable annuity:** The annuitant pays a premium on an ongoing basis prior to retirement and receives an annuity payout at some future date. The annuitant can choose from a menu of investment options, similar to the purchase of mutual funds. However, the annuity is purchased through a salesperson who is licensed to sell insurance products. Compared with mutual funds, deferred variable annuities can be more expensive and have limited investment options.

   Deferred variable annuities can include a death benefit to a beneficiary. In exchange for a fee, the insurance company will pay the entire amount used to purchase the annuity when the annuitant dies, and the value of the contract is less than the initial investment. The annuitant can surrender the contract prior to retirement in exchange for a surrender charge. At retirement, the annuitant can simply start taking a variable income based on investment performance, add a contract rider, or annuitize the contract by converting it to an immediate payout annuity. Few investors actually annuitize a deferred variable annuity.

   Without a rider, there is no guaranteed income stream for life, as the underlying investments could fall in value until they are worthless. Then the annuity payments would stop, possibly while the annuitant is still alive. A guaranteed minimum withdrawal benefit for life rider can be added to construct a guaranteed income stream for life. In up markets, the initial investment may not be depleted, and any remaining value will be paid to the beneficiary. If the investment value is depleted because of poor investment performance, the insurance company will continue to pay the minimum benefit until the annuitant's death.

5. **Advanced life deferred annuity (ALDA):** An ALDA is a hybrid of deferred fixed annuity and immediate fixed annuity and is known as pure longevity insurance. In exchange for an immediate lump-sum payment, ALDA payments begin later in life well after retirement, typically when the annuitant turns 80 or 85. The premiums will be much lower than an immediate payment annuity. There are three reasons for the lower premium: (1) the insurance company can earn a return on the initial lump sum before making the first payment; (2) life expectancy of a person who is 80 years old is much lower than a person aged 65 at a normal retirement age; and (3) the annuitant may die before payments are made.

When selecting between fixed and variable annuities, there are a number of important considerations:

1. **Volatility of the benefit amount:** Investors who have a high risk tolerance might be better suited to a variable annuity, while those who need assurance of benefit payouts are better suited to a fixed annuity.
2. **Flexibility:** Immediate fixed annuities are irrevocable and cannot be undone. Variable annuities are tied to the investment performance of a subaccount, which can allow for withdrawals by the annuitant.
3. **Future market expectations:** If the investor believes that the markets are going to perform better in the future, a variable annuity is a better choice than a fixed annuity. A fixed annuity locks the investor into a portfolio of bond-like assets subject to interest rate risk. An investor in a fixed annuity who expects that interest rates will increase may defer purchasing the annuity until after rates increase. However, there is a risk that life expectancy will be longer in the future, resulting in lower payouts.
4. **Fees:** Variable annuities tend to have higher fees than fixed annuities. Immediate fixed annuities are easier to compare with each other, an important feature when comparing annuity payouts among insurance companies.
5. **Inflation concerns:** Fixed annuities are nominal payouts and do not change with inflation. However, a rider can be added to a fixed annuity to increase benefits in line with inflation. Some variable annuities automatically allow for payments to increase or decrease with inflation.

There are five payout methods:

1. **Life annuity:** Payments are made until the death of the annuitant.
2. **Period-certain annuity:** Payments are made for a specific number of periods, regardless of the life span of the annuitant.
3. **Life annuity with period certain:** Payments are made for the entire life of the annuitant or for a minimum number of years (most common is 10 years) even if the annuitant dies. If the annuitant dies within the minimum number of years, payments continue to the beneficiary for the remainder of the period certain.
4. **Life annuity with refund:** A life annuity with refund guarantees that the annuitant or beneficiary receives payments equal to the total amount paid into the contract, which equals the initial investment less fees.
5. **Joint life annuity:** Payments continue for two or more annuitants, such as a husband-wife couple, as long as either one of them is alive. Payments stop when the surviving annuitant dies.

Individuals can self-insure longevity risk either by making periodic withdrawals from their own investment portfolios or by annuitizing through a life insurance company. In an annuity, each payment is a combination of interest, principal (premium), and mortality credits. Mortality credits are benefits that surviving members of the annuity pool receive from those who have passed away. Self-insurers do not receive mortality credits, only the interest and principal. However, they face longevity risk.

Annuitants pay a higher price for insurance in exchange for the mitigation and possible elimination of longevity risk. In other words, in exchange for lower shortfall risk (lower risk of running out of money during one's lifetime), the investor has less wealth because of annuity premiums. This trade-off is similar to an efficient frontier for a risky portfolio.

The international shift away from defined benefit (DB) pension plans has caused a shift toward annuities. At the individual level, there are five factors that would likely **increase demand** for any annuity:

1. Longer-than-average life expectancy
2. Greater preference for lifetime income
3. Less concern for leaving money to heirs
4. More conservative investing preferences
5. Lower guaranteed income from other sources (such as pensions)

These five factors would be associated with low wealth and low shortfall risk. The decision to retain risk or buy insurance is determined by a household's risk tolerance. At the same level of wealth, a more risk-tolerant household will prefer to retain more risk, either through higher insurance deductibles or by simply not buying insurance. A risk-averse household would have lower deductibles and would purchase more insurance. For all households, insurance products that have a higher load (expenses) will encourage a household to retain more risk. Finally, as the variability of income increases, the need for life insurance decreases because the present value of future earnings (human capital) will be lower with a higher discount rate.

Exhibit 3: Loss Characteristics and Risk Management

Loss Characteristics	High Frequency	Low Frequency
High severity	Risk avoidance	Risk transfer
Low severity	Risk reduction	Risk retention

An investment advisor will often be asked how much life insurance is enough. There are two techniques:

1. The **human life value method** estimates the present value of earnings that must be replaced.
2. The **needs analysis method** estimates the financial needs of the dependents.

II
PM

PORTFOLIO MANAGEMENT FOR INSTITUTIONAL INVESTORS
Cross-Reference to CFA Institute Reading #33

Common Characteristics of Institutional Investors

While investors with private wealth can be very different, institutional investors tend to share common characteristics:

1. Scale—High AUM improves investment capabilities, but capacity of an investment opportunity may be limited.
2. Long-term horizon—There is usually a benefit commitment that lasts over a very long time.
3. Regulatory frameworks—The jurisdictional frameworks vary in complexity.
4. Governance—Clearly defined governance and investment policy.
5. Principal-agent issues:
    ○ Internal agents include investment committee members and investment staff. External agents include third-party asset managers, broker/dealers, consultants, and board members.
    ○ External fund managers design compensation via a high base fee, which is due regardless of fund performance. This conflicts with the interests of investors.

To deal with principal-agent issues, institutional investors use governance models with high levels of accountability. A board or investment committee typically oversees investment functions for the funds.

Investment Horizon and Liquidity Needs
Institutions have long investment horizons and low liquidity needs, except for frozen DB plans that wish to de-risk. Net payouts are a low percentage of AUM. This allows investment in alternative assets that have long investment lockups and uncertain future liquidity events. Banks and insurance companies are more asset/liability focused and are subject to more burdensome capital adequacy requirements.

Legal, Regulatory, and Tax Constraints
The International Organization of Securities Commissions (IOSCO) brings together the world's securities regulators. The focus of its legal and regulatory frameworks includes investor protection, soundness of financial institutions, and financial market integrity. Key drivers behind the framework since the 2007–2009 financial crisis involve enhanced collateral requirements; increased liquidity requirements; central clearing; trading tax implementation; more transparent reporting; and proprietary trading, private equity, and compensation limits.

Overview of Investment Policy

IOSCO's mission determines investment objectives and focuses on risks in different ways:

- Banks and insurance companies may wish to maximize net present value through asset-liability management and the economic relationships among assets and liabilities.
- Defined-benefit pension plans seek 100 percent funded status or a surplus while maintaining an ability to pay retirement benefits. Risk is stated in volatility of the surplus (i.e., assets less liabilities).
- Endowments may prefer to provide inflation-adjusted financial support to their institution. Risk might be stated in volatility of total returns.

- Sovereign wealth objectives will be similar to endowments while risk might focus on the probability of purchasing power loss or an actual reduction in AUM over a period.

Approaches to meeting institutional investor objectives include:

1. **Norway model**—Almost exclusive reliance on traditional equity and fixed income investments (i.e., the 60/40 model) popularized by Norway's pension fund. This approach limits potential value added from security selection skills above market returns. Investment costs are low, investments are transparent, and there is little complexity and risk of poor manager selection.
2. **Endowment model**—High allocation to alternative investments (private investments and hedge funds), significant active management, and externally managed assets popularized by Yale University. Appropriate for investors with a long horizon.
3. **Canada model**—High allocation to alternative investments as in the endowment model, but with greater internal management. Evaluation involves measurement against a passive benchmark of public equities, fixed income, and cash expected to achieve long-term expected return consistent with the institution's objectives and risk tolerance.
4. **Liability-driven investing (LDI) model**—This model is designed to generate returns that cover liabilities. The strategy focuses on maximizing surplus return (excess return of assets over liabilities) and surplus volatility. Some implementations involve both a portfolio to defease the liability and a return-generating portfolio.

Pension Funds

In defined benefit (DB) plans, the plan sponsor commits to paying a specified retirement benefit and assumes the risk of assets backing benefit payments. In defined contribution (DC) plans, contributions are defined but the risk of retirement benefits falls on the beneficiaries. Countries such as Switzerland have hybrid DB and DC plans.

DB and DC Plan Stakeholders

For a DB plan, the stakeholders include the plan sponsor (i.e., the employer) as represented by the Chief Financial Officer (CFO), the Chief Investment Officer (CIO), the board of directors, the investment committee, and investment committee staff. Shareholders also have a stake in the case of a public company plan. Governments and unions are also considered stakeholders.

For a DC plan, the stakeholders include plan beneficiaries (i.e., employees/participants), the employer, the board, and the government. Boards of companies offering DC plans must consider differing participant knowledge about investments and must provide adequate disclosures. The board may wish to consider education programs for the plan.

Liabilities and Investment Horizon

DB plan liabilities are the present value of expected future retirement benefits, which in turn depend on the design specifics of the plan. Key pieces of the equation include:

- Years of service/tenure
- Salary/earnings
- Mortality/longevity

Assumptions in the estimation process include growth rate of salaries, mortality and disability, expected vesting, and the discount rate used in the present value calculation. Vesting means meeting plan requirements to receive benefits, so calculations should include an assumption about employees not meeting the vesting requirement. The discount rate may be a constant actuarial discount rate such as long-term expected return, bond yields, or swap rates.

Higher discount rates result in lower liabilities. The funded ratio may be used to measure asset sufficiency: Funded ratio = Fair value of plan assets/PV of Defined benefit obligations.

Companies with a surplus or a small insufficiency have more flexibility in taking investment risk when the plan is small compared to the balance sheet and when the core business is not cyclical (i.e., to avoid correlation with plan assets). "Younger" plans have greater flexibility because the sponsor has more time to make up downturns in asset value before they must pay benefits.

DC plan liabilities equal its required contributions, but plan sponsors must still meet their fiduciary duties to plan participants.

Liquidity Needs
Liquidity risk in a pension plan depends on:

- Active employees relative to retirees—A more mature plan (i.e., low active employee ratio and high workforce age) has less time to recover from investment losses and becomes less liquid.
- Workforce age—Plans with lower surpluses/higher deficits or participants who can withdraw from the plan have lower liquidity.
- Plan funded status (i.e., surplus or deficit)—A plan with higher liquidity needs must invest more in cash and liquid investments.
- Ability to withdraw from plan—A plan with lower liquidity risk can invest more in growth assets and especially in private equity and credit investments.

External Constraints
In the United States, Employment Income Security Act of 1974 (ERISA) has a fiduciary code; requires specific disclosures; and regulates vesting, funding, and payouts. Other countries may require employers to contribute a minimum percentage if the plan's funded ratio falls below 1:1, or maximum allocations to certain asset classes.

DC plans, also subject to ERISA, require a Qualified Default Investment Alternative with low fees for participants who do not specify an investment allocation. Other regulations may involve participant education.

Governments typically encourage retirement saving by specifying favorable tax treatment, which may take different forms:

- Reduced taxes on retirement plan contributions
- Favorable tax rates on investment income/capital gains
- Lower tax rates on annuitized distributions (rather than higher taxes on lump sums).

International pension plans should, where possible, take advantage of tax treaties that reduce taxes on growth and withdrawals.

Overfunded plans must appear as an asset on the balance sheet and underfunded plans must appear as liabilities. Plan sponsors must report service costs and investment gains/losses as part of net income.

U.S. public pension plans follow Governmental Accounting Standards Board (GASB) rules that require public plan sponsors to report fair market values for plan assets and a blended value for plan liabilities. The blended approach for liabilities requires discounting the funded portion of plan assets based on expected return on plan assets and the unfunded portion based on tax-exempt municipal bond yields. This pushes plan sponsors to invest the funded portion in higher-risk assets (e.g., equities and alternative investments).

Risk Considerations in Private DB Plans
Key considerations include:

- Plan funded status—Companies can minimize the risk of developing a liability by:
  - Liability-driven investing (LDI)—Matching assets to liabilities in terms of quantity, timing, and risk.
  - Increasing investment risk.
  - Reducing return volatility—The employer may have to make higher contributions over time but will have less risk of a balance sheet liability.
- Financial strength of the DB sponsor; stronger sponsors can tolerate greater investment risk.
- Lower correlation of business income with investment returns allows greater investment risk.
- Plan designs; plans that reward stability allow greater investment risk.
- Workforce characteristics; younger workers allow greater investment risk.

Adequately funded plans can avoid liability status by:

- Offering lump sum payments as an incentive for voluntarily leaving the plan
- Transferring risk to a third party

Investment Objectives
DB pension plans set a long-term target return in nominal terms over a specified investment horizon with risk that allows the plan to meet its liabilities.

While some plan sponsors may seek slight overfunding, DB assets should at least grow in line with liabilities in order to avoid underfunding the plan. Therefore, the plan's board or investment committee should consider portfolio risk relative to the sponsor's ability to increase contribution rates if investments underperform.

DC pension plans wish to provide investment options that allow participants to grow assets to support retirement spending needs.

Additionally, DC plans must set appropriate objectives for the default option based on characteristics of existing participants. This typically results in a balanced fund, sometimes separate funds for various life cycle stages for the participants. These funds may be designed to outperform benchmarks consisting of weighted-average individual asset class benchmarks in the policy weights prescribed by the strategic allocation for the life cycle fund.

Sovereign Wealth Funds (SWFs)

SWFs are classified here as:

- **Stabilization funds**—Insulates the country's economy/budget from external shocks or commodity price volatility
- **Development funds**—Directs resources to infrastructure and priority projects
- **Savings funds**—Transforms non-renewable assets into diversified financial assets to help share benefits over generations
- **Reserve funds**—Increases return on reserves or reduces the negative carry costs of holding reserves
- **Pension reserve funds**—Earns a return on pension assets in country-provided plans

Some SWFs cross these boundaries.

Stakeholders

SWF stakeholders include citizens of the sponsoring country; the government; SWF management, investment committees, and boards; and external asset managers. The ultimate beneficiaries are the current and future citizens (or residents) of the country via direct payment receipt, lower taxes, or improved domestic environments. Many SWFs are established to benefit future as well as current generations.

Liabilities and Investment Horizon

Owing to their mission affecting intergenerational well-being, SWF liabilities are not necessarily well-delineated:

- Budget stabilization funds—Such funds may be needed to help fund budget deficits, so they have uncertain liabilities and short horizons.
- Development funds—These funds aim to increase productivity and real GDP growth, so the objective is uncertain, and the horizon may be short or long.
- Savings funds—The objective is to transform natural resource wealth into more sustainable wealth; they may have a spending policy (e.g., tied to domestic natural resource production) or a real return objective.
- Reserve funds—Common in export-intensive countries that have built reserves, these funds have very long investment horizons with nominal or real return targets for invested assets.
- Pension reserve funds—These funds wish to defease or reduce future pension burdens on their populations, so the horizon is long term and often focused on alternative investments.

Liquidity Needs

Stabilization funds invest in assets that have a low risk of significant losses over short time periods in order to maintain high liquidity.

Development funds invest in infrastructure and R&D, so their liquidity and timing varies depending on the project.

Savings funds have stable liquidity needs generally known well in advance, similar to endowments.

Reserve funds have liquidity needs lower than stabilization funds but higher than savings funds.

Pension reserve funds hold more illiquid investments during the accumulation phase and more liquid investments during the decumulation (i.e., payout) phase.

External Constraints

International Forum of Sovereign Wealth Funds (IFSWF) members developed "The Santiago Principles" to describe best practices for a sound legal framework, well-defined mission, independence, accountability, transparency, disclosure, ethics and professionalism, effective risk management, and review.

Asset allocation rules for a specific SWF are often set up based on the mission of the fund. For example, a technology development fund might require its assets to be invested in offshore technology companies to promote diversification from its direct domestic technology investments.

Sovereigns give tax-free status to their funds. However, non-domestic SWFs may be ineligible to claim withholding taxes or tax credits ordinarily available to taxable investors. SWFs should avoid the perception of evading taxes in any non-domestic jurisdictions.

Investment Objectives
Primary objectives are:

- Budget stabilization funds—Real return with a low probability of a negative return in any given year.
- Development funds—Real returns focus on achieving real return greater than real domestic GDP or productivity growth.
- Savings funds—Achieving nominal returns that will protect the real value of assets and fund ongoing government programs.
- Reserve funds—Nominal returns greater than paid on monetary stabilization bonds or preserve and enhance the international purchasing power of foreign reserves.
- Pension reserve funds—Returns that will meet future benefit obligations.

Asset Allocation for SWFs
Asset allocation results from a combination of an individual fund's liquidity needs, investment objectives, and constraints:

- Budget stabilization funds—Dominated by fixed-income investments
- Development funds—Growth assets (e.g., equities and alternatives)
- Savings funds—Growth assets (e.g., equities and alternatives)
- Reserve funds—Similar to savings funds with less allocation to alternatives
- Pension reserve funds—Similar to savings funds with less allocation to alternatives

Endowments and Private Foundations

Endowments invest their assets in capital markets to provide a savings and growth mechanism to fund ongoing activities and special projects for a specific institution. **Foundations** make grants to outside organizations and persons (rather than to a single institution) to carry out charitable activities. There are four different kinds of foundations:

1. **Community**—Usually funded by public contributions and operating for the benefit of a community (e.g., hospitals, schools, churches, etc.)
2. **Operating**—Funded by individuals or families to operate a not-for-profit business for charitable purposes (e.g., operating a museum)
3. **Corporate**—Established by businesses and funded from profits
4. **Private grant-making**—Funded by individuals or families to fund specific types of charities

Most foundations are private grant-making foundations.

Stakeholders
Endowment stakeholders include current and future students; alumni; current and future university faculty, administrators, and board members; and the larger university community.

Foundation stakeholders include founding family members, donors, grant recipients, and the broader community.

Liabilities and Investment Horizon

The investment horizon of an endowment is perpetuity. The spending policy is designed to ensure intergenerational equity and to make smooth payouts despite capital market volatility.

Endowment spending policies are categorized according to the following payout formula:

$$\text{Spending}_{t+1} = w(\text{Spending}_t)(1 + I) + (1 - w)(\text{Spending rate})(\overline{AUM})$$

where

$$I = \text{inflation rate}$$
$$w = \text{weight of prior period spending}$$
$$AUM = \text{assets under management, averaged}$$

- Constant growth rule: $w = 1$ to provide a fixed annual inflation-adjusted amount
- Market value rule: $w = 0$ to provide spending entirely dependent on AUM
- Hybrid rule: $0 < w < 1$

Endowments that support a smaller percentage of an institutional budget can tolerate more portfolio risk.

Foundations in the United States must spend any donations in the year received (i.e., "flow-through"), although this is not as common outside the United States. Further, U.S. private grant-making foundations must pay out 5% of assets (on a trailing 12-month basis) plus investment expenses. They may use a spending formula similar to that of endowments.

Liquidity Needs

Low liquidity needs and long investment horizons allow both endowments and foundations (except limited-life foundations) to accept higher short-term volatility in pursuit of superior long-term returns. Some portion of the funds may be invested in private equity and other alternative investments with long lockup periods and no current income.

Both will be subject to liquidity management needs on derivatives margins and private equity funding.

External Constraints

Legal and regulatory constraints will be similar on both endowments and foundations except for the foundation minimum-spending requirement. Both are governed in the United States by the Uniform Prudent Management of Institutional Funds Act, which requires maintaining purchasing power of the fund (except for limited life foundations) while allowing flexible charity decisions. These institutions are governed in the U.K. by The Trustee Act.

Both UPMIFA and The Trustee Act allow funds to manage toward preserving fund assets in the long run, rather than only allowing payout of investment earnings.

Endowments and foundations operate under three types of tax-exempt status:

1. Gifts and donations—Contributors receive a tax deduction for the donation
2. Asset income and capital gain—Non-taxable, subject to payouts (for foundations only)
3. Distributions—Received tax-free by non-profit institutions but taxable to for-profit entities

Investment Objectives

The IPS for an endowment or foundation should include a spending policy designed to maintain the purchasing power of the assets into perpetuity (except for limited-life foundations) while achieving investment returns sufficient to sustain spending. Therefore, the return objective will at least equal the preferred spending rate in real terms plus an inflation expectation over a three- to five-year period.

A secondary objective would include outperforming a policy benchmark given a tracking error budget.

Asset Allocation

Not surprisingly, endowments follow the endowment spending model and therefore rely on alternative investments. Foundations also follow these models. Larger institutions have greater allocation to alternatives, and private foundations have greater allocation to alternatives than community foundations.

Banks and Insurers

Financial Stability Board, an international body that monitors the global financial system, has designated about 30 of the larger institutions as globally systemically important banks (G-SIBs). Because of their place in the international financial system, they are often regulated to stricter standards than smaller banks.

Insurance companies can have systemic importance, but tend to be regulated differently based on their underlying liabilities.

Stakeholders

Bank stakeholders include internal parties (i.e., employees, management, and boards) as well as external parties (i.e., shareholders, creditors, customers, credit rating agencies, regulators, and communities where they operate).

Most large insurers in North America and Europe have publicly issued securities, so the shareholders are stakeholders. Others are organized as mutual companies where the policyowners receive excess investment returns as dividends to their policy or in cash.

Liabilities and Investment Horizon

Both banks and insurance companies use asset-liability management (ALM) for part of the portfolio and a separate account with greater potential to use riskier assets.

Bank assets include loans, debt, currency, deposits with central banks, accounts receivable, and bullion. Bank liabilities include deposits as well as short- and long-term debt. Deposits include:

- Term (time) deposits—Interest-bearing accounts with a specified maturity date. This category includes savings accounts and certificates of deposit (CDs). Banks have visibility on the duration of these deposits because they require advance notice prior to withdrawal.
- Demand deposits—Easily accessed checking and certain savings accounts that are considered short-term.

The investment horizon for a bank's investment portfolio depends on maturities of its asset base and liability structure although the bank itself has a perpetual horizon. The long-term horizon includes infinite shorter-horizon tactical cycles that correspond roughly to the business cycle.

Insurance companies include both life insurance companies, which have longer-duration liabilities that depend on policy features and finance more predictable claims, and property and casualty (P&C) companies with duration that depends on their features as well as their product mix. In addition, P&C insurance involves events with potentially higher cost (e.g., natural disasters), lower probability, and uncertain timing, leading to a shorter-duration portfolio.

Life insurers bear mortality risk for traditional life insurance and longevity risks for fixed annuities—and bear some risk for variable life and annuities—so they maintain a **reserve account** of assets to fund these liabilities. They maintain a **surplus portfolio** for the excess over amounts needed to fund these liabilities.

Liquidity
In addition to the short-term nature of most of its liabilities, banks must be able to liquidate investments quickly in the event of a crisis. Increased global scrutiny since the financial crisis of 2007–2009 has resulted in higher quality portfolios with greater liquidity.

Retail banks deal with individuals while commercial banks deal with large corporations and governments. Commercial banks have a higher cost of funds and less liquidity; retail banks have a lower cost of funds and better liquidity.

Life insurance companies must also consider the risk that rising/high interest rates will increase net cash outflow as customers surrender their policies in search of higher yields in other investments or lower payments on new policies.

External Constraints
Liabilities to depositors, claims of policyholders, and amounts due to creditors are contractually defined. Both types are regulated at either national or state levels, or both, and are increasingly overseen by supranational regulatory and advisory bodies.

Bank regulations in most jurisdictions focus on capital adequacy, liquidity, and leverage to lower systemic or contagion risk, and typically address diversification, asset quality and maintaining liquidity.

In the United States, the National Association of Insurance Commissioners (NAIC), of which every state is a member, sets accounting policies and financial reporting standards for the industry. This is addressed by the Solvency II framework applicable to EU member states.

Banks and insurance companies as entities operate under IFRS or GAAP but are also subject to statutory accounting standards mandated by regulators. Statutory accounting subtracts intangible assets from asset and common equity accounts and mandates acceleration of certain expenses (e.g., policy underwriting and sales costs). True economic accounting, a third type, marks assets and liabilities to current market values and considers imputed taxes.

Objectives
The primary objective for both banks and insurance companies is to defease liabilities and grow the surplus.

For banks, the "asset-liability management committee" (ALMCo) performs functions of an investment committee in this regard by setting the IPS, monitoring performance, and ensuring compliance with regulatory targets. ALMCo may also compare performance relative to peers with comparable business models and objectives.

An insurance company's risk tolerance may vary relative to the competitive environment for various product lines, regulatory and tax changes, market conditions, and other factors.

Balance Sheet Management and Investment Considerations

The duration model considers financial institution equity as a function of degree of leverage (A/E), relative modified duration of assets/liabilities, and correlation of changes in yields of assets and liabilities:

$$MDUR_E = \left(\frac{A}{E}\right) MDUR_A - \left(\frac{A}{E} - 1\right) MDUR_L \left(\frac{\Delta i}{\Delta y}\right)$$

where

$$
\begin{aligned}
MDUR &= \text{modified duration} \\
A, \ L, \ E &= \text{assets, liabilties, equity} \\
i &= \text{effective yield on liabilities} \\
y &= \text{reference yield on assets}
\end{aligned}
$$

Managing based on this model depends on the following relationships:

- Lower asset duration by holding cash, deposits at central banks, foreign currency reserves, and other liquid (zero duration) assets.
- Lower liability duration by issuing intermediate and longer-term debt, deeply subordinated capital securities, and perpetual preferred stock.
- Reduce asset/liability mismatches by using financial futures and interest rate swaps.

Changes in interest rate levels, however, are only one source of changes in equity value. The formula can be extended to capture all forms of asset and liability volatility by using the portfolio model:

$$
\sigma^2_{\Delta E/E} = \left(\frac{A}{E}\right)^2 \sigma^2_{\Delta A/A} + \left(\frac{A}{E} - 1\right)^2 \sigma^2_{\Delta L/L}
$$
$$
- 2\left(\frac{A}{E}\right)\left(\frac{A}{E} - 1\right) \rho \sigma_{\Delta A/A} \sigma_{\Delta L/L}
$$

where

ρ = correlation (CORR) between percentage value changes in assets and liabilities

Equity volatility can be *decreased* by:

- Decreasing volatility of portfolio investments, loans and derivatives
- Decreasing volatility from unexpected changes to claims, deposits, guarantees, and other liabilities
- Increasing the correlation between asset and liability changes
- Limiting leverage

This can be achieved by increasing:

- Liquidity
- Diversification of portfolio and other assets and liabilities (e.g., underwriting risks)
- Investment quality
- Transparency (vanilla investments that won't have unexpected changes)
- Funding stability

Monetary limits on guarantees, funding commitments, and insurance claims can also decrease equity volatility.

TRADE STRATEGY AND EXECUTION
Cross-Reference to CFA Institute Assigned Reading #34

Motivations to Trade

Profit Seeking

Managers seek to provide risk-adjusted performance in excess of their benchmark, which usually results from trading in superior insights not yet recognized in the market price. Trading strategies attempt to earn the excess return when the market ultimately adopts the insight and buys into the investment.

Transparent (i.e., illuminated or "lit") markets report pre- and post-trade price, volume, and depth. Alternative trading systems (i.e., "dark pools") provide only post-trade data and thus allow more privacy in establishing a strategy. Dark pools, however, run greater risk of unfilled trades.

Alpha decay describes the decrease in potential alpha after making an investment decision and determines the trade urgency (i.e., how patiently or aggressively the portfolio manager believes the strategy should be implemented).

Value strategies, on the other hand, involve undervalued companies regaining a position or improvement in a variety of other slower-developing factors that drive earnings.

Risk Management/Hedging Needs

Whether a manager adjusts a position by trading the security via derivatives depends on:

- The fund's investment mandate (i.e., derivatives acceptability, portfolio targets, etc.)
- Risks being managed or hedged
- A security's liquidity

Managers may instead hedge risks when they don't have a specific outlook in mind.

Managers may also use options to implement a view on price movement, volatility, or changes in risk factors or risk-factor sensitivity.

Cash Flow Needs

PMs may need cash for other opportunities, to meet margin requirements, investment and distribution of client funds, and other operational needs. In a rising market, mutual funds may use ETFs to equitize uninvested cash until the manager can trade the underlying or until the next rebalance.

Mutual funds often fund investor redemptions based on net asset value (NAV) at close of the day when the request is made, if requested before the market close. Mutual funds may then sell derivatives at the market close to fund the redemption request.

Corporate Actions, Index Reconstitution, and Margin

Trading may be required when derivatives expire, as the result of corporate actions (e.g., mergers and acquisitions or spinoffs), or an index changes constituents. Trading may be required for operational needs such as dividend or bond coupon reinvestment.

Trading Strategies and Strategy Selection

Trade Strategy Inputs

Order Characteristics

Order side (i.e., buy or sell) can determine the portfolio manager's trading strategy. Rising prices may result in longer execution times and negative market impact for buyers as they wait for liquidity providers (sellers). Falling prices may result in longer execution times and negative market impact for sellers as they wait for buyers. Trading a list of buys and sells may result in a mismatch and greater time to transact for on one side or another.

Order size, especially relative to the market, may also affect trading strategy. **Market impact** describes adverse price movements that result from trading an order; larger orders often result in greater market impact due to supply/demand imbalances. To reduce market impact, traders will attempt to trade with less urgency. Market impact costs tend to rise as *relative* order size (%ADV) increases.

Security Characteristics

Trading an American depositary receipt (ADR) or global depositary receipt (GDR) may reduce cost and difficulty relative to trading the underlying security on a local market. Custody, compliance, and regulatory costs may also be less with ADRs/GDRs.

Short-term alpha—also known as trade or trading alpha—represents investment price movement over the period between investment decision and trade execution. Price volatility affects **execution risk** (i.e., the risk of not being able to trade at the desired price). Greater liquidity lowers execution risk and market impact of trades.

Bid-ask spreads indicate the quantity of a security that can be traded at any time.

Market Conditions

Liquidity for all securities may be affected by holiday trading or a systemic panic. Security-specific factors also affect liquidity; such as, being removed from or added to an index or, for fixed income securities, becoming the off-the-run security.

Less risk averse managers will be able to trade more patiently than will more risk averse managers.

Market Impact and Execution Risk

The trader's dilemma could be summarized as, "Trading too fast increases market risk, but trading too slow increases execution risk." Trading strategy should optimize the tradeoff between decreasing market impact versus decreasing execution risk.

Reference Prices

Pre-trade benchmarks include:

- Decision price—The price at which the manager decides to trade (buy/sell); may be the previous open or close if the manager has no record of the decision price, which is often the case in quantitative approaches.
- Previous close—A security's closing price on the day before the trade.
- Opening price—A security's opening price on the day of the trade.
- Arrival price—A security's price when a trade arrives in the market; managers basing a trade on mispricing (i.e., alpha trade) or attempting to minimize trading costs often specify the arrival price as a pre-trade benchmark.

Intraday benchmarks are based on a price or prices that occur during the trading day:

- Volume-weighted average price (VWAP)—Managers with both buy and sell orders may specify VWAP as a benchmark in order to trade with market order flow. Managers may use VWAP to ensure they have cash from sell orders to fund purchases.
- Time-weighted average price (TWAP)—Managers use TWAP when they do not wish to participate during price spikes (e.g., opening or closing prices). TWAP helps evaluate performance against reasonable trading prices rather than volume spikes.

Portfolio managers seeking alpha are likely to use target price benchmarks, usually the price perceived as fair value. The manager purchases as many shares as possible below the target price.

Portfolio managers often select a closing price benchmark when they want to minimize tracking error with a benchmark price, which is usually marked at the end of the trading day. Managers using this approach, however, do not know how they are doing relative to the benchmark until the market closes.

Trade Strategies
A portfolio manager's trade motivation, risk aversion, and other factors such as order size and market conditions determine the trading strategy. Overall, however, the idea is to balance the trading objectives against the trading costs and risks.

Types of trading strategies might include:

- Short-term alpha—High urgency
- Long-term alpha—Low urgency
- Risk rebalance trade
- Cash flow-driven trade
    - Client redemption trade
    - New mandate trade

Managers who are evaluated relative to closing prices may choose to sell in a closing auction if one exists, or time the trade close to the benchmark close.

Trade Execution (Strategy Implementation)

Trade Implementation Choices
Order-driven markets may be run by exchanges, brokers, and alternative trading systems that cross-trade and provide rules-based matching. In request-for-quote (RFQ) markets, dealers and market makers provide quotes upon request.

In agency trades, a portfolio manager keeps the risk but uses an agent to find the other side of a trade. Agency trades may incur slightly higher costs to compensate for the added complexity and additional human involvement. In principal trades, also known as broker-risk trades, market makers and dealers assume risks of the trade, for which they receive additional compensation.

Exhibit 1: Principal vs. Agency Trading

	Agency	Principal
Venue	Exchange clearinghouse, ECN, alternative platform	Usually over-the-counter (OTC)
Execution risk	Customer/asset owner	Dealer/Sell-side
Execution cost	Explicit commission or fee; market impact costs likely	Bid-offer spread
Capital required	No inventory required; no balance sheet impact	Dealer holds inventory and trades for their own account; balance sheet impact

Markets with dealer-provided quotes may be called quote-driven markets, over-the-counter (OTC) markets, or off-exchange markets. Customers trade at the quotes provided by dealers who may work for broker/dealers, investment banks, commercial banks, or proprietary trading firms. Stocks, ETFs, and exchange-trade derivatives trade electronically in order-driven markets. High-yield bonds and other less liquid instruments trade in quote-driven markets to overcome less liquid trading.

Market participants often interact with the market book via a broker/dealer or market maker who has **direct market access (DMA)**. Buy-side firms may directly use a broker's technology infrastructure to achieve best price execution or seek profit rather than handing the order over to the broker.

Algorithmic Trading
Profit-seeking algorithms determine what to buy or sell based on real-time market data and, in some cases, artificial intelligence inputs. Orders are then routed through **execution algorithms** that find best-price execution.

Scheduled Execution (POV, VWAP, TWAP)
Scheduled execution algorithms are appropriate when portfolio managers do not expect adverse market moves or quickly decaying alpha or have greater risk tolerance and are more concerned with minimizing market impact.

Percentage of volume (POV) algorithms trade a constant percentage of market volume at various times. This has the advantage of trading into liquidity but also has the disadvantages of trading into rising prices as volume increases or selling into falling prices as volume increases.

VWAP uses historical intraday volume to slice an order into amounts less likely to incur negative market impact. TWAP sends an equal percentage of the order at different times throughout the day in order to minimize market impact. Both VWAP and TWAP are considered time-slicing strategies, which have the advantage of executing a specific number of shares during a specific time. The disadvantage is forcing trades during illiquid periods rather than exploiting liquidity conditions.

Liquidity Seeking
Liquidity seeking algorithms, also called opportunistic algorithms, seek high liquidity markets with a favorable price. These algorithms are appropriate for large orders when the portfolio manager wishes to avoid market price impact, especially as the result of information leakage or episodic trading.

Arrival Price

Arrival price execution strategies front-load trading to ensure as much as possible of the order transacts at the order's arrival price in the market. The algorithms may be time-based or volume-based and are appropriate for urgent trades.

Dark Strategies/Liquidity Aggregators

These strategies transact in dark pools and away from "lit" venues with pre- and post-trade transparency. They are appropriate for securities trading with wide bid-ask spreads or low liquidity, for low-urgency trades, or when the manager can accept greater execution risk.

Smart Order Routers (SORs)

SORs find the best market price (i.e., national best bid and offer or NBBO in the United States). Market order SORs are appropriate when the market moves quickly, the manager is concerned about execution risk, or when the order is relatively small and will have little market impact. Limit orders SORs find the market with the lowest execution risk. They are appropriate when the manager is concerned about information leakage that could result in market impact.

Comparison of Markets

Equities

Alternative trading systems (ATS or "dark pools") may operate as a broker-dealer or may in some cases apply with regulatory authorities to become an exchange. In Europe, these are known as systematic internalizers (SIs) and multi-lateral trading facilities (MTFs). SIs typically involve a single dealer; MTFs involve multiple investment firms or market operators.

Electronic equity trading is common and equity exchanges may use different algorithms based on trade size and liquidity:

- Small trades—Most buy-side traders use electronic trading for liquid securities
- Large trades
  - Urgent, less liquid—High-touch broker risk trades where the broker acts as a dealer or counterparty (i.e., principal)
  - Non-urgent
    - Liquid—Trading algorithms
    - Illiquid—High-touch broker risk trades

Trading in equities has become fragmented across many markets, which has led to more competition and lower trading costs but requires market participants to use algorithms that seek data from multiple markets.

Fixed Income

Connecting buyers and sellers of debt with specific features usually involves a more expensive principal trade along with additional liquidity costs. Banks and other dealers may make the market for bonds upon request from a buyer or seller, increasingly via electronic means such as electronic chat or RFQ platforms.

Only on-the-run Treasury securities and bond and interest rate futures are usually traded algorithmically. Off-the-run, larger trades, and less liquid securities (e.g., high-yield bonds) typically require a higher-touch approach:

- Urgent execution—RFQs executed as broker-risk (i.e., principal) trades

- Non-urgent execution—may occur as an agency trade instead of a principal to source liquidity while avoiding risk of accumulating large positions

Exchange-Traded Derivatives

Exchange-traded derivatives have a large, very liquid market with high market transparency. Although more options are available, most of the trading volume and most algorithmic trading occur in futures:

- Urgent trades first "sweep the book" on market orders and then start sweeping limit orders
- Non-urgent larger trades may be algorithmic; buy-side traders usually use direct access for smaller trades.

Over-the-Counter Derivatives

Dodd-Frank in the United States mandated swap data repositories (SDRs) for entities not subject to mandatory exchange trading and clearing and with at least one U.S. entity. The G-20 countries agreed in 2009 to begin trading all OTC standardized derivatives on exchanges or other electronic platforms that have centralized clearing.

Spot Foreign Exchange (Currency)

The currency market is almost entirely OTC with very little regulation across countries; trading takes place across many electronic and broker markets. International banks and large financial firms make up the interbank market, the top tier of currency exchange. Smaller banks and institutions make up the second tier, which turns to the first tier to deal in larger trades. Commercial companies and retail traders use the third tier, which in turn uses the second tier.

Although the currency market is liquid, market data typically includes only quotes with no volume data and then only on some venues.

- Urgent trades require sending a request for quote (RFQ) to several dealers.
- Non-urgent trades—Larger trades use TWAP or another algorithm, or a high-touch agency approach. Small trades use DMA where the portfolio manager enters a trade executed via the broker's platform.

Trade Evaluation

Trade Cost Measurement

The implementation period (i.e., the **trade horizon**) spans the period from the portfolio manager's investment decision to the trader's completion of the trade. **Trade costs** represent value paid by buyers or sellers but not received by the counterparty. Trade costs for buyers equal the price paid *above* the decision price and for sellers equal the price received *below* the decision price.

Implementation Shortfall

Implementation shortfall (IS) measures the manager's paper return less the actual return. A portfolio manager can use IS analysis to determine how many shares to invest within a specified price range and the amount of cash the manager can invest into the next most attractive idea. Portfolio managers also use IS in post-trade evaluation:

$$IS = r_{\text{Paper}} - r_{\text{Actual}}$$

More specifically, the paper return shows the hypothetical return of a *frictionless* trade at the manager's decision price:

$$r_{\text{Paper}} = S(P_n - P_d) = S(P_n) - S(P_d)$$

where
- S = total of shares ordered
- P_n = current share price
- P_d = price when the trade decision is made

Actual return from the trade equals the difference between the current market value of the trade less the sum of actual transactions less all fees and trading expenses:

$$IS = \sum s_j p_j - \sum s_j P_d + \left(S - \sum s_j\right)(P_n - P_d) + \text{Fees}$$

Execution cost (i.e., the first two terms) relates to shares transacted in the market and corresponds to price drift from buying or selling. **Opportunity cost** (i.e., the second two terms) relates to unexecuted shares due to adverse price movement or to general market illiquidity.

Execution costs can be separated into delay cost and trading cost:

$$
\begin{aligned}
IS &= \text{Delay costs} + \text{Trading costs} + \text{Opportunity costs} + \text{Fees} \\
&= \left[\left(\sum s_j\right)p_0 - \left(\sum s_j\right)P_d\right] + \left[\sum s_j p_j - \left(\sum s_j\right)p_0\right] \\
&\quad + \left(S - \sum s_j\right)(P_n - p_d) + \text{Fees}
\end{aligned}
$$

where
- p_0 = Arrival price

Arrival price, p_0, describes the price at which the trader released the order to the market.

Delay cost results from the lag between the manager giving the order to the trader and the trader determining which broker or algorithm to use in executing it.

Trading costs equal the difference between the sum of actual number of shares transacted at various prices less the value of all share if transacted at the arrival price.

Evaluating Trade Execution

Trade evaluation involves looking at the sources of this friction that created a loss between expected and actual return and determining whether it was reasonable under the conditions present. It may also be known as trade cost analysis (TCA), trade cost evaluation, and post-trade analysis.

Trade Cost Calculations

Trade costs equal:

- Buy order—the transaction price less the reference price
- Sell order—the reference price less the transaction price

Multiple intraday reference prices may be used to measure trading cost and to evaluate performance:

- Arrival price—Used as the reference for providing the trader with funds to complete the transaction
- VWAP over the trading horizon—Used as the reference versus the last execution price to evaluate how a trader performed relative to other market participants

$$\text{Cost/share} = \text{Side} \times (\overline{P} - P*)$$

$$\text{Total cost} = \text{Side} \times (\overline{P} - P*) \times \text{Shares}$$

$$\text{Cost in bps} = \text{Side} \times \frac{(\overline{P} - P*)}{P*} \times 10{,}000$$

where

Buy side $= +1$

Sell side $= -1$

$\overline{P}$ = Average execution price of order

$P*$ = Reference price

Positive values indicate additional cost and underperformance relative to the benchmark. Negative values indicate a savings and outperformance relative to the benchmark.

Investment professionals often reference cost in basis points (bps) because it is standard across different prices. Traders can calculate the arrival cost of the trade in bps:

$$\text{Arrival cost in bps} = \text{Side} \times \frac{(\overline{P} - P_0)}{P_0} \times 10{,}000$$

A similar calculation can be used when the benchmark price is VWAP, TWAP, market close, and so on, by just replacing P_0 in the above equation with the appropriate benchmark.

Market-Adjusted Cost

Market-adjusted price may be used to separate market movement effects over which the trader has little control from market impact from trading that could have been controlled:

$$\text{Index cost (bps)} = \text{Side} \times \frac{\text{Index VWAP} - \text{Index arrival price}}{\text{Index arrival price}} \times 10{,}000$$

$$\text{Market-adjusted cost (bps)} = \text{Arrival cost bps} - \beta \times \text{Index cost (bps)}$$

where

$$\beta = \text{security's beta with the index}$$

In other words, this formula subtracts the systematic component of the market price movement from the total arrival cost, leaving only the market impact cost from the trade.

Added Value

This formula is tricky; a positive value is an undesirable result:

$$\text{Added value (bps)} = \text{Arrival cost (bps)} - \text{Estimated pre-trade cost (bps)}$$

Trade Governance

Trade policy should consider:

- Best execution—*not* lowest cost. Best execution is either the applicable regulatory framework or the best outcome given competing objectives.
- Optimal execution approach—Based on the manager's investment process, asset class, liquidity, and market type.
- Eligible brokers and venues—Due diligence should ensure that portfolio managers and traders use reputable brokers and venues to ensure reliable, efficient order execution.
- Monitoring—Continually ensure that current arrangements meet or exceed requirements.

Establishing Best Execution within a Regulatory Framework

An investment policy statement or trade policy document should describe the relevant regulatory framework's definition of best execution, which involves the most appropriate trade-off among:

- Nature of the trade and order size
- Execution price
- Trading costs
- Execution speed
- Execution risk
- Settlement risk

Best execution should consider cost, speed, likelihood of execution, likelihood of settlement, and any other relevant factors. MiFID II requires investment managers to pay for broker research costs or to levy a special charge to clients for a research payment account.

Determining an Optimal Execution Approach

The firm's trade policy document should consider factors important to the optimal execution approach in each scenario:

- Urgency
- Security characteristics—Average daily volume; degree of customization (e.g., OTC swaps)
- Venue characteristics
- Investment strategy objectives—Short- or long-term
- Trade rationale—Alpha capture, liquidity, risk

Selecting Eligible Brokers and Venues

Broker and venue suitability may vary by asset class, but the underlying principles involve:

- Quality of service—Competitive against an execution benchmark; operational platform allows efficient, reliable settlement
- Financial stability
- Reputation
- Execution speed—Best price; maximum volume
- Competitive cost—Explicit costs such as commissions and exchange fees should be reasonable
- Willingness to commit capital—Broker willingness to act as a dealer to fill the trade

The best approach to maintaining appropriate broker and venue lists is to establish a Best Execution Monitoring Committee responsible for monitoring suitability and updating and distributing the list.

Monitoring Execution Arrangements

Specific monitoring processes vary by asset class and security type, but the general principles include:

- Trade submission—Trading execution strategy consistent with asset class, security type, and alpha/risk forecast horizons.
- Execution quality—The all-in trade costs versus the benchmark and expectation.
- Trading versus opportunity costs—Achieving an optimal balance
- Potential improvement opportunities

Several years of data should be stored and kept accessible; the U.K. requires record maintenance for *five* years and, in the absence of regulatory guidance or firm policies, CFA Institute recommends maintaining records for *seven* years.

These trading records perform the following functions:

- Address client concerns
- Address regulator concerns
- Assist in improving execution quality
- Trader evaluation

PORTFOLIO PERFORMANCE EVALUATION
Cross-Reference to CFA Institute Assigned Reading #35

The Evaluation Process and Attribution

Performance evaluation involves performance measurement, performance attribution to understand how the manager earned return, and performance appraisal to determine whether the manager earned the return through skill or luck.

Performance measurement involves calculating portfolio return and risk:

- **Absolute return** measures portfolio return without comparison to its benchmark return.
- **Excess return** describes the difference between absolute return and benchmark return.

Performance attribution decomposes return and risk into effects from investing style and skill, as well as other exposures:

- Accounts for all portfolio return and risk exposures
- Reflects the investment decision-making process (e.g., whether security selection takes place first at the country level or involves bottom up screening)
- Quantifies results of the manager's active decisions
- Provides complete excess return/risk understanding

Attribution analysis may involve:

- **Returns-based attribution**—Uses total returns to establish sources of return and risk; most appropriate when underlying portfolio return information is not available (e.g., as with hedge funds). This approach is easiest to implement, but the least informative and subject to data manipulation.
- **Holdings-based attribution** relates return and risk to holdings at the beginning of the period. Such attribution is appropriate for passive strategies without much trading. The difference between actual portfolio return and holdings-based return can be attributed to a **timing/trading effect**.
- **Transactions-based attribution** uses the weights and returns of all transactions, including their transaction costs. All excess returns can be calculated and accurately explained, but this is the most difficult and time-consuming approach to implement.

Performance appraisal assesses whether the manager achieved or exceeded expected return targets, added value, and avoided excess risk through skill or simply as the result of luck.

The results of the portfolio evaluation process are used for communicating results to clients and prospective clients, compensating managers, improving portfolio management processes, and finding successful, skillful managers.

Return Attribution Approaches

Arithmetic attribution is appropriate for considering investment returns over a single period, regardless of the length of the period. Arithmetic approaches are typically used for marketing or discussions with clients.

Geometric attribution considers how subperiod returns are compounded over time and is more appropriate when periods or methods depend on each other:

$$G = \frac{1+R}{1+B} - 1 = \frac{R-B}{1+B},$$

where

G = Geometric excess return
R = Portfolio return
B = Benchmark return

Geometric approaches almost always involve smaller return values in absolute terms but are used in conversations among market practitioners for increased clarity of the attribution effects over longer periods. However, zero standard deviation for all returns in a series will result in the same arithmetic and geometric return.

Equity Return Attribution Approaches

The Brinson-Hood-Beebower Approach

The **Brinson-Hood-Beebower (BHB)** approach first considers that portfolio and benchmark returns for a period are each the sum of asset-weighted individual sectors:

$$R = \sum_{i=1}^{n} w_i R_i$$

$$B = \sum_{i=1}^{n} W_i B_i$$

Excess return $= R - B$

where

w_i = portfolio weight of the ith sector
R_i = portfolio return of the ith sector
W_i = benchmark weight of the ith sector
B_i = benchmark return of the ith sector

Allocation effects occur when the portfolio manager portfolio sector weights different from benchmark sector weights:

$$A_i^{BHB} = (w_i - W_i)B_i$$

$$A = \sum_{i=1}^{n} (w_i - W_i)B_i$$

Overallocation to a sector will add value (outperform) when the benchmark return is positive and decrease value when the benchmark return is negative.

Selection effects (security effects) occur when the manager creates a better return from his selections within a sector than occurred in the benchmark, which results from different security weights within a sector:

$$S_i = W_i(R_i - B_i)$$

$$S = \sum_{i=1}^{n} W_i(R_i - B_i)$$

An overallocation will add value (outperform) when the manager overweights a high-performing security in the benchmark and decrease value when the manager underweights a high-performing security in the benchmark.

Allocation and security effects alone do not entirely explain differences between the portfolio and benchmark returns. The **interaction effect** describes the portion of return that results from both differences in portfolio weights and differences between portfolio and benchmark securities:

$$I_i = (w_i - W_i)(R_i - B_i)$$
$$I = \sum_{i=1}^{n}(w_i - W_i)(R_i - B_i)$$

The interaction effect is often presented along with the true security selection effect as the **full selection effect.** Based on the ith sector:

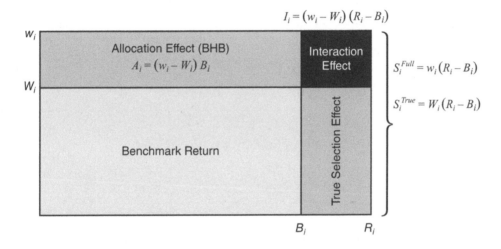

Fundamental Factor Models

Fundamental factor models, such as the Carhart model, can be used to identify the sensitivity of excess return in relation to various fundamental risk-factor differences:

$$R_p - R_f = a_p + \beta_{p1}RMRF + \beta_{p2}SMB + \beta_{p3}HML + \beta_{p4}WML + \epsilon_P$$
$$a_p = R_p - R_f - [\beta_{p1}RMRF + \beta_{p2}SMB + \beta_{p3}HML + \beta_{p4}WML + \epsilon_P]$$

where

R_p, R_f = Portfolio return and risk-free return

a_p = "Alpha" or excess return not expected from systematic risk

$RMRF$ = Excess of a value-weighted index return over risk-free rate

SMB = Average return on small-cap over large-cap portfolios

HML = High minus low; high book-to-market return over low

WML = Last year's winners' returns minus losers' returns

ϵ_P = Return to the portfolio not explained by the model

Positive excess returns result from a combination of overweight positive-beta exposures or underweight negative-beta exposures and the factor returns.

Fixed-Income Return Attribution Approaches

> NOTE: *Candidates should be able to interpret the results of a fixed-income attribution analysis but are not responsible for calculating fixed-income attribution components.*

Exposure Decomposition—Duration Based

Exposure decomposition involves working through a hierarchy of portfolio levels from the top down to explain active management of a portfolio relative to its benchmark. The process involves first grouping component bonds by their characteristics (e.g., duration, sector). Therefore, this is a top-down approach that allows a Brinson-like approach. Exposure decomposition reports are used primarily in marketing and client meetings where they might be more easily understood.

Table 1: Attribution Results: Exposure Decomposition

	Sector	Duration Effect	Curve Effect	Total Interest Rate Allocation	Sector Allocation	Bond Selection	Total
Short	Government						0
	Corporate						0
	Total	0	0	0	0	0	0
Medium	Government						0
	Corporate						0
	Total	0	0	0	0	0	0
Long	Government						0
	Corporate						0
	Total	0	0	0	0	0	0
Total		0	0	0	0	0	0

This type of analysis has **duration effects** that relate to positioning on the yield curve and **duration bucket effects** based on active bets on duration throughout the yield curve. Duration effects relate specifically to returns attributable to shifts in the yield curve across all duration buckets while duration *bucket* effects relate to yield curve shift effects, curve effects, sector allocation effects (i.e., government vs. corporate), and bond selection effects (security selection) within the *same* duration bucket.

Sector allocation attribution assesses the manager's contribution resulting from bond sector exposures (i.e., corporate bonds, government bonds, etc.). For each sector, the portfolio and benchmark contributions to duration (or return) can be determined as the product of sector weight and negative sector duration (or return). This process is repeated for each duration band.

Another sometimes confusing distinction is that **total interest rate allocation** effects equal the sum of duration effects and curve effects within the same duration bucket and sector.

Yield Curve Decomposition—Duration Based

Yield curve decomposition breaks active return contributions into time effects, yield curve effects, and spread effects. These can be aggregated into duration buckets and sector buckets, so yield curve decomposition can be a bottom-up method, although this can also be accomplished using aggregate portfolio data for yield and duration.

Duration-based yield curve decomposition uses active return calculated using negative duration multiplied by specific type of yield change:

- Yield—Active return from weighting decisions on corporate bonds and longer-term maturities, which tend to have higher yields.
- Roll—Longer-maturity bonds sit on a flatter segment of the yield curve and experience less roll effect (change in value based on less time to maturity and a different set of interest rates discounting future cash flows).
- Shift—Difference due to portfolio duration versus benchmark duration.
- Slope—Longer-term yields decrease less than shorter-term yields when yield curves flatten. A positive contribution to active yield would likely result from increasing portfolio weight at the long end of the curve, everything else being equal.
- Curvature—How yield curve shape contributes to active return when a manager over- or underweights the portfolio relative to the benchmark.
- Spread—Overweighting the corporate sector when credit spreads widen leads to a reduction in return.
- Specific spread—The portion of spread due to the idiosyncratic risks of the specific security relative to the overall spread of the sector.
- Residual—The remaining return that duration and convexity were unable to estimate.

Active return from *time* equals the sum of yield and roll active return contributions. Active return from **curve movement** equals the sum of shift, slope, and curvature active return contributions.

Yield Curve Decomposition—Full Repricing

Full repricing considers how the bond revalues when the yield curve changes in various ways. The changes in bond prices can then be aggregated into different duration and sector buckets as well as at the portfolio, benchmark, and total active attribution levels. This is also considered a bottom-up approach, although it may be accomplished top down.

This approach is better aligned with how portfolio managers view the instruments, allowing for a broader range of instruments and types of yield changes. However, the approach is more costly and difficult to use, and more difficult to explain.

Risk and Multi-Level Return Attribution Approaches

Risk Attribution Approaches

Risk attribution identifies sources of volatility for portfolios managed to absolute return mandates and sources of tracking risk for portfolios managed to benchmark-relative mandates. The attribution analysis method selected depends on the type of mandate and the investment decision-making process.

Table 2: Selecting a Risk Attribution Approach

Process	Type of Mandate	
	Absolute	Relative
Bottom up	Position's marginal contribution to total risk	Position's marginal contribution to tracking risk
Top down	Factor's marginal contribution to total risk and specific risk	Attribute tracking risk to relative allocation and selection decisions
Factor based		Factor's marginal contribution to tracking risk and active specific risk

Each position's contribution to tracking risk (TR) equals the active weight of the position multiplied by its contribution to TR. A bottom-up approach cumulates TR for each position to determine portfolio TR regardless of whether in an absolute or benchmark-relative framework:

$$\text{Portfolio tracking risk} = \sum_{i=n}^{N} w_n^{\text{Active}} TR_n$$

Multi-Level Return Attribution Approaches

Macro Attribution

In the **Brinson-Fachler approach**, the **allocation decision** refers to the fund's tactical allocation decisions against its benchmark.

$$A_i^{B-F} = (w_i - W_i)(B_i - B)$$

Although the allocation formula is different, the **manager selection decision** and **interaction effect** are the same:

$$\begin{aligned} S_i &= W_i(R_i - B_i) \\ I_i &= (w_i - W_i)(R_i - B_i) \\ S_i + I_i &= W_i(R_i - B_i) + (w_i - W_i)(R_i - B_i) \\ &= w_i(R_i - B_i) \end{aligned}$$

The **selection effect** captures the return from hiring the manager regardless of the tactical weighting decision. The **interaction effect** captures the decision to overweight the manager. Taken together, the **full selection effect** captures the return benefit of the decision to overweight the specific asset class manager.

Micro Attribution

Micro attribution evaluates portfolio manager decisions at levels below the strategic, tactical, and manager decisions, and is implemented using the Brinson-Fachler approach used for macro attribution. Doing so allows comparison of the manager's asset allocation decisions within each level of the strategy.

The manager's total active return equals the portfolio return, R, less the benchmark return, B. Those returns are the sum of the next level's sector returns.

Benchmarking Investments and Managers

A high-quality benchmark has the following characteristics:

- Specified in advance—Benchmark constituents and their weights should be available before the manager makes allocation and selection decisions.
- Unambiguous—Constituents and their weights should be easy to identify.
- Measurable—Benchmark returns should be easily measured on a reasonably frequent basis.
- Appropriate—The benchmark should reflect the manager's style or area of expertise, and should not involve securities involved in investor-imposed constraints.
- Reflective of current investment opinions—Benchmarks should not include obscure securities; the manager should be able to develop an opinion about the constituents and their factor exposures.
- Investable—The manager must be able to invest in and hold constituents to earn the same gross-of-expenses return as the benchmark, if so chosen.
- Accountable—The manager should accept accountability for results relative to the benchmark.

Liability-Based Benchmarks

Liability-based benchmarks are appropriate when the fund sponsor must defease a specific liability (e.g., pension plan payments). Liability-based benchmarks, then, should focus on cash flows that must be generated to defease the liability. Plans in liability status should help the fund sponsor track progress toward fully funded status.

Plan features that influence construction of the benchmark include:

- Average number of years until retirement for the work force
- Percentage of retired lives in the plan
- Average participant life expectancy
- Whether benefits are indexed to inflation
- Early retirement options
- Sponsor's ability to continue operations (going concern) and increase contributions (diversified, profitable fund sponsor)
- Correlation between changes in plan assets and plan liabilities (lower correlation desirable)

A younger workforce suggests a higher allocation to equity securities. Benefits indexed to inflation would suggest inflation-indexed fixed income securities.

Asset-Based Benchmarks

Types of benchmarks include:

- **Absolute return benchmarks** are often stated as a desire to exceed a return target by a specific number of basis points.
- **Broad market indexes** measure performance of a broad category of assets such as global equity, emerging market bonds, and so on.
- **Investment styles** categorize securities based on natural characteristics (e.g., market capitalization or price-relative metrics) that tend to predict return and dispersion.
- **Factor-based benchmarks** attempt to capture the manager's risk and return decisions through use of a multiple-regression equation that measures sensitivity to types of risk exposure.

- **Returns-based benchmarks** are like factor-based benchmarks, but use sensitivity to style approaches (e.g., the categories in a size versus price-relative performance matrix; a Morningstar style box).
- **Manager metrics** (e.g., universe or peer group) aggregate returns from managers with similar characteristics. A *manager universe* is formed based on asset class and investment approach within a class. A peer group is a subset of managers following similar class and style approaches to the target manager.
- **Custom security-based benchmarks** use conversations with the manager and statistical analysis of risk-return sources to construct a benchmark that better reflects the manager's unique style.

Tests of Benchmark Quality

In this analysis, the market reflects the available processes to achieve the result and the benchmark reflects the manager's process to achieve a specific result (i.e., style):

$$\begin{aligned} P &= M + (B - M) + (P - B) \\ &= M + S + A \end{aligned}$$

Market return, M, the manager's style return, $B - M$, and the manager's active selection decisions, $P - B$, are decomposed. To avoid systematic selection return biases in the benchmark, active management return, A, and style return, S, *should not* be statistically correlated. Excess performance, $E = P - M$, and manager style, S, *should* be statistically correlated with the benchmark.

Benchmarking Alternative Investments

Benchmarking Hedge Fund Investments

Hedge funds cannot be aggregated into a single asset class. Therefore, market benchmarks are not appropriate. The risk-free rate has been advocated for market-neutral hedge funds and absolute return measures have been advocated for opportunistic funds. A benchmark using the risk-free rate plus an absolute spread to compare against the risk-free rate and the manager's skill.

Because even market-neutral strategies may be subject to some systematic risk, spreads relative to the risk-free rate should be adjusted upward to reflect the degree of systematic risk and leverage present in fund investments.

Benchmarking Real Estate Investments

Any externally provided real estate index has returns from unique real estate likely owned by another party. Therefore, such indexes do not represent investable properties although they may, in some cases, represent investable funds. Commercially provided indexes often suffer from one or more of these additional disadvantages:

- Benchmarks focus on one subset of the entire asset class opportunity set or no benchmark adequately addresses the manager's perceived opportunity set.
- The largest index data-providing funds bias index returns to their fund returns.
- Benchmark returns are inherently biased by how data-provided funds report their data.
- Large-city bias may be introduced by indexes weighted by fund or asset size.
- Although transactions-based indexes are becoming more available, most indexes use reported appraisal data that smooths return results.
- Indexes use varying degrees of leverage.

- Real estate indexes may not accurately reflect high transactions costs, lack of transparency, and lack of liquidity available to those wishing to invest in similar properties.
- A difference in return measures complicates comparison:
  - Open-end funds typically use time-weighted return to reflect investor ability to influence their own return.
  - Closed-end funds typically use internal rate of return (IRR) to reflect manager control over return.

Benchmarking Private Equity

Private equity funds typically use IRR because managers determine when to enter and exit.

Private equity, like real estate, suffers from non-investable underlying assets although exposure may be available through an index. Commercially provided indexes also suffer from one or more of these additional disadvantages:

- Valuation methods used by various fund managers may differ.
- Early losses or wins influence IRR.
- The underlying equity investments in cohort firms may be at different stages of development although the index represents investments made in the same year.

To overcome the IRR problem and make private equity investments more comparable to investors, the private market equivalent (PME) methodology replicates the general partner's cash flow contributions and withdrawals in a comparable index of public companies.

Benchmarking Commodity Investments

Commodity investment benchmarks measure return on futures that represent the underlying.

Benchmarking Managed Derivatives

Benchmarks typically relate to a specific manager's strategy and no managed derivatives market index exists. For example, a commercial index exists for an active momentum strategy that uses long and short positions in many futures markets based on a moving-average trading rule, but this does not measure any particular manager's strategy. Commodity trading advisors (CTA) indexes are available based on peer groups of the same strategy, but it is not a market index.

Benchmark Misspecification

A portfolio representing the manager's typical approach to a specific investment universe is called the manager's "normal portfolio" or "normal benchmark." The manager's **true active return** equals the manager's actual portfolio return less the normal portfolio (i.e., manager's benchmark) return.

Benchmark *misspecification* involves a benchmark that doesn't represent the manager's normal portfolio. Misspecification defeats the purpose of performance attribution because the sources of active return become unclear. Misspecification defeats the purpose of performance appraisal because the manager is not measured against decisions representing his normal approach.

Performance Appraisal

Appraisal Measures

Sortino Ratio

The *ex ante* Sortino ratio is indicated by using the expectation value of portfolio return rather than the average return and target as in the *ex post* version:

$$\text{ex ante } SR_D = \frac{E(r_p) - r_T}{\sigma_D}$$

$$\text{ex post } SR_D = \frac{\bar{r}_p - \bar{r}_T}{\sigma_D}$$

where

$$\sigma_D = \left[\frac{\sum_{t=1}^{N} min[0, (r_t - r_T)]^2}{N} \right]^{1/2}$$

$$r_T = \text{Minimum acceptable return; target return}$$

Note that the **target value**, which may be called the **minimum acceptable return (MAR)** value, is often an investor decision criteria and may represent the inflation rate for capital preservation or may be the manager's benchmark return.

The *Sortino* ratio penalizes only downside return and can be used to determine whether the manager is returning the benchmark performance over time. Sortino cannot be compared across investors as can the Sharpe ratio because it uses investor-specific MAR.

Appraisal Ratio

The appraisal ratio compares annualized Jensen's alpha (the return of active management) to the standard deviation of residual risk:

$$R = \alpha + \beta B + \epsilon$$
$$\alpha = R - (\beta B + \epsilon)$$
$$\epsilon = R - (\alpha + \beta B)$$
$$AR = \frac{\alpha}{\sigma_\epsilon}$$

In the CAPM framework, appraisal ratio could also be thought of as the relationship between the manager's return and non-systematic risk.

Capture Ratio and Drawdowns

Capture ratio (CR) represents a manager's success in capturing the benchmark return. Upside capture (UC) and downside capture (DC) relate to "success" at capturing positive and negative benchmark returns, respectively:

$$\text{Capture} = \frac{R_t}{B_t} \begin{bmatrix} UC \text{ if } B_t \geq 0 \\ DC \text{ if } B_t < 0 \end{bmatrix}$$

where

$$R_t = \text{Manager or portfolio return at time } t$$
$$B_t = \text{Benchmark return at time } t$$

The capture statistic is not meaningful without context. A portfolio that goes down during both up and down markets would have a positive capture statistic. A portfolio return may also be positive when benchmark return is negative, leading to a negative capture ratio.

Upside/downside capture ratio (sometimes also called capture ratio) measures upside capture relative to downside capture:

$$CR = \frac{UC}{DC}$$

Upside/downside capture ratios (UDCRs) greater than 1 are *convex* (i.e., *positive asymmetry*); returns from these strategies increase at an increasing rate with the magnitude of benchmark returns. UDCRs less than 1 are *concave* (i.e., *negative asymmetry*); returns from these strategies increase at a decreasing rate with the magnitude of benchmark returns.

Drawdown represents the peak-to-trough loss in portfolio value during a continuous period of negative returns. This formulation of **maximum drawdown** develops a percentage measure:

$$\%DD_{max} = min\left[\frac{(v_t - v_{t^*})}{v_{t^*}}, 0\right]$$

where
$(v_t - v_{t^*})$ = Greatest peak to trough value through time t
v_{t^*} = Peak value at time t

Drawdown percentage like upside downside capture suffers from a measurement base bias because it uses the greater peak value in the denominator.

Drawdown duration measures total time from start of the drawdown until recovery to the previous peak and may be segmented into start-to-trough (*drawdown* phase) and trough-to-full-recovery (*recovery* phase).

Manager Evaluation and Appraisal
Attribution analysis separates the allocation decisions from security selection decisions. The Sharpe, Treynor, and Sortino ratios evaluate how well the manager used different types of risk to add return:

- Sharpe considers the risk-relative return per unit of *total* risk.
- Treynor considers the risk-relative return per unit of *systematic* risk (i.e., benchmark or market risk).
- The Sortino ratio considers *target*-relative return per unit of *downside* risk.
- The appraisal ratio considers manager value per unit of non-systematic risk.

The evaluator can then use information ratio to compare portfolio and benchmark returns, adjusted for the variation of each. The appraisal ratio assesses the manager's selection decisions in terms of their value to the portfolio.

Professional evaluators will also review various qualitative factors such as:

- Direct interviews with management
- Assessment of management's investment goals
- Review of management fees relative to return over time, and so on

INVESTMENT MANAGER SELECTION
Cross-Reference to CFA Institute Assigned Reading #36

A Framework for Investment Manager Search and Selection

Conducting due diligence on an investment manager involves understanding how the manager achieved reported results and whether the manager's people, processes, and portfolio construction techniques can be expected to create acceptable results.

The search and selection process consists of three broad components:

1. The manager universe
2. Quantitative manager performance analysis
3. Qualitative manager capabilities analysis
    - Analytical due diligence (people, philosophy)
    - Operational due diligence (processes, procedures)

Manager Universe

A **manager universe** is a list of feasible managers who survive a filter based on the investment policy statement. For example, selecting or replacing a manager with a specific style tilt will require selection from a strategy universe representing that tilt.

Approaches for assigning managers to a benchmark include:

- Third-party categorization—Investors must understand the provider's criteria or risk misunderstanding how the third-party categorizes managers.
- Returns-based style analysis—Based on *risk exposures* from the manager's actual return series.
- Holdings-based style analysis—Based on categorization of the manager's holdings. Allows categorization of existing factor exposures, but limited transparency may eliminate understanding how those holdings and exposures have changed or might change.
- Manager experience—Based on the manager and observation of portfolios and risk-return *patterns* over time.

The recommended approach suggests building an initial universe from third-party categorization and then refining the feasible set based on risk profile. The feasible set will not be static over time but will evolve with the entry of exceptional managers and exit of underperforming managers.

Errors in Manager Selection

The null hypothesis is that the manager has no skill. The alternative hypothesis is that the manager brings skill to portfolio management:

- Type 1 errors—Rejecting the correct null hypothesis that the manager has no skill and subsequently hiring or retaining a manager who underperforms.
- Type II errors—Failing to reject an incorrect null hypothesis and subsequently not hiring or firing a manager who achieves or exceeds expectations.

Table 3: Type I and Type II Errors

		Realization	
		Below Expectation (no skill)	Meet or Exceed Expectation (skill)
Decision	**Hire/retain**	Type I	Correct
	Not hire/fire	Correct	Type II

Increasing the level of significance (e.g., from 0.01 to 0.05 in a tail) increases the probability of hiring a bad manager; decreasing the level of significance decreases the probability of hiring a bad manager but increases the probability of failing to hire an acceptable manager.

Qualitative Selection Considerations

Investment committees try hard to avoid hiring managers with no skill (i.e., committing a Type I error). Some of the reasons for bias against type I errors may be related to regret avoidance, measurability (i.e., type II errors of not hiring a good manager are seldom measured), and transparency to investors (type I errors must be explained to investors.

Performance Implications of Selection Errors

The costs of Type I and Type II errors tend to be smaller when:

- Differences in sample size are smaller.
- Differences in return distribution means are smaller.
- Differences in return distribution dispersion is greater.
- Markets are more efficient (i.e., less alpha to be obtained results in smaller return distribution differences).

In a mean reverting market, hiring an unskilled manager (a Type I error) has less cost than firing an outperforming manager (a Type II error).

Quantitative Elements of Manager Search and Selection

Style Analysis

Style analysis begins with quantitative measures such as portfolio concentration, industry exposure, capitalization exposure, and other risk factors. Inconsistently implemented philosophy or strategy is likely to result in inconsistent results over time (e.g., style drift) that are hard to repeat and may not always fit well with the rest of the portfolio.

Useful style-based analysis must have the following characteristics:

- Accurate—Reflect actual risk exposures.
- Consistent—Methodology allows comparison across managers and across time.
- Meaningful—Represent the important sources of risk and return.
- Timely—Presented without delay to be useful for making informed, often time-sensitive decisions.

Returns-Based Style Analysis (RBSA)

RBSA is a top-down approach to estimate portfolio sensitivities to factors present in various securities market indexes. This process avoids self-reported or third-party style classifications, each of which must also be analyzed for applicability.

RBSA evaluators have access to data immediately after it becomes available, especially for publicly traded securities, and it is comparable across managers and time periods. However, RBSA effectively uses an average portfolio over the period to establish exposures, which limits identification of management decisions during the period. This distorts recognition and decomposition of how the manager added value.

Holdings-Based Style Analysis (HBSA)

HBSA is a **bottom-up approach** that estimates risk exposures based on portfolio securities at a specific time. Although managers may game this method by trading into outperforming securities near the end of the reporting period, it has the other advantages of RBSA, such as access to immediately available data and comparability across managers and time periods.

HBSA may suffer from additional computational burden and complexity based on the manager's strategy, timing, and frequency of reporting. For example, hedge funds are reluctant to offer position-level information when entering a strategy because they lose the element of surprise. Private equity and venture capital may report with somewhat of a lag once position values become determinable (e.g., financing events). As with RBSA, stale pricing may understate risk exposures due to return smoothing.

Measuring Active Share

Active share measures the difference in portfolio holdings versus benchmark holdings, where $0 \leq$ active share ≤ 1 with 0 being 100 percent indexed and 1 holding no benchmark constituents:

$$AS = 0.5 \sum_{i=1}^{n} w_i - W_i$$

where
w_i, W_i = Portfolio weight and benchmark weight for asset i

Combinations of active share and tracking risk can help categorize managers based on experience.

Table 4: Active Share and Tracking Risk

		Active Share	
		Low	High
Tracking Risk	**Low**	Closet indexer	Diversified stock picker
	High	Sector rotator	Concentrated stock picker

Capture Ratios and Drawdowns in Manager Evaluation

Because a portfolio must experience a greater percentage return to recover from a drawdown than it did to get there, managers with significant drawdowns over time may not be appropriate for investors nearing the end of an investment horizon. Capture ratios help assess drawdowns in the context of meeting an investor's risk and return requirements.

Few strategies provide convexity, depending instead on manager skill for convex results. A long-only strategy that depends on active management may appear convex, but the manager's active skill rather than the strategy produces the result.

Drawdowns have been compared to stress tests for an investment process. Large, unrecovered drawdowns may indicate a flawed or inconsistently implemented investment philosophy or process, or inadequate risk controls and other operational issues.

Qualitative Elements of Manager Due Diligence

Investment Philosophy

The degree of active management that makes sense increases with the perceived inefficiency of the market and the time to equilibrium pricing. Passive strategies seek to earn only the premium associated with market risk while active strategies seek to earn returns in excess of the premium for assuming market risk.

Inefficiencies fall into behavioral and structural categories:

- Behavioral inefficiencies—Arise due to market participant behavior; short-lived.
- Structural inefficiencies—Arise due to internal or external rules and regulations; longer-lived.

Active strategies assume prices converge to intrinsic value estimated by a discounted cash flow model, or through macroeconomic trends driving prices:

- Articulation—The manager and staff understand the philosophy and assumptions.
- Assumptions—Consistent or appropriate for a changing market.
- Repeatability—Strategies based on structural inefficiency are more persistent.
- Persistence—Inefficiencies should be persistent for the manager to repeat the strategy's performance over time.

Strategy capacity (i.e., ability to absorb funding) involves these factors:

- Sufficiency—Frequency and level of returns must cover transactions and other costs.
- Repeatability—Repeatability allows a manager to capture excess returns without learning a new skill set and mastering a new learning curve each time; reduces opportunity for failure.
- Sustainability—The strategy's investments will be sized to avoid attracting too much attention.

Investment Personnel

Investors must assure themselves that the manager and associated employees have the expertise necessary to implement the strategy and process:

- Experience across stressed markets and coming back from drawdowns
- Appropriately sized
- **Key person risk**—The fund should not overly rely on just a few key people
- How the manager attracts and retains people
- Personnel turnover

Investment Decision-Making Process

Signal Creation (Idea Generation)

Efficient market hypothesis (EMH) indicates that exploitable strategies should have information that is:

- Unique—The evaluator should determine the source of the manager's information advantage and whether it is repeatable and sustainable.

- Timely—The evaluator should determine the source of the information advantage and whether it is repeatable and sustainable.
- Interpreted differently—The evaluator should determine if the manager has a unique method of interpreting information and whether it is repeatable and sustainable.

Signal Capture (Idea Implementation)

Signal capture involves translating an investment signal into a profitable investment position:

- Identify the process to translate investment ideas into positions.
- Determine how the manager maintains consistency of ideas with the strategy assumptions.
- Determine whether the process is repeatable.
- Identify the process and chain of accountability for investment decisions.

Portfolio Construction

Portfolios must be constructed consistent with the investment policy and strategy decided and must integrate with employee capabilities:

- Reallocation—A passive strategy will have infrequent reallocation compared to an actively managed portfolio.
- Conviction—Active managers will overweight expected outperformers and underweight expected underperformers.
- AUM—Determine how security selection has changed, if at all, as AUM changes.
- Risk Management—Determine how the manager balances risk of loss with opportunity costs of gain on positions sold too soon.
- Hedging—Examine how the manager establishes hedge ratios and the securities used. Determine how the manager weighs costs and benefits.
- Long/short decisions—Establish how the manager uses short positions.

Liquidity considerations are as important as risk management. Positions or strategies subject to changing market conditions, information, and investor liquidity requirements should offer a liquidity premium:

- Position sizes—Average daily volume (ADV) for each position as well as fund average daily volume weighted by position size.
- Concentrated positions—Determine whether any positions constitute 5% or more of the portfolio.
- Flexibility—Less liquid portfolios will suffer higher transactions costs and market impact.
- Security suspensions—List securities restricted from trading in any way as well as the reasons.
- Demand/supply—Does the manager tend to demand or supply liquidity and how has this changed as AUM changes.

Monitoring the Portfolio

Portfolio monitoring should examine signals from both internal sources (risk-return performance and portfolio construction issues) and external sources (capital market expectations) to determine deviations from the investment process and style drift.

Operational Due Diligence

Operational due diligence involves evaluating the firm's policies and procedures to understand and evaluate risks to the manager's business. For example, managers with cash flow problems may cut staff to a minimum to make more money.

Managers should have a repeatable trading process, free from human error:

- Trading policies, especially regarding use of soft dollars and allocation of bulk trades. Bulk trades should be allocated based on invested capital.
- Protections against unauthorized trading, trading outside risk limits, and so on.
- Procedures for charging and collecting fees and other charges.
- Determine whether the firm can implement and manage any new strategies under consideration.
- Examine use of offsite backup facilities.
- Establish the firm's protections against cyber attacks.

Third-party providers (the "external team") should be able to provide independent verification of the firm's performance reporting. The firm's external team should be capable and reputable. The evaluator should note and request explanation of turnover in the providers.

The firm's risk management manual should establish who is responsible for the function, processes, and procedures for monitoring and curing breaches, and assuring consistency of manager actions with soft/hard trading guidelines.

Firm Considerations

Assessing the business risk of the firm should consider:

- Ownership structure and incentives
- AUM by strategy and total
- The AUM required for each strategy to break even
- Strategies closed to new capital
- Strategies for raising capital and the capital targets

Evaluators should consider whether smaller firms have adequate capital to survive market downturns.

Investors should ensure the firm's interests align with their own interests:

- Disposition of stock incentives held by key people who leave the firm.
- Firms should allow or require key persons to invest in the same strategies as the clients.
- Executives should create a culture of compliance.
- Current and past investigation of employees or litigation for allegations that involve fiduciary duty.

Investment Vehicle

Investor's separately own assets in **separately managed accounts (SMAs)** can potentially provide customized management and other services. **Pooled investment vehicles** pool investor money and manage it with no customization (e.g., mutual funds).

SMAs have the following advantages:

- Ownership—The fund need not sell assets at a loss to satisfy the liquidity demands of other investors.

- Customization—Investors can express individual constraints or preferences.
- Tax efficiency—Allows tax efficient investing and trading including tax loss harvesting and does not subject the investor to the tax consequences of redemption decisions by others.
- Transparency—Investors can see real time, position-level detail with little to no delay.

SMAs are not without their drawbacks:

- Cost—SMAs do not have the economies of scale present with manager-decided trades in a pooled vehicle.
- Tracking risk—Attribution of tracking risk requires separating manager decisions from investor cash flows.
- Investor behavior—Investors have the potential to micromanage portfolio decisions.

The evaluator should choose an investment vehicle based on the investor's policy statement.

Investment Terms
A prospectus, private placement memorandum, and/or limited partnership agreement establish rights and responsibilities. These documents describe liquidity provisions and fees.

Closed-end funds and ETFs allow an investor liquidity to buy or sell shares close to the current price throughout the day; they provide greater execution speed.

Open-end funds may be traded at NAV as of market close, and therefore provide price certainty. However, they may only be traded daily rather than intra-day.

Vehicles that use **limited partnerships** (e.g., hedge funds, private equity, and private real estate) require committing funds and have lockups or redemption gates to discourage early withdrawals. The LP structure allows undisturbed long-term investment but reduces investor liquidity when needed for reallocation, changes in circumstances, or unexpected needs.

Managers charge fees to cover fixed and variable operating costs and to help earn a return on investment of both financial and human capital. The firm may reduce or delay variable commission expenses and bonuses to pay for fixed costs, if necessary.

Fee Structure
Pooled fund structures usually have only AUM-based fees; hedge funds and partnership vehicles have both AUM-based and performance-based fees:

- AUM fees—Fees based on a percentage of assets under management.
- Performance-based fees—These may be absolute return–based or benchmark-relative returns that incentivize performance rather than relying on AUM fees alone.
    - Symmetrical exposure—Influenced by both gains and losses; that is, fees equal the base fee plus a percentage of gains or minus a percentage of losses.
    - Capped symmetrical exposure—Fees equal the base fee plus a percentage of capped gains or minus a percentage of capped losses.
    - Asymmetric (upside) exposure—The higher of base fees or base fees plus percentage of gains. This structure rewards the manager for assuming additional risk but imposes no penalty for bad choices.

Performance (incentive) fees are not simply paid on the gross portfolio return. For example, performance fees may be paid after the return has surpassed each of the following:

1. Management fees (for net-of-fee calculations): AUM-based management fee.
2. **High-water mark (HWM):** The fund's highest NAV after payment of incentive fees. This prevents investors from paying another fee on recouped losses.
3. **Hurdle rate**, which represents a minimum return to investors after recouping their initial investment.

Incentive fees apply to the remaining return, giving total fees:

$$
\text{Fees} = (AUM \times \%F_M) + \max\left[0, \left\{\%F_P \times \left(R_{\text{Gross}}^{>HWM} - F_M - R_{\text{Hurdle}}\right)\right\}\right]
$$

where

$$F_M, F_P = \text{Fees for management and performance}$$

$$R_{\text{Gross}}^{>HWM} = \text{Gross return in excess of the high-water mark}$$

A **clawback provision** applies if GPs have received an incentive on gains but subsequent losses leave the LPs with less than their investment plus agreed minimum return.

Incentive fees encourage risk sharing that reduces return variability on the upside but not on the downside. Risk measures calculated on returns after an incentive fee tend to underestimate downside risk.

II
PM

CASE STUDY IN PORTFOLIO MANAGEMENT
Institutional: Cross-Reference to CFA Institute Assigned Reading #37

Overview: Liquidity Management

Liquidity management for an institutional investor involves meeting cash outflow needs without excessive costs or distressed sales and within the scope of the investment policy.

Liquidity Profiling and Time to Cash

Institutional investors manage liquidity by first determining potential cash inflows and outflows over an investment horizon:

- **Liquidity classification schedule (time-to-cash table)**—Defines "buckets" based on the estimated time to convert assets from a specific category into cash.
- **Liquidity budget**—Describes the percentage of portfolio convertible into cash within the time-to-cash band.

Exhibit 1: Time-to-Cash Table and Liquidity Budget

Time-to-Cash	Liquidity Classification	Liquidity Budget
<1 week	Highly liquid	At least 10%
<1 quarter	Liquid	At least 35%
<1 year	Semi-liquid	At least 50%
>1 year	Illiquid	Up to 50%

In other words, the last line indicates that 50% or more of a portfolio may be invested in illiquid assets. Actual time-to-cash bands are driven by the cash inflows and outflows for the institutional portfolio and the organization(s) for which it provides funding. The institution should also consider the investment vehicles used (i.e., separate accounts, commingled funds, limited partnerships, derivatives, etc.).

Rebalancing and Commitments

In addition to funding commitments, rebalancing may also require liquidity. Having liquid assets and appropriate rebalancing plans in place avoids the need to rebalance illiquid assets at a high cost.

Investors do not control the rate at which cash must be invested or returns harvested for alternative investments such as private equity and real estate. The pacing strategy should consider expected commitments and receipts, rebalancing over time for these classes, and a big enough buffer to allow some overcommitment.

Derivatives can be a cash-efficient way to manage cash flow needs, changing risk exposures, and rebalancing. They can also be used to increase the cash position for rebalancing; for example, use futures to represent the equity position and use undeployed cash to gain exposure to other assets with different liquidity profiles.

Earning an Illiquidity Premium

A liquidity premium compensates an investor for the risk of tying up capital for an uncertain time. The size of this premium increases with the horizon of the investment. One theory suggests that this premium should equal the value of a put option with exercise price equal to the market price of the underlying illiquid asset.

Quinco Case

This case covers illiquidity premium capture, liquidity management, asset allocation, and cash versus derivatives implementation of TAA. Essential facts in the case include:

- Endowment AUM of $8B.
  - $6B unrestricted funding for support/endowment.
  - $2B donor-specific funding restrictions.
- Endowment funds 60% of Quadruvian University annual budget.
- Annual Quadruvium University budget = $583mm.
  - 70% of that amount funds salaries and benefits.
  - QU also pays down debt with part of remainder.
- L-T inflation for universities is expected to be 2–3% annually; the endowment will make 1% of AUM in other contributions
- Endowment investment objective: Support the university spending rate with endowment returns while safeguarding the program over time by preserving the real value of the endowment.
- Quinco's spending rule is designed to shield annual distributions from market fluctuations while producing a 5% long-term spending rate:

$$D_{t+1} = 0.66D_t + 0.34(0.05)\,AUM_t$$

where

D_t, D_{t+1} = Distributions each of prior year, current year, respectively

AUM_t = Market value of assets under management end of prior year

Required return = 5% funding + 2% to 3% inflation + 1% contributions = 8% to 9% nominal rate

Volatility (standard deviation) = 12%–14%

Quinco implements the objective via outside investment advisors.

The investment committee considers increasing the endowment's allocation to alternative assets (i.e., private equity, real assets, and diversifying strategies). The primary objective of a proposed asset allocation change is expected improvement in the portfolio's long-term risk/return profile given capital market expectations (CME):

- Increased risk-adjusted return.
- Lower/relevant Sharpe ratio.
- Monte Carlo analysis showing higher probability of achieving the real L-T return target while preserving the corpus.

Exhibit 2: Proposed vs. Current SAA: Expected Return/Risk Properties

Characteristic	Proposed	Current
Expected nominal return (annual geometric over 10 years)	7.8%	7.5%
Expected real return (annual geometric over 10 years)	5.3%	5.0%
Standard deviation of returns	13.2%	12.5%
Sharpe ratio	0.34	0.33
Probability of 25% erosion in purchasing power over 20 years at 5% spending rate	30%	35%

The focus of this lesson is liquidity management and liquidity premium capture; the focus of examples is on the additional return from accepting less liquidity. The access to alumni networks will likely help the university gain access to information on new technologies, real estate opportunities, and best-in-class asset managers.

There are potential downsides:

- Overcommitment—Overcommitment to avoid cash drag may result in untimely capital calls.
- Capital calls—Higher than expected capital calls can result in overallocation to alternatives.
- Liquidity gates—Protects investors who remain invested against withdrawals, especially during crisis periods.
- Smooth data—Appraisal-based data smooths variances, leading to overallocation.

Asset manager selection also comes into play with important considerations that include:

- Disclosures of confidential information
- Conflicts of interest
- Due diligence
    - Investment due diligence (IDD)
    - Operational due diligence (ODD)

The operational due diligence conversation uncovers a potential problem in fund scalability for the size of their investment.

The board increased QUINCO's active risk budget from 100 bps to 250 bps to allow additional return from tactical asset allocation (TAA):

- Provide exposure to asset classes and/or investment strategies compliant with the investment policy but not in the policy portfolio benchmark.
- Overweight and underweight positions in one or more of the asset classes.

Analysis includes whether the output from valuation models is significantly different to be exploited given the costs of various strategies.

Exhibit 3: Cost Comparison of Potential Alternatives

Component	ETF	Futures	Total Return Swap
Commission	x.xx	x.xx	x.xx
Management fee	x.xx	0.00	0.00
Bid/offer spread	x.xx	x.xx	x.xx
Tracking error	x.xx	x.xx	0.00
Roll costs	0.00	x.xx	0.00
Funding cost	0.00	0.00	x.xx
Total cost	**x.xx**	**x.xx**	**x.xx**

Note that cells with "x" would have a cost associated with them.

The asset manager must balance returns with costs and liquidity considerations, with leverage and without leverage. Leverage may increase the return sufficiently that it changes the strategy decision.

At quarter end, the asset manager considers the results and decides to rebalance. The consideration will involve how far to rebalance (e.g., back to the inside edge of the corridor or back to the SAA), based on cost considerations in the cash versus derivatives markets, and the speed with which the rebalancing can be accomplished.

CASE STUDY IN RISK MANAGEMENT
Private Wealth: Cross-Reference to CFA Institute Assigned Reading #38

Overview of "Eurolandia"

This case uses a family in a hypothetical country to illustrate how risk management methods must change to accommodate changing circumstances. Toward that end, the following sections provide a brief description of each financial stage and identify essential case facts related to the family. Methods are then discussed to mitigate risks to objectives for the family.

Exhibit 4: Marginal Tax Rates	
Yearly Taxable Income	**Marginal Tax Rate**
0 to 15,000	0%
15,000 to 50,000	30%
Greater than 50,000	40%

Eurolandia covers major life risks for its citizens:

- Health insurance—Complete coverage with a small copayment
- Unemployment—Capped at 12,000 per year
- Disability—Capped at 18,000 per year (21,600 for government employees with 10 years of service)

Unemployment and disability payments to individuals are not subject to tax and continue until retirement at age 65.

Early Career Stage

Characteristics of the early career stage include:

- Student loan payback
- Marriage
- Children
- Home purchase
- Little retirement saving
- Possible career-related relocation

The case facts for the Schmitt family at this stage are:

- Paul and Jessica Schmitt, both aged 28 and graduated three years prior with master"s degrees
- Paul earns $45,600 annual as a math teacher; $33,666 after income and social security tax
- Jessica earns $24,000 annual at an IT startup; $20,490 after income and social security tax
- Combined savings of $15,000; no other financial assets or debt
- Old car worth about $7,000

- Rent is $1,000 monthly; other expenses total $1,900
- Vested retirement available to spouse: Paul $11,800; Jessica $21,000

Jessica works for a small startup not subject to paying unemployment insurance premiums. Their advisor forecasts 3% inflation and they each expect their benefit amount will increase at 2% annually.

Exhibit 5: Family Circumstances—Early Career Stage			
	Paul	Jessica	Combined
Gross income	$45,600	$24,000	$69,600
Net income	33,666	20,490	54,156
Living expenses			2,900
Net financial assets			15,000
Car			7,000

After identifying objectives for the Schmitts, a financial advisor would consider potential risks to achieving the objectives.

- Objectives
  - Start a family
  - Buy a 270k home; 25-year mortgage at 3.6%, $1,360 monthly payment
- Risks
  - Earnings
  - Disability
  - Death
  - Auto repair costs
  - Auto liability

Disability Coverages

The formula used for disability and life coverages are related; however, disability insurance helps replace lost income while life insurance covers living expenses.

Exhibit 6: Disability Insurance Coverage—Early Career Stage		
	Paul	Jessica
Annual Income—Net	$33,666	$20,490
Social welfare benefit available	$18,000	$18,000
Shortfall	$15,666	$2,490
Benefit period	37 years	37 years
Annual benefit adjustment (nominal)	2%	2%
Nominal risk-free rate	3%	3%
PV of future earnings replacement	$488,962	$77,717

The disability coverage amount is based on the annual net income after potential applicable benefits are considered and will continue for 37 (i.e., 65 – 28) years:

$$r_{Adj} = \frac{1+r_F}{1+g} - 1 = \frac{1+0.03}{1+0.02} - 1 = 0.98$$

$_{Beg}PV_{Paul}: n = 37; \ PMT = 15{,}666; \ i = 0.98 \ PV = 488{,}962$

$_{Beg}PV_{Jessica}: n = 37; \ PMT = 2{,}490; \ i = 0.98 \ PV = 77{,}717$

This is a present value of annuity due calculation based on the shortfall amount for each spouse. The interest rate calculation reflects the annual inflation rate adjusted for annual increases in the benefit amount.

Life Insurance Coverages

There are two methods of calculating insurance needs:

Exam hint: It is also possible to perform these calculations based on assumed incomes at different life stages, but those calculations are unlikely to be required.

- **Human capital method** (i.e., human life value method)—Estimates the amount of future earnings to replace.
- **Needs analysis method**—Estimates the amount needed to cover survivor's living expenses.

The Schmitts in the early stage in their life had little debt, so the couple decided to cimplify calculations by using the needs analysis method.

Exhibit 7: Life Insurance Coverage—Early Career Stage

	Paul	Jessica
Funeral and burial costs	$15,000	$15,000
Emergency fund	15,000	15,000
Debts to be repaid	0	0
Total cash needs	**30,000**	**30,000**
PV of survivor's annual costs	1,169,000	1,169,000
PV of survivor's income until retirement	758,000	1,246,000
Total capital needs	**411,000**	**–77,000**
Total financial needs	**441,000**	**–47,000**
Cash, savings, investments	15,000	15,000
PV of vested retirement accounts	11,800	21,000
Existing life insurance coverage	0	0
Total Cash Available	**26,800**	**36,000**
Additional life Insurance Needs	**414,200**	**–83,000**

Note that additional life insurance needs equal total financial needs less total cash available; some of the capital needs are met by the $30,000 cash cushion. the current value of Paul's retirement account to Jessica is $21,000 and the current value of Jessica's retirement account to Paul is $11,800. Similarly, the current value of Paul's wage income to Jessica is $1,246,000 and the current value of Jessica's wage income to Paul is $758,000, based on zero net growth for each.

Other Coverages

Car Accident and Repair Costs
Existing coverage protects other people should the Schmitts have an accident (i.e., liability) but does not replace the value of their lost auto (i.e., collision). The Schmitts do not use their low-value car a lot, so the advisor indicates they should save their money rather than spend it on comprehensive coverage.

Lifestyle Risks from Purchasing a Home
The advisor counsels against using their financial assets to make a down payment on a home because it would leave them without an emergency buffer. The advisor suggests six months of expenses should be the target for an emergency fund.

Schmitt Home Purchase
The Schmitts decide to purchase a home for $285,000, with financing as follows:

- $80,000 personal loan from Jessica's parents
- $5,000 in personal funds
- $200,000 mortgage loan with 25-year amortization, 3.6% fixed for five years

The Schmitts insure the property for only $200,000, against the advisor's advice.

Their life insurance needs must increase by $280,000 to reimburse Jessica's parents and pay off the mortgage.

Other Stages
It is not useful to re-create the entire case because it repeats previous calculations. Other considerations not previously discussed include:

- Correlation of Jessica's company stock and warrants with her earnings from employment; these risks should be diversified.
- Continued support for her daughter's college education expenses.
- Continued indefinite support for a special needs child.

One calculation not previously considered is purchasing an annuity that replaces at least some income during retirement years. The annuity is assumed to pay the annual amount needed at the beginning of the period (i.e., an annuity due). The challenge is to find the amount of funds required to generate that level of income. Alternatively, the question could be the annual annuity due that they could receive for some amount of funds contributed.

Considerations with an annuity are that they resolve the longevity risk problem but may return less than a lump-sum withdrawal could return if properly invested. In addition, purchasing an annuity with an annual increase for inflation protects against inflation risk, but further reduces the periodic benefit amount received. If the annuitant (i.e., the person who receives the annuity) dies, the annuity immediately stops unless it is a joint and survivor annuity, which further reduces the periodic payout. Annuities also have counterparty risk; that is, risk the insurance company will not fulfill its obligation to make payments (although this is negligible).

Early payouts from a pension plan and subsequent reinvestment may be considered.